ZAGAT
2013

Portland
City Guide

EDITORS:
Kelly Stewart with Kelly Clarke and Jen Stevenson;
Ben Waterhouse; Becki J. Singer; Liz Crain;
Erin Behan

Published and distributed by
Zagat Survey, LLC
76 Ninth Avenue
New York, NY 10011
T: 212.977.6000
E: feedback@zagat.com
plus.google.com/local

ACKNOWLEDGMENTS

We're grateful to our local editors, Kelly Stewart, a food writer and the editor of *Roast,* a magazine for specialty coffee roasters; Kelly Clarke, a writer and editor who covers food, travel and other cultural topics; Jen Stevenson, author of Portland's 100 Best Places To Stuff Your Faces and web editor of Under The Table With Jen; Ben Waterhouse, a reporter and editor who writes about food, nightlife and the performing arts for local and national outlets; Becki J. Singer, a writer, style advisor and web editor of Shopping's My Cardio; and Liz Crain, small press editor and author of the *Food Lover's Guide to Portland* and the forthcoming *Toro Bravo Cookbook.* We also sincerely thank the thousands of people who participated in this survey – this guide is really "theirs."

We also thank Kara Freewind (editor), Christina Collada and Jamie Selzer, as well as the following members of our staff: Danielle Borovoy (editor), Brian Albert, Sean Beachell, Maryanne Bertollo, Reni Chin, Larry Cohn, Nicole Diaz, Kelly Dobkin, Jeff Freier, Alison Gainor, Michelle Golden, Matthew Hamm, Justin Hartung, Marc Henson, Ryutaro Ishikane, Natalie Lebert, Mike Liao, Vivian Ma, Caitlin Miehl, James Mulcahy, Polina Paley, Josh Rogers, Amanda Spurlock, Chris Walsh, Jacqueline Wasilczyk, Sharon Yates, Anna Zappia and Kyle Zolner.

ABOUT ZAGAT

In 1979, we asked friends to rate and review restaurants purely for fun. The term "user-generated content" had yet to be coined. That hobby grew into Zagat Survey; 34 years later, we have loyal surveyors around the globe and our content now includes nightlife, shopping, tourist attractions, golf and more. Along the way, we evolved from being a print publisher to a digital content provider. We also produce marketing tools for a wide range of corporate clients, and you can find us on Google+ and just about any other social media network.

Our reviews are based on public opinion surveys. The ratings reflect the average scores given by the survey participants who voted on each establishment. The text is based on quotes from, or paraphrasings of, the surveyors' comments. Phone numbers, addresses and other factual data were correct to the best of our knowledge when published in this guide.

JOIN IN

To improve our guides, we solicit your comments – positive or negative; it's vital that we hear your opinions. Just contact us at **nina-tim@zagat.com.** We also invite you to share your opinions at plus.google.com/local

© 2012 Zagat Survey, LLC
ISBN-13: 978-1-60478-527-2
ISBN-10: 1-60478-527-6
Printed in the
United States of America

Contents

Ratings & Symbols

Name	Symbols		Cuisine	Zagat Ratings			
				FOOD	DECOR	SERVICE	COST

Area, Address & Contact
Tim & Nina's ◗ *Pacific NW* ▽ 23 | 9 | 13 | $15
West End | 1195 SW Washington St. (12th Ave.) | 503-123-4567 | www.zagat.com

Review, surveyor comments in quotes
"So local and micro it's unsustainable", this Pacific NW lounge in the West End turns out "artisanal Portland weirdness" (think "deep-fried charcuterie") bolstered by an in-house chicken coop and native weed foraging program; the "nouveau lumberjack" look and "questionable" taxidermy comes with a side of "tatted 'tude", but all is forgiven when the small-batch "hops-like-a-bunny" IPA lands on your "thrice-reclaimed" communal table; P.S. there's a vegan strip club next door with free indoor bike parking.

Ratings
On the Zagat 0 to 30 scale, covering key aspects of each category (e.g. Food, Decor, Service for Dining):

26 - 30 extraordinary to perfection
21 - 25 very good to excellent
16 - 20 good to very good
11 - 15 fair to good
0 - 10 poor to fair
▽ low response | less reliable

Cost
Dining: The price of dinner with a drink and tip. For unrated newcomers, the price range is indicated as I ($25 and below); M ($26-$40); E ($41-$65); VE ($66 or above)

Sites & Attractions: High-season adult admission: $0 (free); I ($10 and below); M ($11-$25); E ($26-$40); VE ($41 or above)

All other costs are indicated as I (inexpensive); M (moderate); E (expensive); VE (very expensive); based on surveyor estimates.

Symbols
◗ dining: serves after 11 PM; shopping: usually open past 7 PM
 closed on Sunday
 closed on Monday
⇗ no credit cards accepted

About This Survey

- 8,534 surveyors
- 627 restaurants, 149 nightspots, 407 shops and 35 attractions
- Winners: **DINING: The Painted Lady** (Food), **Gustav's** (Popularity); **NIGHTLIFE: Ground Kontrol** (Atmosphere), **Crystal Ballroom** (Popularity); **SHOPPING: Made in Oregon** (Popularity), **New Seasons Market** (Popularity, Food & Wine); **ATTRACTIONS: Multnomah Falls** (Appeal, Popularity).

EAT BEAT: Division Street lays claim to Portland's hottest Restaurant Row as newcomers **Cibo, Roe** and **Xico** join top spots **Nuestra Cocina, Pok Pok, Wafu** and **The Woodsman Tavern.** Due to join them: Andy Ricker's upcoming Thai curry house, **Pok Pok Lat Khao,** and Stumptown Coffee's Duane Sorenson's three pots in the fire: the Italian **Ava Genes,** an unnamed, adjoining Roman-style pizzeria and **Woodsman Hall,** a 5,000-sq.-ft., beer-focused wonderland. Meanwhile, Downtown is hot thanks to Vitaly Paley's wood-fired Pacific NW fare at his long-awaited **Imperial** and the adjoining **Portland Penny Diner.** On the street, food carts have been shedding mobility for stability with **The Baowry, Lardo, Nong's Khao Man Gai** and **Shut Up & Eat** going brick-and-mortar. Old-school charm is still lauded, as worth-the-drive **The Painted Lady** is tops for Food, Decor and Service.

DRINKING DENS: Portland's passion for fermenting has extended to grapes, with dual winery/wine bars **Sauvage** and **Southeast Wine Collective** joining the already popular **ENSO** and **Vie de Boheme,** and newcomer **Bar Vivant** adding flair with its txakoli poured from great heights. On the mixed drinks front, Prohibition-cocktail fiends are chomping at the bitters for **Pepe le Moko's** projected late 2012 opening in the Ace Hotel's basement. Evidently, Portland drinkers don't take themselves *too* seriously as arcade/bar **Ground Kontrol** is No. 1 for Atmosphere.

SHOP SCENE: Downtown's West End is on track to be the SW's answer to the Pearl with the arrival of vintage clothier **Animal Traffic** and chic menswear shop **Blackbird,** while the established women's boutique **Parallel** moved in to keep standouts like trendy home goods store **Canoe** and high-end apparel boutique **Frances May** company.

MARKETPLACE: Dough is on the rise with Kim Boyce's **Bakeshop** taking whole grains to the next level, **Fressen Artisan Bakery** turning out German-style soft pretzels and **Spielman Coffee Roasters** pumping out admirable sourdough bagels to pair with its house-roasted brew.

ATTRACTIONS: Standouts include the **Oregon Museum of Science & Industry,** the block-long maze that is **Powell's City of Books,** and **Washington Park**'s many notable sites. A pilgrimage to **Pioneer Courthouse Square,** the **Portland Farmers Market** and the **Governor Tom McCall Waterfront Park** is also de rigueur. To see the area's Most Popular attraction and tops for Appeal, **Multnomah Falls,** you'll have to travel 30 miles east, but it's worth it.

Portland
January 9, 2013

Kelly Stewart, Ben Waterhouse,
Becki J. Singer and Liz Crain

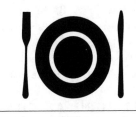

DINING

Most Popular

This list is plotted on the map at the back of this book.

1. Gustav's | *German*
2. Andina | *Peruvian*
3. Flying Pie | *Pizza*
4. Higgins | *Pacific NW*
5. Jake's Famous Crawfish | *Sea.*
6. RingSide Steak | *Steak*
7. Portland City Grill | *American*
8. 3 Doors Down Café | *Italian*
9. Apizza Scholls | *Pizza*
10. Toro Bravo | *Spanish/Tapas*
11. Heathman | *French/Pacific NW*
12. Jake's Grill* | *Seafood*
13. Paley's Place | *Pacific NW*
14. Salty's | *Seafood*
15. Screen Door | *Southern*
16. Pok Pok | *Thai*
17. Painted Lady | *Pacific NW*
18. Nostrana | *Italian*
19. Rheinlander | *German*
20. Fire on the Mountain | *Amer.*

MOST POPULAR CHAINS

1. McMenamins | *Pub Food*
2. Old Spaghetti Factory | *Italian*
3. Pizzicato | *Pizza*
4. Mio Sushi | *Japanese*
5. Original Pancake House | *Amer.*

Top Food

29	Painted Lady	*Pacific NW*

28	Le Pigeon	*French*
	Genoa	*Italian*
	Evoe	*European/Sandwiches*
	Cabezon	*Seafood*
	Lardo	*Sandwiches*
	Andina	*Peruvian*
	Noho's	*Hawaiian*
	Lovely's Fifty Fifty	*Pizza*
	Nostrana	*Italian*
	Apizza Scholls	*Pizza*
	Joel Palmer House	*Pacific NW*

27	Tasty n Sons	*American*
	Paley's Place	*Pacific NW*
	Little Bird	*French*

Clyde's Prime Rib | *Steak*
RingSide Steak | *Steak*
Nicholas | *Lebanese*
Pacific Pie Co.* | *Australian*
Dove Vivi | *Pizza*
Olympic Provisions | *Pacific NW*
Iorio | *Italian*
Toro Bravo | *Spanish/Tapas*
Castagna | *Pacific NW*
Screen Door | *Southern*
DOC | *Italian*
Jam on Hawthorne | *American*
Blossoming Lotus | *Vegan*
Higgins | *Pacific NW*
Bamboo Sushi | *Japanese*

BY CUISINE

AMERICAN (NEW)

27	Tasty n Sons
26	Beaker & Flask
	Portland City Grill
	Clyde Common
	Aviary

AMERICAN (TRAD.)

27	Jam on Hawthorne
26	Observatory
	Papa Haydn
	Country Cat
	Tin Shed

Excludes places with low votes; most lists also exclude food carts and counter-service only places; * indicates a tie with restaurant above

BBQ/SOUTHERN

27 Screen Door
Podnah's Pit
Pine State Biscuits
26 Russell Street BBQ
25 Campbell's Barbecue

BURGERS

27 Killer Burger
26 Helvetia Tavern
Hollywood Burger Bar
Stanich's
Foster Burger

COFFEEHOUSES

27 Pied Cow
25 Barista
Sterling/Coffeehouse NW
Extracto
Stumptown

DELIS/SANDWICHES

28 Evoe
Lardo
27 Otto's Sausage Kitchen
Bunk Sandwiches
26 East Side Delicatessen

FRENCH

28 Le Pigeon
27 Little Bird
Beast
26 Heathman
25 Cocotte

INDIAN

26 East India Co.
Abhiruchi
Bombay Cricket Club
25 Chennai Masala
Bollywood Theater

ITALIAN

28 Genoa
Nostrana
27 Iorio
DOC
Decarli

JAPANESE

27 Bamboo Sushi
Saburo's
26 Yoko's

Yuzu
25 Koji Osakaya

MEXICAN

27 Autentica
26 La Bonita
¿Por Que No?
Nuestra Cocina
King Burrito

PACIFIC NW

29 Painted Lady
28 Joel Palmer House
27 Paley's Place
Olympic Provisions
Castagna

PIZZA

28 Lovely's Fifty Fifty
Apizza Scholls
27 Dove Vivi
Earth Oven Pizza
Vincente's Gourmet Pizza

SEAFOOD

28 Cabezon
27 Jake's Famous Crawfish
26 Jake's Grill
Fish Grotto
25 Fishwife

STEAK

27 Clyde's Prime Rib
RingSide Steak
26 El Gaucho
Sayler's
Laurelhurst Market

THAI

27 Pok Pok
Thai Peacock
Lemongrass
26 Jade Teahouse
Nong's Khao Man Gai

VEGETARIAN

27 Blossoming Lotus
Bye & Bye
26 Portobello
25 Hungry Tiger Too
24 Bay Leaf

BY SPECIAL FEATURE

BREAKFAST

27 Jam on Hawthorne
Pine State Biscuits
Bakery Bar
26 Hollywood Burger Bar
Original Pancake House

BRUNCH

27 Tasty n Sons
Screen Door
Beast
26 Country Cat
Besaw's

BUSINESS DINING

28 Genoa
27 Paley's Place
RingSide Steak
Higgins
Jake's Famous Crawfish

FOOD CARTS

28 Built to Grill
PBJ's Grilled
27 Bora Bora
26 Nong's Khao Man Gai
Aybla Grill

HOTEL DINING

26 El Gaucho (Benson Hotel)
Heathman
Jake's Grill (Governor Hotel)
Clyde Common (Ace Hotel)
25 H5O (Hotel Fifty)

LATE DINING

27 Little Bird
Luc Lac
Bye & Bye
Du Kuh Bee
26 Portland City Grill

MEET FOR A DRINK

27 Bye & Bye
Higgins

Pok Pok
Clarklewis
Pied Cow

NEWCOMERS (RATED)

28 Lardo
27 Dar Salam
26 Jerusalem Cafe
25 Double Dragon
Bollywood Theater

PEOPLE-WATCHING

28 Le Pigeon
Andina
27 Little Bird
Salt & Straw
Pine State Biscuits

ROMANTIC SPOTS

29 Painted Lady
28 Le Pigeon
Andina
Joel Palmer House
27 Toro Bravo

SINGLES SCENES

27 Toro Bravo
Bye & Bye
26 Beaker & Flask
Clyde Common
¡Oba!

WINNING WINE LISTS

29 Painted Lady
28 Genoa
Andina
27 Paley's Place
RingSide Steak

WORTH A TRIP

29 Painted Lady (Newberg)
28 Joel Palmer House (Dayton)
26 Jory (Newberg)
Nick's (McMinnville)
24 Tina's (Dundee)

BY LOCATION

ALBERTA

27 Dar Salam
26 Aviary
Tin Shed
25 Thai Noon
Zilla Sake House

BEAVERTON

27 Decarli
Du Kuh Bee
26 Pho Hung
Pho Van
Abhiruchi

BELMONT

28 Genoa
27 Pied Cow
26 Pad Thai Kitchen
Jerusalem Cafe
Accanto

BUCKMAN/KERNS

28 Nostrana
27 Dove Vivi
Screen Door
Bamboo Sushi
Ken's Artisan Pizza

BOISE-ELIOT

27 Tasty n Sons
Toro Bravo
Lincoln
26 Russell Street BBQ
25 Mint

CENTRAL EASTSIDE/
EASTSIDE INDUSTRIAL

27 Nicholas
Olympic Provisions
Clarklewis
26 Beaker & Flask
Portobello

CLINTON/DIVISION

28 Noho's
27 Pok Pok
26 Broder Cafe
Nuestra Cocina
Petite Provence

CONCORDIA/
WOODLAWN

27 DOC
Beast
Autentica
Firehouse
25 Cocotte

DOWNTOWN

27 Little Bird
Higgins
Thai Peacock
Brazil Grill
El Gaucho

HAWTHORNE

28 Evoe
Lardo
Apizza Scholls
27 Iorio
Castagna

HILLSBORO

27 Earth Oven Pizza
26 Helvetia Tavern
Bambuza
25 Chennai Masala
24 Swagat

HILLSDALE/
MULTNOMAH VILLAGE

26 Original Pancake House
25 Cider Mill & Fryer Tuck
24 Seasons & Regions
Fat City Cafe
23 Salvador Molly's

LOWER BURNSIDE

28 Le Pigeon
26 Farm Cafe
Fire on the Mountain
25 Abby's Table
Burnside Brewing Co.

MISSISSIPPI

28 Lovely's Fifty Fifty
26 Mississippi Pizza Pub
Casa Naranja
25 Equinox
Gravy

NW PORTLAND

27 Paley's Place
RingSide Steak
Olympic Provisions
Bamboo Sushi
Marrakesh

PEARL DISTRICT

28 Andina
26 Piazza Italia
Irving Street Kitchen
Park Kitchen
¡Oba!

SELLWOOD

27 Saburo's
26 Papa Haydn
Gino's
a Cena
25 Bertie Lou's

WEST END

27 Jake's Famous Crawfish
26 East India Co.
Jake's Grill
Clyde Common
Fish Grotto

Top Decor

28 Painted Lady	25 Observatory
27 Departure	Huber's
Jory	Urban Farmer
Marrakesh	Bamboo Sushi
Portland City Grill	Tao of Tea
26 Meriwether's	Portobello*
Pied Cow	Castagna
Irving Street Kitchen	Kells
Genoa	El Gaucho
Andina	Ringside Steak
Serratto	Lemongrass
¡Oba!	Noble Rot
Bluehour	Lincoln
Rheinlander	Brasserie Montmarte
Firehouse	Old Spaghetti Factory

OUTDOORS

Equinox	Pied Cow
Lardo	Produce Row Cafe
Meriwether's	Radio Room
Nel Centro	Tin Shed
Noble Rot	Veritable Quandary

ROMANCE

Aviary	Noisette
Bar Avignon	Paley's Place
Genoa	Portland City Grill
Iorio	Sapphire Hotel
Natural Selection	St. Jack

ROOMS

Bamboo Sushi (NW Portland)	Imperial
Bluehour	Ned Ludd
Departure	Paulée
Gracie's	Woodsman Tavern
Huber's	Xico

VIEWS

Amadeus Manor	Jamison
Departure	Jory
Five Spice	Noble Rot
Hayden's Lakefront Grill	Portland City Grill
Highland Stillhouse	Salty's

Top Service

<u>29</u> Painted Lady

<u>28</u> Genoa

<u>27</u> Jory
Cabezon
Joel Palmer House
Lincoln
Castagna
Pacific Pie Co.*
Higgins

<u>26</u> Iorio
Lovely's Fifty Fifty
Heathman
RingSide Steak
Milo's City Cafe
Clyde's Prime Rib

El Gaucho
Jerusalem Cafe
Paley's Place
Andina
Rheinlander
Jake's Famous Crawfish
H5O
Park Kitchen

<u>25</u> Habibi
Beaker & Flask
Fuller's
Piazza Italia*
Noho's
Beast
Serratto

BEST BUYS: FULL MENU

1. Got Pho?
2. Jam on Hawthorne
3. Fuller's Restaurant
4. Roxy
5. Paradox Cafe
6. Bertie Lou's
7. Pied Cow
8. Fat City Cafe
9. Blueplate Lunch Counter
10. Pho Hung
11. Beaterville
12. Jerusalem Cafe
13. Bridges Cafe
14. Christie's
15. Hollywood Burger Bar
16. Zell's Cafe
17. Marinepolis Sushi Land
18. Gravy
19. Cup & Saucer
20. Dots Cafe

BEST BUYS: SPECIALTY SHOPS

1. Extracto
2. Salt & Straw
3. Ruby Jewel
4. Cool Moon Ice Cream
5. Fifty Licks
6. Potato Champion
7. Voodoo Doughnut
8. Flavour Spot
9. Barista
10. Stumptown
11. Waffle Window
12. Aybla Grill
13. PBJ's Grilled
14. Little Big Burger
15. Whiffies
16. Albina Press
17. Pearl Bakery
18. Nong's Khao Man Gai
19. Baker & Spice
20. Lovejoy Bakers

Dining Special Features

Listings cover the best in each category and include names, locations and Food ratings. Multi-location restaurants' features may vary by branch. These lists include low vote places that do not qualify for tops lists.

BREAKFAST

(See also Hotel Dining)

PBJ's Grilled	**NW Portland**	28
Jam/Hawthorne	**Hawthorne**	27
Po'Shines	**Kenton**	27
Via Delizia	**Pearl Dist.**	27
Pine State Biscuits	**multi.**	27
Bakery Bar	**Kerns**	27
Bunk Sandwiches	**multi.**	27
Milo's City Cafe	**Irvington**	26
Hollywood Burger	**Hollywood**	26
Broder Cafe	**Clinton**	26
Original Pancake	**Multnomah**	26
Besaw's	**NW Portland**	26
Pambiche	**Kerns**	26
FlavourSpot	**multi.**	26
Zell's Cafe	**Buckman**	26
La/Petite Provence	**multi.**	26
Genies Cafe	**Central E**	26
Tin Shed	**Alberta**	26
Arleta Library	**Mt. Scott**	26
Brunch Box	**Downtown**	26
Bijou Cafe	**Old Town-Chinatown**	26
Original Hotcake	**Brooklyn**	25
Stepping Stone	**NW Portland**	25
Mother's	**Downtown**	25
Cricket Cafe	**Belmont**	25
Casa de Tamales	**Milwaukie**	25
Bertie Lou's	**Sellwood**	25
Alameda Cafe	**Beaumont**	25
Christie's	**University Park**	25
Blue Pig	**Hawthorne**	25
Daily Cafe/Pearl	**Pearl Dist.**	25
Bagel & Box	**University Park**	25
Fuller's	**Pearl Dist.**	25
Hungry Tiger Too	**Buckman**	25
Slappy Cakes	**Belmont**	25
Cadillac Cafe	**Irvington**	25
Detour Cafe	**Division**	25
Gravy	**Mississippi**	25
J & M Cafe	**Central E**	25
American Dream	**Mt. Tabor**	25
St. Jack	**Clinton**	24
Helser's/Alberta	**Alberta**	24
Toast	**Woodstock**	24

Beaterville	**Overlook**	24
Fat City	**Multnomah**	24
Isabel	**Pearl Dist.**	24
Byways Cafe	**Pearl Dist.**	24
John St. Cafe	**St. Johns**	24
Bread & Ink	**Hawthorne**	24
Vita Cafe	**Alberta**	24
Bar Carlo	**Foster-Powell**	24
Cup & Saucer	**multi.**	24
Old Wives' Tales	**Buckman**	23
Bridges Cafe	**Boise-Eliot**	23
Roxy	**W End**	22
Tom's	**Division**	22

BRUNCH

Tasty n Sons	**Boise-Eliot**	27
Simpatica	**Central E**	27
Screen Door	**Kerns**	27
Original Dinerant	**Downtown**	27
Blossoming Lotus	**Irvington**	27
Podnah's Pit	**NE Portland**	27
Beast	**Concordia**	27
Autentica	**Concordia**	27
Ocean City	**82nd Ave**	27
Country Cat	**Montavilla**	26
Jory	**Newberg**	26
Veritable Quandary	**Downtown**	26
Besaw's	**NW Portland**	26
Irving St. Kitchen	**Pearl Dist.**	26
Clyde Common	**W End**	26
Accanto	**Belmont**	26
Genies Cafe	**Central E**	26
Wild Abandon	**Belmont**	26
Arleta Library	**Mt. Scott**	26
Portobello	**Central E**	26
Meriwether's	**NW Portland**	25
Cricket Cafe	**Belmont**	25
Casa de Tamales	**Milwaukie**	25
Equinox	**Mississippi**	25
Daily Cafe/Pearl	**Pearl Dist.**	25
Salty's	**NE Portland**	25
Berlin Inn	**Brooklyn**	25
Wong's King	**SE Portland**	25
Hamburger Mary's	**Old Town-Chinatown**	25
Highland Stillhse.	**Oregon City**	25

Seasons/Regions | **Multnomah** 24
Toast | **Woodstock** 24
Cha!Cha!Cha! | **Beaumont** 24
Hall St. Grill | **Beaverton** 24
Cafe Nell | **NW Portland** 24
Blue Olive | **NW Portland** 24
Aquariva | **Johns Landing** 24
Grain & Gristle | **Sabin** 23
Hayden's | **Tualatin** 23
Henry's | **Pearl Dist.** 23
Brix Tav. | **Pearl Dist.** 23
Old Wives' Tales | **Buckman** 23
EaT | **Boise-Eliot** 22
Gracie's | **Goose Hollow** 20
NEW Jamison | **Pearl Dist.** -
NEW Parish | **Pearl Dist.** -

BUSINESS DINING

Genoa | **Belmont** 28
Paley's Pl. | **NW Portland** 27
Little Bird | **Downtown** 27
RingSide Steak | **NW Portland** 27
Higgins | **Downtown** 27
Jake's/Crawfish | **W End** 27
Clarklewis | **E Industrial** 27
Thai Peacock | **Downtown** 27
NEW Via Tribunali | 26
  Old Town-Chinatown
El Gaucho | **Downtown** 26
East India Co. | **W End** 26
Veritable Quandary | **Downtown** 26
Heathman | **Downtown** 26
Portland City Grill | **Downtown** 26
Wildwood | **NW Portland** 26
Serratto | **NW Portland** 26
Murata | **Downtown** 26
Bijou Cafe | 26
  Old Town-Chinatown
Paragon | **Pearl Dist.** 25
Grüner | **W End** 25
Southpark | **Downtown** 25
Huber's | **Downtown** 25
Bluehour | **Pearl Dist.** 25
Seres | **Pearl Dist.** 25
Tucci | **Lake Oswego** 25
Sinju | **multi.** 24
Giorgio's | **Pearl Dist.** 24
Ping | **Old Town-Chinatown** 24
Tina's | **Dundee** 24
McMenamins | **W End** 24
Aquariva | **Johns Landing** 24

Urban Farmer | **Downtown** 23
Hayden's | **Tualatin** 23
Silk | **Pearl Dist.** 23
Red Star Tav. | **Downtown** 23
23Hoyt | **NW Portland** 23
Pazzo | **Downtown** 23
Wilfs | **Old Town-Chinatown** 23
3 Degrees | **S Waterfront** 21
Trader Vic's | **Pearl Dist.** 20
NEW Imperial | **Downtown** -
NEW Jamison | **Pearl Dist.** -
NEW Parish | **Pearl Dist.** -
NEW Riffle NW | **Pearl Dist.** -

CELEBRITY CHEFS

David Anderson
  Genoa | **Belmont** 28
  Accanto | **Belmont** 26
Jason Barwikowski
  Woodsman Tav. | **Division** 24
Oswaldo Bibiano
  Autentica | **Concordia** 27
  NEW Mextiza | **Overlook** 25
  NEW Uno Mas | **Kerns** -
Thomas Boyce
  Bluehour | **Pearl Dist.** 25
Micah Camden
  DOC | **Concordia** 27
  Little Big Burger | **multi.** 25
  NEW Boxer Sushi | **Hawthorne** 25
Tony Demes
  NEW Noisette | **NW Portland** 29
Kevin Gibson
  Evoe | **Hawthorne** 28
John Gorham
  Tasty n Sons | **Boise-Eliot** 27
  Toro Bravo | **Boise-Eliot** 27
Gregory Gourdet
  Departure | **Downtown** 23
Greg Higgins
  Higgins | **Downtown** 27
Christopher Israel
  Grüner | **W End** 25
Daniel Mondok
  NEW Paulée | **Dundee** -
Vitaly Paley
  Paley's Pl. | **NW Portland** 27
  NEW Imperial | **Downtown** -
  NEW Portland Penny | -
  Downtown

Trent Pierce
  Wafu | **Division** | 25
  NEW Roe | **Division** | –
Naomi Pomeroy
  Beast | **Concordia** | 27
Andy Ricker
  Pok Pok | **multi.** | 27
  Ping | **Old Town-Chinatown** | 24
Gabriel Rucker
  Le Pigeon | **Lower Burnside** | 28
  Little Bird | **Downtown** | 27
Johanna Ware
  NEW Smallwares | **Beaumont** | –
Cathy Whims
  Nostrana | **Buckman** | 28
  NEW Oven & Shaker | | 23
    Pearl Dist.

FIREPLACES

Andina | **Pearl Dist.** | 28
RingSide Steak | **NW Portland** | 27
Jake's/Crawfish | **W End** | 27
Papa Haydn | **NW Portland** | 26
Sayler's | **SE Portland** | 26
Heathman | **Downtown** | 26
Fire/Mountain | **NE Portland** | 26
Casa Naranja | **Mississippi** | 26
Meriwether's | **NW Portland** | 25
Salty's | **NE Portland** | 25
Sinju | **Tigard** | 24
Tina's | **Dundee** | 24
Nel Centro | **Downtown** | 24
Five Spice | **Lake Oswego** | 24
Sapphire Hotel | **Hawthorne** | 23
Frank's | **Irvington** | 23
Fratelli | **Pearl Dist.** | 21
NEW Paulée | **Dundee** | –
NEW Smallwares | **Beaumont** | –

FOOD CARTS

Built to Grill | **Downtown** | 28
PBJ's Grilled | **NW Portland** | 28
Bora Bora | **SE Portland** | 27
Nong's Khao Man Gai | **multi.** | 26
Aybla Grill | **multi.** | 26
Viking Soul Food | **Belmont** | 26
Fifty Licks | **Belmont** | 26
Sugar Cube | **Hawthorne** | 26
FlavourSpot | **multi.** | 26
Big-A** Sand. | **E Industrial** | 26
Addy's | **W End** | 26
Brunch Box | **Downtown** | 26

Potato Champion | **multi.** | 25
Koi Fusion | **multi.** | 25
808 Grinds | **W End** | 25
Grilled Cheese Grill | **multi.** | 25
EuroTrash | **multi.** | 25
Sweet Basil | **SW Portland** | 25
Bagel & Box | **University Park** | 25
Kure Juice Bar | **Hawthorne** | 25
Taqueria/Gorditos | **Division** | 25
Whiffies | **multi.** | 24
Pyro Pizza | **multi.** | 23

GREEN/LOCAL/ ORGANIC

Painted Lady | **Newberg** | 29
Natural Selection | **Alberta** | 29
Genoa | **Belmont** | 28
Lovely's Fifty Fifty | **Mississippi** | 28
PBJ's Grilled | **NW Portland** | 28
Joel Palmer Hse. | **Dayton** | 28
Otto's Sausage | **Woodstock** | 27
Paley's Pl. | **NW Portland** | 27
Simpatica | **Central E** | 27
Salt & Straw | **multi.** | 27
Iorio | **Hawthorne** | 27
Castagna | **Hawthorne** | 27
Screen Door | **Kerns** | 27
DOC | **Concordia** | 27
Jam/Hawthorne | **Hawthorne** | 27
Original Dinerant | **Downtown** | 27
Blossoming Lotus | **Irvington** | 27
Ruby Jewel | **Mississippi** | 27
Higgins | **Downtown** | 27
Bamboo Sushi | **multi.** | 27
Prasad | **Pearl Dist.** | 27
Lincoln | **Boise-Eliot** | 27
Beast | **Concordia** | 27
Clarklewis | **E Industrial** | 27
Grand Central | **multi.** | 27
Firehouse | **Woodlawn** | 27
Country Cat | **Montavilla** | 26
Scratch | **Lake Oswego** | 26
Besaw's | **NW Portland** | 26
Farm Cafe | **Lower Burnside** | 26
Papa G's | **Division** | 26
Clyde Common | **W End** | 26
Laurelhurst Mkt. | **Kerns** | 26
Accanto | **Belmont** | 26
Café Castagna | **Hawthorne** | 26
Ned Ludd | **King** | 26
Arleta Library | **Mt. Scott** | 26
Allium | **West Linn** | 25

Paragon | **Pearl Dist.**	25
Cricket Cafe | **Belmont**	25
Casa de Tamales | **Milwaukie**	25
Mint | **Boise-Eliot**	25
Thai Noon | **Alberta**	25
Hotlips Pizza | **multi.**	25
CHA Taqueria | **NW Portland**	25
Southpark | **Downtown**	25
Abby's Table | **Lower Burnside**	25
𝐍𝐄𝐖 Double Dragon | **Central E**	25
Hungry Tiger Too | **Buckman**	25
Dick's Kitchen | **multi.**	25
Detour Cafe | **Division**	25
Kure Juice Bar | **Hawthorne**	25
Seres | **Pearl Dist.**	25
Café Yumm | **multi.**	25
Hammy's Pizza | **Clinton**	24
Cha!Cha!Cha! | **multi.**	24
Cafe Nell | **NW Portland**	24
Tina's | **Dundee**	24
Vita Cafe | **Alberta**	24
Cup & Saucer | **multi.**	24
Vindalho | **Clinton**	24
Hopworks | **multi.**	23
Urban Farmer | **Downtown**	23
𝐍𝐄𝐖 Paulée | **Dundee**	–
𝐍𝐄𝐖 Xico | **Division**	–

GROUP DINING

Noho's | **Beaumont**	28
Nostrana | **Buckman**	28
Jake's/Crawfish | **W End**	27
Vincente's | **Hawthorne**	27
Ya Hala | **Montavilla**	27
Pied Cow | **Belmont**	27
Brazil Grill | **Downtown**	27
Ocean City | **82nd Ave**	27
Rheinlander | **Hollywood**	26
Veritable Quandary | **Downtown**	26
Sayler's | **SE Portland**	26
Russell St. BBQ | **Boise-Eliot**	26
Jake's Grill | **W End**	26
Irving St. Kitchen | **Pearl Dist.**	26
Wildwood | **NW Portland**	26
Serratto | **NW Portland**	26
Clyde Common | **W End**	26
Park Kitchen | **Pearl Dist.**	26
Gustav's | **multi.**	25
Basta's | **NW Portland**	25
Paragon | **Pearl Dist.**	25

Campbell's BBQ | **SE Portland**	25
Salty's | **NE Portland**	25
Alexis | **Old Town-Chinatown**	25
Slappy Cakes | **Belmont**	25
Wong's King | **SE Portland**	25
Pastini Pastaria | **multi.**	25
Hot Pot City | **Downtown**	25
Sinju | **multi.**	24
Seasons/Regions | **Multnomah**	24
Hall St. Grill | **Beaverton**	24
Amalfi's | **Beaumont**	24
Swagat | **multi.**	24
McMenamins | **multi.**	24
Iron Horse | **Sellwood**	24
Aquariva | **Johns Landing**	24
Hopworks | **multi.**	23
Salvador Molly's | **Hillsdale**	23
Urban Farmer | **Downtown**	23
BridgePort | **Pearl Dist.**	23
Davis St. | **Old Town-Chinatown**	23
Old Spaghetti | **Johns Landing**	23
Hayden's | **Tualatin**	23
Red Star Tav. | **Downtown**	23
Henry's | **Pearl Dist.**	23
Pazzo | **Downtown**	23
Wilfs | **Old Town-Chinatown**	23
Hobo's | **Old Town-Chinatown**	22
3 Degrees | **S Waterfront**	21
Rogue | **multi.**	21
Trader Vic's | **Pearl Dist.**	20

HOTEL DINING

Ace Hotel	
Clyde Common | **W End**	26
Stumptown | **W End**	25
Allison Inn & Spa	
Jory | **Newberg**	26
Benson Hotel	
El Gaucho | **Downtown**	26
deLuxe, Hotel	
Gracie's | **Goose Hollow**	20
Edgefield	
McMenamins | **Troutdale**	24
Fifty, Hotel	
H5O | **Downtown**	25
Governor Hotel	
Jake's Grill | **W End**	26
Heathman Hotel	
Heathman | **Downtown**	26
Inn at Red Hills	
𝐍𝐄𝐖 Paulée | **Dundee**	–

Lucia, Hotel
  NEW Imperial | **Downtown** — |
  NEW Portland Penny | — |
    Downtown
McMenamins Crystal Hotel
  McMenamins | **W End** 24 |
McMenamins Kennedy School
  McMenamins | **Concordia** 24 |
Modera, Hotel
  Nel Centro | **Downtown** 24 |
Monaco, Hotel
  Red Star Tav. | **Downtown** 23 |
Nines Hotel
  Urban Farmer | **Downtown** 23 |
  Departure | **Downtown** 23 |
RiverPlace Hotel
  3 Degrees | **S Waterfront** 21 |
River's Edge Hotel & Spa
  Aquariva | **Johns Landing** 24 |
Vintage Plaza, Hotel
  Pazzo | **Downtown** 23 |

LATE DINING

(Weekday closing hour)
Pix Pâtisserie | 2 AM | **Kerns** 28 |
Little Bird | 12 AM | 27 |
  Downtown
RingSide Steak | 12 AM | 27 |
  NW Portland
NEW Luc Lac | varies | 27 |
  Downtown
Bye & Bye | 2 AM | **Alberta** 27 |
Higgins | 12 AM | **Downtown** 27 |
Pok Pok | 12 AM | **Sabin** 27 |
Vincente's | 12 AM | **Hawthorne** 27 |
Pied Cow | varies | **Belmont** 27 |
Ocean City | 12 AM | **82nd Ave** 27 |
Observatory | varies | 26 |
  Montavilla
NEW Baowry | 2:30 AM | 26 |
  St. Johns
El Gaucho | varies | **Downtown** 26 |
Mississippi Pizza | varies | 26 |
  Mississippi
Veritable Quandary | 2:30 AM | 26 |
  Downtown
Portland City Grill | varies | 26 |
  Downtown
Sugar Cube | 12 AM | 26 |
  Hawthorne
Clyde Common | varies | **W End** 26 |
Fire/Mountain | 12 AM | 26 |
  Lower Burnside

Voodoo Doughnut | 24 hrs. | 26 |
  multi.
Le Bistro Montage | varies | 26 |
  E Industrial
Original Hotcake | 24 hrs. | 25 |
  Brooklyn
Potato Champion | 3 AM | 25 |
  Hawthorne
Biwa | 12 AM | **Central E** 25 |
Delta Cafe | 12 AM | **Woodstock** 25 |
Huber's | varies | **Downtown** 25 |
Highland Stillhse. | 12 AM | 25 |
  Oregon City
North 45 | 2 AM | **NW Portland** 25 |
Le Happy | varies | **NW Portland** 25 |
Santeria | 2 AM | **Downtown** 25 |
Cider Mill | 2:30 AM | 25 |
  Multnomah
Gladstone/Pizza | 12 AM | 24 |
  SE Portland
Kenny & Zuke's | 12 AM | 24 |
  Boise-Eliot
Hammy's Pizza | 4 AM | **Clinton** 24 |
Sizzle Pie | varies | **multi.** 24 |
Gilt Club | 2 AM | 24 |
  Old Town-Chinatown
Kells | 12 AM | **multi.** 24 |
Skyline | varies | **Irvington** 24 |
Cassidy's | 2 AM | **W End** 24 |
McMenamins | varies | **multi.** 24 |
Saucebox | varies | **Downtown** 24 |
Zach's Shack | 3 AM | **Hawthorne** 24 |
Whiffies | 3 AM | **Hawthorne** 24 |
Pyro Pizza | 3 AM, 3AM | **multi.** 23 |
Departure | varies | **Downtown** 23 |
Grain & Gristle | 12 AM | **Sabin** 23 |
Sapphire Hotel | 2 AM | 23 |
  Hawthorne
EastBurn | 2 AM | **Buckman** 23 |
NEW Oven & Shaker | 12 AM | 23 |
  Pearl Dist.
Rimsky-Korsakoffee | varies | 23 |
  Buckman
Produce Row | varies | 23 |
  E Industrial
Brix Tav. | varies | **Pearl Dist.** 23 |
Dots Cafe | 2 AM | **Clinton** 23 |
Goose Hollow Inn | varies | 22 |
  Goose Hollow
Hobo's | 2:30 AM | 22 |
  Old Town-Chinatown
Radio Room | 2 AM | **Alberta** 22 |
Lucky Lab | varies | **multi.** 21 |
Rogue | 12 AM | **PSU** 21 |

Virginia Cafe | 2:30 AM | **Downtown** — 21

NEW Riffle NW | 12 AM | **Pearl Dist.** — _|

NEW Smallwares | 2 AM | **Beaumont** — _|

NEW Southland | 1 AM | **NW Portland** — _|

MEET FOR A DRINK

Andina	**Pearl Dist.**	28
Pacific Pie Co.	**Central E**	27
Bye & Bye	**Alberta**	27
Higgins	**Downtown**	27
Pok Pok	**Division**	27
Jake's/Crawfish	**W End**	27
Clarklewis	**E Industrial**	27
Pied Cow	**Belmont**	27
Bunk Sandwiches	**Central E**	27
Observatory	**Montavilla**	26
Beaker/Flask	**Central E**	26
Veritable Quandary	**Downtown**	26
Heathman	**Downtown**	26
Jake's Grill	**W End**	26
Irving St. Kitchen	**Pearl Dist.**	26
Portland City Grill	**Downtown**	26
Wildwood	**NW Portland**	26
Serratto	**NW Portland**	26
Clyde Common	**W End**	26
Park Kitchen	**Pearl Dist.**	26
Accanto	**Belmont**	26
Café Castagna	**Hawthorne**	26
¡Oba!	**Pearl Dist.**	26
Casa Naranja	**Mississippi**	26
Gustav's	**multi.**	25
Allium	**West Linn**	25
Basta's	**NW Portland**	25
Mother's	**Downtown**	25
Paragon	**Pearl Dist.**	25
Grüner	**W End**	25
Zilla Sake Hse.	**Alberta**	25
Biwa	**Central E**	25
CHA Taqueria	**NW Portland**	25
Southpark	**Downtown**	25
Hungry Tiger Too	**Buckman**	25
Huber's	**Downtown**	25
Bluehour	**Pearl Dist.**	25
Hamburger Mary's	**Old Town-Chinatown**	25
Wafu	**Division**	25
Bar Avignon	**Division**	25
Bar Mingo	**NW Portland**	25

Burnside Brew.	**Lower Burnside**	25
Tucci	**Lake Oswego**	25
St. Jack	**Clinton**	24
Original Halibut's	**Alberta**	24
Ping	**Old Town-Chinatown**	24
June	**Buckman**	24
Woodsman Tav.	**Division**	24
Gilt Club	**Old Town-Chinatown**	24
Noble Rot	**Lower Burnside**	24
Jo Bar	**NW Portland**	24
Kells	**multi.**	24
Cafe Nell	**NW Portland**	24
Cassidy's	**W End**	24
Saucebox	**Downtown**	24
Iron Horse	**Sellwood**	24
Five Spice	**Lake Oswego**	24
Hopworks	**multi.**	23
BridgePort	**multi.**	23
Departure	**Downtown**	23
Sapphire Hotel	**Hawthorne**	23
Davis St.	**Old Town-Chinatown**	23
EastBurn	**Buckman**	23
Silk	**Pearl Dist.**	23
Red Star Tav.	**Downtown**	23
Henry's	**Pearl Dist.**	23
23Hoyt	**NW Portland**	23
Brix Tav.	**Pearl Dist.**	23
Wilfs	**Old Town-Chinatown**	23
Dots Cafe	**Clinton**	23
Alameda Brew.	**Beaumont**	22
Goose Hollow Inn	**Goose Hollow**	22
Hobo's	**Old Town-Chinatown**	22
Lucky Lab	**multi.**	21
Coppia	**Pearl Dist.**	21
MacTarnahan's	**NW Portland**	21
Rogue	**multi.**	21
Fratelli	**Pearl Dist.**	21
Trader Vic's	**Pearl Dist.**	20
NEW Cibo	**Division**	_|
NEW Imperial	**Downtown**	_|
NEW Jamison	**Pearl Dist.**	_|
NEW Ox	**Boise-Eliot**	_|
NEW PaaDee	**Kerns**	_|
NEW Riffle NW	**Pearl Dist.**	_|
NEW Smallwares	**Beaumont**	_|
NEW Southland	**NW Portland**	_|
NEW Trigger	**Boise-Eliot**	_|

MICROBREWERIES

Fire/Mountain	**NE Portland**	26
Old Town Pizza	**multi.**	25

Burnside Brew. | **Lower Burnside**	25
Kells | **NW Portland**	24
McMenamins | **multi.**	24
Hopworks | **multi.**	23
BridgePort | **multi.**	23
Alameda Brew. | **Beaumont**	22
Lucky Lab | **multi.**	21
MacTarnahan's | **NW Portland**	21
Rogue | **multi.**	21

NEWCOMERS

Noisette | **NW Portland**	29
Lardo | **Hawthorne**	28
Luc Lac | **Downtown**	27
Shut Up/Eat | **SE Portland**	27
Dar Salam | **Alberta**	27
Via Tribunali | **Old Town-Chinatown**	26
Baowry | **St. Johns**	26
Jerusalem Cafe | **Belmont**	26
Mack/Dub's | **Boise-Eliot**	25
Mextiza | **Overlook**	25
Boxer Sushi | **Hawthorne**	25
Double Dragon | **Central E**	25
Bollywood | **Alberta**	25
Boke Bowl | **E Industrial**	24
Mi Mero Mole | **Division**	24
Oven & Shaker | **Pearl Dist.**	23
Robo Taco | **Central E**	23
Basa Basa | **Kerns**	-
Cibo | **Division**	-
Hokusei | **Belmont**	-
Imperial | **Downtown**	-
Jamison | **Pearl Dist.**	-
Ox | **Boise-Eliot**	-
PaaDee | **Kerns**	-
Parish | **Pearl Dist.**	-
Paulée | **Dundee**	-
Portland Penny | **Downtown**	-
Riffle NW | **Pearl Dist.**	-
Roe | **Division**	-
Slowburger | **Kerns**	-
Smallwares | **Beaumont**	-
Southland | **NW Portland**	-
Trigger | **Boise-Eliot**	-
24th & Meatballs | **Kerns**	-
Uno Mas | **Kerns**	-
Xico | **Division**	-

OUTDOOR DINING

Chez Machin | **Hawthorne**	29
🆕 Lardo | **Hawthorne**	28

Khun Pic's | **Belmont**	28
Noho's | **Beaumont**	28
Pix Pâtisserie | **Kerns**	28
Apizza Scholls | **Hawthorne**	28
Paley's Pl. | **NW Portland**	27
RingSide Steak | **NE Portland**	27
Screen Door | **Kerns**	27
Bye & Bye | **Alberta**	27
Pok Pok | **Division**	27
Via Delizia | **Pearl Dist.**	27
Grand Central | **multi.**	27
Bakery Bar | **Kerns**	27
Pied Cow | **Belmont**	27
🆕 Dar Salam | **Alberta**	27
Firehouse | **Woodlawn**	27
Papa Haydn | **Sellwood**	26
Helvetia Tav. | **Hillsboro**	26
🆕 Baowry | **St. Johns**	26
Jade Teahouse | **Sellwood**	26
¿Por Que No? | **multi.**	26
Veritable Quandary | **Downtown**	26
Piazza Italia | **Pearl Dist.**	26
Nuestra Cocina | **Division**	26
Besaw's | **NW Portland**	26
Pambiche | **Kerns**	26
Farm Cafe | **Lower Burnside**	26
Irving St. Kitchen | **Pearl Dist.**	26
Wildwood | **NW Portland**	26
Laurelhurst Mkt. | **Kerns**	26
Fire/Mountain | **multi.**	26
Park Kitchen | **Pearl Dist.**	26
Aviary | **Alberta**	26
Tin Shed | **Alberta**	26
Casa Naranja | **Mississippi**	26
Ned Ludd | **King**	26
Wild Abandon | **Belmont**	26
Arleta Library | **Mt. Scott**	26
Foster Burger | **Foster-Powell**	26
Barista | **multi.**	25
Meriwether's | **NW Portland**	25
Mint | **Boise-Eliot**	25
La Calaca Comelona | **Belmont**	25
Hotlips Pizza | **Pearl Dist.**	25
Sweet Basil | **Hollywood**	25
DiPrima Dolci | **Overlook**	25
Equinox | **Mississippi**	25
Cha Ba Thai | **Alberta**	25
CHA Taqueria | **NW Portland**	25
Daily Cafe/Pearl | **Pearl Dist.**	25
Salty's | **NE Portland**	25
Hungry Tiger Too | **Buckman**	25

Share your reviews on plus.google.com/local

Berlin Inn	**Brooklyn**	25
Detour Cafe	**Division**	25
Extracto Coffee	**Concordia**	25
Bluehour	**Pearl Dist.**	25
Highland Stillhse.	**Oregon City**	25
Taqueria/Gorditos	**Central E**	25
Bernie's	**Alberta**	25
Burnside Brew.	**Lower Burnside**	25
Tucci	**Lake Oswego**	25
Gladstone/Pizza	**SE Portland**	24
Cha!Cha!Cha!	**multi.**	24
Isabel	**Pearl Dist.**	24
Noble Rot	**Lower Burnside**	24
John St. Cafe	**St. Johns**	24
Laughing Planet	**multi.**	24
McMenamins	**multi.**	24
Nel Centro	**Downtown**	24
Aquariva	**Johns Landing**	24
Zach's Shack	**Hawthorne**	24
Five Spice	**Lake Oswego**	24
Hopworks	**multi.**	23
Perry's/Fremont	**Alameda**	23
BridgePort	**Pearl Dist.**	23
Departure	**Downtown**	23
EastBurn	**Buckman**	23
Hayden's	**Tualatin**	23
Ciao Vito	**Alberta**	23
Henry's	**Pearl Dist.**	23
Produce Row	**E Industrial**	23
Bent Brick	**NW Portland**	23
EaT	**Boise-Eliot**	22
Radio Room	**Alberta**	22
Lucky Lab	**multi.**	21
3 Degrees	**S Waterfront**	21
Rogue	**Central E**	21
Metrovino	**Pearl Dist.**	20
NEW Basa Basa	**Kerns**	-
NEW Jamison	**Pearl Dist.**	-
NEW Slowburger	**Kerns**	-
NEW 24th & Meatballs	**Kerns**	-
NEW Uno Mas	**Kerns**	-

PEOPLE-WATCHING

Le Pigeon	**Lower Burnside**	28
Andina	**Pearl Dist.**	28
Little Bird	**Downtown**	27
Clyde's Prime Rib	**Hollywood**	27
Salt & Straw	**multi.**	27
Toro Bravo	**Boise-Eliot**	27
Bye & Bye	**Alberta**	27
Higgins	**Downtown**	27

Pok Pok	**Division**	27
Jake's/Crawfish	**W End**	27
Clarklewis	**E Industrial**	27
Via Delizia	**Pearl Dist.**	27
Pine State Biscuits	**multi.**	27
Pied Cow	**Belmont**	27
Observatory	**Montavilla**	26
Papa Haydn	**multi.**	26
Helvetia Tav.	**Hillsboro**	26
Hollywood Burger	**Hollywood**	26
El Gaucho	**Downtown**	26
Veritable Quandary	**Downtown**	26
Heathman	**Downtown**	26
Portland City Grill	**Downtown**	26
Wildwood	**NW Portland**	26
Serratto	**NW Portland**	26
Clyde Common	**W End**	26
Park Kitchen	**Pearl Dist.**	26
Café Castagna	**Hawthorne**	26
La/Petite Provence	**multi.**	26
Genies Cafe	**Central E**	26
Tin Shed	**Alberta**	26
¡Oba!	**Pearl Dist.**	26
Voodoo Doughnut	**multi.**	26
Paragon	**Pearl Dist.**	25
Southpark	**Downtown**	25
Sterling/Coffeehse. NW	**NW Portland**	25
Wong's King	**SE Portland**	25
Hamburger Mary's	**Old Town-Chinatown**	25
Gravy	**Mississippi**	25
Stumptown	**multi.**	25
Hot Pot City	**Downtown**	25
Burnside Brew.	**Lower Burnside**	25
Seasons/Regions	**Multnomah**	24
St. Jack	**Clinton**	24
Helser's/Alberta	**Alberta**	24
Sizzle Pie	**multi.**	24
Woodsman Tav.	**Division**	24
Gilt Club	**Old Town-Chinatown**	24
Isabel	**Pearl Dist.**	24
Noble Rot	**Lower Burnside**	24
Jo Bar	**NW Portland**	24
Blue Olive	**NW Portland**	24
Saucebox	**Downtown**	24
Salvador Molly's	**Hillsdale**	23
Urban Farmer	**Downtown**	23
Davis St.	**Old Town-Chinatown**	23
Silk	**Pearl Dist.**	23
Henry's	**Pearl Dist.**	23

23Hoyt | **NW Portland**	23
Roxy | **W End**	22
Hobo's | **Old Town-Chinatown**	22
Radio Room | **Alberta**	22
Trader Vic's | **Pearl Dist.**	20
NEW Cibo | **Division**	-
NEW Imperial | **Downtown**	-
NEW Jamison | **Pearl Dist.**	-
NEW PaaDee | **Kerns**	-
NEW Riffle NW | **Pearl Dist.**	-
NEW Southland | **NW Portland**	-

QUICK BITES

NEW Lardo | **Hawthorne**	28
PBJ's Grilled | **NW Portland**	28
Gandhi's | **Downtown**	28
Otto's Sausage | **Woodstock**	27
Peoples' Sand. | **Old Town-Chinatown**	27
Baker & Spice | **Hillsdale**	27
Staccato Gelato | **multi.**	27
NEW Shut Up/Eat | **SE Portland**	27
Via Delizia | **Pearl Dist.**	27
Grand Central | **multi.**	27
Bora Bora | **SE Portland**	27
Bunk Sandwiches | **multi.**	27
Hollywood Burger | **Hollywood**	26
Jade Teahouse | **Sellwood**	26
Viking Soul Food | **Belmont**	26
Pho Oregon | **82nd Ave**	26
Pearl Bakery | **Pearl Dist.**	26
Fifty Licks | **Belmont**	26
Escape/NY | **NW Portland**	26
Chen's | **Old Town-Chinatown**	26
Pho Hung | **Foster-Powell**	26
Sugar Cube | **Hawthorne**	26
NEW Jerusalem Cafe | **Belmont**	26
East Side Deli | **multi.**	26
FlavourSpot | **multi.**	26
Blueplate | **Downtown**	26
Blind Onion Pizza | **Hollywood**	26
Binh Minh | **multi.**	26
La/Petite Provence | **multi.**	26
Fleur De Lis | **Hollywood**	26
Pho Van | **multi.**	26
Big-A** Sand. | **E Industrial**	26
Yuzu | **Beaverton**	26
Brunch Box | **Downtown**	26
Foster Burger | **Foster-Powell**	26
Bijou Cafe | **Old Town-Chinatown**	26

Grilled Cheese Grill | **Alberta**	25
E-San | **Old Town-Chinatown**	25
EuroTrash | **W End**	25
Hotlips Pizza | **multi.**	25
DiPrima Dolci | **Overlook**	25
Biwa | **Central E**	25
Campbell's BBQ | **SE Portland**	25
Cha Ba Thai | **multi.**	25
Little Big Burger | **multi.**	25
Daily Cafe/Pearl | **Pearl Dist.**	25
Fuller's | **Pearl Dist.**	25
Hush Hush | **Downtown**	25
Dick's Kitchen | **multi.**	25
Got Pho? | **Hollywood**	25
Detour Cafe | **Division**	25
Du's Grill | **Hollywood**	25
Baan-Thai | **PSU**	25
J & M Cafe | **Central E**	25
Wafu | **Division**	25
Taqueria/Gorditos | **multi.**	25
Santeria | **Downtown**	25
Cider Mill | **Multnomah**	25
Café Yumm | **multi.**	25
NEW Boke Bowl | **E Industrial**	24
Sushi Ichiban | **Old Town-Chinatown**	24
Hammy's Pizza | **Clinton**	24
Joe's Burgers | **multi.**	24
Original Halibut's | **Alberta**	24
Cha!Cha!Cha! | **multi.**	24
Sizzle Pie | **multi.**	24
Clay's Smokehse. | **Division**	24
Thai Ginger | **N Portland**	24
Corbett/Hawthorne Fish. | **multi.**	24
McMenamins | **multi.**	24
Iron Horse | **Sellwood**	24
NEW Mi Mero Mole | **Division**	24
Zach's Shack | **Hawthorne**	24
Whiffies | **Hawthorne**	24
Hopworks | **multi.**	23
BridgePort | **Hawthorne**	23
Davis St. | **Old Town-Chinatown**	23
NEW Robo Taco | **Central E**	23
Dots Cafe | **Clinton**	23
EaT | **Boise-Eliot**	22
Roxy | **W End**	22
Goose Hollow Inn | **Goose Hollow**	22
Marinepolis | **multi.**	21
Rogue | **multi.**	21
NEW Basa Basa | **Kerns**	-
NEW Slowburger | **Kerns**	-

NEW 24th & Meatballs | **Kerns** ⎯⎯

NEW Uno Mas | **Kerns** ⎯⎯

ROMANTIC PLACES

Painted Lady	**Newberg**	29
Natural Selection	**Alberta**	29
NEW Noisette	**NW Portland**	29
Le Pigeon	**Lower Burnside**	28
Genoa	**Belmont**	28
Andina	**Pearl Dist.**	28
Joel Palmer Hse.	**Dayton**	28
Paley's Pl.	**NW Portland**	27
Little Bird	**Downtown**	27
RingSide Steak	**NW Portland**	27
Iorio	**Hawthorne**	27
Toro Bravo	**Boise-Eliot**	27
Castagna	**Hawthorne**	27
DOC	**Concordia**	27
Higgins	**Downtown**	27
Pok Pok	**Division**	27
Beast	**Concordia**	27
Decarli	**Beaverton**	27
Clarklewis	**E Industrial**	27
Via Delizia	**Pearl Dist.**	27
Pied Cow	**Belmont**	27
Firehouse	**Woodlawn**	27
NEW Via Tribunali	**Old Town-Chinatown**	26
Papa Haydn	**multi.**	26
El Gaucho	**Downtown**	26
Navarre	**Kerns**	26
Caffe Mingo	**NW Portland**	26
Jory	**Newberg**	26
East India Co.	**W End**	26
Urban Fondue	**NW Portland**	26
Veritable Quandary	**Downtown**	26
Scratch	**Lake Oswego**	26
Heathman	**Downtown**	26
Farm Cafe	**Lower Burnside**	26
Irving St. Kitchen	**Pearl Dist.**	26
3 Doors Down	**Hawthorne**	26
Portland City Grill	**Downtown**	26
NEW Jerusalem Cafe	**Belmont**	26
Serratto	**NW Portland**	26
Clyde Common	**W End**	26
Aviary	**Alberta**	26
Allium	**West Linn**	25
Basta's	**NW Portland**	25
Biwa	**Central E**	25
Equinox	**Mississippi**	25
Salty's	**NE Portland**	25

Eleni's	**multi.**	25
Huber's	**Downtown**	25
Acadia	**Sabin**	25
Amadeus Manor	**Milwaukie**	25
Cocotte	**Concordia**	25
Bar Avignon	**Division**	25
Seres	**Pearl Dist.**	25
Tucci	**Lake Oswego**	25
Sinju	**multi.**	24
St. Jack	**Clinton**	24
Giorgio's	**Pearl Dist.**	24
June	**Buckman**	24
Gilt Club	**Old Town-Chinatown**	24
Cafe Nell	**NW Portland**	24
Tina's	**Dundee**	24
Urban Farmer	**Downtown**	23
Sapphire Hotel	**Hawthorne**	23
Davis St.	**Old Town-Chinatown**	23
Rimsky-Korsakoffee	**Buckman**	23
Le Bouchon	**Pearl Dist.**	23
Pazzo	**Downtown**	23
Wilfs	**Old Town-Chinatown**	23
Hobo's	**Old Town-Chinatown**	22
Coppia	**Pearl Dist.**	21
3 Degrees	**S Waterfront**	21
Fratelli	**Pearl Dist.**	21
Gracie's	**Goose Hollow**	20
NEW Jamison	**Pearl Dist.**	⎯⎯
Luce	**Buckman**	⎯⎯
NEW Ox	**Boise-Eliot**	⎯⎯
NEW Paulée	**Dundee**	⎯⎯
NEW Roe	**Division**	⎯⎯

SINGLES SCENES

Toro Bravo	**Boise-Eliot**	27
Bye & Bye	**Alberta**	27
Bunk Sandwiches	**Central E**	27
Beaker/Flask	**Central E**	26
Clyde Common	**W End**	26
Café Castagna	**Hawthorne**	26
¡Oba!	**Pearl Dist.**	26
Barista	**multi.**	25
Paragon	**Pearl Dist.**	25
CHA Taqueria	**NW Portland**	25
Jo Bar	**NW Portland**	24
Saucebox	**Downtown**	24
BridgePort	**Pearl Dist.**	23
Departure	**Downtown**	23
Davis St.	**Old Town-Chinatown**	23
Henry's	**Pearl Dist.**	23
Brix Tav.	**Pearl Dist.**	23

DINING

SPECIAL FEATURES

Hobo's | **Old Town-Chinatown** 22

Trader Vic's | **Pearl Dist.** 20

🆕 Imperial | **Downtown** -

🆕 Southland | **NW Portland** -

🆕 Trigger | **Boise-Eliot** -

SPECIAL OCCASIONS

Painted Lady | **Newberg** 29

🆕 Noisette | **NW Portland** 29

Le Pigeon | **Lower Burnside** 28

Genoa | **Belmont** 28

Joel Palmer Hse. | **Dayton** 28

Paley's Pl. | **NW Portland** 27

RingSide Steak | **NW Portland** 27

Iorio | **Hawthorne** 27

Toro Bravo | **Boise-Eliot** 27

DOC | **Concordia** 27

Higgins | **Downtown** 27

Jake's/Crawfish | **W End** 27

Beast | **Concordia** 27

Decarli | **Beaverton** 27

Clarklewis | **E Industrial** 27

Gilda's | **Goose Hollow** 27

Brazil Grill | **Downtown** 27

El Gaucho | **Downtown** 26

Jory | **Newberg** 26

East India Co. | **W End** 26

Veritable Quandary | **Downtown** 26

Tabla | **Kerns** 26

Heathman | **Downtown** 26

Irving St. Kitchen | **Pearl Dist.** 26

Serratto | **NW Portland** 26

Park Kitchen | **Pearl Dist.** 26

Café Castagna | **Hawthorne** 26

Meriwether's | **NW Portland** 25

Salty's | **NE Portland** 25

Huber's | **Downtown** 25

Amadeus Manor | **Milwaukie** 25

Tucci | **Lake Oswego** 25

St. Jack | **Clinton** 24

Giorgio's | **Pearl Dist.** 24

Gilt Club | **Old Town-Chinatown** 24

McMenamins | **Troutdale** 24

Aquariva | **Johns Landing** 24

Hobo's | **Old Town-Chinatown** 22

Gracie's | **Goose Hollow** 20

🆕 Imperial | **Downtown** -

🆕 Jamison | **Pearl Dist.** -

🆕 Ox | **Boise-Eliot** -

🆕 Paulée | **Dundee** -

TRANSPORTING EXPERIENCES

🆕 Noisette | **NW Portland** 29

Genoa | **Belmont** 28

Khun Pic's | **Belmont** 28

St. Honoré | **multi.** 28

Joel Palmer Hse. | **Dayton** 28

Paley's Pl. | **NW Portland** 27

Higgins | **Downtown** 27

Beast | **Concordia** 27

Du Kuh Bee | **Beaverton** 27

Via Delizia | **Pearl Dist.** 27

Ya Hala | **Montavilla** 27

Pied Cow | **Belmont** 27

🆕 Dar Salam | **Alberta** 27

🆕 Via Tribunali | **Old Town-Chinatown** 26

Jory | **Newberg** 26

Piazza Italia | **Pearl Dist.** 26

Yuzu | **Beaverton** 26

Barista | **Alberta** 25

Chennai Masala | **Hillsboro** 25

Wong's King | **SE Portland** 25

Tao of Tea | **Old Town-Chinatown** 25

Highland Stillhse. | **Oregon City** 25

Giorgio's | **Pearl Dist.** 24

McMenamins | **Troutdale** 24

Departure | **Downtown** 23

Rimsky-Korsakoffee | **Buckman** 23

TRENDY

Le Pigeon | **Lower Burnside** 28

🆕 Lardo | **Hawthorne** 28

Andina | **Pearl Dist.** 28

Tanuki | **Montavilla** 28

Tasty n Sons | **Boise-Eliot** 27

Olympic Provisions | **E Industrial** 27

Toro Bravo | **Boise-Eliot** 27

Bye & Bye | **Alberta** 27

Bamboo Sushi | **multi.** 27

Pok Pok | **Division** 27

Beast | **Concordia** 27

Clarklewis | **E Industrial** 27

Bunk Sandwiches | **multi.** 27

Beaker/Flask | **Central E** 26

Sugar Cube | **Hawthorne** 26

Clyde Common | **W End** 26

Park Kitchen | **Pearl Dist.** 26

Aviary | **Alberta** 26

iOba! | **Pearl Dist.** 26

Voodoo Doughnut | **multi.** 26

Foster Burger | **Foster-Powell**	26
Barista | **multi.**	25
Paragon | **Pearl Dist.**	25
Grüner | **W End**	25
Biwa | **Central E**	25
Little Big Burger | **Pearl Dist.**	25
NEW Boxer Sushi | **Hawthorne**	25
Sterling/Coffeehse. NW | **NW Portland**	25
Extracto Coffee | **Concordia**	25
Bluehour | **Pearl Dist.**	25
Wafu | **Division**	25
Stumptown | **multi.**	25
NEW Boke Bowl | **E Industrial**	24
Kenny & Zuke's | **Boise-Eliot**	24
Woodsman Tav. | **Division**	24
Noble Rot | **Lower Burnside**	24
Saucebox | **Downtown**	24
Urban Farmer | **Downtown**	23
Departure | **Downtown**	23
Davis St. | **Old Town-Chinatown**	23
Henry's | **Pearl Dist.**	23
23Hoyt | **NW Portland**	23
Brix Tav. | **Pearl Dist.**	23
NEW Basa Basa | **Kerns**	-
NEW Cibo | **Division**	-
NEW Imperial | **Downtown**	-
Luce | **Buckman**	-
NEW Ox | **Boise-Eliot**	-
NEW Riffle NW | **Pearl Dist.**	-
NEW Roe | **Division**	-
NEW Slowburger | **Kerns**	-
NEW Smallwares | **Beaumont**	-
NEW Trigger | **Boise-Eliot**	-
NEW 24th & Meatballs | **Kerns**	-
NEW Uno Mas | **Kerns**	-
NEW Xico | **Division**	-

WINNING WINE LISTS

Painted Lady | **Newberg**	29
NEW Noisette | **NW Portland**	29
Genoa | **Belmont**	28
Andina | **Pearl Dist.**	28

Joel Palmer Hse. | **Dayton**	28
Paley's Pl. | **NW Portland**	27
RingSide Steak | **NW Portland**	27
Iorio | **Hawthorne**	27
Toro Bravo | **Boise-Eliot**	27
Castagna | **Hawthorne**	27
DOC | **Concordia**	27
Higgins | **Downtown**	27
Navarre | **Kerns**	26
Caffe Mingo | **NW Portland**	26
Jory | **Newberg**	26
East India Co. | **W End**	26
Veritable Quandary | **Downtown**	26
Tabla | **Kerns**	26
Gino's | **Sellwood**	26
Heathman | **Downtown**	26
Farm Cafe | **Lower Burnside**	26
Irving St. Kitchen | **Pearl Dist.**	26
Wildwood | **NW Portland**	26
Park Kitchen | **Pearl Dist.**	26
Accanto | **Belmont**	26
Café Castagna | **Hawthorne**	26
a Cena | **Sellwood**	26
Nick's | **McMinnville**	26
¡Oba! | **Pearl Dist.**	26
Southpark | **Downtown**	25
Eleni's | **Pearl Dist.**	25
Bar Avignon | **Division**	25
Bar Mingo | **NW Portland**	25
Tucci | **Lake Oswego**	25
RingSide Fish Hse. | **Downtown**	24
St. Jack | **Clinton**	24
Noble Rot | **Lower Burnside**	24
E'Njoni Cafe | **Humboldt**	24
Tina's | **Dundee**	24
Aquariva | **Johns Landing**	24
Five Spice | **Lake Oswego**	24
Urban Farmer | **Downtown**	23
Pazzo | **Downtown**	23
Coppia | **Pearl Dist.**	21
NEW Imperial | **Downtown**	-
NEW Ox | **Boise-Eliot**	-
NEW Paulée | **Dundee**	-

DINING

SPECIAL FEATURES

Dining Cuisines

Includes names, locations and Food ratings. These lists include low vote places that do not qualify for tops lists.

AMERICAN

Tasty n Sons	**Boise-Eliot**	27
Waffle Window	**multi.**	27
Simpatica	**Central E**	27
Jam/Hawthorne	**Hawthorne**	27
Original Dinerant	**Downtown**	27
Lincoln	**Boise-Eliot**	27
Clarke's	**Lake Oswego**	27
Observatory	**Montavilla**	26
Milo's City Cafe	**Irvington**	26
Papa Haydn	**multi.**	26
Helvetia Tav.	**Hillsboro**	26
Hollywood Burger	**Hollywood**	26
Country Cat	**Montavilla**	26
Beaker/Flask	**Central E**	26
Original Pancake	**Multnomah**	26
Besaw's	**NW Portland**	26
Oswego Grill	**multi.**	26
Portland City Grill	**Downtown**	26
Clyde Common	**W End**	26
Fire/Mountain	**multi.**	26
Park Kitchen	**Pearl Dist.**	26
Zell's Cafe	**Buckman**	26
Aviary	**Alberta**	26
Genies Cafe	**Central E**	26
Tin Shed	**Alberta**	26
Ned Ludd	**King**	26
Wild Abandon	**Belmont**	26
Arleta Library	**Mt. Scott**	26
Bijou Cafe	**Old Town-Chinatown**	26
Original Hotcake	**Brooklyn**	25
Otto	**Hawthorne**	25
H5O	**Downtown**	25
Mother's	**Downtown**	25
Paragon	**Pearl Dist.**	25
Cricket Cafe	**Belmont**	25
Mint	**Boise-Eliot**	25
Bertie Lou's	**Sellwood**	25
Alameda Cafe	**Beaumont**	25
Christie's	**University Park**	25
Blue Pig	**Hawthorne**	25
Equinox	**Mississippi**	25
Daily Cafe/Pearl	**Pearl Dist.**	25
Abby's Table	**Lower Burnside**	25
Fuller's	**Pearl Dist.**	25
Hungry Tiger Too	**Buckman**	25
Slappy Cakes	**Belmont**	25

Huber's	**Downtown**	25
Cadillac Cafe	**Irvington**	25
Detour Cafe	**Division**	25
Bluehour	**Pearl Dist.**	25
Mac!	**Mississippi**	25
Gravy	**Mississippi**	25
J & M Cafe	**Central E**	25
Bar Avignon	**Division**	25
Brass. Montmartre	**Downtown**	25
Cider Mill	**Multnomah**	25
Helser's/Alberta	**Alberta**	24
Toast	**Woodstock**	24
Beaterville	**Overlook**	24
June	**Buckman**	24
Fat City	**Multnomah**	24
Hall St. Grill	**Beaverton**	24
Gilt Club	**Old Town-Chinatown**	24
Noble Rot	**Lower Burnside**	24
John St. Cafe	**St. Johns**	24
Jo Bar	**NW Portland**	24
Skyline	**Sylvan**	24
Bread & Ink	**Hawthorne**	24
Cafe Nell	**NW Portland**	24
Cassidy's	**W End**	24
Tina's	**Dundee**	24
Bar Carlo	**Foster-Powell**	24
Cup & Saucer	**multi.**	24
Whiffies	**multi.**	24
Hopworks	**multi.**	23
Perry's/Fremont	**Alameda**	23
Grain & Gristle	**Sabin**	23
Sapphire Hotel	**Hawthorne**	23
Davis St.	**Old Town-Chinatown**	23
EastBurn	**Buckman**	23
Hayden's	**Tualatin**	23
Red Star Tav.	**Downtown**	23
Henry's	**Pearl Dist.**	23
23Hoyt	**NW Portland**	23
Produce Row	**E Industrial**	23
Brix Tav.	**Pearl Dist.**	23
Wilfs	**Old Town-Chinatown**	23
Bridges Cafe	**Boise-Eliot**	23
Goose Hollow Inn	**Goose Hollow**	22
Hobo's	**Old Town-Chinatown**	22
Tom's	**Division**	22
Sckavone's	**Division**	22
Radio Room	**Alberta**	22

Share your reviews on plus.google.com/local

3 Degrees | **S Waterfront**	21
Sunshine Tav. | **Division**	21
Gracie's | **Goose Hollow**	20
Metrovino | **Pearl Dist.**	20
NEW Jamison | **Pearl Dist.**	–
NEW Paulée | **Dundee**	–

ARGENTINEAN

NEW Ox | **Boise-Eliot**	–

ASIAN

NEW Baowry | **St. Johns**	26
Café Yumm | **multi.**	25
Ping | **Old Town-Chinatown**	24
Bay Leaf | **Division**	24
Isabel | **Pearl Dist.**	24
Saucebox | **Downtown**	24
Five Spice | **Lake Oswego**	24
Departure | **Downtown**	23
NEW Smallwares | **Beaumont**	–

AUSTRALIAN

Pacific Pie Co. | **Central E**	27

BAKERIES

Ken's/Bakery | **NW Portland**	28
St. Honoré | **multi.**	28
Nuvrei | **Pearl Dist.**	28
Baker & Spice | **Hillsdale**	27
Grand Central | **multi.**	27
Bakery Bar | **Kerns**	27
Lovejoy Bakers | **multi.**	27
Little T | **Division**	26
Pearl Bakery | **Pearl Dist.**	26
La/Petite Provence | **multi.**	26
Fleur De Lis | **Hollywood**	26
DiPrima Dolci | **Overlook**	25

BARBECUE

Podnah's Pit | **NE Portland**	27
Russell St. BBQ | **Boise-Eliot**	26
Campbell's BBQ | **SE Portland**	25
Clay's Smokehse. | **Division**	24
Reo's Ribs | **Johns Landing**	22
NEW Southland | **NW Portland**	–

BELGIAN

Potato Champion | **Hawthorne**	25

BRAZILIAN

Brazil Grill | **Downtown**	27

BURGERS

Killer Burger | **multi.**	27
Helvetia Tav. | **Hillsboro**	26
Hollywood Burger | **Hollywood**	26
Stanich's | **Beaumont**	26
Brunch Box | **Downtown**	26
Foster Burger | **Foster-Powell**	26
Little Big Burger | **multi.**	25
Dick's Kitchen | **multi.**	25
Hamburger Mary's | **Old Town-Chinatown**	25
Joe's Burgers | **multi.**	24
Skyline | **Irvington**	24
Dots Cafe | **Clinton**	23
NEW Slowburger | **Kerns**	–

CAJUN

Le Bistro Montage | **E Industrial**	26
Miss Delta | **Mississippi**	25
Acadia | **Sabin**	25
EaT | **Boise-Eliot**	22
NEW Parish | **Pearl Dist.**	–

CHINESE

(* dim sum specialist)

Du Kuh Bee | **Beaverton**	27
Shandong | **Hollywood**	27
Ocean City* | **82nd Ave**	27
Chen's | **Old Town-Chinatown**	26
Wong's King* | **SE Portland**	25
Thien Hong | **NE Portland**	25
Seres | **Pearl Dist.**	25
Hot Pot City | **Downtown**	25
Lucky Strike | **Hawthorne**	25
Mandarin Cove | **Downtown**	24
Beijing Hot Pot | **82nd Ave**	24
August Moon | **NW Portland**	22

COFFEEHOUSES

Spella Caffe | **Downtown**	29
Pied Cow | **Belmont**	27
Barista | **multi.**	25
Ristretto Roasters | **multi.**	25
Sterling/Coffeehse. NW | **NW Portland**	25
Extracto Coffee | **multi.**	25
Stumptown | **multi.**	25
Albina Press | **Humboldt**	25
Rimsky-Korsakoffee | **Buckman**	23

CONTINENTAL

Amadeus Manor | **Milwaukie**	25

DINING

CUISINES

CREOLE

Le Bistro Montage | **E Industrial**   26
Acadia | **Sabin**   25
EaT | **Boise-Eliot**   22
NEW Parish | **Pearl Dist.**   -

CRÊPES

Chez Machin | **Hawthorne**   29
Le Happy | **NW Portland**   25

CUBAN

Pambiche | **Kerns**   26

DELIS

Otto's Sausage | **Woodstock**   27
Papa G's | **Division**   26
East Side Deli | **multi.**   26
Kornblatt's Deli | **NW Portland**   25
Kenny & Zuke's | **multi.**   24

DESSERT

Cool Moon | **Pearl Dist.**   28
Pix Pâtisserie | **Kerns**   28
Salt & Straw | **NW Portland**   27
Ruby Jewel | **multi.**   27
Staccato Gelato | **multi.**   27
Via Delizia | **Pearl Dist.**   27
Pied Cow | **Belmont**   27
Papa Haydn | **multi.**   26
Fifty Licks | **Belmont**   26
Sugar Cube | **Hawthorne**   26
Voodoo Doughnut | **multi.**   26
Whiffies | **multi.**   24
Rimsky-Korsakoffee | **Buckman**   23

DINER

Original Dinerant | **Downtown**   27
Original Pancake | **Multnomah**   26
Blueplate | **Downtown**   26
Original Hotcake | **Brooklyn**   25
Fuller's | **Pearl Dist.**   25
Overlook | **Overlook**   24
Byways Cafe | **Pearl Dist.**   24
Cup & Saucer | **multi.**   24
Roxy | **W End**   22
Tom's | **Division**   22
NEW Portland Penny | **Downtown**   -

ECLECTIC

Scratch | **Lake Oswego**   26
Clyde Common | **W End**   26
Abby's Table | **Lower Burnside**   25

Whiffies | **multi.**   24
Salvador Molly's | **Hillsdale**   23
Old Wives' Tales | **Buckman**   23
NEW Smallwares | **Beaumont**   -

ETHIOPIAN

E'Njoni Cafe | **Humboldt**   24
Horn/Africa | **King**   24
Queen of Sheba | **Boise-Eliot**   23

EUROPEAN

Evoe | **Hawthorne**   28
Grüner | **W End**   25

FONDUE

Urban Fondue | **NW Portland**   26

FRENCH

NEW Noisette | **NW Portland**   29
Le Pigeon | **Lower Burnside**   28
Beast | **Concordia**   27
Heathman | **Downtown**   26
Brass. Montmartre | **Downtown**   25
St. Jack | **Clinton**   24

FRENCH (BISTRO)

Chez Machin | **Hawthorne**   29
Ken's/Bakery | **NW Portland**   28
St. Honoré | **multi.**   28
Little Bird | **Downtown**   27
La/Petite Provence | **multi.**   26
Fleur De Lis | **Hollywood**   26
Cocotte | **Concordia**   25
Le Bouchon | **Pearl Dist.**   23

GERMAN

Otto's Sausage | **Woodstock**   27
Rheinlander | **Hollywood**   26
Gustav's | **multi.**   25
Berlin Inn | **Brooklyn**   25

GREEK

Alexis | **Old Town-Chinatown**   25
Eleni's | **multi.**   25
Overlook | **Overlook**   24
Mad Greek Deli | **multi.**   23

HAWAIIAN

Noho's | **multi.**   28
Ohana | **multi.**   26
Bamboo Grove | **Johns Landing**   26
808 Grinds | **W End**   25
Ate-Oh-Ate | **Buckman**   22

HOT DOGS

Otto's Sausage | **Woodstock**	27
Zach's Shack | **Hawthorne**	24

ICE CREAM PARLORS

Cool Moon | **Pearl Dist.**	28
Salt & Straw | **multi.**	27
Ruby Jewel | **multi.**	27
Staccato Gelato | **multi.**	27
Fifty Licks | **Belmont**	26

INDIAN

Gandhi's | **Downtown**	28
East India Co. | **W End**	26
Abhiruchi | **Beaverton**	26
Bombay Cricket | **Hawthorne**	26
Chennai Masala | **Hillsboro**	25
NEW Bollywood | **Alberta**	25
Namaste | **NE Portland**	24
Swagat | **multi.**	24
Vindalho | **Clinton**	24

IRISH

Kells | **multi.**	24

ITALIAN

Genoa | **Belmont**	28
Built to Grill | **Downtown**	28
Nostrana | **Buckman**	28
Iorio | **Hawthorne**	27
DOC | **Concordia**	27
Decarli | **Beaverton**	27
Gilda's | **Goose Hollow**	27
Firehouse | **Woodlawn**	27
Justa Pasta | **NW Portland**	26
Caffe Mingo | **NW Portland**	26
Piazza Italia | **Pearl Dist.**	26
Gino's | **Sellwood**	26
3 Doors Down | **Hawthorne**	26
Accanto | **Belmont**	26
a Cena | **Sellwood**	26
Nick's | **McMinnville**	26
Portobello | **Central E**	26
Basta's | **NW Portland**	25
Lucca | **Alameda**	25
DiPrima Dolci | **Overlook**	25
Mingo | **Beaverton**	25
Pastini Pastaria | **multi.**	25
Bar Mingo | **NW Portland**	25
Tucci | **Lake Oswego**	25
Giorgio's | **Pearl Dist.**	24
Amalfi's | **Beaumont**	24

Nel Centro | **Downtown**	24
Aquariva | **Johns Landing**	24
Mama Mia | **Downtown**	23
La Buca | **Kerns**	23
Mi Famiglia | **Oregon City**	23
Old Spaghetti | **multi.**	23
Sal's | **NW Portland**	23
Ciao Vito | **Alberta**	23
Pazzo | **Downtown**	23
Coppia | **Pearl Dist.**	21
Fratelli | **Pearl Dist.**	21
NEW Cibo | **Division**	-
Luce | **Buckman**	-
NEW 24th & Meatballs | **Kerns**	-

JAPANESE

(* sushi specialist)

Tanuki | **Montavilla**	28
Bamboo Sushi* | **multi.**	27
Saburo's* | **Sellwood**	27
Murata* | **Downtown**	26
Yoko's* | **SE Portland**	26
Yuzu | **Beaverton**	26
Koji Osakaya* | **multi.**	25
Zilla Sake Hse.* | **Alberta**	25
Biwa | **Central E**	25
NEW Boxer Sushi* | **Hawthorne**	25
Mio Sushi* | **multi.**	25
Du's Grill | **Hollywood**	25
Wafu | **Division**	25
NEW Boke Bowl | **E Industrial**	24
Sushi Ichiban* | **Old Town-Chinatown**	24
Sinju* | **multi.**	24
Masu* | **W End**	24
Mirakutei* | **Lower Burnside**	23
Marinepolis* | **multi.**	21
NEW Hokusei* | **Belmont**	-

KOREAN

Tanuki | **Montavilla**	28
Du Kuh Bee | **Beaverton**	27
Koi Fusion | **multi.**	25
NEW Boke Bowl | **E Industrial**	24
NEW Basa Basa | **Kerns**	-

LEBANESE

Nicholas | **multi.**	27
Ya Hala | **Montavilla**	27
Karam | **Downtown**	25
Habibi | **multi.**	25
Al-Amir | **Downtown**	25

DINING

CUISINES

MEDITERRANEAN

Via Delizia | **Pearl Dist.**	27
Navarre | **Kerns**	26
Aybla Grill | **multi.**	26
Tabla | **Kerns**	26
NEW Jerusalem Cafe | **Belmont**	26
Serratto | **NW Portland**	26
Casa Naranja | **Mississippi**	26
Bombay Cricket | **Hawthorne**	26
EuroTrash | **multi.**	25
Southpark | **Downtown**	25
Bluehour | **Pearl Dist.**	25
Aladdin's Cafe | **Concordia**	24
Blue Olive | **multi.**	24

MEXICAN

Autentica | **Concordia**	27
Bora Bora | **SE Portland**	27
La Bonita | **multi.**	26
¿Por Que No? | **multi.**	26
Nuestra Cocina | **Division**	26
King Burrito | **N Portland**	26
Koi Fusion | **multi.**	25
Casa de Tamales | **Milwaukie**	25
NEW Mextiza | **Overlook**	25
La Calaca Comelona | **Belmont**	25
CHA Taqueria | **NW Portland**	25
La Sirenita | **multi.**	25
Taqueria/Gorditos | **multi.**	25
Santeria | **Downtown**	25
Cha!Cha!Cha! | **multi.**	24
Laughing Planet | **multi.**	24
Iron Horse | **Sellwood**	24
NEW Mi Mero Mole | **Division**	24
NEW Robo Taco | **Central E**	23
NEW Uno Mas | **Kerns**	-
NEW Xico | **Division**	-

MIDDLE EASTERN

NEW Dar Salam | **Alberta**	27
Hush Hush | **Downtown**	25
Hoda's | **Belmont**	24
Horn/Africa | **King**	24

MOROCCAN

Marrakesh | **NW Portland**	27

NOODLE SHOPS

Wafu | **Division**	25
NEW Boke Bowl | **E Industrial**	24
Frank's | **Irvington**	23

NORWEGIAN

Viking Soul Food | **Belmont**	26

NUEVO LATINO

¡Oba! | **Pearl Dist.**	26

PACIFIC NORTHWEST

Painted Lady | **Newberg**	29
Joel Palmer Hse. | **Dayton**	28
Paley's Pl. | **NW Portland**	27
Olympic Provisions | **multi.**	27
Castagna | **Hawthorne**	27
Higgins | **Downtown**	27
Beast | **Concordia**	27
Clarklewis | **E Industrial**	27
Jory | **Newberg**	26
Veritable Quandary | **Downtown**	26
Heathman | **Downtown**	26
Farm Cafe | **Lower Burnside**	26
Irving St. Kitchen | **Pearl Dist.**	26
Wildwood | **NW Portland**	26
Park Kitchen | **Pearl Dist.**	26
Café Castagna | **Hawthorne**	26
Allium | **West Linn**	25
Meriwether's | **NW Portland**	25
Woodsman Tav. | **Division**	24
Tina's | **Dundee**	24
Bent Brick | **NW Portland**	23
NEW Imperial | **Downtown**	-
NEW Ox | **Boise-Eliot**	-

PAN-LATIN

Isabel | **Pearl Dist.**	24

PERUVIAN

Andina | **Pearl Dist.**	28
El Inka | **Gresham**	25

PIZZA

Lovely's Fifty Fifty | **Mississippi**	28
Apizza Scholls | **Hawthorne**	28
Dove Vivi | **Kerns**	27
Earth Oven | **Hillsboro**	27
Vincente's | **Hawthorne**	27
Flying Pie Pizzeria | **multi.**	27
Ken's Artisan Pizza | **Buckman**	27
NEW Via Tribunali | **Old Town-Chinatown**	26
Mississippi Pizza | **Mississippi**	26
Escape/NY | **NW Portland**	26
Blind Onion Pizza | **Hollywood**	26
Lucca | **Alameda**	25

Hotlips Pizza | **multi.**	25
DiPrima Dolci | **Overlook**	25
Al Forno Ferruzza | **Alberta**	25
Old Town Pizza | **multi.**	25
American Dream | **Mt. Tabor**	25
Mellow Mushroom | **Pearl Dist.**	25
Pizzicato | **multi.**	24
Hammy's Pizza | **Clinton**	24
Sizzle Pie | **multi.**	24
Amalfi's | **Beaumont**	24
Pyro Pizza | **multi.**	23
Mi Famiglia | **Oregon City**	23
NEW Oven & Shaker | **Pearl Dist.**	23

POLYNESIAN

Trader Vic's | **Pearl Dist.**	20

PUB FOOD

Highland Stillhse. | **Oregon City**	25
North 45 | **NW Portland**	25
Burnside Brew. | **Lower Burnside**	25
Kells | **multi.**	24
McMenamins | **multi.**	24
Hopworks | **multi.**	23
BridgePort | **multi.**	23
Grain & Gristle | **Sabin**	23
Alameda Brew. | **Beaumont**	22
Goose Hollow Inn | **Goose Hollow**	22
Lucky Lab | **multi.**	21
MacTarnahan's | **NW Portland**	21
Rogue | **multi.**	21
Virginia Cafe | **Downtown**	21
Monteaux's | **Beaverton**	20

SANDWICHES

(See also Delis)

Evoe | **Hawthorne**	28
NEW Lardo | **multi.**	28
PBJ's Grilled | **NW Portland**	28
Peoples' Sand. | **Old Town-Chinatown**	27
NEW Shut Up/Eat | **SE Portland**	27
Bunk Sandwiches | **multi.**	27
East Side Deli | **multi.**	26
FlavourSpot | **multi.**	26
Big-A** Sand. | **E Industrial**	26
Meat Cheese Bread | **Buckman**	26
Addy's | **W End**	26
Grilled Cheese Grill | **multi.**	25
Daily Cafe/Pearl | **Pearl Dist.**	25

NEW Double Dragon | **Central E**	25
Detour Cafe | **Division**	25
NEW 24th & Meatballs | **Kerns**	–

SCANDINAVIAN

Broder Cafe | **Clinton**	26

SEAFOOD

Cabezon | **Hollywood**	28
Jake's/Crawfish | **W End**	27
Ocean City | **82nd Ave**	27
Jake's Grill | **W End**	26
Fish Grotto | **W End**	26
Fishwife | **University Park**	25
Southpark | **Downtown**	25
Salty's | **NE Portland**	25
Wong's King | **SE Portland**	25
Dan/Louis Oyster | **Old Town-Chinatown**	25
RingSide Fish Hse. | **Downtown**	24
Seasons/Regions | **Multnomah**	24
Original Halibut's | **Alberta**	24
Corbett/Hawthorne Fish. | **multi.**	24
Five Spice | **Lake Oswego**	24
EaT | **Boise-Eliot**	22
NEW Riffle NW | **Pearl Dist.**	–
NEW Roe | **Division**	–

SMALL PLATES

(See also Spanish tapas specialist)

Evoe | Euro. | **Hawthorne**	28
Olympic Provisions | Pac. NW | **multi.**	27
Navarre | Eclectic | **Kerns**	26
Accanto | Italian | **Belmont**	26
Aviary | Amer. | **Alberta**	26
Yuzu | Japanese | **Beaverton**	26
CHA Taqueria | Mex. | **NW Portland**	25
Bar Mingo | Italian | **NW Portland**	25
Ping | SE Asian | **Old Town-Chinatown**	24
Noble Rot | Amer. | **Lower Burnside**	24
Sapphire Hotel | Amer. | **Hawthorne**	23
Luce | Italian | **Buckman**	–
NEW Smallwares | Asian | **Beaumont**	–

SOUL FOOD

Po'Shines | **Kenton**	27

SOUTHERN

Screen Door | **Kerns**	27
Bye & Bye | **Alberta**	27
Pine State Biscuits | **multi.**	27
NEW Mack/Dub's | **Boise-Eliot**	25
Miss Delta | **Mississippi**	25
Campbell's BBQ | **SE Portland**	25
Delta Cafe | **Woodstock**	25
Bernie's | **Alberta**	25
NEW Southland | **NW Portland**	-

SPANISH

(* tapas specialist)

Toro Bravo* | **Boise-Eliot**	27
Navarre | **Kerns**	26
Ciao Vito* | **Alberta**	23

STEAKHOUSES

Clyde's Prime Rib | **Hollywood**	27
RingSide Steak | **multi.**	27
El Gaucho | **Downtown**	26
Sayler's | **SE Portland**	26
Laurelhurst Mkt. | **Kerns**	26
Urban Farmer | **Downtown**	23

SYRIAN

Aladdin's Cafe | **Concordia**	24

TEAHOUSE

Tao of Tea | **multi.**	25

TEX-MEX

Iron Horse | **Sellwood**	24
Esparza's | **Buckman**	23
NEW Trigger | **Boise-Eliot**	-

THAI

Khun Pic's | **Belmont**	28
Pok Pok | **multi.**	27
Thai Peacock | **Downtown**	27
Lemongrass | **Kerns**	27
Jade Teahouse | **Sellwood**	26
Nong's Khao Man Gai | **multi.**	26
Pad Thai Kitchen | **Belmont**	26
Red Onion | **NW Portland**	25
Tuk Tuk Thai | **multi.**	25
E-San | **multi.**	25
Thai Noon | **Alberta**	25
Sweet Basil | **multi.**	25
Cha Ba Thai | **multi.**	25
Baan-Thai | **PSU**	25
Thai Ginger | **N Portland**	24
NEW PaaDee | **Kerns**	-

VEGETARIAN

(* vegan)

Natural Selection* | **Alberta**	29
Blossoming Lotus* | **Irvington**	27
Bye & Bye* | **Alberta**	27
Prasad* | **Pearl Dist.**	27
Papa G's* | **Division**	26
Abhiruchi | **Beaverton**	26
Portobello* | **Central E**	26
Hungry Tiger Too* | **Buckman**	25
Kure Juice Bar* | **Hawthorne**	25
Bay Leaf | **Division**	24
Laughing Planet | **multi.**	24
Vita Cafe* | **Alberta**	24
Paradox Cafe | **Belmont**	24

VIETNAMESE

NEW Luc Lac | **Downtown**	27
Jade Teahouse | **Sellwood**	26
Pho Oregon | **82nd Ave**	26
Pho Hung | **multi.**	26
Bambuza | **multi.**	26
Binh Minh | **multi.**	26
Pho Van | **multi.**	26
NEW Double Dragon | **Central E**	25
Got Pho? | **Hollywood**	25
Thien Hong | **NE Portland**	25
Silk | **Pearl Dist.**	23

Dining Locations

Includes names, cuisines and Food ratings. These lists include low vote places that do not qualify for tops lists.

Portland

ALAMEDA/SABIN

Pok Pok	*Thai*	27
Lucca	*Italian/Pizza*	25
Acadia	*Cajun/Creole*	25
Extracto Coffee	*Coffee*	25
Perry's/Fremont	*Amer.*	23
Grain & Gristle	*Pub*	23

ALBERTA

Natural Selection	*Vegan/Veg.*	29
Waffle Window	*Amer.*	27
Salt & Straw	*Ice Cream*	27
Bye & Bye	*Vegan*	27
Pine State Biscuits	*Southern*	27
NEW Dar Salam	*Mideast.*	27
La Bonita	*Mex.*	26
Aviary	*Amer.*	26
La/Petite Provence	*Bakery/French*	26
Tin Shed	*Amer.*	26
Barista	*Coffee*	25
Grilled Cheese Grill	*Sandwiches*	25
Thai Noon	*Thai*	25
Zilla Sake Hse.	*Japanese*	25
Cha Ba Thai	*Thai*	25
La Sirenita	*Mex.*	25
Al Forno Ferruzza	*Pizza*	25
NEW Bollywood	*Indian*	25
Bernie's	*Southern*	25
Helser's/Alberta	*Amer.*	24
Original Halibut's	*Seafood*	24
Blue Olive	*Med.*	24
Vita Cafe	*Vegan/Veg.*	24
Ciao Vito	*Italian/Spanish*	23
Radio Room	*Amer.*	22

BEAUMONT

Noho's	*Hawaiian*	28
Grand Central	*Bakery*	27
Stanich's	*Burgers*	26
Tuk Tuk Thai	*Thai*	25
Ristretto Roasters	*Coffee*	25
Alameda Cafe	*Amer.*	25
Pizzicato	*Pizza*	24

Hoda's	*Mideast.*	24
Cha!Cha!Cha!	*Mex.*	24
Amalfi's	*Italian/Pizza*	24
Alameda Brew.	*Pub*	22
NEW Smallwares	*Asian*	-

BELMONT

Genoa	*Italian*	28
Khun Pic's	*Thai*	28
Pine State Biscuits	*Southern*	27
Pied Cow	*Coffee/Dessert*	27
Aybla Grill	*Med.*	26
Viking Soul Food	*Noodle Shop*	26
Pad Thai Kitchen	*Thai*	26
Fifty Licks	*Ice Cream*	26
NEW Jerusalem Cafe	*Med.*	26
Accanto	*Italian*	26
Wild Abandon	*Amer.*	26
Cricket Cafe	*Amer.*	25
EuroTrash	*Med.*	25
La Calaca Comelona	*Mex.*	25
Dick's Kitchen	*Burgers*	25
Slappy Cakes	*Amer.*	25
Tao of Tea	*Tea*	25
Stumptown	*Coffee*	25
Hoda's	*Mideast.*	24
Laughing Planet	*Mex./Veg.*	24
Paradox Cafe	*Veg.*	24
NEW Hokusei	*Japanese*	-

BETHANY/SYLVAN

Skyline	*Amer.*	24
Mad Greek Deli	*Greek*	23

BOISE-ELIOT

Tasty n Sons	*Amer.*	27
Toro Bravo	*Spanish/Tapas*	27
Lincoln	*Amer.*	27
Grand Central	*Bakery*	27
Russell St. BBQ	*BBQ*	26
Mint	*Amer.*	25
NEW Mack/Dub's	*Southern*	25
Ristretto Roasters	*Coffee*	25
Kenny & Zuke's	*Deli*	24
Cha!Cha!Cha!	*Mex.*	24
Hopworks	*Pub*	23
Queen of Sheba	*Ethiopian*	23

Bridges Cafe	*Amer.*	23
EaT	*Cajun/Creole*	22
NEW Ox	*Argentinean*	-
NEW Trigger	*Tex-Mex*	-

BROOKLYN

Original Hotcake	*Diner*	25
Berlin Inn	*German*	25

BUCKMAN/KERNS

Pix Pâtisserie	*Dessert*	28
Nostrana	*Italian*	28
Dove Vivi	*Pizza*	27
Screen Door	*Southern*	27
Bamboo Sushi	*Japanese*	27
Staccato Gelato	*Ice Cream*	27
Ken's Artisan Pizza	*Pizza*	27
Bakery Bar	*Bakery*	27
Lemongrass	*Thai*	27
Navarre	*Med.*	26
Tabla	*Med.*	26
Pambiche	*Cuban*	26
Laurelhurst Mkt.	*Steak*	26
Zell's Cafe	*Amer.*	26
Meat Cheese Bread	*Sandwiches*	26
Voodoo Doughnut	*Dessert*	26
Grilled Cheese Grill	*Sandwiches*	25
Hungry Tiger Too	*Amer./Vegan*	25
Pizzicato	*Pizza*	24
June	*Amer.*	24
La Buca	*Italian*	23
Mad Greek Deli	*Greek*	23
EastBurn	*Amer.*	23
Esparza's	*Tex-Mex*	23
Rimsky-Korsakoffee	*Coffee/Dessert*	23
Old Wives' Tales	*Eclectic*	23
Ate-Oh-Ate	*Hawaiian*	22
NEW Basa Basa	*Korean*	-
Luce	*Italian*	-
NEW PaaDee	*Thai*	-
NEW Slowburger	*Burgers*	-
NEW 24th & Meatballs	*Italian/Sandwiches*	-
NEW Uno Mas	*Mex.*	-

CENTRAL EASTSIDE/ EAST INDUSTRIAL

Simpatica	*Amer.*	27
Nicholas	*Lebanese*	27
Pacific Pie Co.	*Australian*	27
Olympic Provisions	*Pac. NW*	27
Clarklewis	*Pac. NW*	27
Lovejoy Bakers	*Bakery*	27
Bunk Sandwiches	*Sandwiches*	27
Beaker/Flask	*Amer.*	26
Genies Cafe	*Amer.*	26
Big-A** Sand.	*Sandwiches*	26
Portobello	*Italian/Vegan*	26
Le Bistro Montage	*Cajun/Creole*	26
Potato Champion	*Belgian*	25
Koi Fusion	*Korean/Mex.*	25
Biwa	*Japanese*	25
NEW Double Dragon	*Viet.*	25
J & M Cafe	*Amer.*	25
Taqueria/Gorditos	*Mex.*	25
NEW Boke Bowl	*Japanese/Noodle Shop*	24
Whiffies	*Eclectic*	24
Pyro Pizza	*Pizza*	23
NEW Robo Taco	*Mex.*	23
Produce Row	*Amer.*	23
Rogue	*Pub*	21

CLINTON/DIVISION

Noho's	*Hawaiian*	28
Pok Pok	*Thai*	27
Little T	*Bakery*	26
Broder Cafe	*Scan.*	26
Nuestra Cocina	*Mex.*	26
Papa G's	*Deli/Vegan*	26
La/Petite Provence	*Bakery/French*	26
Little Big Burger	*Burgers*	25
Detour Cafe	*Amer.*	25
Pastini Pastaria	*Italian*	25
Wafu	*Japanese/Noodle Shop*	25
Bar Avignon	*Amer.*	25
Taqueria/Gorditos	*Mex.*	25
Stumptown	*Coffee*	25
Pizzicato	*Pizza*	24
St. Jack	*French*	24
Hammy's Pizza	*Pizza*	24
Bay Leaf	*Asian/Veg.*	24
Woodsman Tav.	*Pac. NW*	24
Clay's Smokeshe.	*BBQ*	24
NEW Mi Mero Mole	*Mex.*	24
Vindalho	*Indian*	24
Dots Cafe	*Burgers*	23
Tom's	*Diner*	22
Sckavone's	*Amer.*	22
Sunshine Tav.	*Amer.*	21

Share your reviews on plus.google.com/local

NEW Cibo | *Italian*	‑
NEW Roe | *Seafood*	‑
NEW Xico | *Mex.*	‑

CONCORDIA/ WOODLAWN

DOC | *Italian*	27
Beast | *French/Pac. NW*	27
Autentica | *Mex.*	27
Firehouse | *Italian*	27
Hotlips Pizza | *Pizza*	25
Extracto Coffee | *Coffee*	25
Cocotte | *French*	25
Aladdin's Cafe | *Med./Syrian*	24
McMenamins | *Pub*	24
Cup & Saucer | *Diner*	24

DOWNTOWN

Spella Caffe | *Coffee*	29
Built to Grill | *Italian*	28
Gandhi's | *Indian*	28
Little Bird | *French*	27
NEW Luc Lac | *Viet.*	27
Original Dinerant | *Diner*	27
Higgins | *Pac. NW*	27
Thai Peacock | *Thai*	27
Brazil Grill | *Brazilian*	27
Bunk Sandwiches | *Sandwiches*	27
El Gaucho | *Steak*	26
Veritable Quandary | *Pac. NW*	26
Aybla Grill | *Med.*	26
Heathman | *French/Pac. NW*	26
Portland City Grill | *Amer.*	26
Murata | *Japanese*	26
East Side Deli | *Sandwiches*	26
Blueplate | *Diner*	26
Brunch Box | *Burgers*	26
H5O | *Amer.*	25
Karam | *Lebanese*	25
Barista	25
Koi Fusion | *Korean/Mex.*	25
Mother's | *Amer.*	25
Koji Osakaya | *Japanese*	25
Southpark | *Med./Seafood*	25
Hush Hush | *Mideast.*	25
Al-Amir | *Lebanese*	25
Huber's | *Amer.*	25
Pastini Pastaria | *Italian*	25
Stumptown | *Coffee*	25
Santeria | *Mex.*	25
Brass. Montmartre | *Amer./French*	25

Hot Pot City | *Chinese*	25
Café Yumm | *Asian*	25
RingSide Fish Hse. | *Seafood*	24
Pizzicato | *Pizza*	24
Joe's Burgers | *Burgers*	24
Laughing Planet | *Mex./Veg.*	24
Mandarin Cove | *Chinese*	24
Saucebox | *Asian*	24
Nel Centro | *Italian*	24
Mama Mia | *Italian*	23
Urban Farmer | *Steak*	23
Departure | *Asian*	23
Red Star Tav. | *Amer.*	23
Pazzo | *Italian*	23
Virginia Cafe | *Pub*	21
NEW Imperial | *Pac. NW*	‑
NEW Portland Penny | *Diner*	‑

82ND AVENUE

Ocean City | *Chinese/Seafood*	27
Pho Oregon | *Viet.*	26
Pho Van | *Viet.*	26
Beijing Hot Pot | *Chinese*	24

FOSTER-POWELL/ MT. SCOTT

Pho Hung | *Viet.*	26
Binh Minh | *Viet.*	26
Arleta Library | *Amer.*	26
Foster Burger | *Burgers*	26
Bar Carlo | *Amer.*	24
Hopworks | *Pub*	23

GOOSE HOLLOW

Gilda's | *Italian*	27
Hotlips Pizza | *Pizza*	25
Goose Hollow Inn | *Pub*	22
Gracie's | *Amer.*	20

HAWTHORNE

Chez Machin | *French*	29
Evoe | *Euro./Sandwiches*	28
NEW Lardo | *Sandwiches*	28
Apizza Scholls | *Pizza*	28
Waffle Window | *Amer.*	27
Iorio | *Italian*	27
Castagna | *Pac. NW*	27
Jam/Hawthorne | *Amer.*	27
Vincente's | *Pizza*	27
Grand Central | *Bakery*	27
¿Por Que No? | *Mex.*	26
3 Doors Down | *Italian*	26

DINING

LOCATIONS

Sugar Cube	Dessert	26
East Side Deli	Sandwiches	26
Café Castagna	Pac. NW	26
Pho Van	Viet.	26
Bombay Cricket	Indian/Med.	26
Otto	Amer.	25
Potato Champion	Belgian	25
Hotlips Pizza	Pizza	25
Blue Pig	Amer.	25
NEW Boxer Sushi	Japanese	25
Mio Sushi	Japanese	25
Kure Juice Bar	Vegan	25
Albina Press	Coffee	25
Lucky Strike	Chinese	24
Cha!Cha!Cha!	Mex.	24
Corbett/Hawthorne Fish.	Seafood	24
Bread & Ink	Amer.	24
McMenamins	Pub	24
Cup & Saucer	Diner	24
Zach's Shack	Hot Dogs	24
Whiffies	Eclectic	24
Pyro Pizza	Pizza	23
BridgePort	Pub	23
Sapphire Hotel	Amer.	23
Lucky Lab	Pub	21

HILLSDALE/ MULTNOMAH VILL.

Baker & Spice	Bakery	27
Grand Central	Bakery	27
Original Pancake	Amer.	26
Cider Mill	Amer.	25
Pizzicato	Pizza	24
Seasons/Regions	Seafood	24
Fat City	Amer.	24
Salvador Molly's	Eclectic	23
Lucky Lab	Pub	21

HOLLYWOOD

Cabezon	Seafood	28
Clyde's Prime Rib	Steak	27
Nicholas	Lebanese	27
Killer Burger	Burgers	27
Shandong	Chinese	27
Hollywood Burger	Burgers	26
Rheinlander	German	26
Blind Onion Pizza	Pizza	26
Fleur De Lis	Bakery/French	26
Gustav's	German	25
Sweet Basil	Thai	25
Mio Sushi	Japanese	25

Got Pho?	Viet.	25
Du's Grill	Japanese	25

HUMBOLDT/KING

Ned Ludd	Amer.	26
Old Town Pizza	Pizza	25
Albina Press	Coffee	25
E'Njoni Cafe	Ethiopian	24
Horn/Africa	Ethiopian/Mideast.	24
McMenamins	Pub	24

IRVINGTON

Blossoming Lotus	Vegan	27
Grand Central	Bakery	27
Milo's City Cafe	Amer.	26
Koji Osakaya	Japanese	25
Cadillac Cafe	Amer.	25
Pastini Pastaria	Italian	25
Cha!Cha!Cha!	Mex.	24
Skyline	Burgers	24
Frank's	Noodle Shop	23
Marinepolis	Japanese	21

JOHNS LANDING/ SOUTH WATERFRONT

Bamboo Grove	Hawaiian	26
Bambuza	Viet.	26
Corbett/Hawthorne Fish.	Seafood	24
Aquariva	Italian	24
Old Spaghetti	Italian	23
Reo's Ribs	BBQ	22
3 Degrees	Amer.	21

KENTON

Po'Shines	Soul Food	27
E-San	Thai	25
Cup & Saucer	Diner	24

LOWER BURNSIDE

Le Pigeon	French	28
Nong's Khao Man Gai	Thai	26
Farm Cafe	Pac. NW	26
Fire/Mountain	Amer.	26
Abby's Table	Amer./Eclectic	25
Burnside Brew.	Pub	25
Sizzle Pie	Pizza	24
Noble Rot	Amer.	24
Mirakutei	Japanese	23

MISSISSIPPI

Lovely's Fifty Fifty	Pizza	28
Ruby Jewel	Ice Cream	27

Mississippi Pizza	*Pizza*	26
¿Por Que No?	*Mex.*	26
FlavourSpot	*Sandwiches*	26
Casa Naranja	*Med.*	26
Koi Fusion	*Korean/Mex.*	25
Miss Delta	*Cajun/Southern*	25
Equinox	*Amer.*	25
Little Big Burger	*Burgers*	25
Mac!	*Amer.*	25
Gravy	*Amer.*	25
Laughing Planet	*Mex./Veg.*	24
Cup & Saucer	*Diner*	24

MONTAVILLA/ MT. TABOR

Tanuki	*Japanese/Korean*	28
Ya Hala	*Lebanese*	27
Flying Pie Pizzeria	*Pizza*	27
Observatory	*Amer.*	26
Country Cat	*Amer.*	26
American Dream	*Pizza*	25
Pizzicato	*Pizza*	24

NE PORTLAND

RingSide Steak	*Steak*	27
Podnah's Pit	*BBQ*	27
Ohana	*Hawaiian*	26
Fire/Mountain	*Amer.*	26
Binh Minh	*Viet.*	26
Cha Ba Thai	*Thai*	25
Salty's	*Seafood*	25
Thien Hong	*Chinese/Viet.*	25
Namaste	*Indian*	24

NORTH PORTLAND

King Burrito	*Mex.*	26
FlavourSpot	*Sandwiches*	26
Tuk Tuk Thai	*Thai*	25
Thai Ginger	*Thai*	24

NW PORTLAND

NEW Noisette	*French*	29
PBJ's Grilled	*Sandwiches*	28
Ken's/Bakery	*Bakery/French*	28
St. Honoré	*Bakery/French*	28
Paley's Pl.	*Pac. NW*	27
RingSide Steak	*Steak*	27
Salt & Straw	*Ice Cream*	27
Olympic Provisions	*Pac. NW*	27
Bamboo Sushi	*Japanese*	27
Grand Central	*Bakery*	27
Marrakesh	*Moroccan*	27

Justa Pasta	*Italian*	26
Papa Haydn	*Amer./Dessert*	26
Caffe Mingo	*Italian*	26
Urban Fondue	*Fondue*	26
Escape/NY	*Pizza*	26
Besaw's	*Amer.*	26
Wildwood	*Pac. NW*	26
Serratto	*Med.*	26
Stepping Stone	*Amer.*	25
Red Onion	*Thai*	25
Basta's	*Italian*	25
Meriwether's	*Pac NW*	25
Ristretto Roasters	*Coffee*	25
Sweet Basil	*Thai*	25
CHA Taqueria	*Mex.*	25
Little Big Burger	*Burgers*	25
Kornblatt's Deli	*Deli*	25
Mio Sushi	*Japanese*	25
Dick's Kitchen	*Burgers*	25
Sterling/Coffeehse. NW	*Coffee*	25
Pastini Pastaria	*Italian*	25
North 45	*Pub*	25
Le Happy	*Crepes*	25
Bar Mingo	*Italian*	25
Pizzicato	*Pizza*	24
Kenny & Zuke's	*Deli*	24
Laughing Planet	*Mex./Veg.*	24
Jo Bar	*Amer.*	24
Kells	*Irish/Pub*	24
Swagat	*Indian*	24
Cafe Nell	*Amer.*	24
Blue Olive	*Med.*	24
McMenamins	*Pub*	24
Sal's	*Italian*	23
23Hoyt	*Amer.*	23
Bent Brick	*Pac. NW*	23
August Moon	*Chinese*	22
Lucky Lab	*Pub*	21
MacTarnahan's	*Pub*	21
NEW Southland	*BBQ/Southern*	-

OLD TOWN- CHINATOWN

Peoples' Sand.	*Sandwiches*	27
NEW Via Tribunali	*Pizza*	26
Chen's	*Chinese*	26
Voodoo Doughnut	*Dessert*	26
Bijou Cafe	*Amer.*	26
E-San	*Thai*	25
Habibi	*Lebanese*	25
Alexis	*Greek*	25

Tao of Tea	*Tea*	25
Hamburger Mary's	*Burgers*	25
Dan/Louis Oyster	*Seafood*	25
Old Town Pizza	*Pizza*	25
Sushi Ichiban	*Japanese*	24
Ping	*SE Asian*	24
Gilt Club	*Amer.*	24
Kells	*Irish/Pub*	24
Davis St.	*Amer.*	23
Wilfs	*Amer.*	23
Hobo's	*Amer.*	22

OVERLOOK

La Bonita	*Mex.*	26
Fire/Mountain	*Amer.*	26
NEW Mextiza	*Mex.*	25
DiPrima Dolci	*Bakery/Italian*	25
Mio Sushi	*Japanese*	25
Overlook	*Diner*	24
Beaterville	*Amer.*	24
Lucky Lab	*Pub*	21

PEARL DISTRICT

Cool Moon	*Ice Cream*	28
Andina	*Peruvian*	28
Nuvrei	*Bakery*	28
Prasad	*Vegan*	27
Via Delizia	*Dessert/Med.*	27
Lovejoy Bakers	*Bakery*	27
Piazza Italia	*Italian*	26
Pearl Bakery	*Bakery*	26
Irving St. Kitchen	*Pac. NW*	26
Park Kitchen	*Pac. NW*	26
¡Oba!	*Nuevo Latino*	26
Barista	*Coffee*	25
Paragon	*Amer.*	25
Hotlips Pizza	*Pizza*	25
Little Big Burger	*Burgers*	25
Daily Cafe/Pearl	*Amer.*	25
Eleni's	*Greek*	25
Fuller's	*Diner*	25
Mio Sushi	*Japanese*	25
Bluehour	*Amer./Med.*	25
Mellow Mushroom	*Pizza*	25
Taqueria/Gorditos	*Mex.*	25
Seres	*Chinese*	25
Sinju	*Japanese*	24
Giorgio's	*Italian*	24
Cha!Cha!Cha!	*Mex.*	24
Isabel	*Asian/Pan-Latin*	24
Byways Cafe	*Diner*	24

Laughing Planet	*Mex./Veg.*	24
BridgePort	*Pub*	23
NEW Oven & Shaker	*Pizza*	23
Silk	*Viet.*	23
Henry's	*Amer.*	23
Le Bouchon	*French*	23
Brix Tav.	*Amer.*	23
Coppia	*Italian*	21
Marinepolis	*Japanese*	21
Rogue	*Pub*	21
Fratelli	*Italian*	21
Metrovino	*Amer.*	20
Trader Vic's	*Polynesian*	20
NEW Jamison	*Amer.*	-
NEW Parish	*Cajun/Creole*	-
NEW Riffle NW	*Seafood*	-

PSU

Nong's Khao Man Gai	*Thai*	26
Hotlips Pizza	*Pizza*	25
Baan-Thai	*Thai*	25
Café Yumm	*Asian*	25
Pizzicato	*Pizza*	24
NEW Joe's Burgers	*Burgers*	24
Rogue	*Pub*	21

SELLWOOD

Killer Burger	*Burgers*	27
Staccato Gelato	*Ice Cream*	27
Grand Central	*Bakery*	27
Saburo's	*Japanese*	27
Papa Haydn	*Amer./Dessert*	26
Jade Teahouse	*Thai/Viet.*	26
Gino's	*Italian*	26
a Cena	*Italian*	26
Bertie Lou's	*Amer.*	25
Eleni's	*Greek*	25
Mio Sushi	*Japanese*	25
La Sirenita	*Mex.*	25
Pizzicato	*Pizza*	24
Cha!Cha!Cha!	*Mex.*	24
Iron Horse	*Tex-Mex*	24

SE PORTLAND

NEW Shut Up/Eat	*Sandwiches*	27
Bora Bora	*Mex.*	27
Sayler's	*Steak*	26
Yoko's	*Japanese*	26
Campbell's BBQ	*BBQ*	25
Wong's King	*Chinese*	25
Gladstone/Pizza	*Pizza*	24

ST. JOHNS/
UNIVERSITY PARK

NEW Baowry | *Asian* — 26
East Side Deli | *Sandwiches* — 26
Fishwife | *Seafood* — 25
Christie's | *Amer.* — 25
Bagel & Box | *Amer.* — 25
John St. Cafe | *Amer.* — 24
McMenamins | *Pub* — 24

SW PORTLAND

Sweet Basil | *Thai* — 25
Joe's Burgers | *Burgers* — 24
Laughing Planet | *Mex./Veg.* — 24

WEST END

NEW Lardo | *Sandwiches* — 28
Ruby Jewel | *Ice Cream* — 27
Jake's/Crawfish | *Seafood* — 27
East India Co. | *Indian* — 26
Nong's Khao Man Gai | *Thai* — 26
Aybla Grill | *Med.* — 26
Jake's Grill | *Seafood* — 26
Clyde Common | *Amer./Eclectic* — 26
Addy's | *Sandwiches* — 26
Fish Grotto | *Seafood* — 26
808 Grinds | *Hawaiian* — 25
Grilled Cheese Grill | *Sandwiches* — 25
Habibi | *Lebanese* — 25
EuroTrash | *Med.* — 25
Grüner | *Euro.* — 25
Stumptown | *Coffee* — 25
Kenny & Zuke's | *Deli* — 24
Sizzle Pie | *Pizza* — 24
Cassidy's | *Amer.* — 24
McMenamins | *Pub* — 24
Masu | *Japanese* — 24
Roxy | *Diner* — 22

WOODSTOCK

Otto's Sausage | *Deli/German* — 27
Delta Cafe | *Southern* — 25
Toast | *Amer.* — 24
Laughing Planet | *Mex./Veg.* — 24

Portland Suburbs

ALOHA/BEAVERTON

Decarli | *Italian* — 27
Du Kuh Bee | *Chinese/Korean* — 27
Pho Hung | *Viet.* — 26

Pho Van | *Viet.* — 26
Abhiruchi | *Indian* — 26
Yuzu | *Japanese* — 26
Mingo | *Italian* — 25
Mio Sushi | *Japanese* — 25
Pastini Pastaria | *Italian* — 25
Café Yumm | *Asian* — 25
Pizzicato | *Pizza* — 24
Hall St. Grill | *Amer.* — 24
Swagat | *Indian* — 24
Marinepolis | *Japanese* — 21
Monteaux's | *Pub* — 20

CLACKAMAS/
HAPPY VALLEY

Gustav's | *German* — 25
Sinju | *Japanese* — 24
Old Spaghetti | *Italian* — 23
Marinepolis | *Japanese* — 21

GRESHAM/
TROUTDALE

Nicholas | *Lebanese* — 27
Flying Pie Pizzeria | *Pizza* — 27
El Inka | *Peruvian* — 25
McMenamins | *Pub* — 24

HILLSBORO

Earth Oven | *Pizza* — 27
Helvetia Tav. | *Burgers* — 26
Bambuza | *Viet.* — 26
Chennai Masala | *Indian* — 25
Swagat | *Indian* — 24
Old Spaghetti | *Italian* — 23

LAKE OSWEGO

St. Honoré | *Bakery/French* — 28
Clarke's | *Amer.* — 27
Flying Pie Pizzeria | *Pizza* — 27
Scratch | *Eclectic* — 26
Oswego Grill | *Amer.* — 26
La/Petite Provence | *Bakery/French* — 26
Tucci | *Italian* — 25
Five Spice | *Asian/Seafood* — 24

MILWAUKIE

Flying Pie Pizzeria | *Pizza* — 27
Ohana | *Hawaiian* — 26
Casa de Tamales | *Mex.* — 25
Amadeus Manor | *Continental* — 25
Cha!Cha!Cha! | *Mex.* — 24

DINING

LOCATIONS

OREGON CITY/ WEST LINN

Allium | *Pac. NW*   25
Highland Stillhse. | *Pub*   25
Mi Famiglia | *Italian/Pizza*   23

TIGARD

Gustav's | *German*   25
Koi Fusion | *Korean/Mex.*   25
Pastini Pastaria | *Italian*   25
Sinju | *Japanese*   24
Joe's Burgers | *Burgers*   24
Marinepolis | *Japanese*   21

TUALATIN

Bambuza | *Viet.*   26
Hayden's | *Amer.*   23

WILSONVILLE

Oswego Grill | *Amer.*   26

Outlying Areas

DAYTON

Joel Palmer Hse. | *Pac. NW*   28

DUNDEE

Tina's | *Pac. NW*   24
NEW Paulée | *Pac. NW*   -

MCMINNVILLE

Nick's | *Italian*   26

NEWBERG

Painted Lady | *Pac. NW*   29
Jory | *Pac. NW*   26

FOOD | DECOR | SERVICE | COST

Dining

Ratings & Symbols

Food, Decor & **Service** are rated on a 30-point scale.

Cost reflects the price of dinner with a drink and tip; lunch is usually 25% to 30% less. For unrated newcomers, the price range is as follows:

I $25 and below	E $41 to $65
M $26 to $40	VE $66 or above
◐ serves after 11 PM	M closed on Monday
S closed on Sunday	

Abby's Table S M *American/Eclectic* 25 | 22 | 25 | $39

Lower Burnside | 609 SE Ankeny St. (6th Ave.) | 503-828-7662 | www.abbys-table.com

"Eaters of all stripes" gather for "flavorful", "family-style" prix fixe feasts that run the gamut from seafood to vegan to "all kinds of '-free' diets" at Abby Fammartino's "local, seasonal" Eclectic-American in Lower Burnside; also bringing folks to the table: the "warm, inviting" "community-minded" atmosphere and "easy-on-the-wallet" prices; P.S. dinner is Wednesday-Saturday only and requires a reservation.

Abhiruchi *Indian* 26 | 19 | 22 | $18

Beaverton | 3815 SW Murray Blvd. (Millikan Way) | 503-671-0432 | www.abhiruchirestaurant.com

"Beautifully seasoned meat and vegetarian" food - and "lots of it" - "never fails to refresh" those tucking into the "authentic" Northern and Southern Indian eats at this Beaverton "strip-mall" joint; so maybe the setting is "not high-end", but "friendly" service and "reasonable" tabs, especially for the "amazing" lunch buffet, make it "worth the drive."

Acadia S *Cajun/Creole* 25 | 22 | 24 | $29

Sabin | 1303 NE Fremont St. (13th Ave.) | 503-249-5001 | www.creolapdx.com

"Mind-blowing" barbecued shrimp and other "dressed up" Cajun-Creole favorites combine with Southern "hospitality" to carve out a "little slice of New Orleans" at this Sabin bistro; there's also a whiff of "Tennessee Williams" in the "romantic" "mood lighting" that makes "every night date night" - though thrifty types love the "wonderful" prix fixe deal Monday evenings.

Accanto *Italian* 26 | 23 | 24 | $31

Belmont | 2838 SE Belmont St. (29th Ave.) | 503-235-4900 | www.accantopdx.com

"Amazing" housemade pastas and other "high-quality" Italian small plates make this "reasonably priced" sister to Belmont's "well-known" Genoa next door a destination in itself; add in "fun cocktails" and "warm" service, and it's a "swell place to meet friends for happy hour" too - and the weekend brunch is one of the "best-kept secrets in town."

a Cena *Italian* | 26 | 22 | 24 | $33 |

Sellwood | 7742 SE 13th Ave. (Lambert St.) | 503-206-3291 |
www.acenapdx.com

"Fantastic" Italian fare, including "fresh homemade" pastas, plus a
"reasonably priced" Boot-heavy wine list make this "warm, intimate" Sellwood nook a "charming" spot for a "romantic evening" or
dinner with the "family"; add in "truly welcoming", "gracious" service, and fans say "you will go back, again and again."

Addy's Sandwich Bar 🗷 *Sandwiches* | 26 | 23 | 25 | $16 |

West End | SW Alder St. & 10th Ave. | 503-267-0994 |
www.addyssandwichbar.com

"Inventive" sandwiches with a lot of "personality" are "lovingly prepared" by namesake proprietress Addy Dittner and her "friendly"
crew at this West End food cart that gets extra props for its "amazing" duck confit; factor in the "low price" and area devotees say it's
a "go-to" for weekday lunch; P.S. closed weekends.

Aladdin's Cafe *Mediterranean/Syrian* | 24 | 21 | 22 | $23 |

Concordia | 6310 NE 33rd Ave. (Holman St.) | 503-546-7686 |
www.aladdinscafe.com

"They know how to prepare lamb" at this "amazing", "inexpensive"
Mediterranean-Syrian in Concordia, whose "authentic", "well-
seasoned" dishes are perfect for sharing; the "homey" ambiance reminds some of "eating in a Middle Eastern living room", and the
service matches the "friendly environment."

Alameda Brewhouse *Pub Food* | 22 | 22 | 23 | $22 |

Beaumont | 4765 NE Fremont St. (49th Ave.) | 503-460-9025 |
www.alamedabrewhouse.com

Backers of this "solid neighborhood brewpub" in Beaumont praise
the "hearty", "quality" grub that admirably "sops up" its "specialized" house-brewed beer; hopsheads particularly "enjoy" the twice-
daily weekday happy hour (with a late-night weekend one, as well),
though "awesome" service and spacious industrial-leaning, "laid-
back" environs make it "family"-friendly too.

Alameda Cafe *American* | 25 | 22 | 24 | $17 |

Beaumont | 4641 NE Fremont St. (47th Ave.) | 503-284-5314 |
www.thealamedacafe.com

This "totally wonderful neighborhood cafe" in Beaumont gets kudos
for its "standout" breakfast and "something-for-everyone" American
offerings in a dressed-up setting that includes white linens and fresh
flowers on every table; prices are reasonable, and the staff is "nice"
even "when you're in a bad mood."

Al-Amir Lebanese Restaurant *Lebanese* | 25 | 22 | 24 | $26 |

Downtown | 223 SW Stark St. (bet. 2nd & 3rd Aves.) | 503-274-0010 |
www.alamirportland.com

"Wonderfully smoky" baba ghanoush and what may be the "best
hummus in Portland" stand out on a Lebanese menu full of "fabulous" dishes deemed "excellent for the price" at this Middle Eastern

mainstay in a "beautiful old" brick building Downtown; "subtle",
"professional" service bolsters the "classy", "quiet" atmosphere,
though it's "quite the party place" on Friday and Saturday nights
thanks to the "interactive (yikes!)" belly dancers.

Albina Press   *Coffeehouse*
25 | 24 | 25 | $11

Hawthorne | 5012 SE Hawthorne Blvd. (50th Ave.) | no phone
Humboldt | 4637 N. Albina Ave. (Blandena St.) | no phone

"Hordes of Mac users" and "studiers" who call this "trendy" Humboldt
cafe (and its larger Hawthorne sibling) home appreciate its offerings of "well-crafted" coffee drinks, tea steeped in French presses
and "delicious" pastries, all at low prices; additional perks are bright,
minimalist digs and "great customer service" – especially welcome
if you're "grumpy and late for work."

Alexis   🅱 *Greek*
25 | 21 | 25 | $21

Old Town-Chinatown | 215 W. Burnside St. (bet. 2nd & 3rd Aves.) |
503-224-8577 | www.alexisfoods.com

The "lengthy, mouthwatering" Hellenic menu featuring "some of the
best calamari around" is "as old school as it gets" and affordable to
boot at this "established" Old Town eatery run by a "wonderful" staff;
though "not much to look at from the outside", the interior boasts
high ceilings and a rustic-"Greek" feel – and the Friday and Saturday
night belly dancing will "keep you entertained."

Al Forno Ferruzza   *Pizza*
25 | 22 | 22 | $16

Alberta | 2738 NE Alberta St. (27th Ave.) | 503-253-6766 |
www.503alforno.com

It's all about "awesome" wood-fired, Sicilian-style pizza and "satisfying" calzones at this inexpensive Alberta pie joint; the staff adds
to the "relaxing" vibe in the "funky" colorful environs that are well
suited for grabbing a beer and watching the "characters wandering
in" from the neighborhood.

Allium   *Pacific NW*
25 | 23 | 23 | $33

West Linn | 1914 Willamette Falls Dr. (bet. 12th & 13th Sts.) |
503-387-5604 | www.alliumoregon.com

"Scrumptious" Pacific NW dishes – including "picture-perfect"
burgers – are made with local ingredients and paired with "delicious"
house-infused cocktails at this West Linn bistro; all in all, neighborhood regulars are "glad to have a quality place like this" with its "cozy",
"pleasant" interior, "beautiful" patio and solid service; P.S. special
themed dinners are offered occasionally.

Amadeus Manor   🅱🅼 *Continental*
25 | 24 | 23 | $34

Milwaukie | 2122 SE Sparrow St. (21st Ave.) | 503-659-1735 |
www.amadeusmanor.com

An "outstanding" symphony of Continental classics (schnitzel, rack
of lamb and "top-notch" desserts) takes center stage at this "romantic" chandelier-lit and Persian rug–strewn stone abode with a
"stunning location" on the Willamette River in Milwaukie; contribut-
ing to the general harmony are moderate prices and fluid service,
making it "perfect for a wedding or special occasion."

	FOOD	DECOR	SERVICE	COST

Amalfi's ⓜ *Italian/Pizza* `24` `21` `23` `$20`

Beaumont | 4703 NE Fremont St. (47th Ave.) | 503-284-6747 |
www.amalfisrestaurant.com

Boosters of this Beaumont "tradition" span generations ("my parents went on their first date here") and celebrate the "tough-to-beat" pizza with a "nice crunch" plus "hearty" "old-time" Italian favorites at a "moderate" cost; service is "prompt", and a remodel "to bring it up to date" conserves its "warm", "inviting" feel.

American Dream Pizza *Pizza* `25` `22` `23` `$18`

Mt. Tabor | 4620 NE Glisan St. (47th Ave.) | 503-230-0699 |
www.americandreampizzapdx.com

"Awesome pizzas" "piled high" with "unique" toppings meet up with "huge" salads, local microbrews and breakfast omelets at this "affordable" Mt. Tabor shop deemed a "worthy choice" in the area; the service gets mixed marks, but it's generally overshadowed by the "funky" hand-painted decor that "looks like a Deadhead designed it."

Andina *Peruvian* `28` `26` `26` `$40`

Pearl District | Pennington Bldg. | 1314 NW Glisan St. (bet. 13th & 14th Aves.) | 503-228-9535 | www.andinarestaurant.com

An array of "lovely flavors" "tickle your taste buds" at this Pearl District "destination", where "adventurous" eaters tuck into "delicious, modern" Peruvian fare – plus a "huge selection" of "inventive, colorful" tapas – and wash it down with "amazing" "regional cocktails" (the "spicy" Sacsayhuamán concoction, pronounced 'sexy woman', is a "must"); "warm" service matches the "boisterous", "gorgeous" environs, and though "pricey", there's no denying it's the "real deal."

Apizza Scholls *Pizza* `28` `18` `21` `$21`

Hawthorne | 4741 SE Hawthorne Blvd. (48th Ave.) | 503-233-1286 |
www.apizzascholls.com

Even those who "don't do lines" eagerly hop on the "infamous", "down-the-block" queue at this Hawthorne pizzeria, where "amazing" pies with a "thin", "slightly charred" crust "reflect an artisan approach" to the craft; sure, there are "dough shortages", "Soup Nazi-esque rules" (e.g. "limit on number of toppings", carryout Monday–Wednesday only) and "no decor" to speak of, but it's "all about the pizza", folks.

Aquariva *Italian* `24` `24` `24` `$32`

Johns Landing | 4650 SW Hamilton Ct. (Moody Ave.) | 503-802-5850 |
www.riversedgehotel.com

The "lovely" views of the Willamette River from the wide terrace of this sleek Johns Landing Italian eatery and wine bar nearly take the attention away from the "delicious", "creative" and moderately priced plates; the "friendly" service is a plus, and the overall experience "rewards those patrons willing to take the trip"; P.S. there's a make-your-own Bloody Mary and mimosa bar during the boozy Sunday brunch.

	FOOD	DECOR	SERVICE	COST

Arleta Library *American*
26 | 21 | 23 | $17

Mt. Scott | 5513 SE 72nd Ave. (Harold St.) | 503-774-4470 | www.arletalibrary.com

"Get there early" for this Mt. Scott American's "fantastic" breakfast including the humbly named Portland's Best Biscuits-n-Gravy and other wallet-friendly brunch and lunch items; the "tiny", "cramped" (some say "uncomfortable") space defines "neighborhood cafe-style dining", as does the "great" staff.

Ate-Oh-Ate *Hawaiian*
22 | 20 | 23 | $19

Buckman | 2454 E. Burnside St. (bet. 24th & 26th Aves.) | 503-445-6101 | www.ate-oh-ate.com

Like a "trip to the islands", this inexpensive stop in Buckman from the crew behind Simpatica and Laurelhurst Market supplies "quality" Hawaiian fare such as plate lunches, poke and and shave ice, plus "ice-cold beer" and rummy cocktails; the "casual" space features counter service, an open kitchen and wooden tables topped with bottles of Sriracha.

August Moon *Chinese*
22 | 19 | 21 | $17

Northwest Portland | 405 NW 23rd Ave. (Flanders St.) | 503-248-9040 | www.augustmoonrestaurant.com

For a "quick, solid Asian lunch" on bustling 23rd Avenue in NW Portland, this "inexpensive" Chinese fits the bill; paper lanterns decorate the "small, cute" space that a few find a bit "shabby", and while service is "fine", many opt for takeout or delivery.

Autentica Ⓜ *Mexican*
27 | 22 | 23 | $27

Concordia | 5507 NE 30th Ave. (Killingsworth St.) | 503-287-7555 | www.autenticaportland.com

Chef Oswaldo Bibiano turns out "exceptional" cuisine with "bright, bold flavors" that's "everything that Mexican food should be" at his midpriced Concordia cantina; "deliciously potent" margaritas, "attentive" service and a "cozy", "stylish" space that includes a lush back garden round out the offerings; P.S. "the mole is a must."

Aviary Ⓢ *American*
26 | 23 | 25 | $43

Alberta | 1733 NE Alberta St. (18th Ave.) | 503-287-2400 | www.aviarypdx.com

Alberta takes flight with this "cutting-edge" upmarket New American where a trio of ex–New York City chefs turns out "sophisticated, nuanced" small plates that "pack maximum flavor" (the dishes that "sound odd are often the best"); wood, candles and "outstanding" service warm up the urban, "bird-sized" space.

Aybla Grill *Mediterranean*
26 | 24 | 25 | $11

Belmont | Good Food Here | SE Belmont St. & 43rd Ave. | 503-222-1531
Downtown | SW Fifth Ave. & Oak St. | no phone Ⓢ
West End | SW Alder St. & 10th Ave. | 503-490-3387
www.ayblagrill.com

Thrifty fans head to this food truck trio with distinctive blue awnings offering "awesome" Med eats like gyros and falafels; factor in affable service and folks "simply can't stay away"; P.S. delivery is a plus.

	FOOD	DECOR	SERVICE	COST

Baan-Thai ⊠ *Thai*   25 | 20 | 21 | $18

PSU | 1924 SW Broadway (bet. College & Hall Sts.) | 503-224-8424
On the edge of Downtown's Portland State University, this "affordable", "real-deal" Thai impresses students with "hot-as-hell" dishes, including some unusual ones that are worth going "out on a limb" for; a "standard" interior and a "slow" but "well-intentioned" crew inspire some to "call way ahead" for takeout.

Bagel & Box ⊠ *American*   25 | 22 | 24 | $14

University Park | 4707 N. Lombard St. (Huron Ave.) | 503-555-5555
"Tasty", low-cost American breakfast eats on the go – from egg sandwiches to local coffee – are the order of the day at this speedy University Park food cart next to Western Meat Market; it was opened by the "nice" crew behind FlavourSpot waffle carts and sources its goods from a variety of area bakeries.

Baker & Spice Ⓜ *Bakery*   27 | 21 | 24 | $12

Hillsdale | 6330 SW Capitol Hwy. (Bertha Ct.) | 503-244-7573 | www.bakerandspicebakery.com
"Deliciously decadent" croissants lead the lineup at Julie Richardson's "hidden gem" of a bakery in a Hillsdale strip mall where fans do "carbo-loading" on "wonderful" pastries, while "to-die-for" homemade soups, "yummy" sandwiches and salads round out the menu; just "be prepared to wait", since the "small", "delightful" space staffed with a "happy" crew has a line out the door nearly every morning.

Bakery Bar *Bakery*   27 | 22 | 22 | $14

Kerns | 2935 NE Glisan St. (bet. 29th & 30th Aves.) | 503-477-7779 | www.bakerybar.com
From-scratch pastries, custom cakes and breakfast standards are made with a "touch of love" at this Kerns bakery, coffee shop and cocktail bar mash-up, slinging inexpensive, "eggs-cellent" sandwiches, "amazing" biscuits and the like, with Stumptown coffee and booze; the modern, industrial environs are "noisy when busy" and include a "huge" front patio.

Bamboo Grove *Hawaiian*   26 | 22 | 23 | $19

Johns Landing | 515 SW Carolina St. (Virginia Ave.) | 503-977-2771 | www.bghawaiiangrille.com
A menu of "delish", "authentic" Hawaiian grinds draws island junkies to this reasonably priced Johns Landing hideaway with solid service; a "big appetite, flip-flops and a pau hana attitude" are advised to match the "fun", "laid-back" environs replete with tiki torches, hanging surf boards and live music on Friday and Saturday nights.

Bamboo Sushi *Japanese*   27 | 25 | 25 | $29

Buckman | 310 SE 28th Ave. (Pine St.) | 503-232-5255
NEW **Northwest Portland** | 836 NW 23rd Ave. (Kearney St.) | 971-229-1925
www.bamboosushi.com
"Incredible", "exquisitely plated" sushi crafted from certified sustainably sourced seafood allows for "guilt-free" dining at this "sceney"

Buckman Japanese with a newer NW 23rd offshoot; even if it's a "little spendy" to some, the "gorgeous" modern space and "professional service" willing to "explain the more exotic" dishes are "definitely worth it."

Bambuza ⊠ *Vietnamese* — 26 | 23 | 22 | $16

South Waterfront | 3682 SW Bond Ave. (Gaines St.) | 503-206-6330
Hillsboro | 19300 NW Cornell Rd. (Amberglen Pkwy.) | 503-747-5882
Tualatin | 7628 SW Nyberg St. (Martinazzi Ave.) | 503-692-9800
www.bambuza.com

"Fast, tasty, inexpensive" and a "favorite lunch spot", this Vietnamese mini-chain ladles up bowls of pho that'll "warm the body from the inside out" plus favorites like summer rolls and banh mi; "accommodating" service and "comfortable" digs mean regulars "always walk away full and happy."

NEW The Baowry ❶ *Asian* — ▽ 26 | 25 | 25 | $24

St. Johns | 8307 N. Ivanhoe St. (Charleston Ave.) | 503-285-4839 | www.baowrypdx.com

Asian steamed buns, or bao, are the thing at this food cart–turned-eatery in St. Johns that attracts a youthful crowd for its namesake rolls and Korean- and Vietnamese-inspired noodles and soups; the interior of the diminutive space stays casual with newsprint tables and a large, scenic garden.

Bar Avignon *American* — 25 | 23 | 23 | $27

Division | 2138 SE Division St. (22nd Ave.) | 503-517-0808 | www.baravignon.com

"Delicious, creative" New American fare complements an "excellent" vino list and "superb" mixed drinks at this affordable Division wine bar; a "quaint", "romantic" setting with "lovely interiors" and "friendly" service cement its status as a neighborhood "gem", as does its "wonderful" weekday happy hour.

Bar Carlo *American* — 24 | 21 | 22 | $17

Foster-Powell | 6433 SE Foster Rd. (65th Ave.) | 503-771-1664 | www.barcarlo.com

"One of the best-kept secrets in town for breakfast" any time of day, this low-cost American with Mexican influences (huevos rancheros, breakfast burrito) wins as a "quality choice" in "up-and-coming" Foster-Powell; the ramshackle space has "lots of room", is "surprisingly kid-friendly" and has a bar that serves "tasty" drinks too; P.S. closed Tuesdays.

Barista *Coffeehouse* — 25 | 23 | 24 | $10

Alberta | 1725 NE Alberta St. (bet. 17th & 18th Aves.) | no phone
NEW **Downtown** | 529 SW Third Ave. (bet. Alder & Washington Sts.) | no phone
Pearl District | 539 NW 13th Ave. (Hoyt St.) | no phone
www.baristapdx.com

When it comes to beans, this coffeehouse trio "handpicks the best of the bunch", and then "knowledgeable, skillful" baristas serve the resulting concoctions "perfectly prepared", with "no Portland pretention" and at "reasonable" prices; while some could "do without the taxidermy hanging from the walls" at Alberta, and others grouse about the "minimal" pastry selection, caffeinados say it all comes back to the "simply awesome" coffee, and "in this town, that's saying a lot."

Bar Mingo *Italian*

| 25 | 23 | 23 | $32 |

Northwest Portland | 811 NW 21st Ave. (bet. Johnson & Kearney Sts.) | 503-445-4646 | www.barmingonw.com

Small plates of "elevated yet rustic" Italian fare plus cocktails and a long list of Boot wines shine at this "trendy", "informal" NW Portland sibling to neighboring Caffe Mingo; service in the bustling, sunset-hued space is "attentive" and "lighthearted", but it's a "popular spot, so be prepared to wait for a table."

NEW Basa Basa *Korean*

| - | - | - | I |

Kerns | The Ocean | 2333 NE Glisan St. (24th Ave.) | 971-271-8260

Part of the Ocean micro-eatery collective in Kerns, this easy-on-the-wallet stop from Caprial and John Pence (of now defunct Caprial's Bistro) focuses on Korean fried chicken wings, which come with a choice of three sauces, macaroni salad and rice; the stark black-and-white space gets a lift from the sleek blond-wood counter seating, and there's more room to stretch on the large front patio.

Basta's Trattoria *Italian*

| 25 | 22 | 23 | $27 |

Northwest Portland | 410 NW 21st Ave. (Flanders St.) | 503-274-1572 | www.bastastrattoria.com

"Traditional" Italian fare that's "inventive" and "fresh" (pastas, sausages, pancetta, bread and desserts are made in-house) delights at this "romantic" NW Portland space, a former A-framed Tastee-Freez; loyalists commend the "good service", "fair prices" and a "parking lot that's a godsend" along busy NW 21st Avenue.

Bay Leaf *Asian/Vegetarian*

| 24 | 20 | 20 | $18 |

Division | 4768 SE Division St. (48th Ave.) | 503-232-7058 | www.bayleafvegetarian.com

Enthusiasts say this "Zen" Division stop is a "fantastic option" for Asian fare with a "vegetarian twist", as classic dishes get a "delicious" meat-free makeover and arrive with "beautiful presentation"; despite some grousing about "slow" service, the "nice" owners, staffers who will "help with non-gluten choices" and "beautiful" tea service leave an overall positive impression; P.S. closed on Tuesdays.

Beaker & Flask ☒ *American*

| 26 | 23 | 25 | $32 |

Central Eastside | 727 SE Washington St. (Sandy Blvd.) | 503-235-8180 | www.beakerandflask.com

"Imaginative cocktails" "teamed with innovative", "grown-up" New American "foodie" fare ("you will eat weird things and they will taste fantastic") are on offer inside a sign-free, "industrial-chic" space in Central Eastside; servers who "truly seem to enjoy being there" and "know their food and booze" are also "key to the experience", which is "not cheap", but most agree it's "worth it."

	FOOD	DECOR	SERVICE	COST

Beast ☑ *French/Pacific NW* — 27 | 22 | 25 | $98

Concordia | 5425 NE 30th Ave. (Killingsworth St.) | 503-841-6968 | www.beastpdx.com

At *Top Chef* alum Naomi Pomeroy's small Concordia fiefdom, diners sit an "elbow away" from each other at communal tables for pricey twice-nightly prix fixe platings of "phenomenal" French- and Pacific NW–inspired cuisine and a "mind-blowing" three-course Sunday brunch that constitute a "carnivorous adventure"; a few find the "no-substitutions" rule "draconian" while others plead "get rid of the uncomfortable chairs", but ultimately it's a "must-try" experience that's "well worth the hype"; P.S. closed Monday and Tuesday.

Beaterville *American* — 24 | 23 | 22 | $14

Overlook | 2201 N. Killingsworth St. (Gay Ave.) | 503-735-4652 | www.beatervillecafeandbar.com

The "car-themed kitsch is everywhere" at this low-cost Overlook American with a "diner feel" and "old-school" breakfasts; maybe there's "no elegance" in the "funky" digs, but it's "fun, especially for automotive fans" or anyone interested in live blues in the adjoining bar.

Beijing Hot Pot *Chinese* — 24 | 21 | 23 | $19

82nd Avenue | 2768 SE 82nd Ave. (bet. Brooklyn & Clinton Sts.) | 503-774-2525 | www.thebeijinghotpot.com

Fans "love the concept" of cooking meats and vegetables in "amazing boiling broth that simmers in the middle of every table" at this "traditional" Chinese on SE 82nd; while the space is unremarkable and the DIY approach can be a "little messy", "excellent" service and the "unique experience" make for a "great date" (and a cheap one).

The Bent Brick *Pacific NW* — 23 | 23 | 23 | $34

Northwest Portland | 1639 NW Marshall St. (17th Ave.) | 503-688-1655 | www.thebentbrick.com

"You will not regret a walk on the wild side" say fans of the "imaginative" Pacific NW "food adventure" awaiting at this NW Portland offshoot of Park Kitchen; its more quotidian charms include moderate prices, "knowledgeable" service and a "romantic" brick-walled setting.

Berlin Inn ☑ *German* — 25 | 22 | 24 | $27

Brooklyn | 3131 SE 12th Ave. (Kelly St.) | 503-236-6761 | www.berlininn.com

"Generous portions" of "genuine" German fare come at a "decent price" at this Brooklyn eatery, along with a selection of Teutonic wine and beer; a "considerate, dedicated and unbelievably friendly" staff adds to the allure, and owing to the "small" space, regulars warn "don't expect a table without reservations"; P.S. closed Monday and Tuesday, and breakfast and lunch is weekend-only.

Bernie's Southern Bistro ☑ *Southern* — 25 | 24 | 24 | $21

Alberta | 2904 NE Alberta St. (29th Ave.) | 503-282-9864 | www.berniesbistro.com

The "excellent renditions of Southern favorites" at this Alberta spot are complemented by "terrific cocktails" such as the "dangerously delicious" Sidecar – all for a "great price"; the service is "hospitable to a fault", and while it "can be hard to get into at peak times", most report "walking out a significantly happier person"; P.S. it's "especially delightful when you can sit on the back deck."

Bertie Lou's *American* | 25 | 21 | 24 | $13 |
Sellwood | 8051 SE 17th Ave. (Spokane St.) | 503-239-1177
At this "greasy spoon" in Sellwood, "amazing" American breakfast and brunch fare is "served up with a smile and a sense of humor"; the prices befit the "funky, laid-back feel", and the "tiny" space gets a lift from "napkin art" hanging on the walls; P.S. closes at 2 PM daily.

Besaw's *American* | 26 | 22 | 23 | $22 |
Northwest Portland | 2301 NW Savier St. (23rd Ave.) | 503-228-2619 | www.besaws.com
"Adored by locals", this "classic" in NW Portland (circa 1903), purportedly bearer of the first liquor license in the state after Prohibition, is "always crowded" thanks to its "reasonably priced" American "comfort food galore", emphasizing local and organic products, and popular weekend brunch; service is "wonderful", and devotees insist it's "worth the wait, and there's always a wait" in the "old-time" setting with a polished mahogany bar.

Big-A** Sandwiches 🅂 *Sandwiches* | 26 | 20 | 23 | $12 |
Eastside Industrial | The Row | 304 SE Second Ave. (Oak St.) | 503-803-0619 | www.bigasssandwiches.com
"It's all in the name" at this cheeky food cart, which recently relocated to the Eastside Industrial pod The Row and crafts "crazy big" sandwiches, most stuffed with piles of meat and homemade béchamel sauce – "expect your fries in the sandwich or just go somewhere else" say aficionados; the "down-to-earth" crew "loves to make conversation" as patrons wait for the "ridiculously cheap" lunch; P.S. it closes when the food runs out.

Bijou Cafe *American* | 26 | 21 | 24 | $17 |
Old Town-Chinatown | 132 SW Third Ave. (Pine St.) | 503-222-3187 | www.bijoucafepdx.com
With its "supernal breakfasts" in a "bright" space, this low-cost Old Town American has been delivering some of the "best eggs in town", an "oyster hash that doesn't skimp on the signature ingredient" and "excellent" coffee since 1978; "doting" servers attend to an "always crowded" room where "local politicians sit arm-and-arm with slightly hungover college kids", so "get there early" or "be prepared to wait."

Binh Minh Bakery & Deli Ⓜ *Vietnamese* | 26 | 19 | 23 | $13 |
Northeast Portland | 6812 NE Broadway (67th Ave.) | 503-257-3868
Binh Minh Sandwiches Ⓜ *Vietnamese*
Foster-Powell | 7821 SE Powell Blvd. (78th Ave.) | 503-777-2245
For a "fabulous" version of the "happy, humble Vietnamese" sandwich, this "fast, simple" duo in NE Portland and Foster-Powell pleases

with "fluffy baguettes of wonder" filled with pickled veggies, herbs and various meats; the service at the counter-service stops is "good", and though "there is no decor", it's "dirt-cheap."

Biwa ● *Japanese* | 25 | 24 | 23 | $22 |

Central Eastside | 215 SE Ninth Ave. (Ash St.) | 503-239-8830 | www.biwarestaurant.com

"All sorts of amazing" izakaya fare – including a "nice assortment of fusion dishes", ramen that competes for the "best in town" and a late-night burger fans "rave about" – combine with "stellar" sake at this Japanese in Central Eastside, run by the "nicest people"; a few complain that multiple plates can get "a little expensive", but the "cozy", subterranean space strikes others as the ideal venue for an "inexpensive date night."

Blind Onion Pizza & Pub *Pizza* | 26 | 20 | 23 | $18 |

Hollywood | 3345 NE Broadway (33rd Ave.) | 503-284-2825 | www.blindonion.com

The "pizza is good" and the "beer is cold" at this longtime Hollywood joint with "delicious", "truly gourmet" specialty pies and "friendly" service; it can get "noisy" and some liken it to "a basement in a '70s fraternity house", but the "filling, satisfying", reasonably priced fare takes precedence.

Blossoming Lotus *Vegan* | 27 | 23 | 23 | $21 |

Irvington | 1713 NE 15th Ave. (B'way) | 503-228-0048 | www.blpdx.com

It "might make a raw foodist out of me yet" say fans of this "amazing" organic vegan specialist in Irvington that proffers "upscale presentations" of "healthy, delicious" cuisine "with a creative twist", complemented by organic wines, at reasonable prices; a "stylish setting" and "excellent service" complete the picture.

Bluehour *American/Mediterranean* | 25 | 26 | 23 | $47 |

Pearl District | 250 NW 13th Ave. (Everett St.) | 503-226-3394 | www.bluehouronline.com

Bruce Carey's "stunning", "spendy" New American–Med in the Pearl District attracts a "see-and-be-seen", "expense-account" crowd that appreciates classic dishes with "just the right amount of innovation", an "attentive, polite" staff and a "most heavenly cheese service"; some label it "pretentious", but when the "clientele is as attractive as the food", you get "atmosphere that's hard to beat"; P.S. "drop by happy hour for fabulous deals at the bar."

Blue Olive *Mediterranean* | 24 | 21 | 22 | $19 |

Alberta | 2712 NE Alberta St. (33rd Ave.) | 503-206-6168
Northwest Portland | 500 NW 21st Ave. (Glisan St.) | 503-528-2822 Ⓜ
www.blueolivepdx.com

For "great Greek family food", this Mediterranean pair gives locals two ways to get their mezza on: at the sleek NW 21st Avenue stop with a bar and sidewalk seating for people-watching or at the smaller, more casual sibling on NE Alberta; both offer "decent" service and relatively low prices.

	FOOD	DECOR	SERVICE	COST

Blue Pig Cafe *American*   25 | 22 | 24 | $17

Hawthorne | 2028 SE Hawthorne Blvd. (12th Ave.) | 503-231-2775 | www.bluepigpdx.com

"Huge portions" of "damn good" breakfast and lunch classics, plus a "creative variety" of weekly specials, are the draw at this sunny Hawthorne American where pig statuettes adorn the room; the "friendly" service can get "slow when they are busy", but despite the wait, many deem it an "A-plus experience all around."

Blueplate Lunch Counter &   26 | 22 | 23 | $14
Soda Fountain 🅱 *Diner*

Downtown | 308 SW Washington St. (3rd Ave.) | 503-295-2583 | www.eatatblueplate.com

It's "just like the good ol' days" at this daytime Downtowner that "exudes old-fashioned charm and comfort" with "slightly upscale" diner classics, including "exceptional blue-plate specials" (naturally), plus "tasty floats", sundaes and some of the "best homemade sodas" around; it's "small" and can "get a bit crowded", but solid service and affordable tabs help; P.S. no alcohol.

NEW Boke Bowl 🅱 *Japanese/Noodle Shop*   24 | 21 | 22 | $15

Eastside Industrial | 1028 SE Water Ave. (Yamhill St.) | 503-719-5698 | www.bokebowl.com

"Simple but delicious" ramen, rice bowls and steam buns, including some with "interesting" combinations, star at this Eastside Industrial Japanese that's especially popular on Thursday nights when it cooks up "oustanding" Korean fried chicken; with affordable prices, solid service and casual warehouse surrounds, it works for both "kids and adults"; P.S. dinner is served Thursday–Saturday only.

NEW Bollywood Theater *Indian*   25 | 23 | 22 | $20

Alberta | 2039 NE Alberta St. (21st Ave.) | 971-200-4711 | www.bollywoodtheaterpdx.com

For a "little taste of Indian street food" diners hit up this Alberta stop where the "delicious" traditional offerings come at budget-friendly prices; old Bollywood flicks play on the back wall in the small, casual space, and the service scores solid marks.

Bombay Cricket Club *Indian/Mediterranean*   26 | 23 | 24 | $29

Hawthorne | 1925 SE Hawthorne Blvd. (19th Ave.) | 503-231-0740 | www.bombaycricketclubrestaurant.com

The "interesting menu" combines "excellent" Indian specialties with "surprisingly good Mediterranean offerings", all offered in "servings so big they crowd the small tables" at this "popular" Hawthorne longtimer; staffers "make you feel like one of the family" in the "tiny" space, and with moderate prices it's a local "favorite."

Bora Bora 🅼 *Mexican*   27 | 23 | 24 | $15

Southeast Portland | 15803 SE Division St. (158th Ave.) | 503-750-1253

Some of the "crispiest, spiciest grilled chicken you'll ever eat" enthuse admirers of the main draw at this inexpensive SE Portland cart that also whips up tacos, ceviche and other Mexican standards; the staff is "friendly", and regulars suggest those "man enough ask for the habanero sauce" to top things off.

NEW Boxer Sushi *Japanese* ▽ 25 | 24 | 26 | $18

Hawthorne | 1524 SE 20th Ave. (Hawthorne Blvd.) | 971-271-8635 | www.boxersushi.com

Prolific restaurateur Micah Camden (Little Big Burger, Yakuza) reels in fish lovers with "amazing fresh sushi" and other specialties at this affordable Hawthorne Japanese; the tiny wood and concrete-enhanced space is dominated by a graffiti-inspired octopus mural, and the counter proves an ideal perch to watch the chefs work their magic.

Brasserie Montmartre *American/French* 25 | 25 | 23 | $29

Downtown | 626 SW Park Ave. (Alder St.) | 503-236-3036 | www.brasserieportland.com

"Traditional French favorites" share menu space with American offerings at this "beautiful" Downtown brasserie with an "easy, relaxed atmosphere", "interesting wine list" and "knowledgeable" staff; other pluses include frequent live music, a "great happy hour" and "good nightlife crowd."

Brazil Grill *Brazilian* 27 | 23 | 25 | $38

Downtown | 1201 SW 12th Ave. (bet. Jefferson & Main Sts.) | 503-222-0002 | www.brazilgrillrestaurant.com

You can "gorge yourself on all sorts of meat" (plus "out-of-this-world" roasted pineapple) at this all-you-can-eat Downtown Brazilian where the "endless" offerings are supplied by "rotating" gaucho servers who carve from skewers tableside; casual, brightly painted digs further make it "group"-friendly, and even though it's not cheap you'll get your money's worth – especially if you "come ravenous" instead of just plain hungry.

Bread & Ink Cafe *American* 24 | 20 | 23 | $17

Hawthorne | 3610 SE Hawthorne Blvd. (36th Ave.) | 503-239-4756 | www.breadandinkcafe.com

"Quality" ingredients and "interesting" preparations "elevate" American standards "to a higher level" say fans of this "reasonably priced" Hawthorne "favorite" that's especially popular for breakfast and brunch; framed art decorates the "pleasant" space, service gets few complaints and the attached Waffle Window is a "nice addition."

BridgePort Ale House Ⓜ *Pub Food* 23 | 22 | 21 | $22

Hawthorne | 3632 SE Hawthorne Blvd. (bet. 36th & 37th Aves.) | 503-233-6540

BridgePort Brewpub *Pub Food*

Pearl District | 1313 NW Marshall St. (14th Ave.) | 503-241-3612 | www.bridgeportbrew.com

"Beer's the thing" at this midpriced duo where "lotsa good" choices "suit all tastes" and are offered alongside "surprisingly decent" pub grub that "hits the spot" and "works well" with the brews; the multi-level Pearl District space is larger with an "industrial-chic" vibe, while the Hawthorne sib is smaller but still "comfortable", and both get a boost from "attentive" service.

Bridges Cafe *American*

23 | 21 | 24 | $14

Boise-Eliot | 2716 NE Martin Luther King Jr. Blvd. (Knott St.) | 503-288-4169 | www.bridgescafeandcatering.net

A "friendly" crew that seems to "genuinely like what they do" makes the "dependable and delicious" organic-leaning fare taste even "better" say fans of this daytime American in Boise-Eliot; the digs are "small", but "reasonable" prices provide further incentive to "go again."

Brix Tavern ☻ *American*

23 | 24 | 24 | $22

Pearl District | 1338 NW Hoyt St. (14th Ave.) | 503-943-5995 | www.brixtavern.com

This Pearl District "find" leads a double life as a "classy" modern restaurant with a "well-executed" menu of American comfort favorites and also as a "large" TV- and game-filled bar; service is "friendly", prices are generally "low" and insiders suggest hopsheads "get the surprise beer in a paper bag" (bartender's choice).

Broder Cafe *Scandinavian*

26 | 22 | 23 | $23

Clinton | 2508 SE Clinton St. (25th Ave.) | 503-736-3333 | www.broderpdx.com

"One of the best breakfast places" cheer fans of this "popular" Clinton Scandinavian that "hits all the right notes" with its "seriously great" morning offerings, especially the "fantastic" aebleskivers (traditional Danish pancakes); it offers lunch and dinner too (Wednesday-Saturday), and prices are affordable, just expect "long waits on the weekends" as the "small, simple" digs have "limited seating."

Brunch Box *Burgers*

26 | 20 | 25 | $12

Downtown | SW Fifth Ave. & Stark St. | 503-477-3286 | www.brunchboxpdx.com

It's all about the "delicious" burgers at this daytime food cart Downtown where devotees suggest you "go decadent" with any of the "insane" creations, including ones with "grilled cheeses as buns"; it also offers turkey and veggie patties when you want to "go light", plus "filling breakfast sandwiches" too, and with "cheap" tabs, it's a "must-try."

Built to Grill ⊠⊅ *Italian*

28 | 23 | 27 | $13

Downtown | 232 SW Washington St. (3rd Ave.) | 503-789-3767

"Ah-maz-ing" classic Italian dishes such as penne alla vodka and panini are the draw at this Downtown food cart; the cash-only policy and "rather limited hours" (it's closed weekends and evenings) are offset by "super-friendly" service and "cheap" tabs.

Bunk Sandwiches *Sandwiches*

27 | 16 | 20 | $13

Central Eastside | 621 SE Morrison St. (bet. 6th & 7th Aves.) | 503-477-9515

NEW **Downtown** | 211 SW Sixth Ave. (Oak St.) | 503-972-8100 www.bunksandwiches.com

"What all sandwich shops aspire to be" enthuse fans of the "meaty" and "bold" sammies made with "unusual" "top-notch" ingredients" ("get anything that says pork belly") at this daytime Downtown and Central Eastside duo; despite the long lines, "they crank out the orders pretty quickly", but the limited seating and "grungy decor" translate into a "better for take-out" experience; P.S. both only serve beer, but a nearby spin-off, Bunk Bar, has a full range of drinks.

Burnside Brewing Co. *Pub Food*   25 | 22 | 24 | $20

Lower Burnside | 701 E. Burnside St. (7th Ave.) | 503-946-8151 | www.burnsidebrewco.com

"Excellent" beers, including "innovative" housemade offerings, pair with "upscale" pub grub that devotees consider "top-notch for a bar" at this Lower Burnside brewpub; "friendly" service, a "cool" indoor-outdoor space and "affordable" prices further explain why brew fiends "can't wait to go back."

The Bye & Bye ● *Vegan*   27 | 26 | 24 | $15

Alberta | 1011 NE Alberta St. (10th Ave.) | 503-281-0537 | www.thebyeandbye.com

At this "hipster Eden" in Alberta, a crowd of "yuppies and bike messenger" types "meets and mingles" over "strong" drinks poured by "nice bartenders" in a "dimly lit" space that sports a "good juke-box", plus "lots of outside seating"; for the vegan community (and even a lone "carnivore" from time to time), it's all about the "mouth-watering" Southern-inspired meatless menu that's "so good you forget it's vegan."

Byways Cafe *Diner*   24 | 19 | 22 | $14

Pearl District | 1212 NW Glisan St. (12th Ave.) | 503-221-0011 | www.bywayscafe.com

"Home cooked at its best" cheer fans of the "comfort-food" breakfasts and lunches at this "popular" Pearl District stop with a "diner vibe" and "kitschy" "retro" stylings; the "staff is friendly" and prices are "reason-able", just "get there early or be prepared to wait" on the weekends.

Cabezon 🅩 *Seafood*   28 | 25 | 27 | $36

Hollywood | 5200 NE Sacramento St. (52nd Ave.) | 503-284-6617 | www.cabezonrestaurant.com

Tucked on a Hollywood side street, this "family-run" "neighborhood gem" offers a "wonderful", daily changing menu of "fresh", "creative" fin fare, as well as a number of "options for those who don't want sea-food"; a "friendly" staff makes you "feel welcome" in the wooden-raftered interior (and, seasonally, at the sidewalk tables), and if some reviewers find the bill a tad "spendy", most agree it's "worth it."

Cadillac Cafe *American*   25 | 24 | 24 | $17

Irvington | 1801 NE Broadway (bet. 17th & 19th Aves.) | 503-287-4750 | www.cadillaccafepdx.com

For some of the "best brekkie" around, and "consistently great lunches" too, diners hit up this "reasonably priced" Irvington American where "all the old standbys" are offered alongside "creative" dishes with "interesting twists" and backed by "especially good" drinks; a "vintage Cadillac on display is a standout" in the casual space, and while it can be "crowded", "courteous, efficient" staffers help.

Café Castagna *Pacific NW*
26 | 24 | 25 | $32

Hawthorne | 1758 SE Hawthorne Blvd. (Poplar St.) | 503-231-9959 | www.castagnarestaurant.com

This "bustling" Hawthorne "gem" turns out "simpler", "less expensive" (and "less weird") Pacific NW fare than its "upscale big sister", Castagna, located next door; the burger in particular is "ludicrously tasty" and the "small but well-chosen" wine list impresses too, as does "warm" service, which extends from the "easy", "airy" room to the "lovely" streetside patio.

Cafe Nell *American*
24 | 22 | 23 | $32

Northwest Portland | 1987 NW Kearney St. (20th Ave.) | 503-295-6487 | www.cafenell.com

"Clearly the place for pretty people with good taste" assess fans of this midpriced American bistro in NW Portland boasting an "ever-changing, seasonal menu" plus "splendid drinks" like a Bloody Mary that's "a meal in itself"; despite the "cool" "NYC-style ambiance", at heart it's just a "cute neighborhood spot."

Café Yumm *Asian*
25 | 20 | 22 | $11

Downtown | 301 SW Morrison St. (3rd Ave.) | 503-222-9866
PSU | 1806 SW Sixth Ave. (Montgomery St.) | 503-226-9866
Beaverton | 14601 SW Millikan Way (Murray Blvd.) | 503-627-9866
www.cafeyumm.com

Fans of "healthy" Asian-inspired fare turn to this low-cost Eugene-born chain that caters to vegans, vegetarians and the gluten-free with a menu of rice bowls, wraps and salads, much of it topped with its signature sauces; the staff is "extremely friendly" and "quick", and even if the "decor is a bit plain", most find it "lives up to its name."

Caffe Mingo *Italian*
26 | 23 | 24 | $33

Northwest Portland | 807 NW 21st Ave. (bet. Johnson & Kearney Sts.) | 503-226-4646 | www.caffemingonw.com

It's like "dining at your Italian grandmother's house" at this "cozy", "casual" ristorante in NW Portland where "lovingly prepared pastas and mains" meet up with a "fantastic wine selection", and prices are "approachable, even on a budget"; service is "warm" and "professional" too, but you'll need to "get there early" or prepare to "wait"; P.S. you can also "chill at their bar next door."

Campbell's Barbecue Ⓜ *BBQ*
25 | 19 | 22 | $19

Southeast Portland | 8701 SE Powell Blvd. (87th Ave.) | 503-777-9795 | www.campbellsbbq.com

"Excellent", "authentic" "Texas-style" 'cue "hits the spot" for fans of this SE Portland joint near I-205 also offering traditional sides and sweet potato pie; an "old-time" atmosphere, affable service and "great" prices have kept its pit fires burning for more than 20 years.

Casa de Tamales Ⓜ *Mexican*
25 | 20 | 23 | $18

Milwaukie | 10605 SE Main St. (Scott St.) | 503-654-4423 | www.canbyasparagusfarm.com

"Homemade tamales" are the standout at this cheery Milwaukie Mexican using "ingredients sourced from local farms", including asparagus from the owners' own Canby farm; prices are reasonable, the staff "knows how to treat people" and on-site cooking classes are a plus.

Casa Naranja *Mediterranean*
26 | 24 | 24 | $18

Mississippi | 4205 N. Mississippi Ave. (bet. Mason & Skidmore Sts.) | 503-459-4049 | www.casanaranjapdx.com

Diners "love the patio with swinging hammocks" in the backyard of this affordable Mississippi hangout turning out "tantalizing" Med-influenced tapas, cocktails and "sultry sangria"; as an added bonus, the "fabulous" staff upholds the warm "family-run" atmosphere.

Cassidy's ● *American*
24 | 22 | 23 | $24

West End | 1331 SW Washington St. (13th Ave.) | 503-223-0054 | www.cassidysrestaurant.com

This "been-around forever" bar and bistro in a gritty area of West End provides "reliable if not grand" American eats and classic cocktails until 2 AM; the dimly lit, wood-paneled environs impart an "old Portland warmth with an edge", and low prices – including two daily happy hours – complete the package.

Castagna ⧄Ⓜ *Pacific NW*
27 | 25 | 27 | $59

Hawthorne | 1752 SE Hawthorne Blvd. (18th Ave.) | 503-231-7373 | www.castagnarestaurant.com

"Brilliant" chef Justin Woodward tinkers with one of the city's most "intriguing menus", an "amazing modernist take on Northwest ingredients and flavors" (the "best option for molecular gastronomy" in town) at this "elegant", "minimalist" Hawthorne spot; sure, it's "pricey", but the "terrific, knowledgeable" service and "wonderful wines" make it "ideal for a special night out."

Cha!Cha!Cha! Taqueria *Mexican*
24 | 20 | 22 | $15

Beaumont | 4727 NE Fremont St. (bet. 47th & 49th Aves.) | 503-595-9131
Boise-Eliot | 3808 N. Williams Ave. (Failing St.) | 503-281-1655
Hawthorne | 3433 SE Hawthorne Blvd. (bet. 34th & 35th Aves.) | 503-236-1100
Irvington | 2635 NE Broadway (27th Ave.) | 503-288-1045
Pearl District | 1208 NW Glisan St. (12th Ave.) | 503-221-2111
Sellwood | 1605 SE Bybee Blvd. (16th Ave.) | 503-232-0437
Milwaukie | 11008 SE Main St. (Jefferson St.) | 503-659-2193
www.chachachapdx.com

"Healthy" takes on "simple", "solid" Mexican standards – including vegan options – come at a "decent price" at this "cute" area chain also offering "strong margaritas" from the bar; a "friendly" staff and "sunny" settings add appeal.

Cha Ba Thai *Thai*
25 | 21 | 22 | $19

Alberta | 3024 NE Alberta St. (31st Ave.) | 503-719-6917
Northeast Portland | 5810 NE Sandy Blvd. (58th Ave.) | 503-282-3970

"Cheap and delicious" takes on Thai standards make this NE pair a hit with neighbors seeking "comfort food on a rainy Portland night"; the Sandy Boulevard stop is "small" and geared to takeout, and although a few report a wait at the newer Alberta outpost, the "huge outdoor seating area" is a draw for a sit-down meal.

CHA Taqueria & Bar *Mexican* 25 | 24 | 24 | $22
Northwest Portland | 305 NW 21st Ave. (Everett St.) | 503-295-4077 | www.chaportland.com

The "upscale" sib of the city's Cha!Cha!Cha! Taqueria chain, this NW Portland Mexican is "not your typical chips and salsa place" with an "excellent" modern menu including "terrific small plates" and "pretty" decor; it can "get packed" but service manages, and the "large", "colorful patio" and "fantastic happy hour" are big bonuses.

Chennai Masala Ⓜ *Indian* 25 | 15 | 20 | $19
Hillsboro | 2088 NW Stucki Ave. (Cornell Rd.) | 503-531-9500 | www.chennaimasala.net

Located in a Hillsboro strip mall, this South Indian earns raves for its "delicious" eats that include "pillow soft" naan and dosas that are "belly heaven"; "arrive early" for the popular lunch buffet, but it's "good for the money" and "worth the drive out of Portland proper"; P.S. a post-Survey expansion and revamp, which added banquettes and wood floors, may outdate the Decor score.

Chen's Good Taste *Chinese* 26 | 17 | 21 | $21
Old Town-Chinatown | 18 NW Fourth Ave. (bet. Burnside & Couch Sts.) | 503-223-3838

"Simple but delectable dishes built around roasted meats" please at this fluorescent-lit Old Town Chinese with "no decor" beyond the row of ducks in the entryway; bargain prices and solid service add up to an experience that's "great for lunch", especially for Downtowners.

Chez Machin *French* ▽ 29 | 22 | 24 | $20
Hawthorne | 3553 SE Hawthorne Blvd. (bet. 35th & 36th Aves.) | 503-736-9381 | www.chezmachincreperie.com

"Dust off your high-school French", because this "adorable" Hawthorne "hole-in-the-wall" serving up a "nice variety" of "amazing" savory and sweet crêpes (plus other "fantastic", "rustic" bistro fare) is just that "authentic"; it's got "wonderful service" to boot, plus a year-round covered patio and a "solid but limited wine list" – all in all, "c'est très, très bon."

Christie's *American* 25 | 24 | 24 | $15
University Park | 5507 N. Lombard St. (Van Houten Ave.) | 503-289-6111 | www.christiesofportland.com

Regulars insist this University Park American "can't be beat" for breakfast and also gratifies with down-home fare for lunch and dinner at "decent prices"; it's a "nice place" with "friendly, attentive" service, and extras include free WiFi and a patio that welcomes pets.

Ciao Vito *Italian/Tapas* 23 | 20 | 22 | $31
Alberta | 2203 NE Alberta St. (22nd Ave.) | 503-282-5522 | www.ciaovito.net

"Swanky" describes this Alberta "hangout" full of "dark nooks and crannies" and "always crowded and popular with those in the know" tucking into "Italian comfort food with a twist"; a few find it "too noisy", but prices are moderate, the mood's "warm and inviting" and a long grappa list and housemade limoncello cap the "classy" package; P.S. a post-Survey changeover brings a Barcelona-born chef to the kitchen and a Spanish influence to the menu, which now includes tapas.

NEW Cibo ⊠ Italian

| - | - | - | M |

Division | 3539 SE Division St. (35th Ave.) | 503-719-5377 | www.cibopdx.com

Its name means 'food' in Italian, and this Division trattoria turns out plenty of midpriced, authentic and often unusual fare such as *cecina* (garbanzo-based flatbread), salt-baked fish and pizzas fired in an imported wood- and gas-fueled oven, a behemoth that's adorned with a cutesy flamey hell demon; a 30-seat wooden bar wraps gracefully around the open kitchen, and the button-bedecked red booths add an element of comfort to the all-around warm room.

Cider Mill Lounge & Fryer Tuck Restaurant ◗ American

| 25 | 16 | 22 | $14 |

Multnomah Village | 6712 SW Capitol Hwy. (Vermont St.) | 503-246-7737 | www.fryertuckchicken.com

This Multnomah Village pub is "greasy heaven" for "chicken and spud lovers" tucking into "homestyle" fried birds, potato wedges and dip, although there's also standard American bar fare on offer; value prices are a plus, however the wood-paneled decor "looks like its been there for decades", despite periodic remodels.

Clarke's ⊠ American

| ∇ 27 | 25 | 26 | $30 |

Lake Oswego | 455 Second St. (B Ave.) | 503-636-2667 | www.clarkesrestaurant.net

A "neighborhood gem" in Lake Oswego, this "excellent" New American is beloved by locals for its upmarket cuisine (think lobster risotto and free-range chicken) offered with Pacific NW wines at a "good price"; quality service and setting qualify it as one of "the best" in the area.

Clarklewis ⊠ Pacific NW

| 27 | 25 | 24 | $38 |

Eastside Industrial | Eastbank Commerce Ctr. | 1001 SE Water Ave. (bet. Taylor & Yamhill Sts.) | 503-235-2294 | www.clarklewispdx.com

The "smell of wood smoke" wafts through this "gorgeous", "stylish" converted Eastside Industrial warehouse offering an "amazing" Pacific NW menu exhibiting an "obsession with freshness and local sourcing"; nitpickers say it's "too dark, too loud" and a little "spendy", but service is "knowledgeable and well paced" and "can probably tell you who raised your lamb."

Clay's Smokehouse Grill Ⓜ BBQ

| 24 | 19 | 23 | $23 |

Division | 2932 SE Division St. (30th Ave.) | 503-235-4755

Customers "craving some sauced-up meat on bread" turn to this low-budget Division barbecue joint with "amazing" in-house smoked meats offered with "all the fixin's"; eclectic Southern ephemera decorates the small storefront that's not exactly "high end", but still delivers "great atmosphere and food."

Clyde Common ● *American/Eclectic*   26 | 23 | 23 | $31

West End | Ace Hotel | 1014 SW Stark St. (bet. 10th & 11th Aves.) | 503-228-3333 | www.clydecommon.com

There's "nothing common" about this American-Eclectic, a "hipster paradise" attached to the West End's Ace Hotel, which turns out a "short menu" featuring "high-quality, local ingredients cooked with care and invention" (even the "popcorn has magic on top") and stars a bar that "can't be overlooked" thanks to barrel-aged cocktails and house-crafted mixers; there's communal dining downstairs and "quieter" upstairs seating, and though a few find it "a bit pricey", the "quirky staff knows their ramps from their nettles."

Clyde's Prime Rib *Steak*   27 | 21 | 26 | $26

Hollywood | 5474 NE Sandy Blvd. (56th Ave.) | 503-281-9200 | www.clydesprimerib.com

"Tasty, juicy" prime rib carved tableside takes center stage at this midpriced Hollywood steakhouse where the "superb" service matches the "exceptional" eats; live music and some of the "best people-watching in town" can be found in the adjoining bar, and though the digs are decidedly "old-school", fans say the "awesome kitsch" alone (with a castlelike exterior and red-velvet booths) warrants a trip.

Cocotte *French*   25 | 24 | 24 | $35

Concordia | 2930 NE Killingsworth St. (30th Ave.) | 503-227-2669 | www.cocottepdx.com

Admirers insist "it's easy to have a love affair" with this "hip, little" Concordia bistro turning out "expertly prepared", "accessible" French fare in an "adorable", "intimate" setting with an open kitchen; moderate bills plus "great cocktails" and "inspiring" wine pairings from a pro staff further its alluring reputation.

Cool Moon Ice Cream *Ice Cream*   28 | 22 | 25 | $8

Pearl District | 1105 NW Johnson St. (11th Ave.) | 503-224-2021 | www.coolmoonicecream.com

The "delicious artisanal flavors" change with the seasons at this Pearl District ice-cream shop where you can "ask for samples – they're happy to let you try to your heart's content"; just know the small space "can be packed" thanks to its fair prices and "excellent" location across from Jamison Square.

Coppia ⊠Ⓜ *Italian*   ▽ 21 | 23 | 23 | $31

Pearl District | 417 NW 10th Ave. (Flanders St.) | 503-295-9536 | www.coppiaportland.com

This "tiny", "peaceful" Pearl District Italian turns out a "limited" but "above-average" lineup of dishes from Piedmont, and its unique menu pairs each with a wine for easy-breezy ordering; a "personable" crew enhances the experience, and insiders insist it's "marvelous for the price."

	FOOD	DECOR	SERVICE	COST

Corbett Fish House *Seafood*
24 | 19 | 22 | $21

Johns Landing | 5901 SW Corbett Ave. (Pendleton St.) | 503-246-4434 | www.corbettfishhouse.com

Hawthorne Fish House *Seafood*

Hawthorne | 4343 SE Hawthorne Blvd. (4th Ave.) | 503-548-4434 | www.hawthornefishhouse.com

"Gluten-free before gluten-free was cool", this seafood pair is proud of its "healthier version" of fried fish, dredged in rice flour and flash-fried in rice-bran oil for a "light, crispy" taste; service is dependable, but like the Wisconsin taverns it emulates, it's "not a fancy place" with budget bills and Green Bay Packers sports memorabilia that makes it feel like being "back in the Midwest."

Country Cat Dinner House *American*
26 | 21 | 24 | $27

Montavilla | 7937 SE Stark St. (80th Ave.) | 503-408-1414 | www.thecountrycat.net

"Excellent Southern-inspired cuisine" "with a locavore twist" is the thing at this Montavilla American serving up "unreal" fried chicken and "incredible" biscuits from "the king of all things pork", Adam Sappington (his wife, Jackie, turns out the "great" desserts); a few say the wood-heavy room "needs warming up", while the "smart, sassy" "über-tatted" staff and "reasonable" bills universally impress; P.S. "sit at the counter" to watch the kitchen "create fabulous works of art."

Cricket Cafe *American*
25 | 20 | 21 | $18

Belmont | 3159 SE Belmont St. (32nd Ave.) | 503-235-9348 | www.cricketcafepdx.com

A few "healthy" choices augment the "hearty, rich" American breakfast standbys at this quirky, cramped Belmont cafe; low price tags and a staff that's always "friendly even on the busiest of Saturdays" spur fans to say it's "worth the long wait to get in on the weekends."

Cup & Saucer *Diner*
24 | 20 | 22 | $14

Concordia | 3000 NE Killingsworth St. (30th Ave.) | 503-287-4427
Hawthorne | 3566 SE Hawthorne Blvd. (bet 35th Pl. & 36th Ave.) | 503-236-6001
Kenton | 8237 N. Denver Ave. (McClellan St.) | 503-247-6011
Mississippi | 3746 N. Mississippi Ave. (bet. Beech & Failing Sts.) | 503-548-4614
www.cupandsaucercafe.com

This "laid-back" local mini-chain of "cute", organic-leaning diners is a home away from home for those craving cheap basic fare – including "lots of vegan options", "plate-sized pancakes" and burgers – available all day; the staff is "genuinely nice", but "bring your patience" for long weekend waits, especially at the Hawthorne original.

Daily Cafe in the Pearl *American*
25 | 23 | 24 | $20

Pearl District | 902 NW 13th Ave. (Kearney St.) | 503-242-1916 | www.dailycafeinthepearl.com

Though this "delightful" light-filled American cafe in the Pearl District is "known for breakfast" and a Sunday brunch that "never disappoints", fans find it's also a "stealth choice for dinner" at a reasonable price on weekdays with the bonus of "friendly" servers who "know the regulars"; given it's such a "little" space, at peak hours you can "expect to wait."

Dan & Louis Oyster Bar *Seafood* | 25 | 22 | 23 | $27 |

Old Town-Chinatown | 208 SW Ankeny St. (bet. 2nd & 3rd Aves.) | 503-227-5906 | www.danandlouis.com

A "true Portland classic", this "touristy" Old Town seafooder (since 1907) makes its name on "ice-cold" Pacific NW oysters, "yummy" "warm-me-up" clam chowder and "pleasant" service; prices are "fair", and most like the walls filled with "lots of history and nautical decor."

ɴᴇᴡ Dar Salam Ⓜ *Mideastern* | 27 | 23 | 24 | $20 |

Alberta | 2921 NE Alberta St. (bet. 29th & 30th Aves.) | 503-206-6148 | www.darsalamportland.com

"Fantastic" and affordable, this Middle Eastern in Alberta dishes up "tasty, unexpected" Iraqi fare, including veg and gluten-free options; the "gracious" Baghdad-born owners decorated the wood-beamed space with photos of their country "from beautiful landscapes to ancient sculptures" for a "nice atmosphere" that includes a patio.

Davis Street Tavern Ⓩ *American* | 23 | 23 | 22 | $27 |

Old Town-Chinatown | 500 NW Davis St. (5th Ave.) | 503-505-5050 | www.davisstreettavern.com

The "delicious", "stepped-up" comfort food at this American in Old Town shines "with some serious refinement" in a "gorgeous, low-lit renovated space with exposed beams" and a "convivial bar"; solid service and reasonable prices heighten the experience.

Decarli Restaurant Ⓜ *Italian* | 27 | 23 | 24 | $29 |

Beaverton | 4545 SW Watson Ave. (bet. Farmington Rd. & 1st St.) | 503-641-3223 | www.decarlirestaurant.com

"An oasis of quality dining in the 'burbs", this midpriced Beaverton Italian showcases a "creative but not intimidating", "locally focused" menu in a modern, airy space with vintage touches like a chandelier from the historic Benson Hotel; the "friendly, informative" staff upholds an ambiance that's "perfect for a little romantic dinner" or "regular weeknight dining."

Delta Cafe ❶ *Southern* | 25 | 22 | 23 | $16 |

Woodstock | 4607 SE Woodstock Blvd. (46th Ave.) | 503-771-3101 | www.deltacafepdx.com

For "tasty, homestyle" Southern fare with Cajun inflections that comes in "big", "price-appropriate" portions, locals point to this "quirky" Woodstock cafe as a "perfect fit for eccentric East Portland"; "helpful" servers contribute to the vibe, although for some it comes down to the "PBR 40s on ice – isn't that why everyone goes?"

Departure ❶ *Asian* | 23 | 27 | 21 | $36 |

Downtown | The Nines | 525 SW Morrison St., 15th fl. (5th Ave.) | 503-802-5370 | www.departureportland.com

"We're not in Portland anymore" assert admirers of this "futuristic space-age" lounge atop Downtown's The Nines Hotel with "spectacular" city and mountain views from its interior seating and two open-air patios; the "stiff" cocktails are "heavy on the wallet", but they keep things "abuzz", while "playful", "tasty" Asian fusion bites impress the "'in' crowd", as does the "fast, sexy" service.

Detour Cafe *American*   25 | 20 | 23 | $22

Division | 3035 SE Division St. (bet. 30th & 32nd Aves.) | 503-234-7499 | www.detourcafe.com

This "cute little mom-and-pop shop" in Division slings low-cost "locally sourced" American daytime fare like skillet breakfasts and sandwiches on house-baked breads washed down with "bottomless" cups of Stumptown coffee; a "friendly" staff and dog-accommodating patio boost its standing.

Dick's Kitchen *Burgers*   25 | 21 | 24 | $18

Belmont | 3312 SE Belmont St. (33rd Ave.) | 503-235-0146
Northwest Portland | 704 NW 21st Ave. (Irving St.) | 503-206-5916
www.dkportland.com

"Exotic", "ethically sourced" burgers like the Dork ("yes, pork + duck") lead the lineup at these "bright", "noisy" modern diners in Belmont and NW Portland also known for their "healthy" bill of fare with vegan, gluten-free and paleo items; prices are affordable too, and most find they work best when you need "something out of the ordinary to slap between two slices of bread."

DiPrima Dolci Ⓜ *Bakery/Italian*   25 | 20 | 24 | $16

Overlook | 1936 N. Killingsworth St. (Denver Ave.) | 503-283-5936 | www.diprimadolci.com

A sweet hunk of Italy, this Overlook bakery and trattoria turns out "old-school" pastries and cookies, "flavorful" panini and "authentic" standards like pizza and meatballs; the bill is modest, and service in the quaint yellow dining area and outdoor patio is "always helpful", so most just "wish Portland had more places like this."

DOC Ⓢ Ⓜ *Italian*   27 | 22 | 24 | $55

Concordia | 5519 NE 30th Ave. (Killingsworth St.) | 503-946-8592 | www.docpdx.com

"Truly fit for foodies", this Concordia "treasure" set in "microscopic" digs earns raves for its Italian-inspired, "locally sourced" fare offered à la carte or as an "exquisite" tasting menu ("the way to go"); it's "expensive for Portland", but also "perfect for a romantic evening that should not be rushed."

Dots Cafe ❶ *Burgers*   23 | 24 | 22 | $15

Clinton | 2521 SE Clinton St. (bet. 25th & 26th Aves.) | 503-235-0203

"Uniquely Portland", this "funky" "neighborhood staple" in Clinton decked out with "lots of black-velvet paintings, '50s kitsch and flocked wallpaper" features a "something-for-everyone" American menu of well-priced burgers, vegan items and such plus "strong drinks" served by an "adept" crew; consensus finds it's "best experienced late at night."

	FOOD	DECOR	SERVICE	COST

NEW Double Dragon *Vietnamese*　　25 | 22 | 23 | $20

Central Eastside | 1235 SE Division St. (Ladd Ave.) | 503-230-8340 |
www.doubledragonpdx.com

"Gourmet banh mi" "served on tender, fresh and crisp baguettes"
rules the roost at this hip, counter-service Central Eastside shop
where the "nontraditional" offerings are stuffed with chicken chorizo, pork belly and the like; prices skew a bit higher than the average
Vietnamese sandwich, but the ingredients are mostly local and sustainable and loyalists insist they "leave full and pleased every time."

Dove Vivi *Pizza*　　27 | 23 | 24 | $19

Kerns | 2727 NE Glisan St. (bet. Lawrence & 28th Aves.) |
503-239-4444 | www.dovevivipizza.com

It's all about the "unique" cornmeal crust ("awesome") at this "fantastic", inexpensive Kerns pizza haven that tops its pies with "unusual but delicious combinations" like pesto and corn and serves by
the pie, half pie or slice; the "small" modern-industrial space doesn't
offer "a lot of seating", but most find it's "worth the wait."

Du Kuh Bee ●🗷 *Chinese/Korean*　　27 | 16 | 23 | $18

Beaverton | 12590 SW First St. (St. Helens Rd.) | 503-643-5388

"Wait in the rain if you must" for a seat at this tiny Beaverton "hole-in-
the-wall" famed for its "amazing" hand-pulled noodles and dumplings
off an "interesting, tasty" Chinese-Korean menu; there's no decor to
speak of, but prices are "dirt-cheap", and "late" hours are a plus.

Du's Grill 🗷 *Japanese*　　25 | 13 | 24 | $11

Hollywood | 5365 NE Sandy Blvd. (54th Ave.) | 503-284-1773 |
www.dusgrill.com

"Follow your nose" to this "tiny, shantylike" Japanese in Hollywood
grilling up some of the "best teriyaki in town" matched with an ice-
berg salad topped with "amazing" dressing; prices are "inexpensive"
and the "staff is always pleasant amid the constant rush", just know
it's closed on weekends.

Earth Oven Pizza 🗷Ⓜ *Pizza*　　27 | 24 | 25 | $21

Hillsboro | 337 E. Main St. (3rd Ave.) | 503-747-7743 |
www.earthovenpizza.com

Loyalists "love the pizza" at this Hillsboro entry turning out "excep-
tionally good" rounds from a wood-burning oven, topped with "healthier" items including dairy- and gluten-free options; it's "fun for
families", and "excellent prices", live music and a "great" beer selection "will make you want to hang there every night."

EastBurn ● *American*　　23 | 24 | 23 | $17

Buckman | 1800 E. Burnside St. (18th Ave.) | 503-236-2876 |
www.theeastburn.com

This Buckman pub is "swinging – literally – inside and out" with hanging chairs on the covered patio, frequent live music and Skee-Ball in
the basement Tap Room; its "above-average" New American menu
boasts a "highly recommended" burger as well as loads of craft beers,
with discounted pints on Tuesdays.

	FOOD	DECOR	SERVICE	COST

East India Co. ⌧ *Indian*　26 | 24 | 24 | $23

West End | 821 SW 11th Ave. (Taylor St.) | 503-227-8815 |
www.eastindiacopdx.com

This "first-rate" West End Indian boasts a "varied menu spanning several regions", "impressive vegetarian" selections and an "accommodating" staff; although a few feel the fare is "Westernized for American tastes", all appreciate the "lovely ambiance" and affordable bills.

East Side Delicatessen　*Sandwiches*　26 | 19 | 24 | $8

Downtown | 1438 SW Park Ave. (Clay St.) | 503-243-3354 ⌧
Hawthorne | 4626 SE Hawthorne Blvd. (46th Ave.) | 503-236-7313
University Park | 4823 N. Lombard St. (Fiske Ave.) | 503-247-3354
www.pdxdeli.com

For "amply filled" sandwiches that are "freshly made" for little dough, this no-nonsense New York–style deli trio fits the bill and offers "great faux-meat options" for vegans and vegetarians too; "quick service" comes "with some personality", and even if "your mind isn't going to be blown, you'll be far from dissatisfied."

EaT: An Oyster Bar　*Cajun/Creole*　22 | 20 | 22 | $21

Boise-Eliot | 3808 N. Williams Ave. (Failing St.) | 503-281-1222 |
www.eatoysterbar.com

"Extremely fresh" oysters, gumbo and po' boys await at this affordable Cajun-Creole in Boise-Elliot with a casual "energy" that makes it a "great place to hang out and relax"; a low-key staff furthers the vibe, which ups a notch for the Sunday jazz brunch.

808 Grinds ⌧ *Hawaiian*　25 | 22 | 24 | $18

West End | SW Ninth Ave. & Washington St. | 503-713-8008
Named for Hawaii's area code, this sunny-yellow food cart says 'aloha' to Downtown's West End via "true" plate lunches (e.g. "waaay mean" grinds like Kalua pork and Spam musubi) made by folks "who know what they're doing"; "fast" service and "affordable" prices also get a big mahalo from the office types who work around its semi-permanent spot; P.S. closed weekends.

Eleni's Estiatorio ⌧Ⓜ *Greek*　25 | 21 | 24 | $30

Sellwood | 7712 SE 13th Ave. (bet. Lambert & Malden Sts.) | 503-230-2165
Eleni's Philoxenia Ⓜ *Greek*
Pearl District | 112 NW Ninth Ave. (bet. Couch & Davis Sts.) |
503-227-2158
www.elenisrestaurant.com

"Crave"-worthy Greek "comfort food" comes in "large portions" with a "nice selection" of wines at this "unpretentious" Sellwood Hellenic and its sleeker Pearl District sister; it's "not cheap", but pays off with "attentive" service and a "delightful atmosphere."

El Gaucho ❶ *Steak*　26 | 25 | 26 | $63

Downtown | Benson Hotel | 319 SW Broadway (bet. Oak & Stark Sts.) |
503-227-8794 | www.elgaucho.com

"Classy in all the right places", this "swanky" steakhouse in Downtown's Benson Hotel boasts "massive, tender" "quality cuts" delivered by "impeccable" "black-tie" servers who perform "tableside extras like Caesar salad and cherries jubilee", making it an "experience more than a meal"; "astronomical" prices lead some to nickname it "El Gouge-o", but most find it a "splurge" that's "worth every penny."

El Inka   *Peruvian*   ▽ 25 | 20 | 25 | $17

Gresham | 48 NE Division St. (Roberts Ave.) | 503-491-0323 | www.elinkarestaurant.com

Hidden in a strip mall, this modest Gresham shop specializes in "delicious" Peruvian fare including a standout fire-roasted chicken available by quarter, half or whole bird and displayed in a glass-fronted rotisserie oven; it's not fancy, but "reasonable" bills make it a mainstay.

E'Njoni Cafe Ⓜ *Ethiopian*   ▽ 24 | 19 | 22 | $18

Humboldt | 910 N. Killingsworth St. (Mississippi Ave.) | 503-286-1401 | www.enjonicafe.com

Loyalists "love" this Humboldt Ethiopian for its "outstanding" eats (including "many vegan dishes") and "reasonably priced buffet" offered on weekends; a "super-nice owner and staff" and "simple" spice-colored space complete the picture; P.S. the buffet is lunch-only Friday and Saturday and all day Sunday.

Equinox Restaurant & Bar   *American*   25 | 23 | 24 | $25

Mississippi | 830 N. Shaver St. (Mississippi Ave.) | 503-460-3333 | www.equinoxrestaurantpdx.com

The "eclectic" New American menu is sensitive to just about "every dietary need" at this well-priced "hidden gem" in Mississippi featuring a noteworthy burger and a "delicious" weekend brunch; a warm setting, "lovely" terrace and full bar complete the offerings.

E-San Thai   *Thai*   25 | 21 | 23 | $17

Kenton | 8233 N. Denver Ave. (McClellan St.) | 503-517-0683
Old Town-Chinatown | 133 SW Second Ave. (Pine St.) | 503-223-4090
www.e-santhai.com

This longtime, family-owned Old Town Thai (and its newer Kenton sibling) is an "excellent" bet for a "variety of Northern and Eastern" dishes on its affordable menu; expect "timely service" and a simple setting filled with "traditional" trappings.

Escape From New York Pizza ⑰ *Pizza*   26 | 19 | 21 | $11

Northwest Portland | 622 NW 23rd Ave. (Irving St.) | 503-227-5423 | www.efnypizza.net

Since 1983 this cash-only NW Portland shop has been slinging some of the "best New York–style pizza" in town with a "full helping of attitude" at "cheap" rates; "you can't get salads" or crazy toppings, just the basics with limited additions, and the somewhat "dinky, dingy" digs only add to the experience.

Esparza's Tex Mex Cafe   *Tex-Mex*   23 | 21 | 21 | $19

Buckman | 2725 SE Ankeny St. (28th Ave.) | 503-234-7909 | www.esparzastexmex.com

For "enormous portions of home-cooked goodness", Tex-Mex seekers head to this "funky" Buckman cantina to chow on everything from buffalo enchiladas to snapper with mashed potatoes among the "kitsch" – a stuffed rattlesnake, hanging marionettes – that's "worth the visit" alone; "from-scratch" margaritas and "casual, friendly" service are improved by the "even better price."

EuroTrash *Mediterranean*   25 | 20 | 23 | $13

Belmont | Good Food Here | SE Belmont St. & 43rd Ave. | 253-861-6733
West End | SW 10th Ave. & Washington St. | 253-861-6733 |
www.eurotrashcart.com

"Foie gras from a cart? Yes, please!" crow converts to this eye-popping pair of pink-and-turquoise trucks in Belmont and Downtown's West End serving "fun, fatty", "random" Med-European street foods in-cluding fried Spanish anchovies and the aforementioned goose liver atop housemade potato chips; prices are low and service brisk, leading some to call it a "must" in the cart-eats scene.

Evoe Ⓜ *European/Sandwiches*   28 | 21 | 25 | $21

Hawthorne | Pastaworks | 3731 SE Hawthorne Blvd. (bet. 37th & 38th Aves.) | 503-232-1010 | www.pastaworks.com

"Every bite" of chef Kevin Gibson's "unusual, creative" sandwiches and small plates is a "burst of flavor" insist insiders who "sit at the counter" of this Hawthorne "gem" and watch as the European-inspired dishes "come together"; it's set in a "simple, small" space in an "odd location" (inside the gourmet grocery Pastaworks), but a "large collection" of wines by the glass, modest prices and that "exquisite" chow over-come all; P.S. closes at 7 PM; closed Monday–Tuesday.

Extracto Coffee Roasters *Coffeehouse*   25 | 21 | 24 | $7

Sabin | 1465 NE Prescott St. (bet. 14th Pl. & 15th Ave.) | 503-284-1380
Concordia | 2921 NE Killingsworth St. (bet. 29th & 30th Aves.) |
503-281-1764
www.extractocoffee.com

Regulars rely on the "delicious" espresso drinks (with "out-of-this-world" foam art) and pour-over coffee at this modern Concordia coffee roaster and Sabin sister cafe boasting a vibe that's "hip but not so hipster that you feel uncomfortable" and plenty of pastries for a nosh; the baristas are "wonderful", and whether inside or out on the patio, it's a "great spot to chill" and "people-watch."

The Farm Cafe *Pacific NW*   26 | 24 | 24 | $24

Lower Burnside | 10 SE Seventh Ave. (bet. Ankeny & Burnside Sts.) |
503-736-3276 | www.thefarmcafe.com

"So Portland it hurts" ("seasonal", "sustainable", "local", it even has some "fine-dining vegan" offerings) is how devotees describe this Lower Burnside eatery featuring a "sumptuous" yet affordable Pacific NW menu; a "sweet, funny" staff keeps things "comfortable" in the "cute" converted Victorian digs that include a "most relaxing" patio, adding up to a "divine" experience.

Fat City Cafe *American*   24 | 19 | 23 | $13

Multnomah Village | 7820 SW Capitol Hwy. (bet. 35th & 36th Aves.) |
503-245-5457 | www.fatcitycafe.net

This "greasy spoon" in Multnomah Village has been serving up "down-home" "all-American" cooking in "big portions" at bargain rates since 1974; it's cluttered with "Oregon kitsch" and lures lots of "locals hanging out", especially on all-you-can-eat-spaghetti Friday nights when kids under 12 eat free (otherwise it's breakfast and lunch only); P.S. don't miss the "awesome cinnamon rolls."

Fifty Licks Ⓜ⇗ *Ice Cream*

| 26 | 19 | 25 | $8 |

Belmont | Good Food Here | SE Belmont St. & 43rd Ave. | 954-294-8868 | www.fifty-licks.com

"Delicious" ice cream in "wonderfully unique" flavors like maple bacon and Stumptown coffee are on offer at this "cute", "friendly" Belmont truck; and there's a brick-and-mortar location planned for SE Clinton in early 2013.

Firehouse *Italian*

| 27 | 26 | 25 | $26 |

Woodlawn | 711 NE Dekum St. (Madrona St.) | 503-954-1702 | www.firehousepdx.com

"Bistro fare meets brick-oven pizza" at this "comfortable, cozy" Woodlawn Italian in the historic Dekum Firehouse that charms with a "bustling open kitchen" and bucolic courtyard; despite the "casual atmosphere", service is "supremely polished" and prices are more than reasonable.

Fire on the Mountain *American*

| 26 | 21 | 22 | $16 |

Lower Burnside | 1708 E. Burnside St. (17th Ave.) | 503-230-9464 ☽
NEW **Northeast Portland** | 3443 NE 57th Ave. (Fremont St.) | 503-894-8973
Overlook | 4225 N. Interstate Ave. (Skidmore St.) | 503-280-9464
www.portlandwings.com

Groupies can't get enough of the "awesome" wings slathered with "all kinds of sauces" ranging from "familiar BBQ" to "bragging-rights hot" at these Deadhead-themed outposts also offering American fare along the lines of sandwiches and deep-fried Oreos plus "tasty" beers from the NE Portland location's microbrewery; they're "usually packed", so service isn't always a strong suit.

Fish Grotto *Seafood*

| 26 | 22 | 24 | $25 |

West End | 1035 SW Stark St. (11th Ave.) | 503-226-4171 | www.fishgrotto.com

Despite the "totally gnarly exterior" on a gritty West End street, this venerable seafooder is a "gem" turning out "fresh, flavorful" fish plates at modest rates in a "dark", handsome dining room; service is solid, the vibe is "very Portland" and the bargain happy hour is a plus.

The Fishwife ⊠Ⓜ *Seafood*

| 25 | 18 | 24 | $18 |

University Park | 5328 N. Lombard St. (bet. Portsmouth & Van Houten Aves.) | 503-285-7150 | www.thefishwife.com

This "very cute, tiny" University Park mainstay wins the hearts of locals with a menu of "excellent" seafood standards such as homemade chowder, fried clam strips and cod sandwiches; fare comes at a "reasonable cost", and its "friendly staff" is a reflection of its family-owned roots.

	FOOD	DECOR	SERVICE	COST

Five Spice Seafood Restaurant + Wine Bar *Asian/Seafood*

| 24 | 25 | 22 | $38 |

Lake Oswego | 315 First St. (A Ave.) | 503-697-8889 | www.fivespicerestaurant.com

"Warm, intimate dining with a one-of-a-kind view" of Lake Oswego means this "pricey-but-worth-it" suburbanite seafooder works for a "nice night out" without the "hustle and bustle of Downtown"; the imaginative Asian-tinged menu offers "interesting cocktails" as well as happy-hour specials and half-price wine nights.

FlavourSpot *Sandwiches*

| 26 | 19 | 24 | $9 |

Mississippi | 810 N. Fremont St. (Mississippi Ave.) | 503-282-9866
North Portland | 2310 N. Lombard St. (Omaha Ave.) | 503-289-9866
www.flavourspot.com

"Fresh, hot and yummy" "waffle sandwiches" in "interesting flavor combinations" (both sweet and savory) keep fans coming to these two food carts in Mississippi and North Portland for a cheap fix; a "friendly" staff and picnic tables for chowing down add to the magnetism.

Fleur De Lis Bakery & Cafe *Bakery/French*

| 26 | 22 | 24 | $12 |

Hollywood | 3930 NE Hancock St. (40th Ave.) | 503-459-4887 | www.fleurdelisbakery.com

"Boy do they know how to bake bread" and "scrumptious pastries" at this French bakery and cafe in Hollywood that also proffers sandwiches, salads and Stumptown coffee in a "restyled library" building; a "pleasant staff" helps to bolster its status as a neighborhood gathering place, as do the affordable tabs.

Flying Pie *Pizza*

| 27 | 21 | 24 | $21 |

Montavilla | 7804 SE Stark St. (78th Ave.) | 503-254-2016
Gresham | 1600 NW Fairview Dr. (Burnside Rd.) | 503-328-0018
Lake Oswego | 3 Monroe Pkwy. (Boones Ferry Rd.) | 503-675-7377
Milwaukie | 16691 SE McLoughlin Blvd. (Naef Rd.) | 503-496-3170
www.flying-pie.com

"You'll never leave hungry" from this "quality" pizza chainlet, where the "out-of-this-world" pies "heaped high" with "fresh" meat and veggies are "not a solo" venture ("bring friends") – and come at tabs that lead frequent fliers to advise "you get way more than you pay for"; they skew "noisy", but the "smiling service is always a plus", as are the "laid-back", "family-oriented" vibe and "offbeat" video games.

Foster Burger *Burgers*

| 26 | 22 | 23 | $15 |

Foster-Powell | 5339 SE Foster Rd. (54th Ave.) | 503-775-2077 | www.fosterburger.com

"Phenomenal" burgers and "to-die-for" black-and-white fries (Parmesan, truffle oil, squid ink aïoli) are at the forefront of this "hip" Foster-Powell joint also featuring milkshakes and cocktails on its "limited" lineup; "great" service and "economical" bills further the appeal, as does a "funky" setting covered in "cool" concert handbills, lending a "very Portland attitude."

	FOOD	DECOR	SERVICE	COST

Frank's Noodle House ⊠ *Noodle Shop*   23 | 18 | 22 | $17

Irvington | 822 NE Broadway (8th Ave.) | 503-288-1007 | www.franksnoodlehouse.com

The "handmade, hand-cut" noodles are "out of this world" at this Irvington Asian where "huge portions" signal an "extraordinary" value for the dollar; expect a "classic, no-frills" setting plus "fast, friendly" service that works especially if you're "in a hurry."

Fratelli *Italian*   21 | 20 | 21 | $36

Pearl District | 1230 NW Hoyt St. (bet. 12th & 13th Aves.) | 503-241-8800 | www.fratellicucina.com

"Romantic" and "rustic", this Pearl District trattoria is beloved for its "hearty Italian-accented dishes" and "warm staff" that "makes you feel at home"; some take issue with "inconsistent" food and service, but on the whole its "longevity speaks for itself."

Fuller's Restaurant ⊭ *Diner*   25 | 21 | 25 | $13

Pearl District | 136 NW Ninth Ave. (bet. Couch & Davis Sts.) | 503-222-5608

This circa-1941 Pearl District diner is the "real McCoy when it comes to great, simply prepared breakfasts" and lunches that "fill you up" for not too much dough; quirky service is "part of the charm" as is the "elbow-to-elbow" seating at the cramped horseshoe counter where you can "sit and chat up your neighbors"; P.S. cash only.

Gandhi's: An East Indian Cafe ⊠ *Indian*   ∇ 28 | 18 | 24 | $12

Downtown | Global Food Ct. | 827 SW Second Ave. (Taylor St.) | 503-219-9224

For a "quick bite" at midday, "locals know" that this Global Food Court stand near Downtown's Lownsdale Square offers "delicious, home-cooked" Indian fare, including some of the "best vindaloo in town", at "value" prices; though a "line" is standard during its limited hours (10 AM-3 PM, weekdays only), the "quality" alone makes it "worth the wait."

Genies Cafe *American*   26 | 22 | 22 | $17

Central Eastside | 1101 SE Division St. (11th Ave.) | 503-445-9777 | www.geniesdivision.com

"Delish" American brunch and lunch classics offered alongside "strong drinks" like the bacon Bloody Mary explain the "kind of crazy" waits for a table at this "noisy" Central Eastside diner that's "full of hungover hipsters on weekends"; even if a "full-sleeve tattoo is required to work there", service is "extra helpful" and the manageable bills mean "you won't need to take out a second mortgage to have breakfast."

Genoa ⋈ *Italian*   28 | 26 | 28 | $85

Belmont | 2832 SE Belmont St. (bet. 28th & 29th Aves.) | 503-238-1464 | www.genoarestaurant.com

A "beloved" Belmont "institution" for "romantic", "unhurried" evenings full of "food artistry", this "formal" Italian "wows" with an "exquisite" five-course prix fixe menu of "imaginatively prepared", "consistently superb" plates; the "impeccable service" includes a sommelier at the "top of his game", and while it's "expensive", it's "well worth it"; P.S. it shares the block with its "casual cousin" Accanto next door.

Gilda's Italian Restaurant *Italian*   ▽ 27 | 22 | 24 | $24

Goose Hollow | 1601 SW Morrison St. (16th Ave.) | 503-224-0051 | www.gildasitalianrestaurant.com

"Is this Italy? if it's not, it is just as good" proclaim fans of this charming, mural-covered Goose Hollow ristorante and its chef who "has a gift when it comes to creating wonderful meals"; solid service and reasonable prices make it a "go-to" for local celebrations and pre-theater meals.

Gilt Club ●𝔖 *American*   24 | 25 | 23 | $29

Old Town-Chinatown | 306 NW Broadway (Everett St.) | 503-222-4458 | www.giltclub.com

Evoking "San Francisco in the 1950s", this "sexy" Old Town "treasure" with "big, comfy" red booths offers "lots of choices for the adventurous foodie" from a well-priced New American menu served till late, plus cocktails that "rock"; the staff is "efficient and charming" too, and even if a few find it a touch "overpriced", "where else can you get fine dining at 2 AM?"

Gino's *Italian*   26 | 22 | 23 | $28

Sellwood | 8051 SE 13th Ave. (Spokane St.) | 503-233-4613 | www.ginosrestaurantandbar.com

"Amazing Italian" prepared "in a rustic style" has made this "funky" trattoria a Sellwood destination for midpriced dining; "prompt", "friendly" service, a 500-plus-bottle wine list (many from the home country) and a sleek, modern environment keep neighbors coming back.

Giorgio's 𝔖𝔐 *Italian*   24 | 24 | 24 | $41

Pearl District | 1131 NW Hoyt St. (12th Ave.) | 503-221-1888 | www.giorgiospdx.com

"Italian mensch" Giorgio Kawas "treats everyone like family" at this "elegant" Pearl District "date-night" standby where "traditional, innovative" Northern Italian dishes with French influences, including "wonderful" handmade pastas, are presented in a "quaint" dining room ("think NYC Little Italy, hex-tile floor and all"); the "mild splurge" comes with "perfect" espresso and "some of the best desserts in town."

Gladstone Street Pizza ● *Pizza*   24 | 21 | 24 | $18

Southeast Portland | 3813 SE Gladstone St. (39th Ave.) | 503-775-1537 | www.gladstonepizza.com

"Awesome" thin-crust pizza with "just the right amount of toppings" is the draw at this "hole-in-the-wall" in SE Portland; there's a full bar serving local beers and liquor, and the affordable pies can be downed in the pint-sized dining room with a view of the open kitchen, on the "great" leafy back patio or at the adjacent lounge.

	FOOD	DECOR	SERVICE	COST

Goose Hollow Inn ● *Pub Food* — 22 | 21 | 21 | $15

Goose Hollow | 1927 SW Jefferson St. (20th Ave.) | 503-228-7010 |
www.goosehollowinn.com

Regulars swear by the Reuben ("hot, filling and dripping with goodness") and other pub classics at this "laid-back" Goose Hollow tavern
with an "old-style junktique" vibe and an outdoor deck; it has a rep for
providing "good, cheap" beer and as a "great place to meet people, including the mayor", Bud Clark, who ran the city from 1985 to 1992.

Got Pho? *Vietnamese* — 25 | 19 | 23 | $12

Hollywood | 3634 NE Sandy Blvd. (37th Ave.) | 503-232-4888 |
www.gotphoonline.com

There's "no glitz" at this "reliable" strip-mall Vietnamese at the
edge of the Hollywood 'hood, just "fantastic" pho and a roster of
other "amazing" eats from banh mi to vermicelli bowls; fans say
that combined with the "nice owners" and low prices, it's a "great
deal all around."

Gracie's Restaurant *American* — ▽ 20 | 23 | 20 | $31

Goose Hollow | Hotel deLuxe | 729 SW 15th Ave. (Yamhill St.) |
503-222-2171 | www.graciesdining.com

Tucked into the "hip", Hollywood-themed Hotel deLuxe, the "beautiful old-time" formal dining room of this Goose Hollow American
exudes a "civilized", "romantic" feel; aficionados say the midpriced
contemporary fare is "great", including a brunch that's "worth trying", while the Rat Pack–esque Driftwood Room bar proffers late-
night eats and drinks.

Grain & Gristle ● *Pub Food* — ▽ 23 | 25 | 24 | $21

Sabin | 1473 NE Prescott St. (15th Ave.) | 503-298-5007 |
www.grainandgristle.com

At the core of this "cozy, casual" open-timbered Sabin pub is its
striking live-edged maple bar stocked with a "small but thoughtfully
chosen beer selection" that complements the well-priced and "meat-
heavy, snout-to-tail" New American fare, notably the "incredible
burger"; the "friendly" but "not-in-your-face" staffers add appeal,
but it's the "hand-butchered meats and housemade pickles" that get
most of the attention.

Grand Central Bakery *Bakery* — 27 | 21 | 23 | $12

NEW **Beaumont** | 4440 NE Fremont St. (bet. 44th & 45th Sts.) |
503-808-9877
Boise-Eliot | 714 N. Fremont St. (Borthwick Ave.) | 503-546-5311
Hawthorne | 2230 SE Hawthorne Blvd. (bet. 22nd & 23rd Aves.) |
503-445-1600
Multnomah Village | 3425 SW Multnomah Blvd. (Capitol Hwy.) |
503-977-2024
Irvington | 1444 NE Weidler St. (15th Ave.) | 503-288-1614
Northwest Portland | 2249 NW York St. (22nd St.) | 503-808-9860
Sellwood | 7987 SE 13th Ave. (Lexington St.) | 503-546-3036
www.grandcentralbakery.com

The "smell" of the "terrific fresh-baked breads and pastries" and
other "delectable baked treats" may be "reason enough to visit" this

"no-fuss" bakery/cafe chain that's committed to organic and local sourcing, but it also offers "fantastic", "reasonably priced" sandwiches; the staff is "super-nice", and the outer NW stop offers a glimpse of bakers at work in a spacious converted warehouse.

Gravy *American*

25 | 21 | 24 | $15

Mississippi | 3957 N. Mississippi Ave. (Shaver St.) | 503-287-8800

"Alarmingly large", "freaking delicious" breakfast classics (including "fantastic" French toast) are the bread and butter of this "friendly", good-value Mississippi American with "farmhouse appeal"; diners grouse that it's "constantly busy", but the majority says it's "worth any wait you might have to endure", just "plan to burn calories afterward"; P.S. closes at 3 PM.

Grilled Cheese Grill *Sandwiches*

25 | 22 | 23 | $16

Alberta | NE Alberta St. & 11th Ave. | 503-206-8959 Ⓜ
Kerns | SE Ankeny St. & 28th Ave. | 503-206-7018 Ⓜ
NEW **West End** | SW Alder St. & 10th Ave. | no phone
www.grilledcheesegrill.com

"Oh the childhood memories" that this trio of bargain carts brings with its "unique spin" on the "perfectly gooey" namesake sandwiches, including "interesting combinations" such as the Original Cheesus, a burger wedged between two grilled cheeses; service is "quick", and fans say "it's fun to sit and eat your lil' sammie" inside the "converted" school bus in Alberta or the double-decker along SE 28th.

Grüner Ⓩ *European*

25 | 23 | 22 | $38

West End | 527 SW 12th Ave. (Alder St.) | 503-241-7163 |
www.grunerpdx.com

Chef Chris Israel recasts "old-world recipes in a refreshing light" to create "genuine, sublime" Alpine-inspired European fare at this "comfortable", "ultrachic" West Ender – even the burger is said to "elevate the form to high art"; the bill is "surprisingly reasonable for this quality", and servers are "considerate and charming to the point of being seductive"; P.S. the attached modern saloon Kask serves handcrafted cocktails alongside well-edited meat and cheese plates.

Gustav's *German*

25 | 24 | 24 | $25

Hollywood | 5035 NE Sandy Blvd. (50th Ave.) | 503-288-5503
Clackamas | 12605 SE 97th Ave. (Sunnyside Rd.) |
503-653-1391
Tigard | 10350 SW Greenburg Rd. (Oak St.) | 503-639-4544
www.gustavs.net

"*Wunderbar!*" declare devotees of this "busy" local chainlet revered for its "gut-busting" platters of "hearty", "full-flavored" German fare, "awesome deals" ("happy hour? yes, please") and "some of the best imported beers" on tap; the "festive" atmosphere is enhanced by "yodeling servers" in "authentic" garb who somehow "make you want to wear lederhosen" too – no wonder it's voted the Most Popular restaurant in Portland.

Habibi Restaurant *Lebanese*
25 | 23 | 25 | $20

Old Town-Chinatown | 221 SW Pine St. (3rd Ave.) | 503-459-4441
West End | 1012 SW Morrison St. (10th Ave.) | 503-274-0628
www.habibirestaurantpdx.com

The "extensive but not expensive" menu of "authentic", "dreamy good" Lebanese fare dazzles at this casual pair where "wonderful" service makes you "feel like family"; while the decor doesn't elicit comment, the overall package has many asking "what's not to like?"

Hall Street Grill *American*
24 | 24 | 24 | $27

Beaverton | 3775 SW Hall Blvd. (Westgate Dr.) | 503-641-6161 | www.hallstreetgrill.com

Locals say it's "always a treat" to visit this "chic", dark wood–accented Beaverton New American serving "delicious" fare that's a "taste extravaganza"; the service is solid, and though some find it a "little spendy", the "amazing" happy hour means you can pay "less" while getting your "drink on and eating a great burger."

Hamburger Mary's *Burgers*
25 | 23 | 23 | $18

Old Town-Chinatown | 19 NW Fifth Ave. (Couch St.) | 503-688-1200 | www.hamburgermarys.com

A "great hamburger dive", this Old Town outpost of a "gay-friendly" national chain goes beyond with deep-fried PB&J, novelty cocktails and nightly events like karaoke – regulars advise that "it gets a little raunchy the later you stay"; service follows suit (the moderate check comes in an "old stiletto") in an atmosphere "made for pure entertainment, relaxation and fun."

Hammy's Pizza ● *Pizza*
24 | 19 | 23 | $19

Clinton | 2114 SE Clinton St. (21st Ave.) | 503-235-1035 | www.hammyspizza.com

This "adorable" Clinton take-out joint is "best known for its delivery" of traditional or vegan pizzas, which runs until 4 AM (2:30 AM for carryout), perfect for when "you're hungry after the bar closes"; a few gripe it's "expensive" for pizza, but it's easy to "give them a call."

Hayden's Lakefront Grill *American*
23 | 23 | 23 | $26

Tualatin | 8187 SW Tualatin-Sherwood Rd. (bet. Boones Ferry Rd. & Martinazzi Ave.) | 503-885-9292 | www.haydensgrill.com

"Not your boring grill food", this suburban American offers a "well-executed" menu of "inventive" fare that's made all the better by the "beautiful view" of Tualatin's Lake of the Commons from the "warm" dining room and "excellent outdoor seating"; to shave a few bucks off the midpriced bill, savvy diners recommend the 3 PM-to-close bar-only happy hour, which comes "at a great price."

Heathman Restaurant & Bar *French/Pacific NW*
26 | 25 | 26 | $47

Downtown | Heathman Hotel | 1001 SW Broadway (Salmon St.) | 503-790-7752 | www.heathmanrestaurantandbar.com

"Elegance without pretense" takes center stage at this "romantic" destination in Downtown's "beautiful" Heathman Hotel, where "inventive" "French-inflected" Pacific NW fare is prepped with a "commitment to fresh, farm-to-table quality" – and whose "terrific" breakfasts, high teas and "cool happy hours" also have a legion of fans; "impeccable" service and a seemingly "bottomless" wine cellar supplement the "high-end enjoyment"; P.S. the post-Survey departure of culinary director Philippe Boulot may outdate the Food score.

Helser's On Alberta *American*   ▽ 24 | 20 | 21 | $20

Alberta | 1538 NE Alberta St. (16th Ave.) | 503-281-1477 | www.helsersonalberta.com

There's "always a crowd" for the "delicious, decadent" American breakfast and brunch at this Alberta eatery, where "friendly" faces deliver specialties such as Scotch eggs and "to-die-for" Dutch baby pancakes in a simple, light-filled space; though inexpensive any time of day, the breakfast special from 7 AM to 9 AM weekdays is a steal.

Helvetia Tavern 🚫 *Burgers*   26 | 20 | 23 | $16

Hillsboro | 10275 NW Helvetia Rd. (Dierdorff Rd.) | 503-647-5286 | www.helvetiatavern.com

It's "worth the trek out of town" for the "huge", "messy five-napkin burgers with special sauce" and a "generous serving" of "incredible" fries or "dope" onion rings at this cash-only Hillsboro American with a "simple", affordable menu; the "very casual, very country" theme extends to both decor (hats line the ceiling) and the sweet servers who "wait on you to the point of harassment."

Henry's 12th Street Tavern *American*   23 | 24 | 21 | $23

Pearl District | 10 NW 12th Ave. (Burnside St.) | 503-227-5320 | www.henrystavern.com

Housed in the Pearl's old Blitz-Weinhard Brewery, this "more upscale tavern" boasts "kazillions" of beers on tap and a laundry list of "solid", affordable American pub offerings in a "cool" labyrinth of exposed-brick chambers; while some find the setting "über-commercial" and the fare "uninspired", for many the "social atmosphere" comes out at the "terrific-value" happy hour and on weekends, when it's filled with "trendy twentysomethings."

H5O bistro & bar *American*   25 | 23 | 26 | $29

Downtown | Hotel Fifty | 50 SW Morrison St. (1st Ave.) | 503-484-1415 | www.h5obistro.com

Hidden inside Downtown's Hotel Fifty, this "posh" American turns out a menu of "innovative" dishes from breakfast through dinner for travelers and locals alike; a "friendly" crew pleases, and devotees say the "decent happy-hour specials" and drink selection impress them "enough to want to return."

Higgins Restaurant & Bar ● *Pacific NW*   27 | 24 | 27 | $46

Downtown | 1239 SW Broadway (Jefferson St.) | 503-222-9070 | www.higginsportland.com

"Uniformly superb" NW dishes comprising the "freshest local ingredients" have kept "godfather of sustainability" Greg Higgins and his Downtown bistro near the "top of the Portland food chain" for nearly two decades; "outstanding" Oregon wines "add another dimension to meals", while the "classy" yet "relaxed" vibe in the "always-busy" dining room ("make reservations!") is echoed by a staff of "total pros"; P.S. the "lively" bar boasts an "astonishing beer list" – and "less expensive" tabs.

The Highland Stillhouse Pub ● Ⓜ Pub Food | 25 | 24 | 22 | $16 |

Oregon City | 201 S. Second St. (McLoughlin Blvd.) | 503-723-6789

"Excellent", well-priced Scottish fare – haggis balls, bangers and beans, pasties – and a "ton of really great scotch and whiskey" have fans of this "friendly", "cozy" nook-filled Oregon City pub feeling "transported to Scotland" (there's even live Celtic music Thursday and Saturday nights); aye, it's so "authentic" you "almost expect" to see a "Highland cow" outside, but patrons settle for "phenomenal views" of the Willamette River from the deck.

Hobo's ● American | 22 | 22 | 22 | $24 |

Old Town-Chinatown | 120 NW Third Ave. (Couch St.) | 503-224-3285 | www.hobospdx.com

An "open and accepting atmosphere" "attracts gay and straight clientele" to this "classy" affordable Old Town eatery and piano lounge serving "wonderful" American victuals; service is "consistently great" (and the bartenders are "hot"), whether you've got "two people or 20."

Hoda's Middle Eastern Cuisine Mideastern | 24 | 19 | 24 | $17 |

Beaumont | 4727 NE Fremont St. (bet. 47th & 49th Aves.) | 503-688-5577 🅑

Belmont | 3401 SE Belmont St. (34th Ave.) | 503-236-8325 www.hodas.com

"Good", inexpensive Middle Eastern fare, including "authentic shawarma" and "homemade pita bread", can be found at this homey Belmont veteran (and its smaller Beaumont outpost); it's run by "nice" family staffers who are "on top of it" and has become a "favorite" for many.

NEW Hokusei Japanese | - | - | - | E |

Belmont | 4246 SE Belmont St. (42nd Ave.) | 971-279-2161 | www.hokuseisushi.com

Omakase is the thing at this upscale Belmont Japanese turning out sushi and traditional fare (slow-roasted pork shoulder, pickled vegetables) in presentations that are both striking and simple; the sleek, industrial surrounds benefit from exposed rafters and glass-clad garage doors that roll up to let the fresh air in.

Hollywood Burger Bar 🅑🏱 Burgers | 26 | 23 | 24 | $15 |

Hollywood | 4211 NE Sandy Blvd. (Hancock St.) | 503-288-6422 | www.hollywoodburgerbar.com

It's "hard to beat" the "great American burgers" and "outstanding" bargain-priced breakfasts at this "quaint", circa-1954 Hollywood diner; the quarters are "small and tight" (mostly counter stools), but the owner and staff "interact energetically with their patrons" and make fast friends of first-timers; P.S. cash only.

FOOD DECOR SERVICE COST

Hopworks Urban Brewery *Pub Food*   23 | 24 | 23 | $18
Foster-Powell | 2944 SE Powell Blvd. (29th Ave.) | 503-232-4677
Hopworks BikeBar *Pub Food*
Boise-Eliot | 3947 N. Williams Ave. (Shaver St.) | 503-287-6258
www.hopworksbeer.com
With salvage-chic decor "built out of spare bicycle parts", "fantastic" beers, "healthy" organic-leaning pub grub (gluten-free and vegan-friendly) and "multiple play areas" for kids, this huge, "laid-back" Foster-Powell brewpub and its smaller sister bar in Boise-Eliot are "perfectly Portland"; it's no surprise that they're "always packed" with "super-noisy" crowds of families.

Horn of Africa Ⓜ *Ethiopian/Mideastern*   24 | 21 | 23 | $20
King | 5237 NE Martin Luther King Jr. Blvd. (bet. Emerson & Sumner Sts.) | 503-331-9844 | www.hornofafrica.net
A "great diversity" of "authentic" Ethiopian and Middle Eastern fare with "wonderful, unusual spices and flavors" for "not a lot of moola" makes this "inviting" eatery in King's Vanport Square complex a hit for both meaty and vegan-friendly bites; "warm" service combined with the "different flavor profile" have fans saying it "will change your life."

Hotlips Pizza *Pizza*   25 | 20 | 23 | $12
Concordia | 5440 NE 33rd Ave. (Killingsworth St.) | 503-445-1020
Goose Hollow | 633 SW 19th Ave. (Morrison St.) | 503-517-9354
Hawthorne | 2211 SE Hawthorne Blvd. (bet. 22nd & 23rd Aves.) | 503-234-9999
Pearl District | 721 NW Ninth Ave. (bet. Irving & Johnson Sts.) | 503-595-2342
PSU | 1909 SW Sixth Ave. (bet. College & Hall Sts.) | 503-224-0311
www.hotlipspizza.com
"There's something for everyone" (vegans and the gluten-free included) at this sustainably minded, "very Portland-y" pizza chain serving pies with "delicious crusts" topped by "fresh, local and in-house ingredients", which "pair nicely" with a housemade soda; the overall decor is "nothing fancy", but the PSU link is good for a cheap "munch while studying", and the Pearl outpost boasts breezy outdoor picnic tables.

Hot Pot City *Chinese*   25 | 19 | 20 | $14
Downtown | 1975 SW First Ave. (Lincoln St.) | 503-224-6696
"It's fun to cook your own" Chinese soups at this "traditional", tidy Downtown hot pot joint where the combos of ingredients (udon, meats, fish, vegetables) from the buffet line seem "limitless"; a few find the service a "little cold", but for most it's a "cheap", "unique and enjoyable" experience for lunch or dinner.

Huber's ● *American*   25 | 25 | 24 | $26
Downtown | 411 SW Third Ave. (bet. Stark & Washington Sts.) | 503-228-5686 | www.hubers.com
"Turkey is king" and tastes exactly "how you always wanted your mom to make it" at this "historic" Downtowner (opened in 1879 and

in the Oregon Pioneer Building since 1910) serving roasted birds with "holiday" trimmings and other midpriced American fare; it's like "stepping back in time" when you sit in the "delightful", "clubby" wood-paneled bar, and for a "cool show", order an "expertly prepared" Spanish coffee – "it is a favorite."

Hungry Tiger Too *American/Vegan*　25 | 19 | 21 | $17

Buckman | 213 SE 12th Ave. (bet. Ash & Pine Sts.) | 503-238-4321 | www.hungrytigertoo.com

A pair of "gr-r-reat" American bar menus, one full of "awesome" organically minded "vegan delights" (including corn dogs and dairy-free soft serve) and the other full of classic carnivorous eats, breakfast through late-night, liven up this "friendly", reasonably priced Buckman diner; its variety of spaces – dining room, bar and "nice patio" – means it "works for just about anything."

Hush Hush Cafe ☒ *Mideastern*　▽ 25 | 20 | 25 | $12

Downtown | 433 SW Fourth Ave. (bet. Stark & Washington Sts.) | 503-274-1888 | www.hushhushcafe.com

"Giant portions" of "consistently excellent" Middle Eastern fare, including some of the "best hummus around" and a veggie meze big enough to "share or save for a second meal", make this small Downtowner an affordable "lunchtime favorite"; "incredibly fast service" adds to the value.

NEW Imperial *Pacific NW*　- | - | - | E

Downtown | Hotel Lucia | 410 SW Broadway (Stark St.) | 503-228-7222 | www.imperialpdx.com

With dramatic red-brick walls, tattoo-inspired wallpaper and bike-chain chandeliers, this hotly anticipated eatery in Downtown's Hotel Lucia from chef Vitaly Paley seems a world away from his more demure Paley's Place; the pricey Pacific NW fare, much of it prepped on a centerpiece wood-fired grill and rotisserie, is just as outsized as the surrounds – and it's on offer for breakfast, lunch and dinner; P.S. Paley's more casual Portland Penny Diner is next door.

Iorio ☒ *Italian*　27 | 24 | 26 | $27

Hawthorne | 912 SE Hawthorne Blvd. (9th Ave.) | 503-445-4716 | www.ioriorestaurant.com

"Bring the one you love" to share "heavenly" meatballs and other "serious" Italian eats (packed with a "lifetime supply of garlic"), backed by Pacific NW and Boot wines, at this "romantic", dimly lit "gem" along a "funky" stretch of Hawthorne; a "capable, attentive" staff and moderate prices cement its status as a "nice neighborhood spot"; P.S. closed Tuesday.

Iron Horse ☒ *Tex-Mex*　24 | 19 | 22 | $22

Sellwood | 6034 SE Milwaukie Ave. (Knight St.) | 503-232-1826 | www.portlandironhorse.com

A "varied" menu of "flavorful", inexpensive Tex-Mex plates (the "chile verde will sizzle your taste buds into submission") delights at this Sellwood "staple"; the staff is "personable", and if the "super-kid-friendly" dining room doesn't entice, there are always the picnic tables on the sidewalk.

Irving Street Kitchen *Pacific NW*
26 | 26 | 25 | $34

Pearl District | 701 NW 13th Ave. (Irving St.) | 503-343-9440 | www.irvingstreetkitchen.com

The "creatively executed", "Southern-inspired" Pacific NW eats ("think upscale soul food") and "strong, inventive" cocktails lure diners to this "warm" room in the Pearl where the wine comes in mason jars and milk-bottle chandeliers hang from the ceiling; a few find it "on the spendy side", but the "exceptional hospitality" and a kitchen where "something good is happening" push it into "gem" territory.

Isabel *Asian/Pan-Latin*
24 | 22 | 21 | $24

Pearl District | 330 NW 10th Ave. (bet. Everett & Glisan Sts.) | 503-222-4333 | www.isabelscantina.com

An outpost of Isabel Cruz's empire, this "wonderful" light-filled glass box in the Pearl is a "funny mix" of Asian and Pan-Latin flavors, but it makes for some "good", reasonably priced meals, including what some say is the "best breakfast in town"; it can get "busy", but the "relaxed" servers maintain a "friendly" vibe.

Jade Teahouse & Patisserie Ⓜ *Thai/Vietnamese*
26 | 25 | 23 | $18

Sellwood | 7912 SE 13th Ave. (Lexington St.) | 503-477-8985 | www.jadeportland.com

For "interesting combinations" of Vietnamese and Thai flavors, this "beautiful", "comfortable" Sellwood counter-service "favorite" delights with "affordable" plates and an "amazing" selection of exotic teas; the "helpful, friendly" staff pleases, as do the "mouthwatering" pastries and cookies.

Jake's Famous Crawfish *Seafood*
27 | 24 | 26 | $38

West End | 401 SW 12th Ave. (Stark St.) | 503-226-1419 | www.jakesfamouscrawfish.com

This "legendary Portland seafood palace" is "still delivering the goods" after 100-plus years in its "clubby" West End digs, where "fresh, delicious" fish comes accompanied by "professional" service; it gets a "little pricey", which explains why the "bargain" lunch specials and "amazing" happy hours are especially "popular" – and that's when you'll see a "healthy amount of locals" among a "lot of tourists" in the eatery that spawned the McCormick & Schmick's chain.

Jake's Grill *Seafood*
26 | 24 | 25 | $35

West End | Governor Hotel | 611 SW 10th Ave. (Alder St.) | 503-220-1850 | www.mccormickandschmicks.com

A "Portland institution for fresh seafood and tasty cocktails", this midpriced "McCormick & Schmick's property" in Downtown's West End pleases both "tourists" and locals with its "wide selection of delicious" offerings that go beyond fish (steaks, pastas, etc.); the "top-notch" service includes "hilarious" bartenders who preside over a "fantastic" happy hour, while the old-school dining room's "original woodwork" adds to the "tremendous atmosphere."

NEW Jamison *American*

`- | - | - | E`

Pearl District | 900 NW 11th Ave. (bet. Johnson & Lovejoy Sts.) | 503-972-3330 | www.jamisonpdx.com

Adjacent to Jamison Square, this charmer sports picture-perfect, light-filled rooms outfitted with a living wall of greenery, wood reclaimed from a Beavercreek barn and a handmade communal bar table; the decor sets the stage for the pricey New American menu from the team behind Davis Street Tavern, and there are deals to be had at happy hour and during the comfort-oriented weekend brunch.

Jam on Hawthorne *American*

`27 | 23 | 25 | $14`

Hawthorne | 2229 SE Hawthorne Blvd. (23rd Ave.) | 503-234-4790 | www.jamonhawthorne.com

Sprawling and "laid-back", this Hawthorne cafe "can't be beat" given its "diverse" menu of inexpensive, "fabulous" American breakfast eats with an "emphasis on the vegan-friendly" served in art-filled chambers; the "sweet" staff adds to the "laid-back" ambiance, and thank heavens for the "superb" multipaged breakfast cocktail menu – sometimes "a normal Bloody Mary just won't cut it."

J & M Cafe ⌷ *American*

`25 | 22 | 25 | $25`

Central Eastside | 537 SE Ash St. (6th Ave.) | 503-230-0463 | www.jandmcafepdx.com

This "light, airy", cash-only Central Eastside nook is one of the city's "best-kept secrets" for breakfast and lunch, serving up affordable, "tasty" American fare like breakfast burritos, scrapple with eggs and hearty sandwiches; "good" service contributes to the "welcoming" vibe, as do the mismatched mugs for self-serve coffee hanging on metal tree branches near the register.

NEW Jerusalem Cafe ⊠ *Mediterranean*

`26 | 21 | 26 | $15`

Belmont | 3801 SE Belmont St. (38th Ave.) | 503-206-7799 | www.thejerusalemcafe.com

Fans declare this cozy, family-owned Belmont Med turns out some of the most "authentic" cuisine "this side of Tel Aviv", delivered by a staff that's "always looking to please"; "reasonable" prices are one more reason it's a "find", whether for a "leisurely lunch" or "casual date."

Jo Bar & Rotisserie *American*

`24 | 22 | 22 | $26`

Northwest Portland | 701 NW 23rd Ave. (Irving St.) | 503-222-0048 | www.papahaydn.com

The "tasty" wood-fired New American plates at this "upscale" lounge are bolstered by a "good cocktail scene" and "people-watching on NW 23rd", although its real ace is the "over-the-top" desserts made in the kitchen it shares with its fine-dining sib, Papa Haydn; "solid" service and a "well-priced happy hour" put the molten chocolate in the cake.

Joel Palmer House ⊠Ⓜ *Pacific NW*

`28 | 24 | 27 | $62`

Dayton | 600 Ferry St. (6th St.) | 503-864-2995 | www.joelpalmerhouse.com

"Mushrooms more ways than Cincinnati has chili" star on the "extraordinary", "expensive-but-worth-it" Pacific NW menu at this Dayton destination where the "foraged 'shroom"–centric dishes are crafted by a chef with a "deft hand" and served in "lovely", "romantic" environs inside a historic house; a "stunning" Oregon-oriented wine list and what seems like "more staffers than tables" shore up its reputation as a "perfect" stop post–Willamette Valley vino tasting.

Joe's Burgers *Burgers* | 24 | 20 | 22 | $14 |

Downtown | 625 SW Fourth Ave. (Alder St.) | 503-248-5637
NEW **PSU** | 540 SW College St. (bet. 5th & 6th Aves.) | 503-432-8022
Southwest Portland | 4439 SW Beaverton-Hillsdale Hwy. (45th Ave.) | 503-892-6686
Tigard | Bridgeport Vill. | 7409 SW Bridgeport Rd. (Upper Boones Ferry Rd.) | 503-598-1111
www.joesburgers.com

"Portland's closest thing to an In-N-Out Burger", this mini-chain scores with a brief menu of "simple", "delicious", affordable burgers and "crispy, hot" fries made from "high-quality ingredients"; the goods are cooked to order but served up "quick" at its "retro" diner Downtown, from a kiosk in Tigard's busy Bridgeport Village, at its new PSU branch or at the the larger SW outpost, which beefs up its offerings with local brews, pool and video games.

John Street Cafe Ⓜ *American* | ∇ 24 | 21 | 26 | $20 |

St. Johns | 8338 N. Lombard St. (John Ave.) | 503-247-1066
Whether for a "comfort date" or a "relaxing" outing with friends, this "adorably quaint" St. Johns American fits the bill with its inexpensive menu of "fantastic" breakfast lunch favorites delivered by an able crew; tables fill up fast in its small dining room and on the plant-filled patio come weekends, so "bring a newspaper or three for the wait"; P.S. closed Monday and Tuesday.

Jory *Pacific NW* | 26 | 27 | 27 | $63 |

Newberg | Allison Inn & Spa | 2525 Allison Ln. (Springbrook Rd.) | 503-554-2526 | www.theallison.com
An "oasis of excellence" in wine country, the Allison Inn & Spa's luxe dining room gets high marks for its "beautiful view" of the Willamette Valley, which makes the perfect backdrop for its "wonderful" Pacific NW cuisine and "enticing" vintages; the "friendly" pro staff also impresses, so even though it's plenty "expensive", most say it's right on "for a special dinner" – especially if you're "someone else's guest."

June Ⓢ Ⓜ *American* | ∇ 24 | 23 | 24 | $43 |

Buckman | 2215 E. Burnside St. (22nd Ave.) | 503-477-4655 | www.junepdx.com
Chef Gregory Perrault's "hyper-seasonal, delicately prepared, delicious" fare has diners "trading bites" at his "relaxed", wood-beamed Buckman New American; it's on the spendy side, but the "warm" staff adds to the solid "value" here – and as a bonus, the "bartender is fantastic."

Justa Pasta Co. *Italian*   26 | 19 | 22 | $22

Northwest Portland | 1336 NW 19th Ave. (Pettygrove St.) |
503-243-2249 | www.justapasta.com

It's "nothing fancy" and you "stand in line to order", but this NW
Portland "hideaway" in a quiet residential neighborhood is lauded
for its "consistently fine" Italian classics, most notably "awesome"
housemade pastas; "value" prices, "generous" wine pours and
"nice" staffers are other reasons loyal lasagna-lovers return on
a "weekly basis."

Karam *Lebanese*   ▽ 25 | 21 | 24 | $22

Downtown | 316 SW Stark St. (3rd Ave.) | 503-223-0830 |
www.karamrestaurant.com

The "subtle flavors" of the Lebanese cooking at this intimate
Downtowner "elevate" it above the norm according to devotees
of its specialties including pita bread that "arrives piping hot
from the oven" and "excellent" kebabs; "warm, personal" service
that has surveyors feeling "like honored houseguests" and low prices
seal the deal.

Kells ◑ *Irish/Pub Food*   24 | 25 | 23 | $21

NEW **Northwest Portland** | 210 NW 21st Ave. (bet. Burnside &
Everett Sts.) | 503-719-7175 | www.kellsbrewpub.com
Old Town-Chinatown | 112 SW Second Ave. (Ash St.) | 503-227-4057 |
www.kellsirish.com

This "convivial" Old Town pub's "good old-fashioned" Emerald
Isle charms include the "fun touch" of coins on the ceiling, a cigar lounge and nightly "traditional" live music; even if "everyone
goes for the Guinness", both its "authentic", reasonably priced
Irish fare and its service are rated "better than average"; P.S. a
NW Portland offshoot opened recently and supplies house-brewed
beer to both locations.

Kenny & Zuke's Bagelworks *Deli*   24 | 19 | 20 | $17

Northwest Portland | 2376 NW Thurman St. (bet. 23rd & 24th Sts.) |
503-954-1737 | www.kzbagelworks.com
Kenny & Zuke's Deli Bar ◑ *Deli*
NEW **Boise-Eliot** | 3901 N. Williams Ave. (bet. Failing & Shaver Sts.) |
503-287-0782 | www.kennyandzukes.com
Kenny & Zuke's Delicatessen *Deli*
West End | 1038 SW Stark St. (bet. 10th & 11th Aves.) | 503-222-3354 |
www.kennyandzukes.com

A "yummy compromise between an authentic deli and a casual
Pacific NW" eatery, this "crazy crowded" West End joint and its
Boise-Eliot and NW Portland brethren serve up "to-die-for"
pastrami in portions that would "make a Jewish grandmother
blush"; some surveyors find prices a "tad high" for the "hands-
off" service, and a few fuss it's "close but no cigar" to the East
Coast originals, but most say it works "when you just have to get
your nosh on"; P.S. the NW location has a bagel focus, and the
new light-filled Deli Bar on Williams offers morning bagels, lunch,
dinner and cocktails.

	FOOD	DECOR	SERVICE	COST

Ken's Artisan Bakery *Bakery/French*
28 | 20 | 21 | $14

Northwest Portland | 338 NW 21st Ave. (Flanders St.) | 503-248-2202 |
www.kensartisan.com

"Crusty" breads, "fabulous" pastries and sandwiches "to die for" are
among the inexpensive offerings at this "small", "charming" NW
Portland bakery and French bistro; "limited" seating has aficionados
advising "get it to go" to avoid the "packed" lunch rush – and "savor
every bite" of that croissant, because you will "want another one";
P.S. it's open Monday nights for pizza.

Ken's Artisan Pizza *Pizza*
27 | 22 | 23 | $23

Buckman | 304 SE 28th Ave. (Pine St.) | 503-517-9951 |
www.kensartisan.com

"Get there early or wait in line" at this "cramped"-but-"vibrant"
Buckman pizzeria where the "artfully constructed" wood-fired pies
sport "perfectly thin", "crisp, crackling" crusts topped with "unusual",
"seasonal" ingredients and "sumptuous extras" like Calabrian chiles
and fresh arugula; such a "buzzing" scene means the "friendly" staff
can get "harried", and the bill can seem "pricey for what you get",
but to most it's "well worth it."

Khun Pic's Bahn Thai 🅂🅼🍴 *Thai*
∇ 28 | 29 | 28 | $18

Belmont | 3429 SE Belmont St. (bet. 34th & 35th Aves.) | 503-235-1610
There's only "one chef" preparing the "authentic" Thai eats to order
and "her husband is the server" at this cash-only stop housed in a
Belmont Victorian; the "incredible location" behind overgrown greenery on a busy road adds to the "amazing", yet low-cost, experience.

Killer Burger 🅂 *Burgers*
27 | 21 | 25 | $13

Hollywood | 4644 NE Sandy Blvd. (47th Ave.) | 971-544-7521
NEW **Sellwood** | 8728 SE 17th Ave. (Linn St.) | 503-841-5906
www.killerburger.biz

"Fun twists on the old-fashioned burger" draw meatheads to
these Hollywood-Sellwood patty places, where the "affordable",
cardiologist-worthy lineup includes a "crazy-but-delicious" option
with peanut butter sauce, pickles and bacon, plus the "addictive" "bottomless" fries come gratis; the "small" Sandy Boulevard outpost can
be "standing-room-only", but "peppy" service keeps tables turning.

King Burrito *Mexican*
26 | 14 | 22 | $15

North Portland | 2924 N. Lombard St. (bet. Greeley & Peninsular Aves.) |
503-283-9757 | www.kingburritomexicanfood.com

"Don't let its looks keep you out", because this "unassuming" North
Portland "dive" is deemed "Mexican-food nirvana"; a "longtime
slinger" of "consistent", "tasty" basic fare – "burritos, tacos and the
occasional menudo" – via an efficient counter crew, it boasts "low"
prices to seal the deal.

Koi Fusion *Korean/Mexican*
25 | 17 | 22 | $12

Eastside Industrial | The Row | 304 SE Second Ave. (Oak St.) |
503-789-0848

(continued)

(continued)

Koi Fusion

Downtown | Global Food Ct. | 827 SW Second Ave. (Taylor St.) |
503-789-0848
Mississippi | 4233 N. Mississippi Ave. (Skidmore St.) | 503-997-6654
Tigard | Bridgeport Vill. | 7413 SW Bridgeport Rd. (Hazelfem Rd.) |
503-997-6654
www.koifusionpdx.com

It's "twisted fusion" at its "best" say "die-hard fans" of this local
Korean-meets-Mexican chain and its carts and kiosks, considered
"must-stop" destinations for "tasty" eats "made with care", whether
"on a bun or in a tortilla"; a "friendly", "efficient" staff adds to the
low-cost experience that's "nice for a change" of pace; P.S. a West
Burnside brick and mortar location is planned for late 2012.

Koji Osakaya *Japanese*   25 | 20 | 23 | $22

Downtown | 1000 SW Broadway (Main St.) | 503-517-8820
Downtown | 606 SW Broadway (Alder St.) | 503-294-1169
Irvington | 1502 NE Weidler St. (15th Ave.) | 503-280-0992
www.koji.com

This local Japanese chain commands a following for its "traditional"
sushi and cooked dishes served in simple settings overseen by a capable crew; fans say they "get their money's worth" given the "large" portions, and recommend it for "business chats" or really "any time."

Kornblatt's Delicatessen *Deli*   25 | 19 | 22 | $16

Northwest Portland | 628 NW 23rd Ave. (Irving St.) | 503-242-0055 |
www.kornblattsdelipdx.com

"Massive sandwiches" piled with "sinful" pastrami, "sassy New
Yorkian waiters" and "all the crunchy pickles you can eat" impress
at this NW Portland Jewish deli; the small, no-frills space is "often a
mob scene", but for most its wallet-friendly "tastes of the East
Coast" are "worth the effort."

Kure Juice Bar *Vegan*   ▽ 25 | 21 | 24 | $14

Hawthorne | 4409 SE Hawthorne Blvd. (44th Ave.) | 503-688-1006 |
www.kurejuicebar.com

"Don't pass up" this humble Hawthorne juice hut proffering "freshly
squeezed" juice and smoothie blends with cheeky names like Tiger's
Blood and Berried Alive (plus acai bowls and parfaits), which have
enthusiasts "going back for more"; prices are relatively reasonable
given that most ingredients are local and organic; P.S. hit their Rose
Garden stand during Trail Blazers games and look for a planned outpost on SW Taylor Street near Pioneer Square.

La Bonita *Mexican*   26 | 21 | 24 | $13

Alberta | 2839 NE Alberta St. (29th Ave.) | 503-281-3662
Overlook | 2710 N. Killingsworth St. (Greeley Ave.) | 503-278-3050
www.labonitarestaurant.net

"Family-owned with a family feel", these "basic" joints in Alberta
and Overlook captivate fans who "love, love, love" the "real Mexican
food made well"; they're certainly "not overpriced" and their counter staffers are "possibly the nicest people on the planet."

	FOOD	DECOR	SERVICE	COST

La Buca *Italian*

▽ 23 | 20 | 23 | $20

Kerns | 40 NE 28th Ave. (Couch St.) | 503-238-1058 |
www.labucaitaliancafe.com

Anchoring a busy corner of NE 28th Avenue's bustling Restaurant Row in Kerns, this bright, casual Italian woos devotees of "so-fresh pastas" and other "above-average" classics; prices are "crazy cheap for the quality", and its "friendly workers" further endear it to a "neighborhood" crowd.

La Calaca Comelona ☒ *Mexican*

▽ 25 | 23 | 23 | $18

Belmont | 2304 SE Belmont St. (23rd Ave.) | 503-239-9675 |
www.lacalacacomelona.com

An "eye-catching" stop in Belmont thanks to its "riotous" mural-splashed facade and Technicolor party bus parked on the front patio, this Mexican mainstay is appreciated for its "off-the-beaten-track menu" of "regional specialties", which are priced a bit higher than its basics like tacos and quesadillas; solid service and "divine" mixed drinks have fans joking "it's better than Frida and Diego combined."

La Provence *Bakery/French*

26 | 22 | 22 | $20

NEW **Lake Oswego** | 16350 SW Boones Ferry Rd. (Clara Ln.) |
503-635-4533

Petite Provence *Bakery/French*

Alberta | 1824 NE Alberta St. (19th Ave.) | 503-284-6564
Division | 4834 SE Division St. (bet. 48th & 49th Aves.) | 503-233-1121
www.provence-portland.com

If you "love French food, you'll love" this "affordable" Alberta and Division duo (with a newer, bigger Lake Oswego third) say fans cheering the "gorgeous pastries" ("you have to get a croissant") and "delicious" bistro fare; "limited seating" means you should expect "long lines", especially on weekends.

NEW Lardo *Sandwiches*

28 | 21 | 27 | $17

West End | 1205 SW Washington St. (12th Ave.) | 503-241-2490
Hawthorne | 1212 SE Hawthorne Blvd. (12th Ave.) | 503-234-7786
www.lardopdx.com

Having originally peddled his "melt-in-your-mouth" pork products and "delicious" fries from one of the "cutest" food trucks, "talented" chef Rick Gencarelli has moved to solid ground with the post-Survey debut of this brick-and-mortar sandwich shop pair in Hawthorne and the West End (not reflected in the Decor score); expect the same "awesome" pig-centric sammies, plus plenty of indoor/outdoor seating and a dozen-plus beers on tap.

La Sirenita *Mexican*

25 | 17 | 22 | $18

Alberta | 2817 NE Alberta St. (28th Ave.) | 503-335-8283
Sellwood | 8029 SE 17th Ave. (Spokane St.) | 503-234-3280

Maybe they're "not places you go to for the atmosphere", but these "one-step-above-the-taco-van" Mexicans in Alberta and Sellwood dispense "awesome" basics that "more than make up for" lacking decor; "quick" service, "cheap" prices and an all-around "authentic flair" seal the deal.

	FOOD	DECOR	SERVICE	COST

Laughing Planet Café *Mexican/Vegetarian*   24 | 20 | 21 | $12

Belmont | 3320 SE Belmont St. (33rd Ave.) | 503-235-6472
Downtown | 1720 SW Fourth Ave. (bet. Harrison & Market Sts.) |
503-224-2326
Woodstock | 4110 SE Woodstock Blvd. (41st Ave.) |
503-788-2921
Mississippi | 3765 N. Mississippi Ave. (bet. Beech & Failing Sts.) |
503-467-4146
Northwest Portland | 922 NW 21st Ave. (bet. Kearney & Lovejoy Sts.) |
503-445-1319
Pearl District | 721 NW Ninth Ave. (bet. Irving & Johnson Sts.) |
503-505-5020
Southwest Portland | 4405 SW Vermont St. (45th Ave.) |
503-244-4254
www.laughingplanetcafe.com

Known for its "cheap", "fat burritos" that "overflow with yummy",
this family-friendly Mexican chain draws crowds for "fresh, fast
and healthy" staples that unite "vegans and meat eaters"; its
"casual", counter-service setups with toy dinosaurs on the tables
cement it as a "place to relax and chill", as do the "well-selected
beers on draft."

Laurelhurst Market *Steak*   26 | 21 | 24 | $43

Kerns | 3155 E. Burnside St. (32nd Ave.) | 503-206-3097 |
www.laurelhurstmarket.com

"It's all about the meat" at this "lively" Kerns steakhouse/butcher
shop, a "carnivore's delight" proffering "unusual" cuts "aged to perfection (and cooked even better)" plus "awesome" sides to go with;
tabs can be a "little pricey" and toe-tappers lament "excruciating"
waits for a table in the "industrial" space, but "exquisite" cocktails
from some of the "best bartenders in town" and "professional" service help quell most beefs.

Le Bistro Montage ⬤ *Cajun/Creole*   26 | 24 | 22 | $19

Eastside Industrial | 301 SE Morrison St. (3rd Ave.) | 503-234-1324 |
www.montageportland.com

"Exceptional mac 'n' cheese" and gator bites star at this "super-
cheap" Cajun-Creole joint "hidden" down a gritty Eastside Industrial
side street, but fans also flock for the "eccentric, entertaining" service, "fun" communal tables and a vibe that "rocks all day long"; ok,
a few are turned off by the "purposefully rude" staff, but all's forgiven with the arrival of "your leftovers wrapped in a foil animal."

Le Bouchon 🆉 Ⓜ *French*   23 | 17 | 24 | $36

Pearl District | 517 NW 14th Ave. (Glisan St.) | 503-248-2193 |
www.bouchon-portland.com

"Practice your French" at this "authentic" midpriced Gallic bistro
turning out "just the classics, executed with love" in a "cramped",
"noisy", "bare-bones" Pearl District storefront; a few carb critics
claim it "could use better bread", but the majority is more focused
on the "pleasant service" overseen by a chef-owner who is a "character" and enhances the "little-trip-to-Paris" atmosphere.

	FOOD	DECOR	SERVICE	COST

Le Happy ●☒ *Crêpes*
25 | 22 | 22 | $16

Northwest Portland | 1011 NW 16th Ave. (Lovejoy St.) | 503-226-1258 | www.lehappy.com

The string light–festooned storefront of this "cutest little crêperie" in NW Portland beckons seekers of "delicious" sweet and savory crêpes offered at "low prices"; a "lively" staff, "strong" drinks from a "fine bar" and late hours on weekends ensure it's a popular local pick, whether for a "kitschy date night" or just to "hang out."

Lemongrass ☒Ⓜ⇆ *Thai*
27 | 25 | 25 | $19

Kerns | 1705 NE Couch St. (17th Ave.) | 503-231-5780

What loyalists laud as some of the "best Thai food in Portland" from "people who have been doing it for a long time" draws heat-seeking diners – the one–20 spice scale is legendary – to this "charming" Kerns eatery set in a "quiet", "wonderful old house"; a cash-only policy and prices slightly higher than your typical take-out joint don't discourage fans from "visiting regularly."

Le Pigeon *French*
28 | 22 | 25 | $46

Lower Burnside | 738 E. Burnside St. (8th Ave.) | 503-546-8796 | www.lepigeon.com

"Impeccable" French cuisine that blends "whimsy, precision and inventiveness" attracts an "eclectic crowd" to this "snug joint" in Lower Burnside, where "loyal minions" snag seats at communal tables or at the counter to watch "highly skilled" (and "tattooed") chef Gabriel Rucker turn out "genius dishes" from an "ever-changing menu"; while some find it "pricey" for the tight fit, most are "drooling to go back."

Lincoln ☒Ⓜ *American*
27 | 25 | 27 | $42

Boise-Eliot | 3808 N. Williams Ave. (Failing St.) | 503-288-6200 | www.lincolnpdx.com

It's "what a bistro bar is supposed to be" say admirers of this Boise-Eliot "gem" that puts forth "excellent-yet-no-fuss" locally sourced American fare in an industrial-leaning space with an open kitchen; the high-flying staff is "knowledgeable and unrushed" and the prices "not expensive" considering the overall "amazing" experience, which has many wishing it were closer so they could "go more often."

Little Big Burger *Burgers*
25 | 20 | 22 | $10

NEW Division | 3810 SE Division St. (38th Ave.) | 503-841-6456
Mississippi | 3747 N. Mississippi Ave. (bet. Beech & Failing Sts.) | 503-265-8781
NEW Northwest Portland | 930 NW 23rd Ave. (bet. Kearney & Lovejoy Sts.) | 971-544-7817
Pearl District | 122 NW 10th Ave. (bet. Couch & Davis Sts.) | 503-274-9008
www.littlebigburger.com

This "hip" local fast-food chain with a penny-pinching, six-item menu slings "fantastic" "made-to-order" sliders that are "tiny but full of flavor" and complemented by "wonderful" white truffle oil-laced fries and ketchup with a "kick"; good thing the service is "rapid", because its no-frills, red-accented shops offer "limited" seating and the line is "often out the door" – it "blows other burger bars away."

Little Bird ● *French*   27 | 24 | 25 | $35

Downtown | 219 SW Sixth Ave. (Oak St.) | 503-688-5952 | www.littlebirdbistro.com

"If you like Le Pigeon, you'll love" this "superb" Downtown bistro since both share "*wunderkind*" chef Gabriel Rucker, who here helms an "interesting" menu of "country French" fare at "friendlier prices" (including a duck confit that "will make a Frenchman cry"); the "just-right", "foxy" setting with dark-red banquettes and an upstairs mezzanine is "usually crowded" and overseen by a staff that "works as an amazing team."

Little T American Baker *Bakery*   ▽ 26 | 19 | 18 | $10

Division | 2600 SE Division St. (bet. 38th & 39th Aves.) | 503-238-3458 | www.littletbaker.com

"Dough master" Tim Healea helms this "sleek" Division Street bakery stocked with "fine" "rustic breads" and "delicious" pastries, plus lunch favorites such as quiche, sandwiches and salads; even the crustiest customers say it turns out some of the "best baguettes and croissants outside of Paris", with "reasonable" prices to ice the cake.

Lovejoy Bakers *Bakery*   27 | 24 | 24 | $12

NEW **Central Eastside** | 2523 SE Ninth Ave. (Division St.) | 971-229-0984 🖪
Pearl District | 939 NW 10th Ave. (Lovejoy St.) | 503-208-3113 www.lovejoybakers.com

This "elegant" Pearl District bakery proffers "delicious, fresh" pastries and breads plus "well-prepared sandwiches and salads" at easygoing tabs, served up by a "cheerful" crew; it boasts pleasant, "bustling" digs with a "great patio", and now it's been joined by a breakfast- and lunch-only cafe housed inside the company's Central Eastside wholesale production facility.

Lovely's Fifty Fifty Ⓜ *Pizza*   28 | 22 | 26 | $25

Mississippi | 4039 N. Mississippi Ave. (bet. Mason & Shaver Sts.) | 503-281-4060 | www.lovelysfiftyfifty.com

At this "cute, kitschy" Mississippi joint, "gorgeous" wood-fired pizzas with "unconventional", locally sourced toppings share space on a gently priced menu with "delicious" salads and "killer" housemade ice cream (including salted caramel – "OMG!") made all the better by "great service"; naturally, it's almost "always jammed" with a "lively" crowd, but no matter: loyalists just "love this place."

Lucca Ⓜ *Italian/Pizza*   ▽ 25 | 23 | 23 | $29

Alameda | 3449 NE 24th Ave. (Fremont St.) | 503-287-7372 | www.luccapdx.com

A "reliable neighborhood Italian", this Alameda "hangout" draws families and others for "delicious" wood-fired pizzas, pastas and the like, delivered by a solid staff; it gets "busy" at prime times, but still many count its dining room with unique woven-wood ceiling panels as a "relaxing place", and all appreciate the moderate prices.

Luce *Italian*

`-` `-` `-` `M`

Buckman | 2140 E. Burnside St. (22nd Ave.) | 503-236-7195

With its quaint corner-store looks (checkerboard floor, shelves offering European culinary sundries for sale) and moderate prices, it'd be easy to miss the punch that this petite Buckman Italian packs with its simply prepared antipasti and entrees like baked stuffed trout and housemade cappelletti; from the husband-and-wife team behind the Kerns favorite Navarre, it's making waves in foodie circles.

Lucky Labrador ◑ *Pub Food*

`21` `21` `22` `$15`

Northwest Portland | 1945 NW Quimby St. (bet. 19th & 20th Aves.) | 503-517-4352

Hawthorne | 915 SE Hawthorne Blvd. (9th Ave.) | 503-236-3555

Multnomah Village | 7675 SW Capitol Hwy. (31st Ave.) | 503-244-2537

Overlook | 1700 N. Killingsworth St. (Taylor St.) | 503-505-9511 www.luckylab.com

"Bring your dog" to these spacious, "down-home" pubs where four-legged friends have the run of outdoor areas and "cool folks" serve the "handcrafted", brewed-in-house beers; the grub is "decent" and affordable, and there's an all around "excellent" vibe – "what else could you want?"

Lucky Strike *Chinese*

`24` `19` `22` `$24`

Hawthorne | Hawthorne Theater | 3862 SE Hawthorne Blvd. (39th Ave.) | 503-206-8292 | www.luckystrikepdx.com

Nestled inside the Hawthorne Theater, this "kitschy" kung pao kitchen slings "delicious", "spicy" Sichuan cuisine and specialty cocktails in "funky" boudoir-meets-bistro environs lit by red chandeliers; though it can be "hard to locate" and offers "limited parking", to most it's "worth the effort", with "reasonable prices" and an "entertaining" atmosphere sweetening the deal.

NEW Luc Lac Vietnamese Kitchen ◑🆅 *Vietnamese*

`27` `20` `17` `$11`

Downtown | 835 SW Second Ave. (Taylor St.) | 503-222-0047 | www.luclackitchen.com

A food cart–turned-restaurant success story, this "friendly" Downtown hot spot dishes up "fresh, body-warming" Vietnamese classics to hordes of hungry office workers and mall shoppers; it can get "crowded" and "noisy", but the tabs are "cheap" – and even more so at happy hour.

Mac! Mac & Cheesery *American*

`25` `22` `23` `$19`

Mississippi | 3936 N. Mississippi Ave. (bet. Failing & Shaver Sts.) | 503-200-5787 | www.macandcheese.biz

"Get your mac 'n' cheese on" at this "quirky" Mississippi cafe, where "interesting combinations" of the "lovely cheesy goodness" are served in "large portions" at a low price; though it gets "busy" at prime times, service is "fast" and "friendly", and waist-watchers joke they'd "go more often if they had a carb-free pasta."

FOOD | DECOR | SERVICE | COST

🆕 Mack & Dub's Excellent Chicken & Waffles Ⓜ *Southern*

▽ 25 | 17 | 23 | $14

Boise-Eliot | 3601 NE Martin Luther King Jr. Blvd. (Fremont St.) | 714-603-5644 | www.mackanddub.com

For some of the "best darn Southern-fried cooking" on the cheap, enthusiasts trek to this Boise-Eliot soul stop for "OMG" down-home faves including crispy chicken and sides; maybe the "decor needs work", but the "super-nice" service bolsters the atmosphere of "eating at home with friends"; P.S. a fire has temporarily shuttered it.

MacTarnahan's Tap Room *Pub Food*

21 | 21 | 22 | $23

Northwest Portland | 2730 NW 31st Ave. (Industrial St.) | 503-228-5269 | www.macsbeer.com

In a "hard-to-find", "industrial" stretch of NW Portland, this "classic" brewpub gets props for its combo of "excellent" craft beer (12 rotating taps) and "decent", affordable grub; "quick" service and "outdoor seating in nice weather" are other pluses, and even if a few find the eats merely "average", they tout the MacTarnahan's Amber Ale as anything but.

Mad Greek Deli Ⓢ *Greek*

23 | 17 | 21 | $14

Bethany | 18450 NW West Union Rd. (185th Ave.) | 503-645-1650
🆕 **Buckman** | 1740 E. Burnside St. (18th Ave.) | 503-232-0274
www.madgreekdeli.com

A "local legend", this affordable, "timeless" Bethany Greek has earned a loyal following for its gyros called some of the "best in town", notable lunch specials and full bar; it's definitely no-frills, but live music on weekends adds interest; P.S. the expansion to Buckman has metro dwellers happy they no longer "have to drive out to the sticks" for their fix.

Mama Mia Trattoria *Italian*

23 | 23 | 23 | $23

Downtown | 439 SW Second Ave. (bet. Stark & Washington Sts.) | 503-295-6464 | www.mamamiatrattoria.com

Romantics go gaga for the "over-the-top", "elegant" decor at this Downtown Italian that's a no-brainer for "special occasions"; "attentive" servers deliver the "generous" portions of "fairly priced", "no-pretenses" standards, which come even cheaper when ordered in the lounge during happy hour.

Mandarin Cove *Chinese*

24 | 20 | 22 | $19

Downtown | 111 SW Columbia St. (1st Ave.) | 503-222-0006 | www.mandarin-cove.com

It's "typical" "Americanized Chinese", but this seasoned joint sates Downtown appetites with "abundant, tasty" fare that loyal followers say is "best for your buck" at lunchtime; the enclosed-atrium dining room dripping with live plants affords a glimmer of a river view, and it's "convenient" before a show at the Keller Auditorium.

Marinepolis Sushi Land *Japanese*

21 | 16 | 18 | $11

Irvington | 1409 NE Weidler St. (14th Ave.) | 503-280-0300
Pearl District | 138 NW 10th Ave. (Davis St.) | 503-546-9933

(continued)

Marinepolis Sushi Land

Beaverton | 4021 SW 117th Ave. (Canyon Rd.) | 503-520-0257
Clackamas | 8424 SE Sunnyside Rd. (bet. 82nd & 84th Aves.) |
503-794-1800
Tigard | 7194 SW Hazelfern Rd. (Bridgeport Rd.) | 503-726-0308
www.sushilandusa.com

As "conveyor-belt sushi" goes, this chain churns out "generic-but-reliable" rolls plus a handful of cooked Japanese dishes, making it a popular stop for a "quick lunch" in unremarkable environs; even those who say the fish is "nothing special" tout it as one to "check out" if you're "on a budget."

Marrakesh *Moroccan*   27 | 27 | 25 | $28

Northwest Portland | 1201 NW 21st Ave. (Northrup St.) | 503-248-9442 |
www.marrakeshportland.com

It's "one-of-a-kind" enthuse aficionados of the "unforgettable" "cultural experience" at this "lively", midpriced NW Portland Moroccan vet offering "superb" traditional cuisine and "not-to-be-missed" belly dancing (Wednesday–Sunday); an affable staff and seating on ornate, "pillow"-piled banquettes complete the atmospheric "fun time"; P.S. with three days notice, larger parties can feast on spit-roasted lamb.

Masu *Japanese*   24 | 24 | 22 | $29

West End | 406 SW 13th Ave. (bet. Burnside & Washington Sts.) |
503-221-6278 | www.masusushi.com

This "airy" second-floor West End Japanese "gem" lures couples and others with "gorgeous sushi" and cooked dishes served by a capable crew in "trendy", "plush" environs; the à la carte items "can add up", but wallet-watchers tout its "excellent" happy-hour deals; P.S. it offers parking validation.

McMenamins Bagdad *Pub Food*   24 | 23 | 22 | $22

Hawthorne | 3702 SE Hawthorne Blvd. (37th Ave.) | 503-236-9234

McMenamins Barley Mill Pub *Pub Food*

Hawthorne | 1629 SE Hawthorne Blvd. (17th Ave.) | 503-231-1492

McMenamins Black Rabbit Restaurant *Pub Food*

Troutdale | Edgefield | 2126 SW Halsey St. (244th Ave.) | 503-669-8610

McMenamins Blue Moon ◑ *Pub Food*

Northwest Portland | 432 NW 21st Ave. (Glisan St.) | 503-223-3184

McMenamins Chapel Pub *Pub Food*

Humboldt | 430 N. Killingsworth St. (Commercial Ave.) | 503-286-0372

McMenamins Kennedy School
Courtyard Restaurant ◑ *Pub Food*

Concordia | McMenamins Kennedy School | 5736 NE 33rd Ave.
(bet. Jessup & Simpson Sts.) | 503-288-2192

McMenamins Ringlers Annex ◑ *Pub Food*

West End | 1223 SW Stark St. (Burnside St.) | 503-384-2700

McMenamins Ringlers Pub ◑ *Pub Food*

West End | 1332 W. Burnside St. (bet. 13th & 14th Aves.) | 503-225-0627

(continued)

(continued)

McMenamins St. Johns *Pub Food*
St. Johns | 8203 N. Ivanhoe St. (Richmond Ave.) | 503-283-8520
McMenamins Zeus Café *Pub Food*
West End | McMenamins Crystal Hotel | 303 SW 12th Ave.
(bet. Burnside & Stark Sts.) | 503-384-2500
www.mcmenamins.com
Additional locations throughout the Portland area

The "solid" if "basic" pub fare "goes down easy" with the "hearty",
housemade craft beer at these "reliable" links ranked as Portland's
Most Popular restaurant chain and owned by the McMenamin
brothers, who specialize in restoring notable buildings and deck-
ing them out with "eclectic" furnishings and colorful murals; opinions on service run the gamut ("swell" to "slow"), but many agree
that the environs are "mellow" and the inexpensive menu offers
"something for everyone."

Meat Cheese Bread ⊠ *Sandwiches*   26 | 17 | 21 | $13
Buckman | 1406 SE Stark St. (14th Ave.) | 503-234-1700 |
www.meatcheesebread.com

"Not just your same old sandwich shop", this Buckman storefront
piles "fantastic", "seasonal" ingredients on housemade bread (the
"name says it all") to formulate "rustic", "thoughtfully designed, delicious" creations; the "cute little" art-strewn space also houses the
Xocolatl de David chocolate lab, and plans are afoot to open an adjacent bar, fittingly dubbed Beer.

Mellow Mushroom *Pizza*   25 | 22 | 23 | $18
Pearl District | 1411 NW Flanders St. (14th Ave.) | 503-224-9019 |
www.mellowmushroom.com

For "delish" pizza and brews, there's this "funky" Pearl District link
of the Atlanta-based chain, which turns out creative pies and 'build-
your-own' salads in "colorful", psychedelic environs; staffers who
make "you feel at home" and reasonable prices are two more reasons locals keep coming to this "fun spot."

Meriwether's Restaurant *Pacific NW*   25 | 26 | 24 | $37
Northwest Portland | 2601 NW Vaughn St. (26th Ave.) | 503-228-1250 |
www.meriwethersnw.com

Renowned for its "breathtakingly beautiful garden" patio ("perfect
for brunch, lunch or summertime evenings") and "serene, romantic"
setting in a historic building on the 1905 World's Fair site, this
bastion charms a mature crowd with Pacific NW cuisine "bursting
with freshness and flavor", much of it made with produce from its
own NW Portland garden; "top-notch drinks" and "attentive, well-
informed" service further justify its tabs "on the pricey side."

Metrovino *American*   ∇ 20 | 20 | 19 | $47
Pearl District | 1139 NW 11th Ave. (Northrup St.) | 503-517-7778 |
www.metrovinopdx.com

The "unique approach to wine sampling" at this Pearl District New
American comes courtesy of a high-tech preservation system that

allows sippers to snag "tastes" of bottles they otherwise "would never pay for" and pair those quaffs with "unexpectedly decent" fare; a few balk at "big prices", but the sleek, "quite nice" dining room with wraparound windows adds value.

NEW Mextiza *Mexican*

∇ 25 | 21 | 22 | $22

Overlook | 2103 N. Killingsworth St. (Detroit Ave.) | 503-289-3709 | www.mextiza.com

The chef-owner of popular Autentica "does it again" with this affordable Overlook cantina that early-goers are calling one of Portland's "new Mexican stars"; servers "help you navigate" the "stellar" but sometimes unfamiliar fare, as well as the broad tequila selection arrayed behind the bar.

Mi Famiglia *Pizza/Italian*

23 | 19 | 18 | $17

Oregon City | 701 Main St. (7th St.) | 503-594-0601 | www.mi-famiglia.com

A "best-kept secret" in sleepy Oregon City, this "warm, inviting", family-owned pizzeria dishes up "homestyle" Italian fare in addition to its pies "crafted with care" (including gluten-free options) that emerge from the open kitchen's wood-fired oven; tabs are low and service "friendly", and the "locals"-oriented crowd makes it a "fun place to go after work."

Milo's City Cafe *American*

26 | 23 | 26 | $17

Irvington | 1325 NE Broadway (14th Ave.) | 503-288-6456 | www.miloscitycafe.com

There's "usually a long line" on weekend mornings at this "local" Irvington American known for its "freakin' fantastic" breakfasts and "unusual" specials, delivered by a "quick" staff that "treats you like family"; a "relaxed", "hometown feel" pervades its airy, bright space, and it's "well-priced" to boot.

NEW Mi Mero Mole Ⓜ *Mexican*

∇ 24 | 16 | 24 | $12

Division | 5026 SE Division St. (bet. 50th & 51st Aves.) | 503-232-8226 | www.mmmtacospdx.com

"Honest, humble" Mexican street fare, "no disguise needed" draws adventure-seekers to this economical Division eatery dishing up a rotating selection of housemade *guisados* (stews and stir-fries) on fresh tortillas to fill tacos, burritos, quesadillas and plates; "nice" staffers and tequila- and mezcal-based cocktails liven up the dark surroundings, as does the Aztec-inspired mural on the wall.

Mingo *Italian*

25 | 21 | 22 | $37

Beaverton | 12600 SW Crescent St. (Hall Blvd.) | 503-646-6464 | www.mingowest.com

"Good Italian food in Beaverton? – you bet!" promise partisans of this midpriced suburban "go-to" for "solid, soulful" trattoria "standouts" "prepared with care", like penne al sugo di carne (pasta with beef braised in chianti and espresso); in summer, the garage doors roll up to catch the breeze, plus ample patio seating means you can "sit outdoors and enjoy."

Mint *American*

`25` `23` `24` `$26`

Boise-Eliot | 816 N. Russell St. (Albina Ave.) | 503-284-5518 | www.mintand820.com

An "intelligently prepared", midpriced New American menu that capitalizes on "whatever's fresh and local" (the lamb burger is a "winner") at this Boise-Eliot bistro nearly takes a backseat to the "fantastic" adjoining bar, 820, with its long list of "delicious" specialty cocktails; the "modern, clean" interior pleases, as does the "nice" patio, and "solid service" is the crowning touch.

Mio Sushi *Japanese*

`25` `21` `23` `$20`

Hawthorne | 3962 SE Hawthorne Blvd. (40th Ave.) | 503-230-6981

Hollywood | 4204 NE Halsey St. (42nd Ave.) | 503-288-4778 🛃

Northwest Portland | 2271 NW Johnson St. (23rd Ave.) | 503-221-1469 🛃

Overlook | 2735 N. Killingsworth St. (Greeley Ave.) | 503-286-5123 🛃

Pearl District | 1317 NW Hoyt St. (bet. 13th & 14th Aves.) | 503-224-7905 🛃

Sellwood | 1710 SE Tacoma St. (17th Ave.) | 503-445-0411 🛃

Aloha | 1255 NW 185th Ave. (Walker Rd.) | 503-617-9432 🛃

Beaverton | 12600 SW Crescent St. (Hall Blvd.) | 503-469-0881 🛃

www.miosushi.com

"You know what you're getting" at this Japanese chain: a "nice variety" of "fresh" sushi rolls served "fast" by a "friendly" staff in "bright", "Formica-heaven" setups; "decent prices" get even more so at its happy hour that "rocks", but just be aware that its "family-friendly" rep can translate into a "dinnertime crush"; P.S. you can buy fish retail at the chain's NW 16th Avenue warehouse/market.

Mirakutei *Japanese*

▽ `23` `16` `24` `$29`

Lower Burnside | 536 E. Burnside St. (6th Ave.) | 503-467-7501

Chef Hiro Ikegaya, of the lauded, now-shuttered Hiroshi, turns out sushi that shows "quality" in both "preparation and presentation" at this Lower Burnside Japanese, but devotees also herald its "fine small dishes" and "exceptional" ramen; service is "attentive and friendly", and while the interior is small and unassuming, so are the "reasonable prices."

Miss Delta *Cajun/Southern*

▽ `25` `22` `23` `$16`

Mississippi | 3950 N. Mississippi Ave. (Shaver St.) | 503-287-7629 | www.missdeltapdx.net

For Cajun and "Southern food done right", Dixiephiles head for this petite Mississippi Avenue queen that's "the place" when you "crave hush puppies, fried catfish and jambalaya"; service is solid, and for deep discounts on already-cheap fare, there's the daily happy hour (twice daily on Friday and Saturday).

Mississippi Pizza Pub ● *Pizza*

`26` `21` `22` `$16`

Mississippi | 3552 N. Mississippi Ave. (bet. Beech & Fremont Sts.) | 503-288-3231 | www.mississippipizza.com

"Super-yummy", low-cost pies (including "awesome vegan and gluten-free" options) plus "eclectic live music" for both "little ones" and adults make this pizzeria a "unique" Mississippi option; the overall "pleasant" mood is boosted by solid service, and as added incentive, there are "strong" drinks coming out of its full bar–endowed lounge, and "you can't beat Quizissippi on Wednesday nights."

Monteaux's Public House 🖂 *Pub Food* | 20 | 19 | 19 | $20 |

Beaverton | 16165 SW Regatta Ln. (Schendel Ave.) | 503-439-9942 | www.monteauxs.com

Notable burgers and a "surprising beer selection" draw Beaverton locals to this "modern" pub that "never gets boring" thanks to its monthly specials that focus on specialties from various world regions; it gets "busy", but the "staff makes the effort to get to know you" all the same, and easygoing tabs sink even lower during happy hour.

Mother's Bistro & Bar Ⓜ *American* | 25 | 23 | 23 | $26 |

Downtown | 212 SW Stark St. (2nd Ave.) | 503-464-1122 | www.mothersbistro.com

Devotees say it's "just like mom's cooking, only better" at this "busy, buzzy", midpriced Downtown American that offers a "dose of comfort" via "robust", "slow-cooked" classics for lunch and dinner and a "killer" breakfast (reserve ahead "for the sake of your sanity"); the chandeliered decor nods to "country elegance", and an "accommodating" staff adds to the overall "homey" vibe at a place that's become "iconic Portland."

Murata 🖂 *Japanese* | ∇ 26 | 19 | 20 | $49 |

Downtown | 200 SW Market St. (2nd Ave.) | 503-227-0080

"Mr. Murata is a master" enthuse habitués of this "incredibly authentic" Downtown Japanese who come for "divine" sushi and "melt-in-your-mouth" sashimi at "expensive" prices; perspectives vary on the service ("thoughtful" vs. "brusque"), and many find the sake cup–size room's decor "lacking", but the overall pleasing effect is that of "stepping into a family-run *ryokan*"; P.S. be sure to make reservations and "ask for a tatami room."

Namaste *Indian* | 24 | 19 | 23 | $15 |

Northeast Portland | 8303 NE Sandy Blvd. (82nd Ave.) | 503-257-5059 | www.namasteindiancuisine.com

"All-you-can-eat" enthusiasts say *'namaste'* to this basic NE Portland Indian whose "large" lunch and dinner buffets satisfy with a variety of "well-seasoned" dishes that "accommodate everyone, even vegans"; "outstanding-value" rates and solid service, plus the ability to host celebrations of all sizes, add up to a "user-friendly" experience.

Natural Selection 🖂Ⓜ *Vegan/Vegetarian* | ∇ 29 | 27 | 29 | $41 |

Alberta | 3033 NE Alberta St. (31st Ave.) | 503-288-5883 | www.naturalselectionpdx.com

"Wonderfully complex flavors" arrive in each "amazing", "plant-based" course at this upscale, midpriced, European-influenced Alberta vegetarian, which caters to the vegan and gluten-free; an "incredibly friendly, helpful" staff works the sleek, dark wood-clad room notable for its rustic rolling bar cart and open kitchen; P.S. closed Sunday–Tuesday.

Navarre *Mediterranean*   ▽ 26 | 21 | 24 | $33

Kerns | 10 NE 28th Ave. (Burnside St.) | 503-232-3555

"Eccentric in a good way", this Kerns "delight" charms with a "dazzling array" of "inventive, seasonal" Mediterranean small plates with origins in Spain, Italy and France, made for pairing with pours from a "well-chosen" wine list that includes more than 50 by-the-glass options; the staff seems "happy to have you", and though the decor's on the "sparse" side and the prices "far from cheap", most agree it's "easy to love."

Ned Ludd *American*   26 | 24 | 24 | $33

King | 3925 NE Martin Luther King Jr. Blvd. (Failing St.) | 503-288-6900 | www.nedluddpdx.com

"Gorgeous wood-fired" dishes are the crux of this "rustic"-meets-"luxurious" King "go-to date-night spectacular" dedicated to "inventive", "strictly seasonal", midpriced New American cuisine, most of which is cooked in a handsome brick oven; that members of the "kind, wise" staff even "chop their own" firewood furthers its status as "unique."

Nel Centro *Italian*   24 | 22 | 23 | $32

Downtown | Hotel Modera | 1408 SW Sixth Ave. (Columbia St.) | 503-484-1099 | www.nelcentro.com

Located within the Hotel Modera, this "dramatic", "hip" Downtown Italian stages "innovative", "well-executed" fare, with the added bonus of a courtyard patio enhanced with a lush living wall and nighttime fire pits; service is solid, and the happy hour is touted as "one of Portland's great bargains."

Nicholas Restaurant *Lebanese*   27 | 19 | 24 | $19

Central Eastside | 318 SE Grand Ave. (Pine St.) | 503-235-5123
Hollywood | 3223 NE Broadway (33rd Ave.) | 503-445-4700
Gresham | 323 N. Main Ave. (3rd St.) | 503-666-3333
www.nicholasrestaurant.com

"Delicious" Lebanese dishes, including "huge" pitas "hot from the oven", draw droves to this affordable family-run trio, where "friendly" staffers preside over the "somewhat frenetic" scene; the Gresham outpost boasts "more space" than the "packed" Portland links, but patrons say they'll endure no-frills surrounds with "tight seating" in exchange for the "awesome aromas and flavors."

Nick's Italian Cafe Ⓜ *Italian*   26 | 21 | 23 | $36

McMinnville | 521 NE Third St. (Evans St.) | 503-434-4471 | www.nicksitaliancafe.com

"Nick's gone but the food's still good" at this "authentic" McMinnville Italian, a "destination in wine country" for its "OMG minestrone" and fresh pasta dishes in a homey, casual setting; it's still family-run and service is "wonderful", but be prepared for price tags that skew "expensive."

	FOOD	DECOR	SERVICE	COST

Noble Rot *American*
24 | 25 | 23 | $30

Lower Burnside | Burnside Rocket | 1111 E. Burnside St. (11th Ave.) | 503-233-1999 | www.noblerotpdx.com

"What more could you ask for?" muse boosters of this "hip", "noisy" Lower Burnside wine bar boasting "stunning" city panoramas from a fourth-floor perch with patio and "simple" New American small plates that are "big on satisfying taste buds"; the staff is "ridiculously well informed" about the vintages, and the "semi-spendy" tabs come with the territory; P.S. ask about the 5 PM Tuesday tours of the rooftop garden.

Noho's Hawaiian Cafe *Hawaiian*
28 | 22 | 25 | $18

Beaumont | 4627 NE Fremont St. (47th Ave.) | 503-445-6646
Clinton | 2525 SE Clinton St. (26th Ave.) | 503-233-5301
www.nohos.com

It's "like a mini-vacation to the islands" at this "authentic" Hawaiian duo, where the "brilliant" barbecue "always hits the spot" ("Kalua pig makes for a mighty fine Friday night"), as do the "not-too-expensive" prices; while "helpful" servers and surfer-abilia can be expected at both, Beaumont features a "great patio", while alcohol-free Clinton can feel a bit "crowded" – though "the food really makes up for it."

NEW Noisette 🅂🅜 *French*
▽ 29 | 24 | 26 | $69

Northwest Portland | 1937 NW 23rd Pl. (Vaughn St.) | 503-719-4599 | www.noisetterestaurant.com

"*This* is what a real French restaurant should be" coo connoisseurs of "accomplished" chef Tony Demes' NW Portland "don't-miss", whose "exceptional", expensive tasting menu, "well-sourced, creatively prepared" à la carte dishes and wine list that "does them justice" remind some of his erstwhile 1990s eatery, Couvron; it's all set in a "petite" space overseen by an "exceptional" staff, further reasons it's a "treat" for a "special occasion, or just a serious foodie" experience.

Nong's Khao Man Gai 🅂 *Thai*
26 | 14 | 25 | $11

NEW Lower Burnside | 609 SE Ankeny St. (6th Ave.) | 503-740-2907
NEW PSU | 411 SW College St. (4th Ave.) | 503-432-3286
West End | SW Alder St. & 10th Ave. | 971-255-3480
www.khaomangai.com

There's only "one dish, perfectly done" at Nong Poonsukwattana's wildly popular West End cart ("when she sells out, she is out") and its Lower Burnside spin-off: that "amazing" namesake Thai chicken-and-rice dish, which "never disappoints"; prices are low, service is "great" and, for a little variety, the PSU location has an expanded menu that packs similar "simple-but-complex" flavors.

North 45 Pub ❶ *Pub Food*
25 | 23 | 21 | $23

Northwest Portland | 517 NW 21st Ave. (bet. Glisan & Hoyt Sts.) | 503-248-6317 | www.north45pub.com

"Yummy" mussels are a highlight at this affordable travel-themed NW Portland pub boasting appealing "daily specials" and a notable selection of local and Belgian brews, best imbibed on the "nice" back patio–cum–beer garden; service is solid, but the nonsporting suggest "avoid on nights when there's a Timbers game."

Nostrana *Italian*
28 | 24 | 23 | $37

Buckman | 1401 SE Morrison St. (14th Ave.) | 503-234-2427 | www.nostrana.com

"Wonderful" thin-crust pizza "baked to blistered perfection" in a wood-fired oven attracts acolytes to Cathy Whims' "unpretentious" (some say "pricey") Buckman Italian that also wins converts for "authentic" dishes constructed from "high-quality ingredients handled simply"; though the oft-"crowded" digs can get "noisy at times", the "welcoming, knowledgeable" staff lends the "soaring", "lodge"-like space a "convivial" vibe.

Nuestra Cocina 🗷 Ⓜ *Mexican*
26 | 23 | 24 | $31

Division | 2135 SE Division St. (22nd Ave.) | 503-232-2135 | www.nuestra-cocina.com

"If you're looking for the typical greasy taco or enchilada, keep moving" advise aficionados of this Division crowd-pleaser whose "innovative", "upscale Mexican with NW flair" includes housemade tortillas and "ever-changing moles"; the open kitchen and bar "add to the general feeling of vibrancy", as does the "stellar" service, while "perfect margaritas" make the "long waits" for "worth-the-price" fare "less painful."

Nuvrei *Bakery/French*
▽ 28 | 18 | 17 | $13

Pearl District | 404 NW 10th Ave. (Flanders St.) | 503-546-3032 | www.nuvrei.com

"How can a French-patisserie addict not go here?" muse croissant fiends of this "incredible" Pearl District bakery, a longtime wholesale outfit that expanded into a full-fledged, albeit "tiny", cafe offering low-cost breakfast and lunch; never mind that it's "tough to find a seat" here, the coffee is "good" and the sandwich bread alone is "worth the visit."

¡Oba! *Nuevo Latino*
26 | 26 | 25 | $34

Pearl District | 555 NW 12th Ave. (Hoyt St.) | 503-228-6161 | www.obarestaurant.com

A "vacation for your taste buds" is provided by the "inventive, perfectly executed" Nuevo Latino plates on offer at this "lively" midpriced Pearl District resto-lounge; while "professional" service draws "romantic" types and other serious diners to the expansive "cheerful and colorful" dining room, "dangerous margaritas" fuel a "high-energy" bar scene that's "young", "hip" and "happy."

The Observatory ◑ *American*
26 | 25 | 25 | $21

Montavilla | 8115 SE Stark St. (81st Ave.) | 503-445-6284 | www.theobservatorypdx.com

"Go early to avoid crowds" and enjoy the "fantastic happy hour" at this "all-around-wonderful" Montavilla American slinging "excellent" eats like the "to-die-for" chicken-fried chicken; "delicious" cocktails poured at the large back bar plus a dark, handsome look make it a "date destination", though "families enjoy" it too.

	FOOD	DECOR	SERVICE	COST

Ocean City ● *Chinese/Seafood* — ▽ 27 | 20 | 23 | $22

82nd Avenue | 3016 SE 82nd Ave. (Brooklyn St.) | 503-771-2299 |
www.oceancityportland.com

For "fresh", "fantastic", "worth-the-drive" dim sum, this upscale
Chinese seafood specialist on SE 82nd Avenue comes "highly recommended", even if "language barriers" can make "grabbing a random item from the cart" the "most fun kind of Russian roulette"; it
strikes a few as a "bit pricey", but it also draws comparisons to the
"best" of its kind "in San Francisco."

Ohana Hawaiian Cafe *Hawaiian* — 26 | 23 | 25 | $20

Northeast Portland | 6320 NE Sandy Blvd. (bet. 63rd & 64th Aves.) |
503-335-5800
Milwaukie | 10608 SE Main St. (Scott St.) | 503-305-8170
www.ohanahawaiiancafe.com

Pop "back to Hawaii" via the "authentic", "just-plain-delicious" island
favorites – "excellent" pork, "exceptional" desserts like shave ice and
haupia – at these inexpensive NE Portland and Milwaukie oases; service manages to be "friendly and attentive without hovering" and the
"brightly decorated", casual interiors further the escapist fantasies.

Old Spaghetti Factory *Italian* — 23 | 25 | 23 | $22

Johns Landing | 715 SW Bancroft St. (Bond Ave.) | 503-222-5375
Hillsboro | 18925 NW Tanasbourne Dr. (bet. 188th Ave. & Stucki Pl.) |
503-617-7614
Clackamas | 12725 SE 93rd Ave. (bet. SE Sunnybrook &
SE Sunnyside Rds.) | 503-653-7949
www.osf.com

"Unique" dining room touches like a centerpiece "trolley replica"
play second fiddle to the "gorgeous" waterfront location at this "dependable" Johns Landing Italian (with outposts in Hillsboro and
Clackamas) that spawned the international chain; thanks to the
"budget" price, pastas "to suit kids' tastes" and a staff that's always
"on top of it", it remains a "family favorite."

Old Town Pizza *Pizza* — 25 | 22 | 22 | $20

King | 5201 NE Martin Luther King Jr. Blvd. (Sumner St.) | 503-200-5988
Old Town-Chinatown | 226 NW Davis St. (3rd Ave.) | 503-222-9999
www.oldtownpizza.com

A "worthwhile experience for the native and tourist", this "rustic",
allegedly haunted Old Town "institution" delivers "lots of history
with your pizza", which fans call "delicious" and definitely "worth
braving the ghosts" for; cynics find the "unique" atmosphere a "bit
cheesy", but none quibble with the "reasonable" prices and "friendly"
service; P.S. the lodgelike King offshoot boasts an in-house brewery,
Old Town Brewing Company.

Old Wives' Tales *Eclectic* — 23 | 18 | 20 | $18

Buckman | 1300 E. Burnside St. (13th Ave.) | 503-238-0470 |
www.oldwivestalesrestaurant.com

"Always a good bet" for "from-scratch" vittles, this longtime Buckman
cafe can be counted on for "sizable portions" of well-priced Eclectic

vegetarian, chicken and seafood dishes, presenting a "worry-free" option for vegans and the gluten-free; some find the digs a bit "too rustic" and service just "ok", but the children's play area is an indisputable "big plus" for families.

Olympic Provisions *Pacific NW*
27 | 22 | 24 | $27

Eastside Industrial | 107 SE Washington St. (2nd Ave.) | 503-954-3663
Northwest Portland | 1632 NW Thurman St. (17th Ave.) | 503-894-8136
www.olympicprovisions.com

Fans of these "cool" but "cozy" European-style salumerias in NW Portland and Eastside Industrial like that they have a "big-city deli and butcher-shop feel" and are perfect for "cultured and on-a-budget" diners; the star of the show here is the housemade charcuterie "raised to absurdly delicious levels" and assembled on "well-crafted, simple" Pacific NW–influenced plates that "change often"; P.S. counters at both locations mean you can nab "superb" sausages and "life-altering" frankfurters to go.

The Original Dinerant *Diner*
▽ 27 | 26 | 24 | $19

Downtown | 300 SW Sixth Ave. (Oak St.) | 503-546-2666 | www.originaldinerant.com

A "menu to suit any palate" lures a Downtown crowd to this nouveau diner slinging affordable classics inspired by "seasonal", "local ingredients" plus a few oddities that'll "make you smile" (e.g. Fruit Loops pancakes); the "super-cool, modern" bi-level space is outfitted with booths, counter seating and a bar dispensing housemade sodas plus cocktails, beer and wine; P.S. open till 4 AM Friday and Saturday.

The Original Halibut's *Seafood*
24 | 17 | 23 | $21

Alberta | 2525 NE Alberta St. (26th Ave.) | 503-808-9601 | www.theoriginalhalibuts.com

The "crazy good" baskets of "moist, delicious" fish 'n' chips run from the expected halibut to catfish, cod and salmon and comprise most of the reasonably priced menu at this "retro-feeling" Alberta seafooder; the chef-owner "makes it fun" and "adding to the excitement" are live blues musicians most Thursday through Saturday nights at the adjacent bar, which also serves as overflow seating for this shoebox-sized eatery.

Original Hotcake House ❶ *Diner*
25 | 16 | 20 | $13

Brooklyn | 1002 SE Powell Blvd. (10th Ave.) | 503-236-7402

"When you absolutely have to have pancakes at 3 AM", this "old-school" 24/7 SE Powell diner is *the* place for "huge portions" of "carb-overload" breakfasts at "small prices"; the "long line" to order at the counter "moves fast", and though its "greasy-spoon" looks are "nothing special", it's "so busy you never really see the decor" anyway.

The Original Pancake House Ⓜ⇼ *American*
26 | 20 | 24 | $19

Multnomah Village | 8601 SW 24th Ave. (Barbur Blvd.) | 503-246-9007 | www.originalpancakehouse.com

For a "true Portland classic", there's this "nostalgic" SW "favorite" (the actual 'original' in the national franchise), which still flips a "wonderful variety of pancakes" as it has since 1953; a few say "you pay for it both in price and by waiting to get a table", but addicts point to the "unmatched" Dutch baby pastry as proof that it's "just what a breakfast place should be", with "aproned" waitresses to match; P.S. this location is cash or check only and closed Monday and Tuesday.

Oswego Grill American
26 | 25 | 25 | $30

Lake Oswego | 7 Centerpointe Dr. (Kruse Oaks Blvd.) | 503-352-4750
Wilsonville | 30080 SW Boones Ferry Rd. (Wilsonville Rd.) | 503-427-2152
www.oswegogrill.com

Both this perennially "packed" Lake Oswego American and its Wilsonville sib put a "fresh" take on "traditional steakhouse favorites", dished up with "amazing personal service"; the "romantic, enticing" vibe has frequenters recommending it for "special occasions", and though a few find it "a little pricey", tabs go "low, low, low" during the "amazing" bar-only happy hours.

Otto Ⓜ American
▽ 25 | 16 | 26 | $20

Hawthorne | 1852 SE Hawthorne Blvd. (19th Ave.) | 503-517-7770 | www.ottopdx.com

Bordering busy Hawthorne Boulevard, this relaxed bistro whips up an ever-changing roster of New American dishes and cocktails considered "fantastic for the price point" and based on "seasonal, local goods"; the simple, stripped-down space is overseen by an "accommodating" crew.

Otto's Sausage Kitchen & Meat Market Deli/German
27 | 16 | 23 | $12

Woodstock | 4138 SE Woodstock Blvd. (bet. Martins St. & Woodstock Blvd.) | 503-771-6714 | www.ottossausage.com

The low-priced housemade sausages "rock" and the hot dogs are some of the "best in the city" at this "superb" German deli in Woodstock that's become a "Portland tradition and treasure"; manned by a "fantastic" staff, it offers an "amazing meat counter" inside serving market fare and sandwiches and a "not-to-be-missed" outdoor grill whose sizzling specialties can be eaten on sidewalk picnic tables.

NEW Oven & Shaker ◐ Pizza
23 | 24 | 22 | $25

Pearl District | 1134 NW Everett St. (bet. 11th & 12th Aves.) | 503-241-1600 | www.ovenandshaker.com

Champions of this "lively", "casual" Pearl District pizzeria from Cathy Whims celebrate its "innovative" wood-fired pies offered at a "great price" and praise its "insanely delicious cocktails" – a mix that's enjoyed amid "a lot of flair and pomp"; pie-sanos proclaim "if you can get past the blaring music" and the wait, "it's worth it."

Overlook Restaurant Diner
24 | 21 | 25 | $19

Overlook | 1332 N. Skidmore St. (Interstate Ave.) | 503-288-0880

This Greek-American diner in Overlook earns regulars' affections by "delivering exactly what's promised": "plentiful" staples at low cost; sure, the "retro decor is "dated", but "it makes no pretense to be something it isn't", and the "friendly" staff boosts the "homey feeling."

NEW Ox M *Argentinean*
— | — | — | E

Boise-Eliot | 2225 NE Martin Luther King Jr. Blvd. (bet. Russell & Thompson Sts.) | 503-284-3366 | www.oxpdx.com

The custom-made, wood-fired grill stars at this pricey Boise-Eliot Argentinean that's pulling in crowds for its sizzling mash-up of South American and Pacific NW cuisines; like its namesake, the interior is sturdy and serviceable with an exposed-brick wall and simple, dark-hued tables that lend an everyday vibe; P.S. cool your heels at the slender adjacent bar during the inevitable wait.

NEW PaaDee *Thai*
— | — | — | M

Kerns | 6 SE 28th Ave. (Burnside St.) | 503-360-1453 | www.paadeepdx.com

This airy Thai eatery mixes materials (wicker birdcage lights, concrete floors) to au courant modern-industrial effect along busy 28th Avenue's Restaurant Row in Kerns; it dishes up authentic, midpriced fare that goes beyond corner takeout and has cocktails to match.

Pacific Pie Company *Australian*
27 | 22 | 27 | $17

Central Eastside | 1520 SE Seventh Ave. (bet. Clay St. & Hawthorne Blvd.) | 503-381-6157 | www.pacificpieco.com

"Heavenly" Australian savory meat pies with "buttery, flaky crusts" are the specialty of this "modern"-looking Central Eastsider, which also bakes up sweet versions (Key lime, apple), all presided over by a "friendly, helpful" staff; the Down Under theme continues with a few native wines and beers, and the "value" deepens during happy hour.

Pad Thai Kitchen *Thai*
26 | 20 | 23 | $20

Belmont | 2309 SE Belmont St. (23rd Ave.) | 503-232-8766

It's "your standard Thai place" in Belmont, but with "fresh" offerings including drunken noodles that beckon "like right now" – as does the outdoor seating; the "friendly, timely" service and reasonable rates have area curry-hounds adding it to their "go-to" lists.

The Painted Lady M *Pacific NW*
29 | 28 | 29 | $85

Newberg | 201 S. College St. (2nd St.) | 503-538-3850 | www.thepaintedladyrestaurant.com

"You're in for a remarkable" evening (and the Portland area's top-rated Food, Decor and Service) the "minute you step inside the picket fence" at this wine-country "jewel" set in a "romantic" Newberg Victorian, where the "world-class" Pacific NW tasting menus are "fascinating in their variety, seasonality and freshness"; "well-orchestrated" service and "fabulous" local vinos add to the "stellar" experience; P.S. rezzies required and closed Monday and Tuesday.

Paley's Place Bistro & Bar *Pacific NW*
27 | 24 | 26 | $58

Northwest Portland | 1204 NW 21st Ave. (Northrup St.) | 503-243-2403 | www.paleysplace.net

With the "intimate" confines of a "charming" Victorian dwelling serving as his backdrop, "master chef" Vitaly Paley prepares "sophisticated", "always-surprising" Pacific NW fare replete with European flourishes and made from the "freshest" local ingredients in NW Portland; happily, he's backed by a "professional" staff and a "consummate hostess" "running the front of the house with ease" – his wife, Kimberly; P.S. reservations are "essential", especially for seats on the "gracious veranda."

Pambiche *Cuban* | 26 | 22 | 23 | $21 |

Kerns | 2811 NE Glisan St. (28th Ave.) | 503-233-0511 | www.pambiche.com

A "little piece of Havana", this "vibrant", "well-priced" destination at the end of Kerns' Restaurant Row vends "some of the best Cuban north of Miami", including "all the traditional favorites", plus desserts "worth skipping dinner for", all set down by "friendly" servers; "claustrophobic introverts should beware", as patrons "literally rub elbows" in the "tiny", "packed-to-the-gills" dining room, but some relief's to be had if you "snag an outdoor table."

Papa G's Vegan Organic Deli *Deli/Vegan* | ∇ 26 | 17 | 24 | $13 |

Division | 2314 SE Division St. (23rd Ave.) | 503-235-0244 | www.papagees.com

"Excellent" all-organic vegan options, including raw and gluten-free fare, have enthusiasts praising the "good folks doing right" at this Division BYO counter serve; service earns high marks in the casual, wood-heavy space, and though it's generally inexpensive, some warn it can get "a little pricey" – but "only because you'll probably end up wanting a little bit of everything."

Papa Haydn *American/Dessert* | 26 | 23 | 24 | $27 |

Northwest Portland | 701 NW 23rd Ave. (Irving St.) | 503-228-7317
Sellwood | 5829 SE Milwaukie Ave. (bet. Knight & Ramona Sts.) | 503-232-9440
www.papahaydn.com

"You won't leave without satisfying your sweet tooth" say fans of this "classic" Portland duo that boasts an "extensive selection" of "decadent", "high-quality" treats considered a "feast for your eyes as well as your mouth", plus "delicious" American grub too; service is "attentive" and "low lighting" lends a "romantic" vibe, so even if a few find the more savory eats a bit "pricey" "for what you get", many remind "it's all about the desserts" anyway, insisting they're "well worth it."

Paradox Cafe *Vegetarian* | 24 | 19 | 23 | $12 |

Belmont | 3439 SE Belmont St. (35th Ave.) | 503-232-7508 | www.paradoxorganiccafe.com

Fans call this daytime Belmont cafe the "vegetarian granddaddy of the Portland scene" for its "tasty" "classics", including many vegan offerings (plus a few meat-centric dishes too); decor is basic, but service is "usually swift", and it all comes at a "great price."

Paragon *American* | 25 | 24 | 25 | $25 |

Pearl District | 1309 NW Hoyt St. (13th Ave.) | 503-833-5060 | www.paragonrestaurant.com

Get transported to "locavore heaven", courtesy of the "tasty" "locally sourced" eats at this midpriced Pearl District American; other pluses include "professional" servers and "great outdoor seating."

NEW The Parish *Cajun/Creole*

| - | - | - | M |

Pearl District | 231 NW 11th Ave. (Everett St.) | 503-227-2421 |
www.theparishpdx.com

Upscale Cajun-Creole standards (think frogs' legs, gumbo, jamba-laya) at modest tabs are on the menu at this Pearl District new-comer from the crew behind Boise-Eliot's EaT: An Oyster Bar; evocative touches like an antique Southern church pulpit add to the Big Easy ambiance, and there's a wraparound oak bar where congre-gants can watch bivalve shuckers in action.

Park Kitchen *Pacific NW*

| 26 | 20 | 26 | $42 |

Pearl District | 422 NW Eighth Ave. (bet. Flanders & Glisan Sts.) |
503-223-7275 | www.parkkitchen.com

"When you feel like coloring outside the lines" there's this moderate Pearl District New American, whose devotees tout the "well-executed", "seasonally driven" fare highlighting "true NW original-ity" and the "short but impressive wine list"; "kind", "unfussy service" enhances "small", "cozy" digs that come with views of the "lively open kitchen", or you can "take advantage of their outdoor seating" and "watch locals play bocce across the street."

Pastini Pastaria *Italian*

| 25 | 21 | 23 | $20 |

Division | 2027 SE Division St. (20th Ave.) | 503-595-6400
Downtown | 911 SW Taylor St. (9th Ave.) | 503-863-5188
Irvington | 1426 NE Broadway (15th Ave.) | 503-288-4300
Northwest Portland | 1506 NW 23rd Ave. (Quimby St.) | 503-595-1205
Beaverton | Cedar Hills Crossing | 3427 SW Cedar Hills Blvd.
(Hall Blvd.) | 503-619-2241
Tigard | Bridgeport Vill. | 7307 SW Bridgeport Rd. (72nd Ave.) |
503-718-2300
www.pastini.com

"Consistently great", "pasta-centric Italian" fare gets respect at these "casual", "relaxing" trattorias that are "not too spendy" and are tended by a "caring, friendly" crew; a "kinda chic vibe" works for business lunches as well as families, but be warned it can get "crowded" so you "may have to wait."

NEW Paulée *Pacific NW*

| - | - | - | E |

Dundee | Inn at Red Hills | 1410 N. Hwy. 99 W. (Alder St.) |
503-538-7970 | www.pauleerestaurant.com

This expensive wine country destination at Dundee's Inn at Red Hills turns out a daily changing Pacific NW menu that highlights local ingre-dients (some from local farms, some grown on-site) and pairs it with an extensive vino selection, including many by the glass; a showpiece cellar separates the wood-and-stone-enhanced dining room from the casual bar, which has a rustic patio with a fireplace (drinks only).

Pazzo Ristorante *Italian*

| 23 | 22 | 22 | $38 |

Downtown | Hotel Vintage Plaza | 627 SW Washington St. (B'way) |
503-228-1515 | www.pazzo.com

Set in Downtown's Hotel Vintage Plaza, this "reliable" Italian serves "elegantly prepared" plates to a crowd that's "mainly couples on dates and business travelers"; it can be a touch "pricey" for the genre, but the atmosphere is "welcoming" and service "accommodating"; P.S. there's also a "beautiful" bar and an attached bakery/cafe so fragrant it "could charge for sniffs."

PBJ's Grilled Ⓜ⇗ *Sandwiches* | 28 | 23 | 27 | $12 |

Northwest Portland | 919 NW 23rd St. (Lovejoy St.) | 702-743-0435 | www.pbjsgrilled.com

It's not the normal "PB&J in your lunch box" at this tiny cash-only NW Portland food cart known for "interesting combinations", resulting in both "savory and sweet" sandwiches that are "awesome, 'nuff said"; add in solid service and cheap prices and you'll "leave longing for your next visit"; P.S. closed Monday and Tuesday.

Pearl Bakery *Bakery* | 26 | 19 | 22 | $11 |

Pearl District | 102 NW Ninth Ave. (Couch St.) | 503-827-0910 | www.pearlbakery.com

"Just try to walk by this place and not be drawn in by the smell" challenge fans of this "can't-miss" Pearl District bakery that satisfies with "excellent breads" "right out of the oven", "good sandwiches" and "unbelievable" baked goods at reasonable prices; it's counter-serve only, but service is generally "friendly", and it's an overall "nice place to grab a bite."

The Peoples' Sandwich ▽ | 27 | 24 | 26 | $12 |
of Portland *Sandwiches*

Old Town-Chinatown | 53 NW First Ave. (Couch Ave.) | 503-222-0525 | www.sandwichofportland.com

"Delicious" sandwiches crafted with NW-sourced proteins pull partisans to this Communist-themed shop in Old Town, where the homemade "DicTater chips never fail to please" and vegans have "super-good" options too; the staff is "always great", and affordable prices further convince people to "come back."

Perry's on Fremont ⓈⓂ *American* ▽ | 23 | 23 | 24 | $26 |

Alameda | 2401 NE Fremont St. (24th Ave.) | 503-287-3655 | www.perrysonfremont.com

Regulars consider this Alameda American the "perry perry best" thanks to a "consistently good", "something-for-everyone" menu and the "always-there" owners who "welcome you like you are part of their family"; the casual space is augmented by a patio, and a kids' menu adds family-friendly appeal.

Pho Hung *Vietnamese* | 26 | 20 | 24 | $14 |

Foster-Powell | 4717 SE Powell Blvd. (47th Ave.) | 503-775-3170

Beaverton | 13227 SW Canyon Rd. (bet. Hocken & Lloyd Aves.) | 503-626-2888

www.pho-hung.com

"Generous" portions of "off-the-hook" pho and other "delicious" Vietnamese specialties are the draw at this Foster-Powell stop (with a Beaverton sib); the simple, minimalist space is enhanced by a staff that "treats you like family" and it all comes at "good prices."

Pho Oregon *Vietnamese*
26 | 21 | 22 | $16

82nd Avenue | 2518 NE 82nd Ave. (Brazee St.) | 503-262-8816
"Delicious pho" "always satisfies" at this cavernous NE 82nd Avenue Vietnamese; "service is friendly and fast" in the simple, no-frills space, and "good prices" extend the appeal.

Pho Van *Vietnamese*
26 | 22 | 22 | $17

82nd Avenue | 1919 SE 82nd Ave. (bet. Division & Stark Sts.) | 503-788-5244
Hawthorne | 3404 SE Hawthorne Blvd. (34th Ave.) | 503-230-1474 Ⓜ
Beaverton | Beaverton Town Sq. | 11651 SW Beaverton-Hillsdale Hwy. (bet. Hwy. 217 & Lombard Ave.) | 503-627-0822
www.phovanrestaurant.com
You'll feel like "you've had a night out in Saigon" at this Vietnamese trio, where "well-prepared" "traditional" dishes, like "soul-warming pho", are punctuated by "intense flavors"; service is "prompt", and the overall "upmarket" environs "relaxing."

Piazza Italia *Italian*
26 | 22 | 25 | $26

Pearl District | 1129 NW Johnson St. (bet. 11th & 12th Aves.) | 503-478-0619
"Are we in Italy?" quip fans at this midpriced Pearl District Italian, where "authentic" and "delicious" classics are presented "in broken Itanglish" by a staff that may "hug and kiss you" or even "dance with you if the mood strikes"; it's "small, noisy and crowded", and the "soccer-themed decoration" extends to the matches on TV, but it all complements the "old-world" vibe – just "make reservations."

Pied Cow Coffeehouse ❶ *Coffeehouse/Dessert*
27 | 26 | 20 | $14

Belmont | 3244 SE Belmont St. (33rd Ave.) | 503-230-4866
"Beautiful" meets "bohemian" at this Belmont coffeehouse set in a grand Victorian, where regulars "fall in love" with the "exquisite desserts" and other "sweet and savory nosh plates"; the "romantic" patio doubles as a "hookah garden", and while it can "get crowded", it's still a "date"-worthy choice, especially on "summer nights."

Pine State Biscuits *Southern*
27 | 18 | 22 | $13

Alberta | 2204 NE Alberta St. (22nd Ave.) | 503-477-6605
Belmont | 3640 SE Belmont St. (37th Ave.) | 503-236-3346
www.pinestatebiscuits.com
"One-of-a-kind" cheer fans of this "reasonably priced" Belmont and Alberta duo known for "seriously good" biscuits, "simple, slathered or sandwiched" "with a tower of toppings" ("nothing cures what ails you like a Reggie Deluxe"), plus other "delicious" Southern offerings; the staff is "nice considering how slammed" they get, but veterans suggest you "go early" or be "willing to fight" the crowds; P.S. both close at 2 PM daily, but Alberta reopens from 6 PM–1 AM Friday and Saturday.

Ping 🅱Ⓜ *SE Asian*
24 | 24 | 24 | $25

Old Town-Chinatown | 102 NW Fourth Ave. (Couch St.) | 503-229-7464 | www.pingpdx.com
"Vibrant, varied and often unexpected flavors" come in a "parade of small plates" at this Chinatown izakaya where the variety is like a

	FOOD	DECOR	SERVICE	COST

"best-of collection" of Asian "street food"; both the casual, wood-accented space and service earn solid marks and prices are affordable.

Pix Pâtisserie ⬤ Dessert

| 28 | 21 | 23 | $14 |

Kerns | 2225 E. Burnside St. (bet. 22nd & 24th Aves.) | 971-271-7166 | www.pixpatisserie.com

After a post-Survey relocation (not reflected in the Decor score), this Kerns patisserie offers the same "amazing desserts" paired with an "interesting array" of drinks in new digs shared with Spanish pintxos spot Bar Vivant; a curved bar separates the two sides, and "helpful" staffers remain "focused on delivering a great experience."

Pizzicato Pizza

| 24 | 20 | 22 | $16 |

Beaumont | 4217 NE Fremont St. (bet. 42nd & 43rd Aves.) | 503-493-2808
Kerns | 2811 E. Burnside St. (28th Ave.) | 503-236-6045
Division | 2045 SE Division St. (20th Ave.) | 503-764-9786
Downtown | 705 SW Alder St. (B'way) | 503-226-1007 🅢
Hillsdale | 6358 SW Capitol Hwy. (bet. Bertha Ct. & Burlingame Ave.) | 503-452-7166
Mt. Tabor | 6042 SE Division St. (bet. 60th & 61st Aves.) | 503-546-1686
Northwest Portland | 505 NW 23rd Ave. (Glisan St.) | 503-242-0023
PSU | 1708 SW Sixth Ave. (Mill St.) | 503-227-5800
Sellwood | 1630 SE Bybee Blvd. (Milwaukie Ave.) | 503-736-0174
Beaverton | 10719 SW Beaverton-Hillsdale Hwy. (107th Ave.) | 503-574-3115
www.pizzicatopizza.com
Additional locations throughout the Portland area

"Consistently good" "gourmet" pizzas featuring "some interesting toppings" are served alongside salads and sandwiches at this home-grown Portland-area pie chain; service is "personable", and though what's "cheap" to some is considered "expensive" by others, most agree it works for a no-fuss "family night."

Podnah's Pit Barbecue BBQ

| 27 | 20 | 23 | $21 |

Northeast Portland | 1625 NE Killingsworth St. (bet. 16th & 17th Aves.) | 503-281-3700 | www.podnahspit.com

"Real BBQ lovers" should "prepare for an orgy" of "true Texas-style" 'cue that's "as good as it smells" (including an "incredible" brunch) at this "simple" NE Portland joint; "friendly" service can occasionally be "slow", but you'll "get a lot for your money", which helps keep it "popular" – so go early as it tends to "run out of the good stuff early."

Pok Pok Thai

| 27 | 20 | 23 | $24 |

Division | 3226 SE Division St. (32nd Ave.) | 503-232-1387 | www.pokpokpdx.com
Pok Pok Noi ⬤⊟ Thai
Sabin | 1469 NE Prescott St. (bet. 14th Pl. & 15th Ave.) | 503-287-4149 | www.pokpoknoi.com

A "culinary mecca" say fans of this "gutsy" Division Thai and its "more casual, less crowded" Sabin offshoot where chef-owner Andy Ricker turns out "lip-smacking", "mind-blowing street food", like "unbelievably good chicken wings", plus "creative beverages" featuring "brilliant" drinking vinegars; sure, they're a "little pricey" for the genre, and the "cramped" Division digs are "mad busy", but the "hipster staff" is "prompt" and many agree they're area "musts"; P.S. sib Whiskey Soda Lounge (across the street from Pok Pok) offers drinks and nibbles.

¿Por Que No? *Mexican* | 26 | 23 | 22 | $13 |

Hawthorne | 4635 SE Hawthorne Blvd. (bet. 46th & 47th Aves.) | 503-954-3138
Mississippi | 3524 N. Mississippi Ave. (bet. Beech & Fremont Sts.) | 503-467-4149
www.porquenotacos.com

"Don't let the line scare you" because the "tough-to-beat" tacos and other "authentic", "well-executed" Mexican cooking is "worth the wait" say fans of these affordable Mississippi and Hawthorne "institutions"; it's a "tight squeeze", especially at the Mississippi branch, and you "order before you sit", whether in the "whimsical" dining rooms or on the patios, both of which are ideal destinations for some "dangerously delicious" margaritas.

Portland City Grill ◐ *American* | 26 | 27 | 25 | $42 |

Downtown | U.S. Bancorp Tower | 111 SW Fifth Ave., 30th fl. (Burnside St.) | 503-450-0030 | www.portlandcitygrill.com
"Breathtaking" "skyline" views lure "high-rise romantics", "tourists" and more to this "upscale" New American with Asian notes on the 30th floor of Downtown's U.S. Bancorp Tower where the "wide range" of offerings, including many surf 'n' turf options, are "all done well" and set down by a "knowledgeable", "polite" staff; it's not cheap, so bean-counters suggest the "best time to come" is during the "popular" "value"-filled happy hour, when people-watching is "tops."

NEW Portland Penny Diner Ⓢ *Diner* | - | - | - | I |

Downtown | Hotel Lucia | 410 SW Broadway (Stark St.) | 503-228-7222 | www.portlandpennydiner.com
Chef Vitaly Paley's diner in the hip Hotel Lucia serves up affordable all-day chow with local flair plus creative cocktails and milkshakes; outside, there's a giant spinning penny, which references the 1845 coin toss that gave the city its name; P.S. closes at 7 PM on week-nights, but on Fridays and Saturdays it's open late.

Portobello Vegan Trattoria Ⓜ *Italian/Vegan* | 26 | 25 | 23 | $26 |

Central Eastside | 1125 SE Division St. (12th Ave.) | 503-754-5993 | www.portobellopdx.com
You "don't feel deprived eating vegan" swear fans of this Central Eastside Italian known for a "creative" meat-free menu, including some "amazing" dishes; service is "warm", as is the cozy wood-lined dining room, and prices are affordable.

Po'Shines Cafe de la Soul ⒮Ⓜ *Soul Food* ▽ | 27 | 21 | 26 | $15 |

Kenton | 8139 N. Denver Ave. (Kilpatrick St.) | 503-978-9000 | www.poshines.com
"Fantastic soul food", including some of the "best catfish" around, makes this Southern gem in Kenton "one heck of a stop"; "service is welcoming", prices are low and fans note that it manages to remain "busy" despite a "no-booze" policy, which is "impressive for Portland."

	FOOD	DECOR	SERVICE	COST

Potato Champion Ⓜ *Belgian*
25 | 17 | 20 | $8

NEW **Eastside Industrial** | The Row | 304 SE Second Ave. (Oak St.) | no phone 🅢

Hawthorne | Cartopia | SE Hawthorne Blvd. & 12th Ave. | 503-683-3797 ◗Ⓜ

"Wonderfully flavorful" Belgian-style pommes frites get a boost from "extensive gourmet dipping sauces" at this "inexpensive" Hawthorne and Eastside Industrial truck duo, where you can also sample poutine that supporters say bests "much of the stuff in Montreal"; the picnic-style seating and late hours (till 3 AM nightly) at the Hawthorne branch make it an appealing option "after the bars close."

Prasad *Vegan*
▽ 27 | 21 | 25 | $22

Pearl District | Yoga Pearl | 925 NW Davis St. (bet. 9th & 10th Aves.) | 503-224-3993 | www.prasadcuisine.com

Those seeking "awesome food and awesome yoga in the same space" can find nirvana at this simple Pearl District cafe inside Yoga Pearl that offers "great vegan organic bites" and juices; prices are moderate and service earns high marks, just be prepared for "limited seating."

Produce Row Cafe ◗ *American*
23 | 23 | 24 | $16

Eastside Industrial | 204 SE Oak St. (2nd Ave.) | 503-232-8355 | www.producerowcafe.com

This Eastside Industrial American, an "oldie but goodie", typifies "authentic slacker Portland" and puts out "solid" eats complemented by "great beer" in a "cozy" space so "cool" "even squares feel hip"; an "attentive" staff furthers the "welcoming" vibe, prices are walletfriendly and it's got "one of the best patios in town."

Pyro Pizza ◗Ⓜ *Pizza*
23 | 19 | 24 | $15

NEW **Eastside Industrial** | The Row | 304 SE Second Ave. (Oak St.) | 503-929-1404 🅢

Hawthorne | Cartopia | SE Hawthorne Blvd. & 12th Ave. | 503-929-1404 www.pyropizzacart.com

Fans marvel they "make great wood-fired pizzas out of a cart" at this Hawthorne pie shop in the popular Cartopia pod and its Eastside Industrial spin-off; service is "fast", and late hours at the Hawthorne stop (till 3 AM nightly) further the appeal.

Queen of Sheba *Ethiopian*
23 | 15 | 22 | $22

Boise-Eliot | 2413 NE Martin Luther King Jr. Blvd. (Sacramento St.) | 503-287-6302 | www.queenofsheba.biz

The "delicious", "authentic" Ethiopian cooking is "worth a try" applaud fans of this affordable Boise-Eliot hole-in-the-wall; the "simple" surrounds remind some of a "cafeteria", but service is "friendly."

Radio Room ◗ *American*
22 | 23 | 22 | $18

Alberta | 1101 NE Alberta St. (11th Ave.) | 503-287-2346 | www.radioroompdx.com

An "awesome" rooftop patio and one with a fire pit draw guests to this "cool" Alberta American where the gently priced bar fare "can hold its own"; it also offers a twice-daily happy hour and an "excellent Bloody Mary bar" on weekends, so fans deem it a "great place to hang out."

	FOOD	DECOR	SERVICE	COST

Red Onion *Thai*

25 | 21 | 22 | $25

Northwest Portland | 1123 NW 23rd Ave. (Marshall St.) | 503-208-2634 | www.redonionportland.com

The "well-presented", "authentic" fare "goes beyond the ordinary" at this NW Portland Thai; statues decorate the simple space, tabs are "value"-priced and devotees assure you'll be "glad" you came.

Red Star Tavern & Roast House *American*

23 | 21 | 23 | $30

Downtown | Hotel Monaco | 503 SW Alder St. (bet. 5th & 6th Aves.) | 503-222-0005 | www.redstartavern.com

Tucked into Downtown's Hotel Monaco, this "casual" tavern turns out solid New American fare, buoyed by a "great selection of local beer and well-made cocktails"; the atmosphere is "comfortable", service is "friendly" and if a few penny-pinchers sniff it's "just ok for the price", supporters still "keep it in the mix."

Reo's Ribs *BBQ*

22 | 16 | 20 | $18

Johns Landing | 6141 SW Macadam Ave. (Carolina St.) | 503-310-3600 | www.reosribs.com

A SW Portland "institution", this affordable BBQ joint in Johns Landing is known for "smoky ribs" and other "tasty" standards (that, and the owner is Snoop Dogg's uncle); "welcoming" staffers work the "hole-in-the-wall" digs, and even if a few critics say it can be "hit-or-miss", fans counter it's "worth the trip."

Rheinlander Ⓜ *German*

26 | 26 | 26 | $30

Hollywood | 5035 NE Sandy Blvd. (50th Ave.) | 503-288-5503 | www.rheinlander.com

"It's Oktoberfest all year long" at this "good old-fashioned" Hollywood beer hall (sib to Gustav's) that "will sweep you to Bavaria" with its "wonderful German specialties" (the "fondue is legendary"), and "great selection" of brews, all delivered by an "attentive" crew in "lively" environs complete with a "strolling accordion player"; it's "accommodating to groups", and with moderate prices it works both as a "family place" or for an "adult night out."

NEW Riffle NW ● *Seafood*

- | - | - | E

Pearl District | 333 NW 13th Ave. (Flanders St.) | 503-894-8978 | www.rifflenw.com

Seafood is the thing at this big-ticket Pearl District hot spot where the ocean-centric theme extends from the fare on your plate to the nautical stylings (reclaimed dock wood, netted light fixtures) decorating the dining room; cocktails get attention for their ice, which is hand-cut from giant blocks, and the chef's counter and raw bar provide front-row seats to the kitchen action.

Rimsky-Korsakoffee House ●⊟ *Coffeehouse/Dessert*

23 | 24 | 18 | $14

Buckman | 707 SE 12th Ave. (Alder St.) | 503-232-2640

"Unlike any other place in Portland" say fans of this "quirky" Buckman coffeehouse set in an old house, where "delicious" desserts are served in "eclectic" environs decorated with random knickknacks and oddities (hanging ornaments, 'haunted' tables that rotate or vibrate); "live classical music" on the weekends adds to the experience, just bring cash (no cards) and don't forget to check out the famous bathroom upstairs.

RingSide Fish House *Seafood*

24 | 24 | 24 | $41

Downtown | 838 SW Park Ave. (bet. Taylor & Yamhill Sts.) | 503-227-3900 | www.ringsidefishhouse.com

"Quality" seafood stars at this "upscale" Downtowner (sib to RingSide Steakhouse), where a "knowledgeable" crew dispenses "simple", but "delicious" dishes backed by an extensive wine list and cocktails made with "house-infused liquors"; if a few find it "overpriced", "fantastic" happy-hour specials help, as do prix fixe options that are especially appealing "before going to a show" at the nearby Arlene Schnitzer Concert Hall.

RingSide Steakhouse *Steak*

27 | 25 | 26 | $51

Northeast Portland | Glendoveer Golf Course | 14021 NE Glisan St. (bet. 140th & 141st Aves.) | 503-255-0750
Northwest Portland | 2165 W. Burnside St. (22nd Ave.) | 503-223-1513 ●
www.ringsidesteakhouse.com

A "perennial that gets better with age" say fans of this circa-1944 NW Portland chophouse and its newer NE double at the Glendoveer Golf Course, where "mouthwatering" steaks "come out sizzling", the "to-die-for" onion rings are "alone worth the trip" and the extensive wine list (Burnside has a 10,000-bottle cellar) features "quality" choices; "attentive" tuxedoed waiters "add to a retro vibe" in the "dark", "old-school" environs ("think Sinatra"), and while tabs are expectedly "pricey", the "deal"-filled happy hour is more "affordable."

Ristretto Roasters *Coffeehouse*

▽ 25 | 23 | 25 | $10

Beaumont | 3520 NE 42nd Ave. (Fremont St.) | 503-284-6767
Boise-Eliot | 3808 N. Williams Ave. (Falling St.) | 503-288-8667
NEW Northwest Portland | 2181 NW Nicolai St. (Sherlock Ave.) | 503-227-2866
www.ristrettoroasters.com

There's "less flannel shirt and more edge" at this trio of "cool" Portland coffeehouses that hand-roast single-origin beans in small batches to serve up "fantastic" coffee, which can be paired with "good" pastries from Bakeshop; they're a "bit off of the beaten path" in Beaumont, Boise-Eliot and NW Portland, but any way you pour it, "the espresso is fabulous."

NEW Robo Taco *Mexican*

▽ 23 | 17 | 22 | $11

Central Eastside | 607 SE Morrison St. (6th Ave.) | 503-232-3707

"Authentic tacos" and other solid Mexican grub comes cheap at this tiny, stripped down Central Eastside joint that's friendly to carnivores and vegetarians alike; the staff "treats you well" and late hours (till 3:30 AM) Thursday–Saturday make it popular with night owls, although there's currently no alcohol.

	FOOD	DECOR	SERVICE	COST

NEW Roe ☒Ⓜ Seafood

	-	-	-	E

Division | 3113 SE Division St. (31st Ave.) | 503-232-1566 |
www.roe-pdx.com

Situated in the back of Division's ramen slinger Wafu, Trent Pierce's 30-seat modern seafooder is open Thursday–Saturday night by reservation only, the better to allow him to personally source and forage from the Oregon coast for his pricey à la carte and tasting menus; an open kitchen gives a peek behind the scenes, and the moody, dimly lit room befits its semi-hidden location.

Rogue Hall ❶ Pub Food

	21	19	21	$17

PSU | 1717 SW Park Ave. (Montgomery St.) | 503-219-8000

Rogue Distillery & Public House Pub Food

Pearl District | 1339 NW Flanders St. (Glisan St.) | 503-222-5910

Green Dragon Bistro & Brewpub Pub Food

Central Eastside | 928 SE Ninth Ave. (Yamhill St.) | 503-517-0660
www.rogue.com

"Worth it for the beer alone", these "casual" Rogue-branded brewpubs also churn out "creative pub fare" like a "fine, heart-stopping hamburger" "easily paired" with the "so good" house-brewed ales, stouts and porters, while at the Green Dragon branch, there's a "daunting" selection of 60-plus taps; "cool atmosphere", outdoor breathing room and central locations render the trio as ideal "hangouts" that can bring on total "beervana."

The Roxy ❶Ⓜ Diner

	22	22	21	$12

West End | 1121 SW Stark St. (bet. 11th & 12th Aves.) | 503-223-9160 |
www.theroxydiner.com

"For hangover food and socialization", this "cheap" 24-hour West End diner fills the bill (the "spectacular" burger is a standout) in a "quirky-as-all-get-out" environment where a "cross-section of Portland" is on vivid display; still, the "efficient" servers "don't put up with" much as they help folks "sober up" after a "night out at the clubs."

Ruby Jewel Ice Cream

	27	20	23	$7

Mississippi | 3713 N. Mississippi Ave. (Beech St.) |
503-505-9314
NEW West End | 428 SW 12th Ave. (Washington St.) |
971-271-8895
www.rubyjewel.net

"Amazing" homemade ice cream crafted with local ingredients is offered in "unique" flavors at this playful Mississippi scoop shop (with a newer West End sequel), where you can "build your own" cookie sandwiches and sundaes; it's all dispensed by a "kind" staff, so enthusiasts say "you won't be disappointed."

Russell Street Bar-B-Que BBQ

	26	19	23	$22

Boise-Eliot | 325 NE Russell St. (Martin Luther King Jr. Blvd.) |
503-528-8224 | www.russellstreetbbq.com

Diners "craving comfort food" point to this Boise-Eliot "family favorite" where the "all-around tasty" barbecue (including options for

FOOD DECOR SERVICE COST

vegetarians) comes via "friendly, timely" staffers; "super-casual" surrounds mean you can "go in jeans", and prices are fittingly affordable.

Saburo's Sushi House *Japanese* | 27 | 19 | 20 | $25 |

Sellwood | 1667 SE Bybee Blvd. (Milwaukie Ave.) | 503-236-4237 | www.saburos.com

"The lines don't lie" at this unflaggingly "popular" Sellwood "dive", where in-the-know locals queue up to devour "über-fresh" "fist-sized" sushi so "enormous" you'd "better do jaw stretches" in preparation; the "cramped" dining room is always "super packed", but given the "price-to-quality ratio" many say it's "completely worth it."

Sal's Italian Kitchen *Italian* | ▽ 23 | 22 | 23 | $32 |

Northwest Portland | 33 NW 23rd Pl. (Burnside St.) | 503-467-4067 | www.salskitchen.com

Shoehorned into a humble strip mall off trendy NW 23rd Avenue, this casual Italian (sib to Pizzicato and Lovejoy Bakers) dishes "authentic" eats, including specials that often "hit the spot", all bolstered by a "good wine list"; moderate prices further make it a "local" "go-to."

Salt & Straw *Ice Cream* | 27 | 23 | 25 | $7 |

Alberta | 2035 NE Alberta St. (21st Ave.) | 503-208-3867
NEW **Northwest Portland** | 838 NW 23rd Ave. (bet. Johnson & Kearney Sts.) | 971-271-8168
www.saltandstraw.com

"Now this is an ice-cream parlor" cheer fans of this Alberta and NW duo, a "must-try" thanks to "dreamy", "interesting" "housemade" flavors, all handed out by a "lovely staff"; sure, certain options are a "little too crazy" for some, and "lines can be out the door", but given the "darn good" offerings, admitted "addicts" still say "it's worth the wait"; P.S. a Division third is slated for spring 2013.

Salty's on the Columbia River *Seafood* | 25 | 24 | 24 | $42 |

Northeast Portland | 3839 NE Marine Dr. (33rd Dr.) | 503-288-4444 | www.saltys.com

"Unsurpassed views of the Columbia River" coupled with "melt-in-your-mouth" seafood and "excellent" service make this "upscale" NE Portland chain link ideal for a "quiet, intimate dinner"; a few find it a "little spendy" and say it's "not fantastic", but fans abound for its "amazing" Sunday buffet brunch.

Salvador Molly's Restaurant *Eclectic* | 23 | 22 | 23 | $19 |

Hillsdale | 1523 SW Sunset Blvd. (Capitol Hwy.) | 503-293-1790 | www.salvadormollys.com

You'll find "lots of variety" at this budget-friendly Hillsdale Eclectic where the "adventuresome" menu features dishes "from all corners of the world", including "island cuisine" and Asian fusion offerings; inside has "pirate-themed decor" and "servers are happy to see you", so despite sometimes "crowded" conditions, it remains an area "favorite"; P.S. try to "conquer the Great Balls of Fire" habanero fritters contest "if you dare."

	FOOD	DECOR	SERVICE	COST

Santeria ● *Mexican*
▽ 25 | 16 | 18 | $12

Downtown | 703 SW Ankeny St. (Burnside St.) | 503-956-7624 |
www.thesanteria.com

This "dive-y" pinto bean–sized Mexican Downtown dishes "authentic" standards like "generously proportioned" burritos "in the last place you'd expect it" – down a shabby alley and in a space that shares a bathroom with strip joint Mary's Club; it "can get crowded", but "low" prices and late hours keep it "popular."

Sapphire Hotel ● *American*
▽ 23 | 26 | 23 | $23

Hawthorne | 5008 SE Hawthorne Blvd. (50th Ave.) | 503-232-6333 |
www.thesapphirehotel.com

Previously the lobby of a seedy hotel, this now "charming" Hawthorne lounge offers midpriced American small plates and "interesting cocktails"; service is "friendly", and many take advantage of the "cool" "vibrant atmosphere."

Saucebox ● *Asian*
24 | 22 | 21 | $28

Downtown | 214 SW Broadway (bet. Burnside & Oak Sts.) |
503-241-3393 | www.saucebox.com

"Portland luminaries" frequent this "swank" "see-and-be-seen" Downtown "icon" known as much for its "fantastic happy hour" and "awesome" DJ-fueled "night scene" as for its "beautifully presented" Pan-Asian fare and "exquisite" cocktails; opinions on service vary from "slow" to "good", and if you don't like it "loud", "get there early" or request the more "serene dining room."

Sayler's Old Country Kitchen *Steak*
26 | 20 | 24 | $35

Southeast Portland | 10519 SE Stark St. (105th Ave.) | 503-252-4171 |
www.saylers.com

For "old-time steakhouse ambiance" and "tender" chops, this SE Portland "legend" (since 1946) is the place, with a "dining room that looks like a diner" and "homestyle" fare that's reminiscent of "grandma's table"; solid service and "decent prices" further help it add up to a "great place to take the Midwest in-laws" (they'll be impressed by the relish tray).

Sckavone's *American*
▽ 22 | 21 | 24 | $18

Division | 4100 SE Division St. (41st Ave.) | 503-235-0630 |
www.sckavones.com

Once a pharmacy, this Division American now run by the original owner's grandson turns out comfort food "just like mom's" in a "comfortable" setting with an "old soda fountain" vibe; the staff is generally "friendly", and prices are affordable.

Scratch ⑤Ⓜ *Eclectic*
▽ 26 | 19 | 27 | $28

Lake Oswego | 149 SW A Ave. (2nd St.) | 503-697-1330 |
www.scratchfoodsllc.com

If you have a "hankering" for "simple, yet lovely" "farm-to-plate" cuisine, fans suggest you "scratch that itch" at this petite Lake Oswego Eclectic, where the seasonal, internationally influenced menu changes monthly and includes many gluten-free choices; it's not cheap, but service scores highly, and enthusiasts say it has all the makings of an "unpretentious" "fine-dining" experience.

Screen Door *Southern* | 27 | 23 | 23 | $22 |

Kerns | 2337 E. Burnside St. (24th Ave.) | 503-542-0880 | www.screendoorrestaurant.com
"Fantastic" "down-home" cooking "with a NW twist" supported by "good ol' Southern hospitality" have folks banging down the door of this "extremely popular", spacious Kerns "comfort-food" mecca for favorites like buttermilk-fried chicken that "rivals anything below the Mason-Dixon"; the awfully "decent" tabs are just gravy, as is the "off-the-charts" weekend brunch that's "worth the wait – and there will be a wait."

Seasons & Regions | 24 | 20 | 24 | $26 |
Seafood Grill *Seafood*

Multnomah Village | 6660 SW Capitol Hwy. (30th Ave.) | 503-244-6400 | www.seasonsandregions.com
Fans call this "quaint little" Multnomah Villager with a "heated, screened-in patio" "a diamond in the rough" and say it charms with its "delicious" seafood dishes (and "lots of other options", like vegetarian and gluten-free) that are composed partly of ingredients from its own 13-acre Estacada farm; further reasons to visit are the "smiling staff" and easygoing prices, especially on its daily 'cheap food menu' offered 3-5:30 PM and late-night.

Seres Restaurant *Chinese* | ▽ 25 | 22 | 23 | $38 |

Pearl District | 1105 NW Lovejoy St. (11th Ave.) | 971-222-7327 | www.seresrestaurant.com
This "glassy", "modern" Pearl District Chinese offers mostly organic, locally sourced Sichuan-style fare that's "generously portioned and beautifully presented" and ferried by a "considerate" staff; "prices match" the "upscale" setting, but if you're on a budget, try the "killer" happy hour.

Serratto *Mediterranean* | 26 | 26 | 25 | $33 |

Northwest Portland | 2112 NW Kearney St. (21st Ave.) | 503-221-1195 | www.serratto.com
A "quaint little piece of Italy" in NW Portland, this Boot-leaning Mediterranean "never fails to please", especially with its "amazing" wood-fired pizza and "outstanding" housemade pasta; servers are "the kind you can trust to recommend the best dish", and the "loft-like" space is "equally charming in winter and summer", though perhaps most during the "terrific happy hour."

Shandong *Chinese* | ▽ 27 | 23 | 24 | $18 |

Hollywood | 3724 NE Broadway (bet. 37th & 38th Aves.) | 503-287-0331 | www.shandongportland.com
Devotees of this Chinese Hollywood haunt praise the "awesome" hand-pulled noodles that servers will toss and cut tableside and other "excellent" dishes like the signature Shandong beef; a polished setting pushes it up a few notches, though not at the risk of reasonable tabs.

NEW Shut Up & Eat Ⓜ *Sandwiches* ▽ 27 | 24 | 24 | $13

Southeast Portland | 3848 SE Gladstone St. (39th Ave.) | 503-719-6449 | www.shutupandeatpdx.com

Giant, inexpensive Italian-inspired sandwiches (meatball subs, cheesesteaks) on bread from Pearl Bakery are the order of the day at this former food cart in SE Portland, which also has breakfast hand-helds and wine, beer and cocktails on its menu; the casual, diner-style environs (not reflected in the Decor score) include counter seating and windows that look out onto a busy corner.

Silk Ⓢ *Vietnamese* 23 | 24 | 21 | $27

Pearl District | 1012 NW Glisan St. (10th Ave.) | 503-248-2172 | www.silkbyphovan.com

This "elegant" Pearl District cousin to the Pho Van chainlet turns out "fragrant", "unusual" Vietnamese "delicacies" (including a "refreshing" banana blossom salad) as well as "giant" bowls of "superb" pho delivered by a "friendly" staff; though you'll pay "extra for the ambiance", regulars say the "inventive" cocktails and "well-priced" happy hour make it "worth writing home about."

Simpatica Dining Hall Ⓜ *American* ▽ 27 | 20 | 24 | $49

Central Eastside | 828 SE Ash St. (8th Ave.) | 503-235-1600 | www.simpaticacatering.com

"Creative", "well-presented" prix fixe Friday and Saturday dinners (by reservation only) and "amazing" walk-in Sunday brunches are the hallmarks of this three-meal-a-week Central Eastside New American, "a Portland original" with a "focus on local foods and producers"; a staff that "has its act together" patrols the shabby-chic space located a few steps below the sidewalk, which is outfitted with communal tables where "strangers become friends."

Sinju *Japanese* 24 | 25 | 23 | $34

Pearl District | 1022 NW Johnson St. (bet. 10th & 11th Aves.) | 503-223-6535
Happy Valley | Clackamas Town Ctr. | 11860 SE 82nd Ave. (Monterey Ave.) | 503-344-6932
Tigard | Bridgeport Vill. | 7339 SW Bridgeport Rd. (Hazelfern Rd.) | 503-352-3815
www.sinjurestaurant.com

Both the "beautiful" sushi and "tasty cocktails" go down easy at this Japanese trio with an "upscale" atmosphere that includes reservation-only tatami rooms at the Pearl locale; service is "polite", and though it's a "bit spendy" for some, aficionados say "that's the price you have to pay for quality."

Sizzle Pie ➊ *Pizza* 24 | 20 | 21 | $16

Lower Burnside | 624 E. Burnside St. (bet. 6th & 7th Aves.) | 503-234-7437
NEW **West End** | 926 W. Burnside St. (bet. 9th & 10th Aves.) | 503-234-7437
www.sizzlepie.com

The "twentysomething creative" masses flock to these West End-Lower Burnside pizzerias for "cheap beer" and "innovative", creatively named pies, like The Ol' Dirty with salami, ricotta and pepperoncini (there's gluten-free and "ample" vegan choices as well); the "music is spot on", and the staff "gets the food out with speed and kindness" whether late-night or on weekend mornings when specials like the Drugs Benedict appear.

Skyline Restaurant ⊄ *American*

24	18	22	$15

Sylvan | 1313 NW Skyline Blvd. (Cornell Rd.) | 503-292-6727
Skyline Burgers ❶ *Burgers*
Irvington | 2200 NE Broadway (22nd Ave.) | 503-808-1553

It's like "you stepped into 1950" (actually, it opened in 1935) at this "classic" cash-only roadside joint serving "good burgers, better fries and great sodas and shakes" "without all the bells and whistles" atop Sylvan's scenic Skyline Boulevard; with solid service, it's a "great deal all around", and for city-folk, there's a newer Irvington offshoot.

Slappy Cakes *American*

25	23	24	$19

Belmont | 4246 SE Belmont St. (43rd Ave.) | 503-477-4805 | www.slappycakes.com

You "make your own fun" – and "your own pancakes" – at this "reasonably priced", industrial-sleek Belmont American where kids of all ages order batter, fillings and toppings to assemble on the in-table griddles with the help of the "fun, engaging" staff; folks who don't want to get "messy" can order off the regular menu, but most are excited about rolling up their sleeves for this "brilliant (and delicious) twist on classic breakfast dining."

NEW Slowburger *Burgers*

-	-	-	I

Kerns | The Ocean | 2329 NE Glisan St. (bet. Sandy Blvd. & 24th Ave.) | 503-555-1212

Slow Bar's popular half-pound burgers are the object of obsession at this new single-subject spot in Kerns' Ocean restaurant collective, where the five budget-friendly patties on offer include veg and seasonal options and there's beer on tap too; the slender space features counter seating, a roll-up door and outdoor seating around a fire pit.

NEW Smallwares ❶ *Asian*

-	-	-	M

Beaumont | 4605 NE Fremont St. (46th Ave.) | 971-229-0995 | www.smallwarespdx.com

Johanna Ware's "bold" Beaumont Asian is considered a "PDX plum" for its array of "refreshingly adventurous" spice-spiked small plates at moderate prices, which are accompanied by "killer cocktails"; true to its name, the modern black, white and red space is small, but there's also a back lounge, Barwares, where the kitchen dishes out the zesty eats until 2 AM.

NEW Southland Whiskey Kitchen ❶ *BBQ/Southern*

-	-	-	M

Northwest Portland | 1422 NW 23rd Ave. (Quimby St.) | 503-224-2668 | www.southlandwhiskeykitchen.com

Smoked meats, burgers, fried chicken and other moderately priced Southern-themed vittles are the focus of this barbecue entry in NW

Portland; the casual environs gain warmth from exposed brick and parqueted walls crafted from reclaimed barn wood, and true to the moniker, more than 100 varieties of whiskey and bourbon gleam from behind the bar.

Southpark Seafood Grill & Wine Bar *Mediterranean/Seafood*

| 25 | 24 | 24 | $39 |

Downtown | 901 SW Salmon St. (9th Ave.) | 503-326-1300 | www.southparkseafood.com

"Beautifully located for dinner and a concert or show", this "upscale" Downtown Mediterranean wins applause for its "stellar" cuisine, particularly the "locally sourced" seafood, plus a "large" "creative" wine list overseen by a "well-versed" staff; some feel it's a "little pricey", but the "upbeat", "open" setting works as well for "power lunches" and "romantic dinners" as it does pre- or post-theater munchers; P.S. the wine bar has its own small-plates menu.

Spella Caffe ⓩ *Coffeehouse*

| ▽ 29 | 15 | 22 | $5 |

Downtown | 520 SW Fifth Ave. (bet. Alder & Washington Sts.) | 503-752-0264 | www.spellacaffe.com

On the "cutting edge" of Portland's coffee scene is Andrea Spella's Downtown cafe, which is "heaven for espresso lovers" thanks to his "kind, funny, welcoming" crew that's "very good at what they do"; with only a few counter stools in the "unassuming, closet-sized" space and limited pastries, it's no place to linger, just a brief "haven from the bustle."

Staccato Gelato *Ice Cream*

| ▽ 27 | 23 | 26 | $11 |

Kerns | 232 NE 28th Ave. (Everett St.) | 503-231-7100
Sellwood | 1540 SE Bybee Blvd. (16th Ave.) | 503-517-8957
www.staccatogelato.com

A "fun place for dessert, coffee and catching up", these Kerns-Sellwood scoop shops shine for their "amazing handmade gelato" in intriguing flavors (18 daily) like Thai iced tea and honey lavender, as well as fresh-baked donuts Friday–Sunday (Sellwood also offers simple breakfast and lunch eats); the bright, laid-back spaces fit the dessert shop vibe, as do the "friendly" employees.

Stanich's ⓩ *Burgers*

| 26 | 17 | 20 | $15 |

Beaumont | 4915 NE Fremont St. (49th Ave.) | 503-281-2322 | www.stanichs.com

"What could be better?" than the signature burger (topped with ham, bacon and egg) and "delicious homemade fries" ask grill groupies who gladly suffer "long waits" at this "cheap" Beaumont "institution"; the "old" tavern (since 1949) is a bit of a "dark" "dive" with sports pennants "hanging on every inch of the walls", but that makes it all the more "fun to take visitors."

Stepping Stone Cafe *American*

| 25 | 18 | 20 | $14 |

Northwest Portland | 2390 NW Quimby St. (24th Ave.) | 503-222-1132 | www.steppingstonecafe.com

"Holy pancakes!" say brunch buffs grappling with the "manhole cover"–sized 'mancakes' and other hearty, "cheap" American fare at this "perfectly Portland" "favorite" in the NW; a generally "nice" staff holds its own, but "long waits" are still the norm in the "busy", "eclectic" old-time cafe environs.

Sterling Coffee Roasters *Coffeehouse* 25 | 23 | 26 | $13
Northwest Portland | 417 NW 21st Ave. (bet. Flanders & Glisan Sts.) | 503-248-2133
Coffeehouse Northwest *Coffeehouse*
Northwest Portland | 1951 W. Burnside St. (Trinity Pl.) | 503-248-2133
www.sterlingcoffeeroasters.com

"Friendly", dapper baristas make all the difference at this chic coffee-shop pair set along busy West Burnside and NW 21st Avenue that's famed for its "great" house-roasted Sterling coffee and espresso drinks; thrifty and "tasty snacks" from Bakeshop and Two Tarts pastries, plus Steven Smith teas, and a "pleasant" ambiance complete the picture; P.S. the NW 21 Avenue locale becomes M Bar at night.

St. Honoré *Bakery/French* 28 | 23 | 21 | $15
Northwest Portland | 2335 NW Thurman St. (23rd Pl.) | 503-445-4342
Lake Oswego | 315 First St. (A Ave.) | 503-445-1379
www.sainthonorebakery.com

"Authentic Parisian-style breads and pastries" and "superb" sandwiches draw dilettantes to this "unpretentious" counter-serve boulangerie pair in NW Portland and Lake Oswego, where the tiny cafe tables and glass display cases conjure "a real taste of France"; though you'll "pay handsomely for your treats", it's a bargain when you consider "the plane fare you could have incurred"; P.S. a Division outpost is expected in spring 2013.

St. Jack *French* 24 | 22 | 24 | $50
Clinton | 2039 SE Clinton St. (21st Ave.) | 503-360-1281 | www.stjackpdx.com

The "closest Portland comes to an authentic Parisian bistro (without the imperious waiters)" is this "lovely", airy Clinton "gem" that starts with a small breakfast and lunch patisserie lineup, then moves on to "elegantly prepared" Lyonnaise *plats* at dinner (don't miss the baked-to-order madeleines); it's "on the expensive side", but it's "hip" and "romantic", down to the "epic" cocktails that can be quaffed at the zinc bar.

Stumptown Coffee Roasters *Coffeehouse* 25 | 21 | 23 | $10
Belmont | 3356 SE Belmont St. (34th Ave.) | 503-232-8889
Division | 4525 SE Division St. (46th Ave.) | 503-230-7702
Downtown | 128 SW Third Ave. (Pine St.) | 503-295-6144
West End | Ace Hotel | 1026 SW Stark St. (bet. 10th & 11th Aves.) | 503-224-9060
Stumptown Annex *Coffeehouse*
Belmont | 3352 SE Belmont St. (34th Ave.) | 503-467-4123
www.stumptowncoffee.com

Those "craving a great cup of joe" that's "worth getting up for" rely on the "skilled baristas" at this inexpensive local Portland-area "alternative to corporate coffee", which sweetens the deal with pastries from Little T American Baker; the Downtown and West End branches attract a "good crowd of cooler-than-thou bike messengers, professionals and cutting-edge young things" while the Belmont extension offers whole beans, gear and free public tastings.

Sugar Cube ●Ⓜ *Dessert* ▽ 26 | 19 | 23 | $10

Hawthorne | 1212 SE Hawthorne Blvd. (12th Ave.) | 503-890-2825 | www.thesugarcubepdx.com

Shakes, malts and treats from the oven lure sweet tooths to this "OMG yum" cart permanently parked in the Lardo parking lot on Hawthorne from "rising star" pastry chef Kir Jensen who uses seasonal and local ingredients to craft quirky creations like chocolate caramel potato chip cupcakes; tabs are inexpensive and scoops from local ice-cream maker Salt & Straw round out the offerings.

Sunshine Tavern Ⓜ *American* ▽ 21 | 23 | 20 | $23

Division | 3111 SE Division St. (31st Ave.) | 503-688-1750 | www.sunshinepdx.com

This "casual", windowed Division tavern (little sister to Lincoln) draws a neighborhood crowd to its stepped-up, NW-leaning American menu of burgers, sandwiches, salads and entrees, all at wallet-friendly prices; it's child-friendly too (there are vintage arcade games and a shuffleboard table), but it's adults only on the slushy margarita machine, ample beer list and "spot-on" cocktails.

Sushi Ichiban *Japanese* 24 | 21 | 23 | $20

Old Town-Chinatown | 24 NW Broadway (Couch St.) | 503-224-3417

One of the "best sushi-go-arounds around" say afishionados of the train that circles the bar counter delivering "fresh" finned fare, which adds to the eclectic feel of this Old Town Japanese storefront; regulars like to "ask servers for suggestions of their favorites" and take advantage of discounts on Wednesday and Saturday nights.

Swagat *Indian* 24 | 21 | 21 | $19

Northwest Portland | 2074 NW Lovejoy St. (21st. Ave.) | 503-227-4300
Beaverton | 4325 SW 109th Ave. (110th Ave.) | 503-626-3000
Hillsboro | 1340 NE Orenco Station Pkwy. (Cornell Rd.) | 503-844-3838
www.swagat.com

The lunchtime buffet featuring a "vast array of quality dishes" is "super legit" at this "authentic", long-running Indian chainlet known as an all-around "great deal"; there's plenty of "space to sit" in the interiors that are well appointed with native artwork, and the "friendly" servers uphold the "pleasant atmosphere."

Sweet Basil Thai Cuisine *Thai* 25 | 22 | 24 | $24

Hollywood | 3135 NE Broadway (bet. 30th & 32nd Aves.) | 503-281-8337
Northwest Portland | 1639 NW Glisan St. (17th Ave.) | 503-473-8758
Southwest Portland | 1010 SW Gibbs St. (11th Ave.) | 503-608-7668 🗷
www.sweetbasilor.com

For "creative, attractive" Thai dishes that "taste as good as they look", and are "reasonably priced" to boot, locals look to these "classy" bistros that go "way beyond the typical noodle joint"; the Hollywood locale is known for its "lovely" outdoor patio that allows for "serene", "romantic" dining beneath a "canopy of vines", but the NW branch and weekdays-only SW food cart, with an abbreviated menu, also please.

Tabla Mediterranean Bistro _Mediterranean_

26 | 22 | 25 | $35

Kerns | 200 NE 28th Ave. (Davis St.) | 503-238-3777 | www.tmbistro.com

The "pick of the litter" along NE 28th's Restaurant Row is this "neighborhood bistro" that impresses with "imaginative" Mediterranean, particularly the "elegant homemade pastas" that are part of the nightly three-course set-menu "bargain" (oenophiles say spring for the "accompanying wine pairings"); the floor staff is "knowledgeable" and "relaxed", but for a view of the action, "sit at the back bar and chat with the chefs"; P.S. a post-Survey chef change may outdate the Food score.

Tanuki 🚫Ⓜ _Japanese/Korean_

∇ 28 | 21 | 25 | $21

Montavilla | 8029 SE Stark St. (81st Ave.) | 503-477-6030 | www.tanukipdx.com

In its low-key, roomy Montavilla digs, this izakaya showcases inexpensive Japanese- and Korean-inflected bites (including an omakase that "will blow your mind"), which are complemented by a full bar; the environs are dimly lit and outfitted with pinball machines, a TV showing cult Asian films and a cold case for munchies to go; P.S. it's 21-and-over only.

Tao of Tea _Tearoom_

25 | 25 | 24 | $17

Belmont | 3430 SE Belmont St. (35th St.) | 503-736-0119
Old Town-Chinatown | Lan Su Chinese Garden | 239 NW Everett St. (3rd Ave.) | 503-228-8131
www.taooftea.com

Be "transported to another place" at these "serene" Belmont and Chinatown oolong oases (the latter is inside the Lan Su Chinese Garden) with an "incredible variety" of teas and "lovely, thoughtfully prepared" small plates; also adding to the "restful" vibe are easygoing prices, fluid service and a "relaxing" traditionally attired setting; P.S. you'll need to be a member or pay admission to access the garden location.

Taqueria Los Gorditos _Mexican_

25 | 18 | 23 | $14

Central Eastside | 1212 SE Division St. (12th Ave.) | 503-445-6289 🥡
Division | SE Division & 50th Sts. | 503-875-2615 🚫🥡
NEW **Pearl District** | 922 NW Davis St. (bet. 9th & 10th Aves.) | 503-805-5323
www.losgorditospdx.com

"Truly delightful Mexican food" is the draw at this simple family-run Division eatery and food cart (there's a newer Pearl stop too) that's "worth the wait" for classics like "great" burritos and "fantastic" sopes that please "omnivores, vegivores, every '-ore' imaginable"; it's "cheap" too, especially considering the "huge servings", which helps keep things hopping.

Tasty n Sons *American*

27 | 24 | 23 | $26

Boise-Eliot | 3808 N. Williams Ave. (Failing St.) | 503-621-1400 | www.tastynsons.com

"Wildly inventive", "blissful" taste combinations star at this "hip", "friendly" Boise-Eliot New American (Toro Bravo's "casual", "value"-priced cousin) that offers brunch plates all day, adding bar bites for the afternoon happy hour and more serious small and large plates at dinner; there can be "insane" waits for a berth in the "noisy" "warehouse"-like space, and food comes out as it's ready, but fans' sole focus is the "drop-dead deliciousness"; P.S. a West End branch is expected spring 2013.

Thai Ginger *Thai*

24 | 22 | 22 | $15

North Portland | 2020 N. Rosa Parks Way (Denver Ave.) | 503-283-9731

This no-frills North Portland Thai delivers just "what you expect": "delicious", "flavorful" straightforward fare that won't dent your wallet in a simple strip-mall setting; the solid service accommodates both eat-in and takeout with aplomb.

Thai Noon *Thai*

25 | 21 | 23 | $16

Alberta | 2635 NE Alberta St. (26th Ave.) | 503-282-2021 | www.thainoon.com

"You're in for a treat" at this cheery Alberta Thai where "wonderful presentation" enhances the "consistently amazing" food available at "family-restaurant prices" and served at wooden tables; adding to its charms are "friendly, efficient" servers who are happy to oblige vegan and gluten-free palates plus upgrades like organic veggies.

Thai Peacock *Thai*

27 | 21 | 23 | $23

Downtown | 219 SW Ninth Ave. (Burnside St.) | 503-228-2310 | www.thaipeacockrestaurant.com

For "curry in a hurry, this is the place" claim connoisseurs of this "small, cozy" Downtown Thai who've "never had less than a delicious food experience" thanks to the "wonderful" staples at affordable prices; smooth service and a prime location a block off Burnside are additional feathers in its cap.

Thien Hong Ⓜ *Chinese/Vietnamese*

25 | 18 | 20 | $21

Northeast Portland | 6749 NE Sandy Blvd. (bet. 67th & 68th Aves.) | 503-281-1247

"If you crave salt-and-pepper squid", this NE Portland Chinese-Vietnamese fries some of the "best in town" say ecstatic addicts who also recommend going "with a group of people to venture beyond the standards" on the sizable menu; there's no decor to speak of, but service is fine and prices are low.

Three Degrees Waterfront Bar & Grill *American*

▽ 21 | 21 | 21 | $24

South Waterfront | RiverPlace Hotel | 1510 SW Harbor Way (Montegomery St.) | 503-295-6166 | www.threedegreesportland.com

Occupying an airy, elegant space in the South Waterfront's RiverPlace Hotel, this New American boasts a "wonderful outdoor veranda "overlooking the riverfront" that's "great for people-watching"; otherwise, the "steady, quality cuisine" that accompanies the scenery is a good value, especially during the weekday happy hour.

3 Doors Down Café 🅼 *Italian*   26 | 22 | 24 | $30

Hawthorne | 1429 SE 37th Ave. (Hawthorne Blvd.) | 503-236-6886 | www.3doorsdowncafe.com

"Mama mia itsa good" rave partisans of this "midpriced" Italian off Hawthorne serving up "generous" portions of "simple comfort" fare such as its "addictive" vodka pasta and "terrific" banana cream pie; despite "noisy" "tight quarters", the setting retains a "warm", "cozy" quality and service is "attentive", and "good news": it now takes reservations for parties of any size.

Tina's *Pacific NW*   24 | 21 | 23 | $41

Dundee | 760 Hwy. 99 W. (7th St.) | 503-538-8880 | www.tinasdundee.com

Pinot partisans drink up this wine country "local favorite" tucked in a small, humble Dundee roadhouse with "excellent", "seasonal" Pacific NW plates from chef-owners Tina and David Bergen served alongside the "valley's finest" vintages (BYO with a corkage is also an option); though prices skew high, the staff is "friendly", and it's "nice" to "swap stories and compare" vinos after a day in the tasting rooms.

Tin Shed Garden Cafe *American*   26 | 20 | 24 | $15

Alberta | 1438 NE Alberta St. (14th Pl.) | 503-288-6966 | www.tinshedgardencafe.com

"Go hungry" and "leave totally fulfilled and happy" at this über-popular, "fairly priced" Alberta American that's one of the "best breakfasts in town" – though there's lunch and dinner daily too; the "small" eclectic space has a "fabulous friendly vibe" (dogs and kids get their own menu and there are many gluten-free options), and there's also a "great patio."

Toast *American*   24 | 19 | 23 | $17

Woodstock | 5222 SE 52nd Ave. (Mitchell St.) | 503-774-1020 | www.toastpdx.com

This "tiny" "diner-style cafe" in Woodstock serves seasonally grounded breakfasts brimming with "imagination and flair" (and a succinct American dinner menu Wednesday through Saturday) with a side of "friendly service" that contributes to a "down-home feeling"; the "neighborhood" crowd also toasts the easygoing prices, which help make it "worth the wait on weekends."

Tom's Restaurant *Diner*   22 | 15 | 22 | $19

Division | 3871 SE Division St. (39th Ave.) | 503-233-3739

A "great breakfast for a great price" can be had at this Division "hole-in-the-wall", where folks devour "diner food" and guzzle coffee in a "laid-back" setting with buttoned banquettes and counter stools; regulars "like the service" too, and the adjoining bar has strong drinks, pool, karaoke, video lottery and plenty of TVs for game night.

Toro Bravo *Spanish/Tapas*
27 | 23 | 23 | $39

Boise-Eliot | 120 NE Russell St. (bet. Martin Luther King Jr. Blvd. & Rodney Ave.) | 503-281-4464 | www.torobravopdx.com

This "bustling" Boise-Eliot tapas bar "extraordinaire" transports diners "to Seville" with "fantastically prepared" Spanish fare ("for surprises" and the "best value", the chef's tasting menu is recommended) and an "extremely reasonable" wine list; "perpetual waits" are a "drawback" for some, but most agree it's "so much fun", and the "servers know when to show up" so seemingly "nothing can go wrong"; P.S. "get a drink" upstairs at Secret Society.

Trader Vic's *Polynesian*
20 | 22 | 21 | $37

Pearl District | 1203 NW Glisan St. (12th Ave.) | 503-467-2277 | www.tradervicspdx.com

A "kitschy tiki theme replete with thatch ceiling" gives Portlanders a South Seas feeling, right down to the long list of "strong" cocktails and somewhat pricey fare at this Pearl District link of the rebooted pioneering franchise; add in solid service and eats, including some "excellent" pupus and it makes a fun "first date."

NEW Trigger *Tex-Mex*
- | - | - | M

Boise-Eliot | Wonder Ballroom | 128 NE Russell St. (bet. Martin Luther King Jr. Blvd. & Rodney Ave.) | 503-327-8234 | www.triggerpdx.com

From the masterminds behind Bunk Sandwiches comes this Tex-Mex-inspired spot in the basement of Boise-Eliot's Wonder Ballroom that's in the spirit with cattle skulls, wood paneling and cherry-red chairs at the bar and counter; the modestly priced urban-cowboy eats feature housemade tortillas, grilled meats and lots of queso, while the pair of frozen margarita machines behind the bar offers liquid refreshment with a kick.

Tucci ◩ *Italian*
▽ 25 | 25 | 23 | $43

Lake Oswego | 220 SW A Ave. (2nd St.) | 503-697-3383 | www.tucci.biz

"As close to Italy as you're likely to get in the 'burbs", this pricey Lake Oswego Italian does a "terrific job" with housemade pastas, meat and fish that are served with "attention to flavor and presentation" and matched by a Boot-centric wine list; the "pleasant", "upscale" Euro setting is also appreciated as a "refreshing change of pace" for the neighborhood, plus there's patio seating.

Tuk Tuk Thai *Thai*
25 | 22 | 23 | $20

Beaumont | 4239 NE Fremont St. (43rd Ave.) | 503-282-0456
North Portland | 3226 N. Lombard St. (Emerald Ave.) | 503-719-7796
www.tuktukthairestaurant.com

These low-priced Beaumont and North Portland neighborhood joints please with their "excellent" Thai renditions, including popular dishes such as flaming beef, pumpkin curry and salt-and-pepper calamari that's "to die for"; the simple, brightly colored spaces buoy spirits as does the "always friendly" service.

	FOOD	DECOR	SERVICE	COST

NEW 24th & Meatballs *Italian/Sandwiches*

| − | − | − | I |

Kerns | The Ocean | 2329 NE Glisan St. (24th Ave.) | 503-282-2557 |
www.24thandmeatballs.com

This inexpensive meatball-focused Italian in the Ocean collective in Kerns puts its money on balls – everything from classic Italian to vegan and served alone, in sliders, with spaghetti – and isn't afraid of anatomical puns if the stocking of Cock and Bull ginger beer and its slogan is any indication; the sliver of a room is kitted out with boxing posters and has counter and sidewalk seating.

23Hoyt *American*

| 23 | 24 | 22 | $30 |

Northwest Portland | 529 NW 23rd Ave. (Hoyt St.) | 503-445-7400 |
www.23hoyt.com

"Swanky" yet "rustic" environs – "huge windows", "beautiful art", taxidermy, firewood – are cut from the same cloth as the "imaginative" American food made from "familiar ingredients" at this "friendly", midpriced "modern tavern" from restaurateur Bruce Carey on NW 23rd Avenue; as at some of his other restaurants (e.g. Bluehour, Saucebox), the popular "bargain" happy hour is ideal for "socializing after work."

NEW Uno Mas *Mexican*

| − | − | − | I |

Kerns | The Ocean | 2329 NE Glisan St. (24th Ave.) |
503-208-2764

From the salsas to the plates, color is everywhere at this taqueria from Oswaldo Bibiano (Autentica, Mextiza), which offers homemade tortillas, an extensive menu of fillings (carnita, tripe, chorizo) and economical tabs at its home in the Ocean, a micro-eatery collective in Kerns; its bright-yellow stools lined up underneath communal metal countertops add to the festive feel, as does the list of Mexican-minded beers – most of which are offered in 32-oz. bottles.

Urban Farmer *Steak*

| 23 | 25 | 23 | $46 |

Downtown | Nines Hotel | 525 SW Morrison St., 8th fl. (5th Ave.) |
503-222-4900 | www.urbanfarmerrestaurant.com

"For steak and swank in the heart of the city", rib-eye revelers like to "see and be seen" at this "high-design" steakhouse Downtown that evokes prairieland via tall grasses, cowhide furniture and a "vast open" 'sky' (it's located in the eighth-floor atrium of the Nines Hotel); "well-prepared" chops with accompaniments sourced from "local purveyors" and "professional" service lead to "corporate card"–appropriate bills, but lunch and happy hour are cheaper.

Urban Fondue *Fondue*

| 26 | 23 | 23 | $35 |

Northwest Portland | 2114 NW Glisan St. (21st Ave.) | 503-242-1400 |
www.urbanfondue.com

"Birthday" celebrations, "bachelorette party dinners" and special occasions are often celebrated at this "fun" NW Portland dipping-and-dunking destination that offers a memorable, midpriced "fondue experience"; the sexy red booths, flattering lighting and "courteous" service also make it suitable for "date nights"; P.S. it's attached to Bartini.

	FOOD	DECOR	SERVICE	COST

Veritable Quandary ● *Pacific NW*   26 | 24 | 25 | $35

Downtown | 1220 SW First Ave. (bet. Jefferson & Madison Sts.) | 503-227-7342 | www.veritablequandary.com

"One of the classiest acts in Portland", this "romantic", brick-walled Downtowner near the riverfront has been "consistently" turning out "imaginative" midpriced Pacific NW fare to "movers and shakers" and theatergoers for more than four decades; the "top-notch" staff is also an asset, as are "strong drinks" at the "happening bar" plus a "delightful" patio.

Via Delizia *Dessert/Mediterranean*   ▽ 27 | 25 | 24 | $16

Pearl District | 1105 NW Marshall St. (11th Ave.) | 503-225-9300 | www.viadelizia.com

"The gelato and pastries are divine" (as are the cappuccinos) at this "inexpensive" Pearl District cafe that also serves a full range of "excellent" Mediterranean cuisine from breakfast through dinner, and is presided over by a "delightful raconteur" of an owner and a staff that "makes you feel welcome"; it's decorated to resemble a quaint European garden, complete with a life-sized faux tree hung with lanterns, but note that guests can also dine on the sidewalk patio.

NEW Via Tribunali *Pizza*   ▽ 26 | 26 | 23 | $19

Old Town-Chinatown | 36 SW Third Ave. (Ash St.) | 503-548-2917 | www.viatribunali.net

It's "the smell of the wood-fired oven" blistering up "fantastic" Neapolitan pizzas that causes pie-sani to "fall in love" with this Old Town outpost of a Seattle-based mini-chain, which offers a few calzones, salads and pastas too; equally "delightful" is the bi-level space that boasts "great" mood lighting, but it all comes back to the pizza that's a steal when you consider the "cost of a flight" to Italy.

Viking Soul Food Ⓢ Ⓜ *Norwegian*   ▽ 26 | 24 | 25 | $14

Belmont | Good Food Here | 4262 SE Belmont St (43rd Ave.) | 503-704-5481 | www.vikingsoulfood.com

For a "happy meal" of lefse, "order one savory and one sweet" from this Belmont Norwegian food cart say "converts" who praise the signature flatbread filled with "amazing concoctions" (i.e. "not your grandma's"); low prices and "cool people" who dish out of a vintage Airstream trailer in the Good Food Here pod keep 'em coming back for more.

Vincente's Gourmet Pizza ● *Pizza*   27 | 23 | 24 | $26

Hawthorne | 1935 SE Hawthorne Blvd. (20th Ave.) | 503-236-5223 | www.vincentesgourmetpizza.com

Pizza fanatics "aren't sure how they do it", but this well-priced Hawthorne dough-slinger turns out just the thing for when that slice or whole-pie "craving" hits, and to lubricate things there's an "excellent beer selection"; it's quirky with random interior flourishes like stones and plates on the walls, but there are cozy booths that make it ideal for a "date or group of friends."

	FOOD	DECOR	SERVICE	COST

Vindalho ⓜ Indian

| 24 | 23 | 24 | $29 |

Clinton | 2038 SE Clinton St. (21st Ave.) | 503-467-4550 |
www.vindalho.com

It's as if "Pacific NW and Indian cuisine had a love child" say disciples impressed by the "contemporary" menu at this "big, airy" "modern"-looking Clinton retreat where "exotic flavors" "marry beautifully" with local, "seasonal ingredients"; it's "reasonably priced", too, for a meal above and "beyond the quick curry dash."

Virginia Cafe ● Pub Food

| 21 | 17 | 19 | $17 |

Downtown | 820 SW 10th Ave. (Taylor St.) | 503-227-0033 |
www.virginiacafepdx.com

"Turn back the clock" and dive into some "decent" pub grub and stiff drinks at this "dark" Downtown tavern, a "Portland icon" that traces its lineage to 1914 (though it moved to new digs several years back); its reputation for always offering a "good value" grows exponentially at happy hour, daily 4–7 PM.

Vita Cafe Vegan/Vegetarian

| 24 | 21 | 22 | $15 |

Alberta | 3023 NE Alberta St. (31st Ave.) | 503-335-8233 |
www.vita-cafe.com

This "hipster" joint in Alberta is known for its "killer spread" of veg-etarian and vegan "comfort food" and "generous" pours of vegan wine, although it also serves meat and eggs (free-range, natural and hormone-free) and regular vino too; the setting – casual with wooden tables and benches – can be "busy" at times, but service is solid and the dollar kids' menu 5–7 PM daily is a draw.

Voodoo Doughnut ●⇗ Dessert

| 26 | 22 | 22 | $9 |

Old Town-Chinatown | 22 SW Third Ave. (Burnside St.) | 503-241-4704

Voodoo Doughnut Too ●⇗ Dessert

Kerns | 1501 NE Davis St. (bet. 12th & 16th Aves.) |
503-235-2666
www.voodoodoughnut.com

"A culinary example of just how weird Portland can be", these color-ful 24/7 Old Town–Kerns dessert dens are "worth a stop" even "just to gawk" at the "huge" corner-curling lines for "extremely imagina-tive", often "hilarious", pastries like the "to-die-for" bacon-maple bar and "as-good-as-advertised" signature Voodoo Doll; all in all, the "novelty" makes it a "must-visit", especially for "visitors."

Waffle Window American

| 27 | 21 | 24 | $11 |

NEW Alberta | 2624 NE Alberta St. (26th Ave.) | 503-265-8031
Hawthorne | 3610 SE Hawthorne Blvd. (36th Ave.) |
503-239-4756
www.wafflewindow.com

"The pearly gates open and choruses ring out" in praise of the "crazy-good" waffles paired with "interesting" sweet and savory toppings at these affordable Hawthorne-Alberta batter bastions; the Hawthorne original is strictly takeaway (or try grabbing a table at the attached Bread & Ink Cafe), while the newer, unrated Alberta spot has seating.

	FOOD	DECOR	SERVICE	COST

Wafu Ⓜ *Japanese/Noodle Shop* | 25 | 23 | 23 | $20 |

Division | 3113 SE Division St. (31st Ave.) | 503-236-0205 |
www.wafupdx.com

For a "righteous bowl of noodles", enthusiasts belly up to the bar or a
high-top table at this sleek, sparse Division Japanese izakaya and fall
"in love with" the "delicious ramen"; it also offers some "unusual"
small plates, and to wash it all down there's lots of Japanese beer, craft
cocktails, sake and whiskey; P.S. a seafood spot, Roe, is hidden in back.

Whiffies *Eclectic* | 24 | 15 | 22 | $9 |

NEW Eastside Industrial | The Row | 304 SE Second Ave. (Oak St.) |
503-946-6544
Hawthorne | Cartopia | SE Hawthorne Blvd. & 12th Ave. |
503-946-6544 ●Ⓜ
www.whiffies.com

"You can't go wrong with fried pie" posit loyal followers of these affordable, "tasty" food carts (located in Hawthorne's picnic table–
bedecked Cartopia pod and in Eastside Industrial's The Row) with
an often changing menu of both "dessert and savory varieties" that
"warm the body from the inside out on a cold day"; "nice people"
boost its standing, and the Hawthorne stop is a "must-go-to place
when out late" thanks to its 3 AM closing time.

Wild Abandon *American* | 26 | 21 | 25 | $23 |

Belmont | 2411 SE Belmont St. (bet. 23rd & 25th Aves.) | 503-232-4458 |
www.wildabandonrestaurant.com

"Eat everything you can with wild abandon" at this "sweet, funky"
Belmont American that's got a "dark", "loungey velvet-walled '70s
glam feel" and "great", low-priced European-inflected fare (including the "fabulous" brunch and happy hour); a "wonderful", "friendly
staff" and a back patio that's the "place on a warm summer evening"
push it into "favorite" territory.

Wildwood *Pacific NW* | 26 | 24 | 24 | $41 |

Northwest Portland | 1221 NW 21st Ave. (bet. Northrup & Overton Sts.) |
503-248-9663 | www.wildwoodrestaurant.com

Foragers of "quintessential Pacific NW cuisine" find it at this "pricey"
NW Portland mainstay of "honest, ingredient-driven" fare whose
"knowledgeable" staff can help parse a wine list "as diverse as the
menu"; the "dramatic" bentwood dining room can skew "noisy",
causing some to recommend the "intimate" bar with its own menu and
a "fantastic happy hour", or there's always the street-facing patio.

Wilfs Restaurant & Bar Ⓐ *American* | 23 | 23 | 23 | $31 |

Old Town-Chinatown | Union Station | 800 NW Sixth Ave. (Irving St.) |
503-223-0070 | www.wilfsrestaurant.com

The 1950s "are alive and well" in this "dark" lounge inside Union
Station offering "excellent" midpriced American "classics" like Caesar
salad, steak Diane and bananas Foster, which are all made tableside;
the staff maintains a "sense of humor" while creating a "destination" worthy of a "special occasion", or just a "great start to your
ride", with "good bar jazz" Wednesday–Saturday night.

	FOOD	DECOR	SERVICE	COST

Wong's King Seafood *Chinese*
| 25 | 21 | 21 | $24 |

Southeast Portland | 8733 SE Division St. (87th Ave.) | 503-788-8883
"Authentic" dim sum plus an "extensive" list of Chinese standards
draw throngs to this SE Portland dining hall "institution" with a for-
midable weekend "wait" that's "part of the ritual"; service is "no-
frills", but "efficient" and fare comes at "reasonable prices", so sit
back and take in the "hectic whirlwind" that's "like being in the middle of Hong Kong."

The Woodsman Tavern *Pacific NW*
| 24 | 23 | 24 | $36 |

Division | 4537 SE Division St. (46th Ave.) | 971-373-8264 |
www.woodsmantavern.com
Stumptown Coffee founder Duane Sorenson is the brains behind this
Division "source of hyper-buzz", where a "professional" staff of "hairy
guys and pretty gals" proffers "delicious" Pacific NW plates and inventive cocktails at modest tabs; the "cavernous" space features dark
woods and vintage mountain landscapes that feed the rustic vibe.

NEW Xico *Mexican*
| - | - | - | M |

Division | 3715 SE Division St. (37th Ave.) | 503-548-6343 |
www.xicopdx.com
Pronounced 'chee-ko', this stylish Mexican in Division's Glasswood
building has sustainability on the brain with ecologically friendy design and much of its provender sourced locally (except coffee, which
comes via direct trade from Oaxaca); its modestly priced dishes include tacos with homemade tortillas and *pollo* bathed in a red mole
sauce; P.S. lunch is available at a to-go window Wednesday–Sunday,
while takeaway chicken dinners are on offer daily.

Ya Hala ⌦ *Lebanese*
| 27 | 23 | 24 | $20 |

Montavilla | 8005 SE Stark St. (80th Ave.) | 503-256-4484 |
www.yahalarestaurant.com
The "superb" Lebanese fare at this big, "busy" Montavilla "favorite"
with dramatic curtains and faux wall finishes has meze mavens feeling like they've "stepped into the warm home" of a family in Beirut;
affordable tabs and "excellent" service make it a lock for a "big group"
where "everyone shares a little."

Yoko's *Japanese*
| 26 | 21 | 23 | $18 |

Southeast Portland | 2878 SE Gladstone St. (bet. 28th Pl. & 29th Ave.) |
503-736-9228
This SE Portland Japanese "neighborhood" "favorite" wins a following with its affordable, "unusual and interesting sushi" and "nice
sake selection"; the "small" simple room means there can be occasional "waits", but the "great" staff contributes to an overall experience that's "worth going out of your way for."

Yuzu ⌦ *Japanese*
| 26 | 22 | 23 | $20 |

Beaverton | 4130 SW 117th Ave. (Canyon Rd.) | 503-350-1801
A "best-kept secret in Beaverton", this "true Japanese izakaya" "hidden" in a suburban strip mall courts a doting fan base who call it
"one of the more authentic" stops around for ramen and other "tra-

ditional" small plates, some of which are listed in Japanese on the wall; it's very "small", but so are the prices, making it a "great place to relax and have a beer with friends."

Zach's Shack ● *Hot Dogs* 24 | 20 | 23 | $15

Hawthorne | 4611 SE Hawthorne Blvd. (bet. 46th & 47th Aves.) | 503-233-4616 | www.zachsshack.com

"A place for just hot dogs?" – "yum" say those "blown away" by the "awesome combinations" available at this affordable Hawthorne "treasure" in a casual setting that's somewhere "between a frat boy's room and a food cart"; add a "great staff", "Ping-Pong on the back patio" and late-night hours, and you've got the "perfect spot to end a long night of drinking."

Zell's Cafe *American* 26 | 20 | 24 | $15

Buckman | 1300 SE Morrison St. (13th Ave.) | 503-239-0196 | www.zellscafe.com

This Buckman "gem" dishes up an "absolute must" of a breakfast (lunch too) that "starts with complimentary warm scones" and continues with "high-quality" classic American dishes at "fair prices"; the "quaint", bustling dining room and well-worn wood bar give off a "true Portland vibe" that feels "like home."

Zilla Sake House *Japanese* 25 | 24 | 20 | $26

Alberta | 1806 NE Alberta St. (18th Ave.) | 503-288-8372 | www.zillasakehouse.com

With an "awesome" "sake bible" that has "few if any peers in Portland", this Alberta Japanese pours on the charm, while its limited menu of "interesting, well-executed" sushi matches it drink for drink; restrained prices and a casual vibe (with bar, table and booth seating) complete the picture.

NIGHTLIFE

Most Popular

This list is plotted on the map at the back of this book.

1 Crystal Ballroom
2 Deschutes Brewery
3 Aladdin Theater
4 Doug Fir
5 Acropolis Steak/Strip

6 C.C. Slaughters
7 Darcelle XV Showplace
8 Horse Brass Pub*
9 Widmer Brothers
10 Jimmy Mak's

Top Atmosphere

27 Ground Kontrol

26 Boiler Room Bar
Crystal Ballroom
Jimmy Mak's
Driftwood Room

Rainbow Room
Circa 33
Vie de Boheme
Shanghai Tunnel
Kask

BY SPECIAL APPEAL

BEER SPECIALISTS

25 Horse Brass Pub
24 Hop & Vine
Saraveza
Bailey's Taproom
23 APEX

COCKTAIL SPECIALISTS

26 Circa 33
Kask
25 Secret Society
24 Teardrop Cocktail Lounge
Rum Club

DANCE CLUBS

25 Whiskey Bar
24 Fez Ballroom
23 Boxxes Video Lounge
Escape
22 Holocene

DIVES

26 Shanghai Tunnel
23 Fox & Hounds
Matador
22 Dante's
A & L Sports Pub

GAY BARS

26 Rainbow Room
24 C.C. Slaughters
Scandals

23 Boxxes Video Lounge
Fox & Hounds

MUSIC/PERFORMANCE VENUES

26 Crystal Ballroom
Jimmy Mak's
Doug Fir
25 Wonder Ballroom
Mississippi Studios

SPORTS BARS

24 4-4-2 Soccer Bar
23 Spirit of 77
22 Blitz
On Deck Sports Bar
A & L Sports Pub

STRIP CLUBS

24 Devil's Point
23 Lucky Devil Lounge
22 Silverado
21 Acropolis Steak/Strip
16 Mary's Club

SWANKY

26 Driftwood Room
Kask
24 Vault Martini
Teardrop Cocktail Lounge
East Chinatown Lounge

Excludes places with low votes; * indicates a tie with place above

Top Decor

26 Kask
   Driftwood Room
   Pope House Bourbon
   Circa 33

25 Doug Fir

   Lovecraft
   Ground Kontrol
   Secret Society
   Vie de Boheme
   Crystal Ballroom

Top Service

28 Kask

27 Every Day Wine

26 Saraveza
   Vie de Boheme

25 BeerMongers

   Hop Haven
   Bushwhacker Cider

24 Local Lounge
   Olive or Twist
   Portland U-Brew & Pub

Nightlife Special Appeals

Listings cover the best in each category and include names, locations and Atmosphere ratings. Multi-location nightspots' features may vary by branch. These lists include low vote places that do not qualify for top lists.

AFTER WORK

Prost! | **Mississippi**	26
Pope Hse. | **NW Portland**	26
Journeys | **Multnomah**	26
Horse Brass Pub | **Belmont**	25
Deschutes | **Pearl Dist.**	25
Widmer Bros. | **Boise-Eliot**	24
Side St. Tav. | **Belmont**	24
Vault Martini | **Pearl Dist.**	24
Sweet Hereafter | **Belmont**	24
Grand Central | **Central E**	24
Bailey's Taproom | **Downtown**	24
Bar Bar | **Mississippi**	24
Rontoms | **E Burnside**	24
Gold Dust | **Hawthorne**	24
Breakside Brew. | **Woodlawn**	24
Night Light Lounge | **Clinton**	24
Bartini | **NW Portland**	24
Tugboat Brew. | **Downtown**	24
Rose & Thistle | **Irvington**	23
APEX | **Central E**	23
Spirit of 77 | **Lloyd**	23
Swift Lounge | **Irvington**	23
Bonfire Lounge | **Kerns**	23
Aalto Lounge | **Belmont**	23
15th/Hawthorne | **Hawthorne**	23
Slow Bar | **Central E**	23
Amnesia Brew. | **Mississippi**	22
Local Lounge | **King**	22
Thirsty Lion | **Downtown**	22
Blitz | **multi.**	22
On Deck | **Pearl Dist.**	22
East End | **E Industrial**	22
Buffalo Gap | **Johns Landing**	22
Ash St. Saloon | **Downtown**	20

COMEDY CLUBS

(Call ahead to check nights, times, performers and covers)

Helium | **Central E**	24
Harvey's | **Old Town-Chinatown**	23

DANCE CLUBS

Whiskey Bar | **Old Town-Chinatown**	25
Groove Suite | **Old Town-Chinatown**	24

Fez Ballrm. | **W End**	24
Boxxes | **W End**	23
Escape | **Downtown**	23
Holocene | **Central E**	22
NEW Jones | **Old Town-Chinatown**	-

DIVES

Shanghai Tunnel | **Downtown**	26
Devil's Point | **Foster-Powell**	24
Sloan's Tav. | **Boise-Eliot**	23
Fox & Hounds | **Old Town-Chinatown**	23
Matador | **NW Portland**	23
Dante's | **Old Town-Chinatown**	22
A & L Sports Pub | **Mt. Tabor**	22
Acropolis | **Sellwood**	21
Cheerful Tortoise | **PSU**	20
Mary's Club | **Downtown**	16

DJS

Ground Kontrol | **Old Town-Chinatown**	27
Whiskey Bar | **Old Town-Chinatown**	25
Groove Suite | **Old Town-Chinatown**	24
Dig a Pony | **Central E**	24
Fez Ballrm. | **W End**	24
East Chinatown Lounge | **Old Town-Chinatown**	24
Someday | **Old Town-Chinatown**	24
Valentines | **Old Town-Chinatown**	23
Boxxes | **W End**	23
Escape | **Downtown**	23
Local Lounge | **King**	22
Holocene | **Central E**	22
NEW Jones | **Old Town-Chinatown**	-

DRINK SPECIALISTS

BEER
(* Microbrewery)

Prost! | **Mississippi**	26
Horse Brass Pub | **Belmont**	25

Deschutes* | **Pearl Dist.**	25
Widmer Bros.* | **Boise-Eliot**	24
Upright Brew.* | **Boise-Eliot**	24
Hop & Vine | **Overlook**	24
Saraveza | **Humboldt**	24
Bailey's Taproom | **Downtown**	24
Coalition Brew.* | **Kerns**	24
Breakside Brew.* | **Woodlawn**	24
Tugboat Brew.* | **Downtown**	24
Bazi Bierbrasserie | **Hawthorne**	23
APEX | **Central E**	23
Pints* | **Old Town-Chinatown**	23
Bushwhacker Cider* | **Brooklyn**	23
Portland U-Brew* | **Sellwood**	23
15th/Hawthorne | **Hawthorne**	23
Amnesia Brew.* | **Mississippi**	22
Hop Haven | **Irvington**	22
Cascade* | **Central E**	22
Laurelwood* | **Hollywood**	22
Raccoon Lodge* | **Raleigh Hills**	21
BeerMongers | **Central E**	20
NEW NWIPA | **Foster-Powell**	-

COCKTAILS

Driftwood Rm. | **Goose Hollow**	26
Circa 33 | **Belmont**	26
Kask | **W End**	26
Secret Society | **Boise-Eliot**	25
Olive or Twist | **Pearl Dist.**	25
NEW Interurban | **Mississippi**	25
820 | **Boise-Eliot**	25
Vault Martini | **Pearl Dist.**	24
Teardrop | **Pearl Dist.**	24
Dig a Pony | **Central E**	24
Rum Club | **Central E**	24
Gold Dust | **Hawthorne**	24
NEW Box Social | **Boise-Eliot**	23
Branch Whiskey Bar | **Alberta**	23
Spirit of 77 | **Lloyd**	23
Whiskey Soda Lounge | **Division**	23
NEW Barwares | **Beaumont**	23
NEW Hale Pele | **Irvington**	-

WINE BARS

Vie de Boheme | **Central E**	26
Every Day Wine | **Alberta**	26
Journeys | **Multnomah**	26
ENSO | **Buckman**	25
Ambonnay | **E Industrial**	24
Hop & Vine | **Overlook**	24
NEW Sauvage | **Central E**	-
NEW Southeast Wine | **Division**	-

GAY/LESBIAN

Rainbow | **Old Town-Chinatown**	26
Darcelle | **Old Town-Chinatown**	25
C.C. Slaughters | **Old Town-Chinatown**	24
Scandals | **W End**	24
Sloan's Tav. | **Boise-Eliot**	23
Boxxes | **W End**	23
Fox & Hounds | **Old Town-Chinatown**	23
Crush | **Buckman**	23
Local Lounge | **King**	22
Silverado | **Downtown**	22
Embers | **Old Town-Chinatown**	22

HOTEL BARS

(See also Hotel Dining in Dining
Special Features)

deLuxe, Hotel Driftwood Rm. | **Goose Hollow**	26
McMenamins Crystal Hotel Al's Den | **Pearl Dist.**	24
McMenamins Kennedy School Boiler Rm. Bar | **Concordia**	26

MUSIC CLUBS

Crystal Ballroom | **Pearl Dist.**	26
Jimmy Mak's | **Pearl Dist.**	26
Doug Fir | **Lower Burnside**	26
Wonder Ballrm. | **Boise-Eliot**	25
Mississippi Studios | **Mississippi**	25
Aladdin Theater | **Brooklyn**	24
Alberta Rose Theatre | **Alberta**	24
Someday | **Old Town-Chinatown**	24
Star Theater | **Old Town-Chinatown**	23
Hawthorne Theatre | **Hawthorne**	23
Kelly's Olympian | **Downtown**	23
Dante's | **Old Town-Chinatown**	22
Roseland | **Old Town-Chinatown**	21
Ash St. Saloon | **Downtown**	20

NEWCOMERS

Whiskey Rm. | **Alberta**	25
Interurban | **Mississippi**	25
Box Social | **Boise-Eliot**	23
Barwares | **Beaumont**	23
Bar Vivant | **Kerns**	-
Hale Pele | **Irvington**	-
Jones | **Old Town-Chinatown**	-

NIGHTLIFE

SPECIAL APPEALS

NWIPA | **Foster-Powell** −]
Sauvage | **Central E** −]
Southeast Wine | **Division** −]

OUTDOOR SPACES

(* Rooftop)

Circa 33 | **Belmont** 26]
Prost! | **Mississippi** 26]
Pope Hse. | **NW Portland** 26]
Doug Fir | **Lower Burnside** 26]
Journeys | **Multnomah** 26]
Moon & Sixpence | **Hollywood** 25]
Liberty Glass | **Mississippi** 25]
Whiskey Bar | **Old Town-** 25]
   Chinatown
Binks | **Alberta** 25]
NEW Interurban | **Mississippi** 25]
820 | **Boise-Eliot** 25]
Red Fox | **Humboldt** 25]
Lion's Eye | **82nd Ave** 24]
Scandals | **W End** 24]
Leisure Public Hse. | **St. Johns** 24]
Hop & Vine | **Overlook** 24]
Grand Central | **Central E** 24]
Rum Club | **Central E** 24]
Bailey's Taproom | **Downtown** 24]
Bar Bar | **Mississippi** 24]
Rontoms | **E Burnside** 24]
Coalition Brew. | **Kerns** 24]
Breakside Brew. | **Woodlawn** 24]
Night Light Lounge | **Clinton** 24]
Fixin' To | **St. Johns** 24]
Funhouse | **Central E** 23]
Rose & Thistle | **Irvington** 23]
Valentines | **Old Town-Chinatown** 23]
Star Theater | 23]
   Old Town-Chinatown
Duff's | **Central E** 23]
APEX | **Central E** 23]
Lucky Devil Lounge | **Brooklyn** 23]
Bushwhacker Cider | **Brooklyn** 23]
Swift Lounge | **Irvington** 23]
Hawthorne Theatre | **Hawthorne** 23]
Whiskey Soda Lounge | **Division** 23]
NEW Barwares | **Beaumont** 23]
15th/Hawthorne | **Irvington** 23]
Amnesia Brew. | **Mississippi** 22]
Hop Haven | **Irvington** 22]
Thirsty Lion | **multi.** 22]
Cascade | **Central E** 22]
Blitz | **multi.** 22]

On Deck* | **Pearl Dist.** 22]
Buffalo Gap | **Johns Landing** 22]
Laurelwood* | **Hollywood** 22]
Barrel Rm. | **Old Town-Chinatown** 21]
Raccoon Lodge | **Raleigh Hills** 21]
Ash St. Saloon | **Downtown** 20]
Gypsy | **NW Portland** 19]
NEW Bar Vivant | **Kerns** −]

PEOPLE-WATCHING

Circa 33 | **Belmont** 26]
Prost! | **Mississippi** 26]
A Roadside Attraction | **Central E** 25]
Horse Brass Pub | **Belmont** 25]
Deschutes | **Pearl Dist.** 25]
C.C. Slaughters | 24]
   Old Town-Chinatown
Dig a Pony | **Central E** 24]
Bailey's Taproom | **Downtown** 24]
Bar Bar | **Mississippi** 24]
Gold Dust | **Hawthorne** 24]
APEX | **Central E** 23]
Boxxes | **W End** 23]
Crush | **Buckman** 23]
Escape | **Downtown** 23]
Amnesia Brew. | **Mississippi** 22]

PUB GRUB

Jimmy Mak's | **Pearl Dist.** 26]
Driftwood Rm. | **Goose Hollow** 26]
Circa 33 | **Belmont** 26]
Shanghai Tunnel | **Downtown** 26]
Pope Hse. | **NW Portland** 26]
Doug Fir | **Lower Burnside** 26]
Secret Society | **Boise-Eliot** 25]
Moon & Sixpence | **Hollywood** 25]
Bar Lolo | **Alberta** 25]
Binks | **Alberta** 25]
NEW Interurban | **Mississippi** 25]
Horse Brass Pub | **Belmont** 25]
820 | **Boise-Eliot** 25]
Deschutes | **Pearl Dist.** 25]
Red Fox | **Humboldt** 25]
Widmer Bros. | **Boise-Eliot** 24]
Teardrop | **Pearl Dist.** 24]
Sweet Hereafter | **Belmont** 24]
Dig a Pony | **Central E** 24]
Hop & Vine | **Overlook** 24]
Rum Club | **Central E** 24]
Saraveza | **Humboldt** 24]
Bar Bar | **Mississippi** 24]

Share your reviews on plus.google.com/local

Gold Dust | **Hawthorne** 24
Breakside Brew. | **Woodlawn** 24
4-4-2 Soccer Bar | **Hawthorne** 24
Night Light Lounge | **Clinton** 24
Fixin' To | **St. Johns** 24
Rose & Thistle | **Irvington** 23
Branch Whiskey Bar | **Alberta** 23
Bazi Bierbrasserie | **Hawthorne** 23
Spirit of 77 | **Lloyd** 23
Bonfire Lounge | **Kerns** 23
Whiskey Soda Lounge | **Division** 23
15th/Hawthorne | **multi.** 23
Slow Bar | **Central E** 23
Amnesia Brew. | **Mississippi** 22
Thirsty Lion | **multi.** 22
Buffalo Gap | **Johns Landing** 22
Laurelwood | **multi.** 22
A & L Sports Pub | **Mt. Tabor** 22
Bunk Bar | **Central E** 21
Acropolis | **Sellwood** 21
Raccoon Lodge | **Raleigh Hills** 21
NEW Bar Vivant | **Kerns** -
NEW Sauvage | **Central E** -

ROMANTIC

Driftwood Rm. | **Goose Hollow** 26
Secret Society | **Boise-Eliot** 25
A Roadside Attraction | **Central E** 25
Liberty Glass | **Mississippi** 25

Rum Club | **Central E** 24
Gold Dust | **Hawthorne** 24

SPORTS BARS

4-4-2 Soccer Bar | **Hawthorne** 24
Sloan's Tav. | **Boise-Eliot** 23
Spirit of 77 | **Lloyd** 23
Thirsty Lion | **multi.** 22
Blitz | **multi.** 22
On Deck | **Pearl Dist.** 22
A & L Sports Pub | **Mt. Tabor** 22
Cheerful Tortoise | **PSU** 20

STRIP CLUBS

Darcelle | 25
  Old Town-Chinatown
Devil's Point | **Foster-Powell** 24
Lucky Devil Lounge | **Brooklyn** 23
Silverado | **Downtown** 22
Acropolis | **Sellwood** 21
Mary's Club | **Downtown** 16

SWANKY

Driftwood Rm. | **Goose Hollow** 26
Kask | **W End** 26
Doug Fir | **Lower Burnside** 26
Vault Martini | **Pearl Dist.** 24
Teardrop | **Pearl Dist.** 24
East Chinatown Lounge | 24
  Old Town-Chinatown

NIGHTLIFE

SPECIAL APPEALS

Nightlife Locations

Includes names and Atmosphere ratings. These lists include low vote places that do not qualify for tops lists.

Portland

ALBERTA

Every Day Wine	26
NEW Whiskey Rm.	25
Bar Lolo	25
Binks	25
Alberta Rose Theatre	24
Branch Whiskey Bar	23

BEAUMONT

NEW Barwares	23

BELMONT

Circa 33	26
Horse Brass Pub	25
Side St. Tav.	24
Sweet Hereafter	24
Aalto Lounge	23

BOISE-ELIOT

Secret Society	25
Wonder Ballrm.	25
820	25
Widmer Bros.	24
Upright Brew.	24
NEW Box Social	23
Sloan's Tav.	23

BROOKLYN

Aladdin Theater	24
Lucky Devil Lounge	23
Bushwhacker Cider	23

BUCKMAN/KERNS

ENSO	25
Coalition Brew.	24
Crush	23
Bonfire Lounge	23
LaurelThirst Public Hse.	23
NEW Bar Vivant	-

CENTRAL EASTSIDE/ EAST INDUSTRIAL

Vie de Boheme	26
A Roadside Attraction	25
Ambonnay	24
Helium	24
Dig a Pony	24
Grand Central	24
Rum Club	24
Funhouse	23
Duff's	23
APEX	23
Andrea's	23
Lovecraft	23
Slow Bar	23
Cascade	22
Blitz	22
East End	22
Holocene	22
Bunk Bar	21
BeerMongers	20
NEW Sauvage	-

CLINTON/DIVISION

Night Light Lounge	24
Whiskey Soda Lounge	23
NEW Southeast Wine	-

CONCORDIA/ WOODLAWN

Boiler Rm. Bar	26
Breakside Brew.	24

DOWNTOWN

Crystal Ballroom	26
Shanghai Tunnel	26
Bailey's Taproom	24
Tugboat Brew.	24
Kelly's Olympian	23
Escape	23
Thirsty Lion	22
Silverado	22
Ash St. Saloon	20
Mary's Club	16

E. BURNSIDE

Rontoms	24

82ND AVENUE

Lion's Eye	24

FOSTER-POWELL

Devil's Point	24
NEW NWIPA	-

GOOSE HOLLOW

Driftwood Rm.	26

HAWTHORNE

Greater Trumps	26
Back Stage Bar	25
Gold Dust	24
4-4-2 Soccer Bar	24
Bazi Bierbrasserie	23
Hawthorne Theatre	23
15th/Hawthorne	23

HOLLYWOOD

Tony Starlight's	26
Moon & Sixpence	25
Laurelwood	22

HUMBOLDT/KING

Red Fox	25
Saraveza	24
Local Lounge	22

IRVINGTON/LLOYD

Rose & Thistle	23
Spirit of 77	23
Swift Lounge	23
15th/Hawthorne	23
Hop Haven	22
NEW Hale Pele	-

JOHNS LANDING

Buffalo Gap	22

LOWER BURNSIDE

Doug Fir	26

MISSISSIPPI

Prost!	26
Liberty Glass	25
Mississippi Studios	25
NEW Interurban	25
Moloko	24
Bar Bar	24
Amnesia Brew.	22

MT. TABOR

A & L Sports Pub	22

MULTNOMAH VILL.

Journeys	26

NW PORTLAND

Pope Hse.	26
Voicebox Karaoke	25
Uptown Billiards	25
Bartini	24
Matador	23
Blitz	22
Gypsy	19

OLD TOWN-CHINATOWN

Ground Kontrol	27
Rainbow	26
Darcelle XV	25
Whiskey Bar	25
Groove Suite	24
C.C. Slaughters	24
Backspace	24
East Chinatown Lounge	24
Someday	24
Valentines	23
Star Theater	23
Fox & Hounds	23
Pints	23
Harvey's	23
Dante's	22
Boiler Rm.	22
Embers	22
Roseland	21
Barrel Rm.	21
NEW Jones	-

OVERLOOK

Hop & Vine	24
Alibi Tiki Lounge	23

PEARL DISTRICT

Jimmy Mak's	26
Olive or Twist	25
Deschutes	25
Vault Martini	24
Teardrop	24
Blitz	22
On Deck	22

PSU

Cheerful Tortoise	20

RALEIGH HILLS

Dublin Pub	22
Raccoon Lodge	21

SELLWOOD

Portland U-Brew	23
Laurelwood	22
Acropolis	21

ST. JOHNS

Leisure Public Hse.	24
Fixin' To	24

WEST END

Kask	26
Scandals	24

Al's Den	24
Fez Ballrm.	24
Boxxes	23

Portland Suburbs

TIGARD

Thirsty Lion	22
Blitz	22

Nightlife

Ratings & Symbols

Atmosphere, Decor & **Service** are rated on a 30-point scale.

Cost reflects the price of a typical single drink.

⌐ℒ below $7   ⌐Eℒ $11 to $14
⌐Mℒ $7 to $10   ⌐VEℒ $15 or above

Aalto Lounge   23 | 22 | 21 | M
Belmont | 3356 SE Belmont St. (34th Ave.) | 503-235-6041 |
www.aaltolounge.com
If there's a "Nordic vibe" at this "cool", "dark-but-not-dank" Belmont
wine and cocktail bar "frequented by artists and other Portland co-
gnoscenti", it comes from the furnishings, inspired by namesake Alvar
Aalto and other midcentury modern designers; the "generous" happy
hour and "awesome DJs" are "added perks."

A & L Sports Pub   22 | 18 | 22 | I
Mt. Tabor | 5933 NE Glisan St. (60th Ave.) | 503-234-7607
"It sure ain't fancy", but that doesn't bother the "Steelers fans" who
flock to this "awesome", roomy Mt. Tabor sports bar equipped with
"plenty of TVs", which is among Portland's only dedicated altars to
Pittsburgh's finest, and pool tables; the "cheap" grub and solid beer
selection are enough to pull in even nonbelievers "on a night that
sports are, or aren't, playing."

Acropolis Steakhouse Strip Club   21 | 16 | 21 | I
Sellwood | 8325 SE McLoughlin Blvd. (Umatilla St.) | 503-231-9611 |
www.acropolispdx.com
"Go for the girls, stay for the incredible Acrop burger" at this "classic", kinda "run-down" Sellwood strip club known nearly as much for
its "surprisingly good", "super-cheap" steaks and patties and "incredible beer selection" as for its nude entertainment; of course, the
"talented, acrobatic", "gorgeous" dancers and "friendly" service
from "hot waitresses" make it an "absolute must" for bachelor parties or "any wild weekend."

Aladdin Theater   24 | 21 | 22 | I
Brooklyn | 3017 SE Milwaukie Ave. (bet. Franklin St. & Powell Blvd.) |
503-234-9694 | www.aladdin-theater.com
"It's like being in a genie bottle" enthuse admirers of the "beautiful"
decor – not to mention the "narrow" chairs – at this "landmark"
former movie house in Brooklyn that presents national touring artists and comedians in a "cozy" auditorium with "perfect acoustics";
there's "not a bad seat in the house", but you'll have to "get there
early" to nab one (ditto a streetside parking spot), and to dodge the
"long" beer lines, those in the know duck through a "semi-secret door"
to the attached lounge.

	ATMOS.	DECOR	SERVICE	COST

Alberta Rose Theatre
24 | 22 | 22 | I

Alberta | 3000 NE Alberta St. (30th Ave.) | 503-719-6055 | www.albertarosetheatre.com

A "gem of Alberta", this "sweet, intimate" renovated 1920s movie house now presents live music, comedy and vaudeville in a "truly special" 300-seat room that has Portlanders "pleased as punch"; the "friendly" staff serves an "interesting variety" of beer, wine and "affordable" snacks, and they "know how to deal" with large crowds too.

The Alibi Tiki Lounge
23 | 22 | 20 | M

Overlook | 4024 N. Interstate Ave. (bet. Mason & Shaver Sts.) | 503-287-5335 | www.alibiportland.com

"Cheeky good fun" can be had at this "dark" Overlook tiki lounge, a circa-1922 "classic" where "kitschy" stylings like island-themed murals, thatch and beachy accoutrements pair with "strong" tropical drinks that fuel "nonstop karaoke"; it can get "packed", but "friendly" staffers and "good prices" help, further ensuring it's a "favorite" when you want to "get drunk and sing your heart out."

Al's Den
24 | 22 | 22 | M

West End | McMenamins Crystal Hotel | 303 SW 12th Ave. (Stark St.) | 503-384-2700 | www.mcmenamins.com

Tucked beneath West End's Crystal Hotel, this "funky, dark, creatively adorned" bar and music venue from the McMenamins entertainment empire looks like "your parents' basement – if your parents are Salvador Dali and Joni Mitchell"; in most respects it's "fairly typical" of the brothers' shtick, with the bonus of "friendly" bartenders and "amazing" free nightly performances by local bands.

Ambonnay Champagne Bar
24 | 22 | 22 | E

Eastside Industrial | Olympic Mills Commerce Ctr. | 107 SE Washington St. (bet. 2nd & Water Aves.) | 503-575-4861 | www.ambonnaybar.com

This "small", sparkling-only wine bar hidden away in the Eastside Industrial's Olympic Mills Commerce Center is a "one-of-a-kind champagne-tasting experience" that eschews a romantic feel for "industrial chic"; by-the-bottle prices are steep, but the "totally committed" owner pours more reasonably priced "bubbly flights" as well as rotating by-the-glass selections that make it easy to "taste and discover new" favorites.

Amnesia Brewing
22 | 18 | 20 | I

Mississippi | 832 N. Beech St. (bet. Albina & Mississippi Aves.) | 503-281-7708

"Part of the local beervana lore", this "prototypical" microbrewery in Mississippi attracts sudsophiles with its "top-quality beers made on-site" and "cheap" burgers and dogs "right off the grill"; the "ample" covered patio is a "favorite summertime hangout" that's accepting of smokers and dogs but not children (inside or out), while the "warehouse"-like interior "feels like a home away from home", whether for regulars or "out-of-towners."

	ATMOS.	DECOR	SERVICE	COST

Andrea's Cha Cha Club
| 23 | 20 | 21 | M |

Central Eastside | Grand Cafe | 832 SE Grand Ave. (Belmont St.) | 503-230-1166

Fans of this "small", low-ceilinged hall in the basement of the Central Eastside's Grand Cafe claim it's the "hottest spot north of Havana" for its prime "Latin dancing" and salsa music (occasionally live) four nights a week; lessons aren't cheap, but the price includes a drink and plenty of opportunities to tango with the club's "wonderful" patrons.

APEX ⊄
| 23 | 21 | 22 | I |

Central Eastside | 1216 SE Division St. (bet. 12th & 13th Aves.) | 503-273-9227 | www.apexbar.com

The "daunting", "seemingly endless" selection of "mostly affordable" and often obscure beers at this "cyclist"-friendly Central Eastside taproom includes 50 on draft, all listed on a "huge" screen along with alcohol-by-volume info; regulars know to ask the "friendly, knowledgeable" staff for "spot-on recommendations" and sip out on the "big patio"; P.S. cash only.

A Roadside Attraction ⊄
| 25 | 23 | 20 | I |

Central Eastside | 1000 SE 12th Ave. (Yamhill St.) | 503-233-0743

Whether due to the "urban-industrial" feel of the year-round outdoor patio fire pit, the overflowing "kitsch" statuary that "looks like an episode of *Hoarders* exploded" and themed "nooks to hang out in", this eccentric Central Eastside "hideaway" is just "another thing that makes Portland weird"; the "friendly, yakity" staffers deliver "decent drinks at decent prices", but come packing, as it's cash only.

Ash Street Saloon
| 20 | 16 | 21 | I |

Downtown | 225 SW Ash St. (bet. 2nd & 3rd Aves.) | 503-226-0430 | www.ashstreetsaloon.com

"A bit seedy, a bit rock 'n' roll", this historic "rough-neck dive bar" in the heart of Downtown draws "interesting regulars" and sundry "unsavory characters" seeking "super-cheap" beer and "stiff drinks" from a "prompt" staff during its four-hour happy hour; the scene changes when the "seven-night-a-week live music starts blasting" (usually local rock or hip-hop) and the crowds are "standing-room-only at times."

Backspace
| 24 | 22 | 22 | I |

Old Town-Chinatown | 115 NW Fifth Ave. (bet. Couch & Davis Sts.) | 503-248-2900 | www.backspace.bz

This airy, all-ages Old Town institution, a "haven" for the city's "young creatives", serves as an art gallery, Internet cafe with LAN gaming center, bar and music venue, providing a "model for how a third place should function"; the "friendly" staff serves a "great cup of coffee" and kombucha to software developers by day and beer and wine to crowds of mixed-age "music lovers" after dark – "who thought being a geek could be so cool?"

	ATMOS.	DECOR	SERVICE	COST

Back Stage Bar
25 | 24 | 20 | M

Hawthorne | McMenamins Bagdad Theater | 3702 SE Hawthorne Blvd.
(37th Ave.) | 503-236-9234 | www.mcmenamins.com
Hidden behind Hawthorne's Bagdad Theater, this billiards hall boasts
"incredible" atmosphere compliments of its seven-story-high ceiling and renovations by the McMenamin brothers, with all their usual
wild artwork and historical consciousness; service can run "slow"
and "prices are on the high side", but there's no denying it's a "unique"
venue for a round of snooker.

Bailey's Taproom
24 | 21 | 24 | I

Downtown | 213 SW Broadway (Ankeny St.) | 503-295-1004 |
www.baileystaproom.com
"Tourists, beer geeks and business guys alike" crowd into this "nononsense" Downtown "beer-drinker's bar" for "reasonably priced"
pints pulled from 20 taps of "mainly West Coast" brews that "you can't
get just anywhere", monitorable via "real-time updates" of keg remainder on an electronic board; manned by "über-knowledgeable"
"beer-tenders", it's got "big windows, plenty of light" and board
games, but "no food" – although Santeria will deliver Mexican vittles.

Bar Bar
24 | 21 | 22 | I

Mississippi | 3939 N. Mississippi Ave. (bet. Failing & Shaver Sts.) |
503-288-3895 | www.mississippistudios.com
With an "awesome" patio and a long-lasting happy hour, this "cozy,
intimate" bar/burger joint attached to Mississippi Studios is a "fun
place to be"; true, the vibe can be "über-*Portlandia*", but given the
"funny, friendly" bartenders mixing value-priced cocktails in pint
glasses with cheap patties to soak 'em up, it's a "total win."

Bar Lolo
25 | 24 | 24 | M

Alberta | 2940 NE Alberta St. (30th Ave.) | 503-288-3400 |
www.barlolo.com
Like a "refreshing" trip to Spain, this casual, colorful Alberta tapas bar
offers up "different twists on the usual cocktails" and "amazing" sangria, and the drinks get "cheap" during the happy hours; it's "quiet,
friendly" and "suitable for the family dinner or the romantic moment."

Barrel Room
21 | 18 | 17 | M

Old Town-Chinatown | 105 NW Third Ave. (bet. Couch & Davis Sts.) |
503-242-0700 | www.barrelroompdx.com
Youthful types "drink, dance, laugh and embarrass friends" at this
"crowded, sweaty" Old Town club and show bar where the "party
doesn't really get started till after 10 PM" and there's almost "always a long line"; inside it's the "dueling pianos and band that make
the night so much fun", while outside "girls shake it" on picnic tables.

Bartini
24 | 22 | 21 | M

Northwest Portland | 2108 NW Glisan St. (bet. 21st & 22nd Aves.) |
503-224-7919 | www.bartinipdx.com
At this "tiny", "kitschy-classy" NW Portland martini bar attached to
Urban Fondue, a "myriad" of choices from the "incredibly long

list of fun martinis" come half-price during the "ridiculous" twice-nightly happy hours that leave tipplers both "shaken and stirred"; perhaps owing to the "loud", "convivial" scene, service can be "inconsistent", but still it's a go-to when you're "looking for a night out with the girls."

ᴺᴱᵂ Bar Vivant

- | - | - | M

Kerns | 2225 E. Burnside St. (22nd Ave.) | 971-271-7166 | www.pixpatisserie.com

From the enormous silhouette of a bull that crowns its roof to the bottle-lined walls and napkin-littered floor, this Kerns tapas and champagne bar is one big love letter to Spain; behind the bar, cheerful, bearded servers carve jamón serrano and pour glasses of cider and bubbly Txakoli from great heights and shake up craft cocktails; P.S. it shares a space with Pix Patisserie.

ᴺᴱᵂ Barwares

▽ 23 | 22 | 20 | M

Beaumont | 4605 NE Fremont St. (bet. 46th & 47th Aves.) | 971-229-0995 | www.smallwarespdx.com

A sidekick to chef Johanna Ware's Asian-leaning Smallwares, this "unpretentious" Beaumont addition offers "delicious", "creative" drinks and bites at a "good price" for "foodies and cocktail hounds alike"; it's "cozy" with a fireside couch, bar and table seating, which, in combination with a solid staff, has some looking forward to "many return trips."

Bazi Bierbrasserie

23 | 21 | 23 | M

Hawthorne | 1522 SE 32nd Ave. (bet. Hawthorne Blvd. & Market St.) | 503-234-8888 | www.bazipdx.com

"Belgian-style beers" from both sides of the Atlantic are the specialty of this Hawthorne converted loading dock where "obscure" and sometimes "pricey" brews come in "proper glasses" and get mixed into "tasty" cocktails; it's "family-friendly", a "super spot" to take in a Timbers game and offers the bonus of pub grub that's a "few notches higher" than the norm.

The BeerMongers

20 | 18 | 25 | I

Central Eastside | 1125 SE Division St. (bet. 11th & 12th Aves.) | 503-234-6012 | www.thebeermongers.com

"Knowledgeable", "helpful" staffers win high praise at this Central Eastside bar and bottle shop where "coolers full of remarkable beers from around the globe" and a "short but well-rounded tap list" have attracted a "cult following", especially given the "rock solid prices"; sure, the "tiny", "industrial" space looks "little more than a garage", but that doesn't deter hopsheads who vow they'll "definitely go back."

Binks

25 | 22 | 24 | I

Alberta | 2715 NE Alberta St. (bet. 27th & 28th Aves.) | 503-493-4430 | www.binksbar.com

"Bless its fireplace and jukebox" declare acolytes of this "mellow" Alberta "friendly neighborhood" watering hole that also wins followers with its "amazing" pizza and "to-die-for" house-infused spirits; the "prices are right", and a "friendly", "efficient" staff makes its "great mix of people" "feel like family."

Blitz-Ladd
22 | 21 | 20 | M

Central Eastside | 2239 SE 11th Ave. (Sherman St.) | 503-236-3592
Blitz-99W
Tigard | 10935 SW 68th Pkwy. (Pacific Hwy.) | 503-719-5157
Blitz-Pearl
Pearl District | 110 NW 10th Ave. (bet. Couch & Davis Sts.) | 503-222-2229
Blitz-21
Northwest Portland | 305 NW 21st Ave. (bet. Everett & Flanders Sts.) | 503-208-3227
www.blitzbarpdx.com

These "college bars on steroids" boast "plenty of TVs", "bar games everywhere" (including "serious Ping-Pong and shuffleboard") and "jam-packed" crowds; sure, they host a "bro-ish" scene and service is "spotty", but if you "get there early for big games" and prepare for a "meat markety" vibe in the evenings, they're "fun and people usually get a little crazy."

Boiler Room
22 | 18 | 21 | I

Old Town-Chinatown | 228 NW Davis St. (bet. 2nd & 3rd Aves.) | 503-227-5441 | www.boilerroomportland.com

"You're guaranteed an audience" at this "friendly" Old Town karaoke bar, where a "packed" crowd "awkwardly dances" to amateur crooning seven nights a week; "the drinks are strong", there's the option to "shoot some pool" as well as the "major plus" of a photo booth to provide further distraction; P.S. surveyors say that Monday's comedy open-mike night is "one of the best-kept secrets in town."

Boiler Room Bar
26 | 24 | 21 | M

Concordia | McMenamins Kennedy School | 5736 NE 33rd Ave. (NE Jarrett St.) | 503-249-3983 | www.mcmenamins.com

An "array of twisted and interconnected pipes" creates a "comfy cage" for tossing back a drink or two at this former boiler room in the heart of Concordia's Kennedy School entertainment complex, which is part of the McMenamins empire; the "limited seating" and occasionally "slow" service aside, the chambers make for a "blessedly quiet" venue for "chill patrons" looking to "hang out with friends."

Bonfire Lounge
23 | 21 | 21 | I

Kerns | 2821 SE Stark St. (bet. 28th & 29th Aves.) | 503-232-3704 | www.bonfirepdx.com

"Hippies and hipsters" are drawn to this Kerns lounge for its "cheap booze and cheaper food" ("hearty" fare like burritos, sandwiches, burgers) at happy hour and beyond; its "dark", "low-key" space boasts "minimal decor" beyond the pool table, but there are picnic tables outside for prime "people-watching."

	ATMOS.	DECOR	SERVICE	COST

🆕 Box Social
23 | 23 | 22 | M

Boise-Eliot | 3971 N. Williams Ave. (bet. Failing & Shaver Sts.) |
503-288-1111 | www.bxsocial.com

"Imaginative", "fabulous" cocktails and bar snacks to "soak 'em up"
please fans of this Boise-Eliot lounge run by "accommodating" folks;
its candlelit, "speakeasy-esque" space is long on romance, and frequenters recommend it "for an early evening drink."

Boxxes Video Lounge
23 | 20 | 23 | I

West End | 330 SW 11th St. (Stark St.) | 503-226-4171 |
www.boxxes.com

It's "gay-boy heaven" at this West End club where a "young, vibrant
crowd" populates the sunken dance floor and smokers mingle on the
covered patio, "even in the crappy NW weather"; the "wonderful"
bar service and "cheap" well drinks draw straight revelers on some
nights, while "fun drag shows" and "gay porn on the TV screens"
leave no doubt as to its persuasion.

Branch Whiskey Bar
23 | 22 | 23 | M

Alberta | 2926 NE Alberta St. (bet. 29th & 30th Aves.) | 503-206-6266 |
www.branchwhiskeybar.com

"Feel free to geek out" at this Alberta pub, where "helpful", "experienced" bartenders pour "affordable whiskey drinks" along with pricier treasurers from the "well-curated collection" of bottles on the
back shelf; the "pretty cool build-out" includes a wood-finished bar
and a quiet courtyard in back.

Breakside Brewery
24 | 23 | 24 | I

Woodlawn | 820 NE Dekum St. (Durham Ave.) | 503-719-6475 |
www.breaksidepdx.com

This "industrial" brewpub with roll-up garage doors in "out-of-the-
way" Woodlawn is a "standout in the town that does microbreweries best"; "creative", "delicious" house beers are served alongside
solid guest taps by employees who "know their beer and seem to
genuinely enjoy their jobs", and the "gluttonous" fare runs from
sandwiches to burgers to mac 'n' cheese.

Buffalo Gap
22 | 19 | 22 | M

Johns Landing | 6835 SW Macadam Ave. (California St.) | 503-244-7111 |
www.thebuffalogap.com

If this "relaxing, enjoyable" Johns Landing bar and eatery "feels like
home", maybe it's because it was both a boarding house and a brothel
in previous incarnations – today there's "happening" live music upstairs, pool and arcade games downstairs and "above-average",
family-friendly American dishes throughout; surveyors appreciate
the "decent" prices and say they detect "no gaps in service."

Bunk Bar
21 | 18 | 21 | M

Central Eastside | 1028 SE Water Ave. (bet. Taylor & Yamhill Sts.) |
503-894-9708 | www.bunkbar.com

This noctural offshoot of Bunk Sandwiches in the Central Eastside
draws lunch and dinnertime crowds for "heavenly" sandwiches

paired with a "frosty pint and a game of pinball" and accompanied by "laid-back" service; later on, the "dark, cold" (and to some "ugly") converted warehouse fills up with "young, hip" music-lovers who frequent it for "loud" shows by local rockers and "reasonably priced drinks."

Bushwhacker Cider
23 | 20 | 25 | I

Brooklyn | 1212 SE Powell Blvd. (bet. 12th & 13th Aves.) | 503-445-0577 | www.bushwhackercider.com

"Absolutely the best place in town for cider", this Brooklyn brewery pours an "amazing" selection of draft and bottled alcoholic juice (100-plus varieties, including house brews) at "reasonable" rates; though the space is "just a garage" decorated with a few dartboards, it's manned by a "friendly, helpful" staff that "plays good music" and helps make it a "cool place to hang out."

Cascade Brewing Barrel House
22 | 19 | 21 | M

Central Eastside | 939 SE Belmont St. (10th Ave.) | 503-265-8603 | www.cascadebrewingbarrelhouse.com

It's a "sour beer-lover's heaven" at this "spare" Central Eastside brewpub that offers a "wide array" of barrel-aged suds in the "old-world style", many "incorporating interesting fruits and herbs"; a few grumble that the pours are "a bit pricey" and the bartenders sometimes "charge for tastes", but factor in its "efficient", "knowledgeable" service and "large, inviting" street-front patio, and most say it "really satisfies."

C.C. Slaughters
24 | 22 | 21 | I

Old Town-Chinatown | 219 NW Davis St. (bet. 2nd & 3rd Aves.) | 503-248-9135 | www.ccslaughterspdx.com

There's "lots of energy" at this "loud", "crowded" Old Town gay club renowned for "no cover" and "cheap" drinks; the "attentive" "shirtless bartenders" pour "strong" cocktails for a "gorgeous" crowd of "young(er) guys" dancing under lasers and disco balls and eyeing one of the "best drag shows" on Sunday nights; P.S. the more sedate Rainbow Room is next door.

Cheerful Tortoise
20 | 16 | 20 | I

PSU | 1939 SW Sixth Ave. (bet. College & Hall Sts.) | 503-224-3377 | www.cheerfultortoise.com

"A PSU tradition", this bar on the edge of its Downtown campus has been the default meeting place of undergrads since time immemorial with plenty of beers on tap and loads of TVs; look past the "smelly carpet" and "sticky" tables and you'll find "friendly servers and bartenders" and appropriately cheerful undergrads gathered for "local sports", karaoke and an enormous circular fireplace to drive away the winter chill.

Circa 33
26 | 26 | 24 | M

Belmont | 3348 SE Belmont St. (bet. 33rd & 34th Aves.) | 503-477-7682 | www.circa33bar.com

This "cool, dark" Prohibition-themed Belmont lounge boasts a towering liquor shelf accessed by a library ladder, as well as "outstanding" classic cocktails at moderate prices; the service is "usually excellent", and the "awesome" semi-covered alleyway patio and "back-area speakeasy" hidden behind a swinging bookshelf are added benefits.

Coalition Brewing

| 24 | 20 | 23 | I |

Kerns | 2724 SE Ankeny St. (bet. 27th & 28th Aves.) | 503-894-8080 | www.coalitionbrewing.com

Housed in a "simple", "garage-style" concrete room, this "so-tiny", "friendly" Kerns brewpub serves reasonably priced pints of "its own brews on tap", ranging from "piney" quaffs to "unusual creations" that include collaborations with home brewers; a "neighborhood crowd" spreads out in its "huge outdoor seating" area shared by the double-decker Grilled Cheese Grill bus, and there's a "limited food menu" as well.

Crush

| 23 | 21 | 22 | M |

Buckman | 1400 SE Morrison St. (14th Ave.) | 503-235-8150 | www.crushbar.com

A "cool neighborhood gay bar", this "fun, kitschy" Buckman lounge decorated with glass art, neon and plywood draws a mixed crowd to its eclectic theme nights (samba parties, drag shows, amateur burlesque, lots of charity events); add in "reasonably" priced drinks, a "wide variety of food" and a staff that "clearly likes working" here and it's a "great place for meeting friends."

Crystal Ballroom

| 26 | 25 | 21 | I |

Pearl District | 1332 W. Burnside St. (bet. 13th & 14th Aves.) | 503-225-0047 | www.danceonair.com

One of Portland's "favorite" ballrooms for nearly a century and voted the city's Most Popular nightlife venue thanks in part to its "unique", "bouncy" "gymnasium-sized" floating dance floor, this "absolutely fantastic" Pearl District venue has the McMenamin brothers' "eccentric decor" touch and hosts concerts by major national touring acts; service is "intermittently spotty", but "cheap" beers brewed on-site make it a "fun place to hang and watch bands play."

Dante's

| 22 | 19 | 20 | M |

Old Town-Chinatown | 350 W. Burnside St. (3rd Ave.) | 503-226-6630 | www.danteslive.com

"Fire dancers, need I say more?" query denizens of this Old Town hot spot, a "dungeonlike" "divey rock venue" with "fire coming out of the tables" that's "always packed" for concerts, live-band karaoke and its weekly 'Sinferno' cabaret; the staff is "friendly" if sometimes "slow" and its "late-night pizza" is "pretty good" – just "don't expect to sit" or "leave with working eardrums."

Darcelle XV Showplace

| 25 | 21 | 23 | M |

Old Town-Chinatown | 208 NW Third Ave. (Davis St.) | 503-222-5338 | www.darcellexv.com

A "blast from the golden age of drag", this "real hoot" of an Old Town "institution" attracts crowds "of all stripes", including "lots of bachelorette parties", for founder Walter Cole's "tacky, tawdry and tantalizing" nightly revue and midnight weekend male stripper performances; there's a cover and two-item minimum, but the drinks are "strong" and the "wild, wicked" shows "must be experienced at least once."

Deschutes Brewery Portland Public House

25 | 24 | 23 | M

Pearl District | 210 NW 11th Ave. (Davis St.) | (503) 296-4906 | www.deschutesbrewery.com

Oversized glasses full of "top-notch" beer brewed just behind the bar quench thirsts at this "spacious" Pearl District outpost of the Bend brewery in a "huge" converted auto-body shop that affects a "cozy mountain cabin feel" via a "large fireplace", "big beams of wood" and carvings of NW landscapes; "dependably good" pub grub delivered by "friendly, quick" servers who "work hard" also merits a go.

Devil's Point

24 | 21 | 22 | I

Foster-Powell | 5305 SE Foster Rd. (bet. Bush St. & 54th Ave.) | 503-774-4513 | www.devilspointbar.com

"The Cirque du Soleil of stripping", this Foster-Powell strip bar sets itself apart from the rest of Portland's skin scene with "whipping, flipping, balletic" pole numbers by "attractive dancers of the natural and tattooed variety", accompanied by "cheap drinks" and "personable" service; the red bordelloesque digs are "cramped", but that's "part of the charm", and "be sure to come Sunday" for 'Stripparaoke', when patrons take the stage.

Dig a Pony

24 | 25 | 20 | M

Central Eastside | 736 SE Grand Ave. (Morrison St.) | 971-279-4409 | www.digaponyportland.com

This "happening little" "hipster heaven", a "thoughtfully" restored Central Eastside turn-of-the-century pharmacy, draws "Portland's 'in' crowd" with its "fancy cocktails", "good" beer selection and nightly DJs; the "friendly" bartenders do their best to keep it "chill", but on weekends many are there simply to "dance, dance, dance" and partake in serious "people-watching."

Doug Fir Restaurant & Lounge

26 | 25 | 21 | I

Lower Burnside | 830 E. Burnside St. (bet. 8th & 9th Aves.) | 503-231-9663 | www.dougfirlounge.com

"If REI and IKEA had a lovechild" it would be this streamlined "log cabin of the future", a "hipster" "hangout" next to Lower Burnside's Jupiter Hotel with an expansive grub menu, space-ship windows, globe lights, plenty of stacked wood and an indoor fireplace and outdoor patio pit; downstairs hosts "affordable" concerts by local and national indie artists that sound "surprisingly good for being in a concrete box."

Driftwood Room

26 | 26 | 24 | M

Goose Hollow | Hotel deLuxe | 729 SW 15th Ave. (bet. Morrison & Yamhill Sts.) | 503-222-2171 | www.graciesdining.com

Perhaps the "Portland bar that most closely resembles a *Mad Men* set", this curvaceous, wood-paneled "retro" watering hole in Goose

Hollow's classic Hollywood–themed Hotel deLuxe is perfectly "elegant" and "discreet"; expect to find visitors and "post-theater" crowds gathered for slightly spendy and "fabulous champagne cocktails" and the like poured by an affable bar staff.

Dublin Pub

22 | 20 | 22 | I

Raleigh Hills | 6821 SW Beaverton-Hillsdale Hwy. (Oleson Rd.) | 503-297-2889 | www.dublinpubpdx.com

"Tons o' taps", a "laid-back atmosphere" and a "variety of things to do" (pool, foosball, darts) please patrons of this "affordable", "above-average" Raleigh Hills pub helmed by a "sociable" staff; a few are "not sure how Irish it really is", but most appreciate the "awesome" live music, "decent" food and "Old Country" looks featuring "old Irish sayings" on the walls.

Duff's Garage Bar & Grill

23 | 21 | 22 | I

Central Eastside | 1635 SE Seventh Ave. (Market St.) | 503-234-2337 | www.duffsgarage.com

A "sideburned and tattooed" crew motor into this inexpensive Central Eastside "honky-tonk" for "some of the best" blues, rockabilly and surf shows around, revved up by "cold beer" and "hard liquor" slung by "pleasant, friendly" bartenders; sporting a "tiny dance floor" and stage, the small "garage" space is decked with a jumble of highway signs, racing pennants, wood paneling and retro booths.

East Chinatown Lounge

24 | 18 | 20 | M

Old Town-Chinatown | 322 NW Everett St. (3rd Ave.) | 503-226-1569 | www.eastchinatownlounge.com

This "dark", "chill" Chinatown hideaway looks a bit like something out of *A Clockwork Orange* with its glowing-red accent lights and ultrasleek, modernist lines; also au courant are the "on-point" DJs, who spin house beats while bartenders sling midpriced drinks "late" into the night.

East End

22 | 20 | 22 | I

Eastside Industrial | 203 SE Grand Ave. (Ash St.) | 503-232-0056 | www.eastendpdx.com

The "dark, dingy" "tiny basement of a venue" at this "rad" bi-level Eastside Industrial bar is a "sweaty scene for truly underground acts, varying from indie to electronic to all around adventursome"; upstairs there's "ample seating" for "a beer and a bite" and "friendly" service during the four-hour happy hour, but most stop in for the "chance that your face will be melted and your eardrums blown" by the music.

820

25 | 23 | 22 | M

Boise-Eliot | 820 N. Russell St. (bet. Indiana & Michigan Aves.) | 503-284-5518 | www.mintand820.com

Although known for its "talented mixologists" slinging "killer cocktails", this intimate Boise-Eliot martini lounge also offers "excellent", "reasonably priced" New American fare from adjoining Mint plus a "super" happy hour; with its curvaceous bar and mood lighting, it's "upscale without being too pretentious", and a prime "first-date spot."

Embers

| 22 | 18 | 22 | M |

Old Town-Chinatown | 110 NW Broadway (Couch St.) | 503-222-3082

"The granddaddy of the gay bar scene in Portland", this "friendly" Chinatown club brings in a "mixed crowd" with its "bumping" dance floor, "hell-of-a-lot-of-fun" drag shows and "well-poured" drinks; a few say it's "in need of a face-lift", while fans counter it's "trashy in a good way" and add the aquarium bar "full of fancy goldfish" "deserves a visit" in itself.

ENSO Urban Winery & Tasting Lounge

| 25 | 20 | 19 | M |

Buckman | 1416 SE Stark St. (bet. 14th & 15th Aves.) | 503-683-3676 | www.ensowinery.com

Oenophiles "really like" what the "passionate" owners are doing at this "hip", "priced right" Buckman micro-winery: to wit, sourcing grapes from area vineyards, then fermenting them to create their own "terrific" small-batch bottlings; it also offers a "varied" selection of other labels plus a "small" but "wise" beer menu to pair with bites of charcuterie and cheese in the "reclaimed industrial space" that sports a rolling garage door that "opens the room up" nicely.

Escape ⌽

| 23 | 21 | 22 | I |

Downtown | 333 SW Park Ave. (bet. Oak & Stark Sts.) | 503-227-0830

"Gay, straight, it doesn't matter" at this cash-only, weekend-only, alcohol-free Downtown dance club with a small cover and a "nice, responsible" staff that creates a "fun, accepting environment" for "underage kids" of all orientations; an "always packed" light-up dance floor invites dance-pop fans to "get down and shake it", while there's a separate room for those who prefer industrial music and the like.

Every Day Wine

| 26 | 23 | 27 | M |

Alberta | 1520 NE Alberta St. (bet. 15th & 16th Aves.) | 503-331-7119 | www.everydaywine.com

"Awesomely inexpensive wine finds" are the draw at this Alberta vino bar where a "personable" owner pours single glasses or can assemble themed flights from any of the more than 400 wines on the shelves; otherwise it's "no-frills", i.e. there's no menu, but "you can bring your own food" to pair with the "wonderful" wine.

Fez Ballroom

| 24 | 22 | 21 | M |

West End | 316 SW 11th Ave. (Burnside St.) | 503-221-7262 | www.fezballroom.com

This "wild" Middle Eastern–looking West End club offers a "wide open" layout with "plenty of room to dance" during weekly theme nights such as '80s, Goth, music videos and the long-running 'Shut Up and Dance' with DJ Gregarious; its "friendly" staff, "great" drinks and cheap covers draw "diverse crowds" who appreciate its "variety."

	ATMOS.	DECOR	SERVICE	COST

The Fixin' To
24 | 21 | 22 | M

St. Johns | 8218 N. Lombard St. (Richmond Ave.) | 503-477-4995 |
www.thefixinto.com

"Interesting" cocktails and "good drink deals" are draws at this St.
Johns bar where patrons can play a "little shuffleboard", snack on
Southern-themed grub ("bring on the Frito pie") or just make some
"friendly conversation" with the staffers under antlers and antique
beer signs; all in all, locals deem it a "cool hang", adding the heated
patio is a further "plus."

4-4-2 Soccer Bar
24 | 21 | 22 | I

Hawthorne | 1739 SE Hawthorne Blvd. (18th Ave.) | 503-238-3693 |
www.442soccerbar.com

It's "soccer nirvana" at this "international" Hawthorne sports
pub where games from "all over the world" are broadcast over-
head, and affordable, "authentic" Bosnian fare and 24-oz. mugs of
Czechvar sate a "noisy but well-behaved crowd" that knows to "call
servers over with a yellow or red card"; all the "jerseys and scarves"
on the wall complete the "feel-like-you're-in-Europe" vibe – it's a
"must" for any fan.

Fox & Hounds
23 | 21 | 23 | M

Old Town-Chinatown | 217 NW Second Ave. (bet. Davis & Everett Sts.) |
503-243-5530

Known as a "comfortable neighborhood gay bar", this sparsely decorated yet "intimate" stop provides a welcome "relaxing, quiet" oasis amid the chaos of Old Town; "reasonable prices" and "nice"
bartenders also help to bring in an "older", "bear"-heavy clientele
for beers, billiards and fried bites.

Funhouse Lounge
23 | 22 | 22 | M

Central Eastside | 2432 SE 11th Ave. (bet. Caruthers & Division Sts.) |
503-841-6734 | www.funhouselounge.com

A circus theme ("check out the clown room") sets the tone at this
"spacious" Central Eastside bar and performance venue, which has
an "excellent" entertainment schedule that "embodies the personality of Portland" and includes "hilarious improv", karaoke, live music and trivia; drinks like canned beer are "cheap", and there's
slightly pricier cocktails as well – either work to wash down vittles
from the small menu.

Gold Dust Meridian
24 | 23 | 21 | M

Hawthorne | 3267 SE Hawthorne Blvd. (bet. 32nd Pl. & 33rd Ave.) |
503-239-1143 | www.golddustmeridian.com

This Hawthorne bar – a "groovy candlelit lounge" featuring a
pitched ceiling, loads of teak and booth seating in an immacu-
lately preserved midcentury building – is frequently "crowded"
thanks to its "creative drinkage", including "absolutely delicious"
champagne cocktails and "amazing" 'family bowl' drinks for two;
surveyors say service can be "hit-or-miss" but is generally
"nice", and the "great" happy-hour prices that last until 8 PM
daily are solid gold.

	ATMOS.	DECOR	SERVICE	COST

Grand Central Restaurant & Bowling Lounge

24 | 23 | 21 | M

Central Eastside | 808 SE Morrison St. (bet. 8th & 9th Aves.) | 503-236-2695 | www.thegrandcentralbowl.com

"A bowling alley for people who don't like bowling", this "upscale" Central Eastside complex pairs a dozen glitzy lanes with a large bar featuring "TVs galore" plus a mezzanine-level billiards lounge overlooking the pins; it's "a little expensive", but for those keeping score, a "solid" food menu and a "friendly" staff that's often "willing to be a part of your fun" adds up to an all-around "good place to take a date or the family."

Greater Trumps

▽ 26 | 23 | 23 | M

Hawthorne | McMenamins Bagdad Theater | 1520 SE 37th Ave. (bet. Clay St. & Hawthorne Blvd.) | 503-235-4530 | www.mcmenamins.com

"Sacred ground for Portland cigar smokers" is this Hawthorne stogies-and-port specialist inhabiting a "small" Victorian-looking cubby next to the Back Stage Bar in the McMenamins' Bagdad Theater; aficionados hail it as one of the last bastions in the city where one can both drink and smoke indoors – indeed, the "friendly" staff will even let you "bring your own" smokes (cigars only).

Groove Suite

▽ 24 | 21 | 21 | M

Old Town-Chinatown | 433 NW Fourth Ave. (Glisan St.) | 503-227-5494 | www.groovesuite.net

Both literally and figuratively "underground", this "gem" of a dance club hides in a basement behind an inconspicuous door on the edge of Chinatown and hosts "killer house and electronic artists"; the "cool" mural-covered space is "not too stuffy" despite its subterranean location, and though drinks can be a bit "expensive", the cover is not.

Ground Kontrol

27 | 25 | 21 | I

Old Town-Chinatown | 511 NW Couch St. (bet. 5th & 6th Aves.) | 503-796-9364 | www.groundkontrol.com

It's a "retro gamer's heaven" at this "chaotic", "futuristic"-looking bi-level Old Town "barcade", voted Portland's No. 1 for Atmosphere in Nightlife thanks to a "fantastic collection of classic video games" and some of the "best maintained" pinball machines around that come outfitted with beer holders so you can "let out your drunken inner child"; bonus: there's also "food to soak up" the "cheap" suds, and twice-monthly free-play nights with a live DJ take it to the next level.

Gypsy

19 | 17 | 19 | I

Northwest Portland | 625 NW 21st Ave. (bet. Hoyt & Irving Sts.) | 503-796-1859 | www.gypsyrestaurantandlounge.com

"Drunken warblers" and "fishbowls of liquor" are standard fare at this "divey" NW Portland bar known for its karaoke, "big strong drinks", pinball and pool; for those into the "meat-market" scene, the "ok" fried food and "lackadaisical" service aren't a concern once the "girls gone wild" vibe kicks in late nights.

𝗡𝗘𝗪 Hale Pele
`- | - | - | M`

Irvington | 2733 NE Broadway (27th Ave.) | 503-427-8454 |
www.halepele.com

Formerly Thatch Tiki Bar, this Irvington cocktail lounge reopened
under the ownership of Blair Reynolds, a man so obsessed with
tiki culture that he started his own line of syrups for tropical
drinks, which are employed in the slightly pricey but exquisitely
prepared concoctions like the 151 Swizzle, mai tai and zombie; it's
decorated in bamboo and palm fronds with a clutter of Reynolds'
personal collection of Polynesian kitsch, and come nightfall the
bar's booths fill with Hawaiian-shirted customers perusing a short
menu of themed grub.

Harvey's Comedy Club
`23 | 19 | 20 | M`

Old Town-Chinatown | 436 NW Sixth Ave. (Glisan St.) | 503-241-0338 |
www.harveyscomedyclub.com

Portland's oldest and, until recently, only stand-up venue, this Old
Town stalwart features a lineup of "hilarious" "local and nationally
known talent"; the usual comedy club stereotypes of "expensive"
food, sometimes "slow" servers and "too close" seating apply, but
it's "great for a de-stressing night out" when you want "funny jokes
rather than a big name."

Hawthorne Hophouse
`23 | 22 | 24 | M`

Hawthorne | 4111 SE Hawthorne Blvd. (41st Ave.) |
503-477-9619

Fifteenth Avenue Hophouse

Irvington | 1517 NE Brazee St. (bet. 15th & 16th Aves.) |
971-266-8392
www.oregonhophouse.com

These nearly identical "hopshead havens" in Hawthorne and
Irvington feature "fantastic, always changing" taps of NW craft
brews "that can't be found at every Portland" beer stop, and what's
more, the prices are "reasonable"; topping off its charms, the staff
is "nice", and if the simple decor is a "bit out of the box", folks raise
a toast to its "low-key atmosphere."

Hawthorne Theatre
`23 | 20 | 21 | I`

Hawthorne | 1507 SE Hawthorne Blvd. (39th Ave.) | 503-233-7100 |
www.hawthornetheater.com

As one of Portland's few all-ages music venues, this "vintage"
vaudeville theater with an "upgraded" sound system in Hawthorne
presents intimate, often "affordable", concerts by "sick bands",
mostly metal and hardcore acts; the adults-only lounge upstairs offers karaoke, poker, comedy and burlesque to a much older crowd.

Helium Comedy Club
`24 | 21 | 21 | M`

Central Eastside | 1510 SE Ninth Ave. (bet. Clay St. & Hawthorne Blvd.) |
888-643-8669 | www.heliumcomedy.com

"Laugh so hard it hurts" at this 275-seat, golden yellow–hued Central
Eastside comedy club that's an offshoot of a well-known Philadelphia
venue, allowing management to book "top names" as well as "up-

and-comers that will eventually be A-listers"; despite the "expensive" food, two-item minimum and scattered service complaints, fans say it "classes up" the city's yuk scene.

Holocene

22 | 20 | 20 | M

Central Eastside | 1001 SE Morrison St. (10th Ave.) | 503-239-7639 | www.holocene.org

This "popular" Central Eastside "hipster meat market" with a "cool", airy "warehouse feel" pulls a "younger crowd" with its "eclectic, electric and booty-shaking" DJs and "cutting-edge" live bands; the "friendly" bartenders mostly manage to "keep on top of the crowds", but those seeking a more "chill" experience head to the lower lounge.

Hop & Vine

24 | 23 | 23 | M

Overlook | 1914 N. Killingsworth St. (bet. Concord & Denver Aves.) | 503-954-3322 | www.thehopandvine.com

There's more attention paid to hops than vines but there's an "awesome" selection of both at this "busy" Overlook watering hole; the "wonderful staff" is always ready with a recommendation to sip in its "dark" interior, enormous backyard garden or off-site, since it doubles as a to-go shop.

Hop Haven Beer Bar & Bottle Shop

22 | 20 | 25 | I

Irvington | 2130 NE Broadway (bet. 21st & 22nd Aves.) | 503-287-0244

The "sports focus" at this "laid-back" Irvington beer bar and bottle shop combo is a welcome curveball for the genre, allowing customers to watch several games on TV while they nurse "reasonably" priced brews from a "nice selection" of bottles and "limited" but rotating taps; the "beautiful cast" of bartenders have their own fan followings, as does Thursday night trivia, an "awesome" "pop-culture showdown."

Horse Brass Pub

25 | 23 | 21 | M

Belmont | 4534 SE Belmont St. (bet. 45th & 47th Aves.) | 503-232-2202 | www.horsebrass.com

"Dark" and woody, this Belmont pub decorated with "vintage breweriana" helped "pioneer the craft beer movement" in Oregon and remains a "beer pilgrimage shrine" with its "fabulous" suds, including cask-conditioned varieties, dispensed by "knowledgeable" bartenders from a forest of 59 tap handles; a "diverse mix of people, young and old, hip and non-hip", also toasts the "British vibe" of its darts, televised sports matches and food menu.

NEW Interurban

25 | 24 | 24 | M

Mississippi | 4057 N. Mississippi Ave. (bet. Mason & Shaver Sts.) | 503-284-6669 | www.interurbanpdx.com

It's the "Wild West meets Mississippi Avenue" at this raucous "modern-day saloon" from Dan Hart (Prost) that inhabits both floors of an old brick building; a stuffed antelope watches over the bar where "excellent", "well-informed" bartenders mix "outstanding" midpriced concoctions, including Manhattans in a sharing-sized bottle, but they never forget its roots as a "real whiskey bar."

	ATMOS.	DECOR	SERVICE	COST

Jimmy Mak's

| 26 | 23 | 23 | M |

Pearl District | 221 NW 10th Ave. (bet. Davis & Everrett Sts.) | 503-295-6542 | www.jimmymaks.com

"The sound is great" and "so is the pour" at this "relaxing" Pearl District jazz club and Greek restaurant, where the bands play within arm's length of the tables, "friendly, smiley" waiters work the "busy" crowds and portraits of music icons hang on the walls; regular gigs by dynamite drummer Mel Brown and touring national and international acts make it a must for "anyone even remotely interested in jazz."

NEW Jones

| - | - | - | M |

Old Town-Chinatown | 107 NW Couch St. (bet. 1st & 2nd Aves.) | 971-271-7178 | www.jonesbarportland.com

From the owner of the Boiler Room comes this fluorescent-hued '80s- and '90s-themed dance club in Old Town decked out with disco balls, cassette tapes and an enormous Lite-Brite wall; drinks are reasonably priced, and though the crowd is mixed, some of the revelers shaking side-ponytails to Madonna remixes may not remember when *Like a Prayer* hit double platinum.

Journeys

| 26 | 23 | 24 | M |

Multnomah Village | 7771 SW Capitol Hwy. (bet. 34th & 35th Ave.) | 503-929-0229 | www.journeyspdx.com

A "delightful" "little joint" in Multnomah Village, this "cozy" wine/beer bar is set in the ground floor of a converted bungalow and has the bonus of "nice", "dog-friendly" lawn seating; with a staff that "makes you feel like family" and "respectable" rotating tap selections and "great" wine offerings, it's the "kind of place to visit again and again."

Kask

| 26 | 26 | 28 | E |

West End | 527 SW 12th Ave. (bet. Glisan & Hoyt Sts.) | 503-241-7163 | www.grunerpdx.com

Rated No. 1 for Decor among Portland nightspots, this "small, crowded" West End cocktail bar, cousin of adjacent "alpine" restaurant Grüner, maintains a "calm", earthy atmosphere with a live-edge wooden bar thronged with "hip", "urban thirtysomething Portlanders"; they come for the small plates and "expensive but delicious" drinks that are "finely crafted" ("smashed ice, artisanal bitters") by "seasoned", "attentive" bartenders who earn the top Service slot and are "not too bad to look at either."

Kelly's Olympian

| 23 | 22 | 20 | I |

Downtown | 426 SW Washington St. (bet. 4th & 5th Aves.) | 503-228-3669 | www.kellysolympian.com

"Go for the vintage motorcycles" hanging from the ceiling, stay for the "cheap" drinks and live rock 'n' roll at this "ultimate dive" operating Downtown since 1902; a "mix of punks, business types and street urchins" gathers for Pabst and "strong" pours of Jack Daniels served by "hot, sassy" bartenders, while local acts tear it up in the adjacent performance space.

LaurelThirst Public House
`23` `20` `23` `I`

Kerns | 2958 NE Glisan St. (30th Ave.) | 503-232-1504 | www.laurelthirst.com

"The *Miss Congeniality* of Portland bars", this "funky", "cozy" Kerns pub may not be much to look at, but "it's a dear local favorite" with nightly live music that varies from acid-bluegrass to gypsy-swing; the "nice selection of craft beers" is reasonably priced, and it's "always packed to the rafters" by the time the entertainment hits the stage.

Laurelwood Public House & Brewery
`22` `20` `23` `M`

Hollywood | 5115 NE Sandy Blvd. (bet. 51st & 52nd Aves.) | 503-282-0622
NEW Sellwood | 6716 SE Milwaukie Ave. (bet. Bybee Blvd. & Claybourne St.) | 503-894-8267
www.laurelwoodbrewpub.com

A Hollywood fixture, this stop is known for its "great self-brewed beers" at "ok prices" and a "parent's dream come true" of a kids' play area, and its newer Sellwood branch mimics much of that experience; the staff "goes out of its way to treat you right", and the child-free get the run of the seasonal rooftop deck at the Sandy Boulevard locale.

Leisure Public House
`24` `24` `24` `M`

St. Johns | 8002 N. Lombard St. (Mohawk Ave.) | 503-289-7606 | www.leisurepublichouse.com

Though the staffers are quite "friendly" at this "easygoing", "well-priced" St. Johns "hangout", they can't compare to the "cute", beloved pub cat, Masha; add in a "curvy" bamboo bar and "big open" patio with a heated, covered section plus bocce and Ping-Pong, and it works for a "killer date" or just a place to "meet your buddies for a PBR."

The Liberty Glass
`25` `24` `22` `M`

Mississippi | 938 N. Cook St. (Mississippi Ave.) | 503-517-9931
Set in a converted pink house, this "neighborhoody" Mississippi hang is a "welcome escape" that's often "full of locals" imbibing "stiff" mid-priced drinks delivered by a "fast and friendly" crew; the "comfortable" surrounds feature "charming, homey" touches like water served in camping cups and a claw-foot tub in the upstairs bathroom, and the "chill" atmosphere makes it "easy to meet people and chat."

Lion's Eye
`▽ 24` `22` `23` `I`

82nd Avenue | 5919 SE 82nd Ave. (Woodstock Blvd.) | 503-774-1468
Fans "cannot say enough" about this "neighborhood" tavern on 82nd Avenue with "super-friendly" bartenders that's "unlike anything else in an area" known for its "sleazy" bars; there's plenty of booth and stool seating in the basic interior that's enlivened by "funky artwork", but patrons mostly have their eye on the affordable "fantastic beers on tap", pool tables and a "patio that rules" in summer.

Local Lounge
`22` `21` `24` `M`

King | 3536 NE Martin Luther King Jr. Blvd. (bet. Beech & Fremont Sts.) | 503-282-1833 | www.local-lounge.com
This "awesome gay hangout" in King is also "breeder-friendly" and boasts a "great happy hour" presided over by a "nice" staff with

plenty of bar and table seating; there's usually a weekend DJ and weeknights often have a theme, but mostly it's just a "place to hang with the local" LGBT crowd.

The Lovecraft

23 | 25 | 20 | M

Central Eastside | 421 SE Grand Ave. (bet. Oak & Stark Sts.) | 971-270-7760 | www.thelovecraftbar.com

"Creepy" and "weird", this "eclectic", "horror"-themed Eastside Industrial haunt (named in honor of weird fiction author H.P. Lovecraft) draws an "interesting crowd" with its "dark", "spooky" stylings (think "cthulhu tentacles and pentagrams" and there's a "pet scorpion on the bar") and variety of entertainment, including movies, live music and burlesque; the moderate prices don't scare most, and even if it's not everyone's "scene", it's still a "great place to meet other creatures of the night."

Lucky Devil Lounge

23 | 21 | 23 | I

Brooklyn | 633 SE Powell Blvd. (bet. Grand & 7th Aves.) | 503-206-7350 | www.luckydevillounge.com

An "entertaining and classy" strip club (there's red velvet wallpaper), this Brooklyn establishment at the foot of the Ross Island Bridge is known almost as much for its poker games, "excellent" drink prices, "lovely" staff and heated patio as for its "beautiful" dancers; still, the "excellent performers" keep the main focus on them, using the monkey bars built into the ceiling above the stage "to their advantage."

Mary's Club

16 | 15 | 19 | I

Downtown | 129 SW Broadway (bet. Ankeny & Burnside Sts.) | 503-227-3023 | www.marysclub.com

The city's oldest and most storied strip club, this Downtown family-owned "landmark" once had Courtney Love on its "tiny" stage, and today's dancers "seem to enjoy themselves"; if it's "dark" and "trashy" it's also "unabashedly real", which is "why people go", plus there are "cheap" drinks and a mural of Mt. Fuji painted by cult artist Montyne.

The Matador

23 | 22 | 21 | I

Northwest Portland | 1967 W. Burnside St. (Trinity Pl.) | 503-222-5822 | www.thematadorbar.com

Fans have "never had a bad time" at this "dark" NW Portland "dive bar" frequented by a "wide variety of patrons", including "punks, hipsters and college kids" all enjoying the "cheap drinks", plus "pool, a photo booth and other diversions"; staffers "treat their regulars well (and everyone else too)", and though it can get "packed", it remains a "neighborhood attraction."

Mississippi Studios

25 | 22 | 22 | M

Mississippi | 3939 N. Mississippi Ave. (bet. Failing & Shaver Sts.) | 503-288-3895 | www.mississippistudios.com

"Good music at a reasonable price" might as well be the motto of this "intimate" Mississippi "listening room", known for its "wide variety" of local and touring artists flattered by the club's "very good sound" system; plenty of seating and "impressively quick" service have aficionados declaring it "all around fab"; P.S. Bar Bar next door has a "great" patio and "tasty" burgers.

Moloko

| 24 | 20 | 20 | M |

Mississippi | 3967 N. Mississippi Ave. (Shaver St.) | 503-288-6272 | www.molokopdx.com

Though a bit "hard to find", this Mississippi storefront marked only with whimsical neon symbols hides a "chill" lounge where a "diverse" crowd relaxes at mod-white tables, gazes at the curvy bar's "fantastic" saltwater fish tanks or hangs on the "awesome" covered patio; topping off the experience are "tasty" drinks made by "friendly" mixologists from "house-infused liquors."

Moon & Sixpence British Pub

| 25 | 22 | 22 | I |

Hollywood | 2014 NE 42nd Ave. (bet. Sandy Blvd. & Tillamook St.) | 503-288-7802

"Exactly what you'd want" in an English pub, this inexpensive Hollywood tavern attracts locals for "proper" pints of cask-conditioned ales, "solid" grub and frequent live Celtic music; adding to the "fun", there's "sweet beer-garden action" on the back patio and a separate room for darts "where no one will see you completely miss the board."

Night Light Lounge

| 24 | 22 | 23 | M |

Clinton | 2100 SE Clinton St. (21st Ave.) | 503-731-6500 | www.nightlightlounge.net

"Watch the parade of cyclists and pedestrians" from the indoor banquettes that line the windows or sidewalk tables of this "comfortable" Clinton "watering hole" with a partially covered heated patio and the added distraction of board games; the "high-quality" staff "treats all with respect", the "interesting food and drink choices" are moderately priced and there's a "fine happy hour."

NEW NWIPA

| - | - | - | I |

Foster-Powell | 6350 SE Foster Rd. (65th Ave.) | 971-279-5876 | www.nwipapdx.com

This classy beer bar and bottle shop in up-and-coming Foster-Powell specializes in its namesake India pale ales and offers hops-heavy brews from four taps and three fridge cases, often at below supermarket prices; the sunny space has greater culinary ambitions than most alehouses, serving NW mussels and artisan charcuterie from behind its enormous antique bar.

Olive or Twist

| 25 | 24 | 24 | M |

Pearl District | 925 NW 11th Ave. (bet. Johnson & Lovejoy Sts.) | 503-546-2900 | www.oliveortwistmartinibar.com

"A *Cheers* version of a martini bar", this Pearl District lounge is helmed by a "really nice and inviting" crew yet it's also "dripping with class" in its sleek banquettes, fresh flowers and lots of art; for serious 'tini tipplers, it's all about the "wonderful" cocktails that are moderately priced and made with such "skill" you'll "feel rich sitting there."

	ATMOS.	DECOR	SERVICE	COST

On Deck Sports Bar
22 | 20 | 19 | M

Pearl District | 910 NW 14th Ave. (bet. Kearney & Lovejoy Sts.) | 503-227-7020 | www.ondecksportsbar.com

The "giant" rooftop deck at this Pearl District sports bar offers "stunning" views of the city, but for views of the game, fans must head inside the "smooth", "upscale" space where there's an "incredible" number of screens; a few deride it as "fratish" with "hit-or-miss" service and "typical" grub, but most say it's a fine "hangout."

Pints
▽ 23 | 19 | 22 | I

Old Town-Chinatown | 412 NW Fifth Ave. (bet. Flanders & Gilson Sts.) | 503-564-2739 | www.pintsbrewing.com

This "small" Old Town brewpub pours seven local and English-style ales from its own small-batch facility from 11:30 AM onward (3 PM Saturday) in stylish brick-walled environs, while proffering coffee and lattes weekday mornings; the service is "friendly", prices are reasonable and there's live music most weekend nights.

Pope House Bourbon Lounge
26 | 26 | 24 | M

Northwest Portland | 2075 NW Glisan St. (bet. 20th & 21st Aves.) | 503-222-1056 | www.popehouselounge.com

"Bourbons upon bourbons" fill the shelves of this "cozy" Kentucky-themed bar in a "cute" NW Portland Victorian house, but the "wonderful" selection of "reasonably priced" whiskey is only part of the draw; added attractions are the Southern-leaning food menu and "innovative" in-house ice cream served by "hilarious", "personable" servers.

Portland U-Brew & Pub
23 | 21 | 24 | M

Sellwood | 6237 SE Milwaukie Ave. (Tolman St.) | 503-943-2727 | www.portlandubrewandpub.com

"Make your beer and reap the benefits" at this Sellwood stop with separate brewpub and brewing supply areas that are a "home away from home" for the DIY crowd (peek down through the open floor to gander at the brewing area); service from the staff is "excellent" whether it's providing home-brewers with ingredients and equipment or pouring a pint at the bar.

Prost!
26 | 24 | 24 | I

Mississippi | 4237 N. Mississippi Ave. (Skidmore St.) | 503-954-2674 | www.prostportland.com

"Step into Deutschland" at this Mississippi bier bar that goes "all out for authenticity" with an affordable, "top-notch" selection of hard-to-find German brews served in appropriate, eclectic glassware; the "impeccable, cheerful" staff also delivers brats and the like, either inside the warm space or on the "phenomenal" patio; P.S. it's ok to bring in food from the adjacent carts.

Raccoon Lodge
21 | 20 | 21 | M

Raleigh Hills | 7424 SW Beaverton-Hillsdale Hwy. (bet. Scholls Ferry Rd. & 76th Ave.) | 503-296-0110 | www.raclodge.com

This "nifty little" pub in Raleigh Hills offers a family-friendly "modern hunting lodge" vibe upstairs, complete with log walls and a fireplace, and a TV-heavy sports lounge in the basement; the "decent pub food" and plenty of Cascade Brewing Barrel House's own "experimental" brews (a sister company) complete the picture.

Rainbow Room
26 | 23 | 22 | M

Old Town-Chinatown | 219 NW Davis St. (bet. 2nd & 3rd Aves.) | 503-248-9135 | www.ccslaughterspdx.com

This "chill" Old Town lounge with a back-lit bar is a "great escape" from the noise and crowds of its next-door partner, gay dance club C.C. Slaughters; "great drinks" at moderate prices and an atmosphere that's conducive to getting "to know the staff and the locals" please those looking for a "LGBT-friendly" hangout.

Red Fox
25 | 23 | 23 | I

Humboldt | 5128 N. Albina Ave. (Sumner St.) | 503-282-2934 | www.redfoxpdx.com

"Grab a table outside" and "the night is complete" say fans of this "dark and cozy" Humboldt "hangout" tucked behind a corner grocery; "cheap drinks" and solid service enhance the appeal, and locals like that it's often "quiet enough" to "have a conversation with friends."

Rontoms
24 | 23 | 18 | M

E. Burnside | 600 E. Burnside St. (6th Ave.) | 503-236-4536 | www.rontoms.net

The "huge" back patio complete with a "sweet" Ping-Pong table "can't be beat" at this East Burnside "hangout", though the "cozy", fireplace-enhanced inside draws "lots of hipsters" and assorted other "characters" too; "friendly" service can be "slow" when "crowded", but prices are "reasonable" and on Sunday nights "legit local bands" play.

Rose & Thistle Public House
23 | 22 | 23 | M

Irvington | 2314 NE Broadway (bet. 22nd & 24th Aves.) | 503-287-8582

A "Portland classic", this longtime "English-style pub" in Irvington appeals with a "great beer selection", "friendly" service and grub that expats swear "reminds of home"; add in affordable prices and a "comfortable" patio and fans say it "has everything."

Roseland ⊘
21 | 17 | 18 | M

Old Town-Chinatown | 8 NW Sixth Ave. (Burnside St.) | 971-230-0033 | www.roselandpdx.com

"Big show or small show" this "funky" Old Town concert venue "works" say music lovers cheering the "pretty good acoustics", "reasonable" prices and "cozy" space that affords a "good full-house feel"; still, others bemoan "crowded" conditions and warn that "limited" seats (in the 21-plus upstairs balcony only) mean you should "plan on standing unless you arrive early"; P.S. it's cash-only on drinks and tickets, although food can go on credit.

Rum Club
24 | 23 | 23 | M

Central Eastside | 720 SE Sandy Blvd. (bet. Stark & Washington Sts.) | 503-467-2469 | www.rumclubpdx.com

"Mixology is spoken" at this Central Eastside lounge behind Beaker & Flask where bartenders pour "delicious" "cutting-edge" cocktails, many of which feature rum, of course; the "small" space is enhanced by "friendly" staffers who willingly "guide you through" all the choices, and if "drinks aren't cheap", they "are a good value."

Saraveza
24 | 23 | 26 | I

Humboldt | 1004 N. Killingsworth St. (Michigan Ave.) | 503-206-4252 | www.saraveza.com

A vintage "Midwestern vibe" and "collection of breweriana" provides the backdrop for a "huge" selection of the "latest and greatest" beers at this "Wisconsin-themed" Humboldt bar and bottle shop; the "knowledgeable staff" will help "if you can't decide" what to pick, prices are affordable and sports fans keep it especially "busy on football Sundays" when it's "home central for Packers fans."

NEW Sauvage
- | - | - | M

Central Eastside | 537 SE Ash St. (6th Ave.) | 503-807-5565 | www.sauvagepdx.com

Hidden behind an unmarked Central Eastside door, this 'enopub' dotted with glass carboy light fixtures occupies a subway-tiled corner of the Fausse Piste winery and gets a touch of polish with salvaged-wood tables amid stacked oak barrels; it offers affordably priced wines (its own, plus local and international selections) by the glass and bottle, plus Spanish- and French-influenced small plates based on local ingredients.

Scandals
24 | 22 | 23 | I

West End | 1125 SW Stark St. (bet. 11th & 12th Sts.) | 503-227-5887 | www.scandalspdx.com

This "low-key" gay "hideaway" draws a "friendly crowd" of "all ages" to the heart of Downtown's West End to play billiards and darts or just "hang out" in the "relaxed" surrounds; "moderate" prices and "quick" service are other pluses, and regulars "love" the patio seating.

Secret Society
25 | 25 | 21 | M

Boise-Eliot | 116 NE Russell St. (Rodney Ave.) | 503-493-3600 | www.secretsociety.net

Housed in a century-old former Masonic lodge, this "cozy" Boise-Eliot "hideaway" will have you feeling "like a classy dame in some hip old movie" with its "well-made" "throwback cocktails" and "old-school" vibe; "tiny" digs mean it can "fill up quickly", but prices are moderate and it still works for a "romantic date"; P.S. the attached ballroom hosts live music.

Shanghai Tunnel
26 | 24 | 22 | M

Downtown | 211 SW Ankeny St. (2nd Ave.) | 503-220-4001

"Don't let the [small] bar in the entrance fool you" say enthusiasts who spill that the "real event is down the secret stairway in the back" leading to an "awesome" "dark, dank" basement (part of the city's existing Shanghai Tunnel system) that's decorated with paper lanterns and a samurai mural; "cheap drinks", "lots of pinball" and "great beer on tap" complement bartenders who are "funny and on top of their game even on a busy night."

Side Street Tavern

24 | 20 | 24 | I

Belmont | 828 SE 34th Ave. (bet. Belmont & Morrison Sts.) | 503-236-7999 | www.sidestreetpdx.com

A "sweet little joint" on a quiet Belmont corner, this bar caters to an "interesting mix of people" that appreciates the "honest drinks", like cocktails featuring "fresh-squeezed juices" and playful Pabst-centered offerings with garnishes ranging from orange slices to fake mustaches, all at affordable prices; "friendly staffers", a "low-key" vibe and a "great jukebox" further afford it "favorite" status.

Silverado ⊅

22 | 18 | 21 | M

Downtown | 318 SW Third Ave. (bet. Oak & Stark Sts.) | 503-224-4493 | www.silveradopdx.com

Some of the "hottest dancers in town" are the "main draw" at this "welcoming" gay club "meets strip joint" Downtown where the "thumpin' music" helps fuel a "high-energy vibe" that softens somewhat in the lounge area; either way, the drinks are "stiff" and the prices moderate, so don't be surprised when it's "crowded"; P.S. it's cash-only but there are ATMs.

Sloan's Tavern

∇ 23 | 18 | 23 | I

Boise-Eliot | 36 N. Russell St. (Williams Ave.) | 503-287-2262

A "nice little hangout", this "divey" Boise-Eliot gay bar distinguishes itself with its "friendly" staff, "neighborhood" vibe – and, of course, the semi truck "built into the wall"; a jukebox topped with an animated jazz octet furthers the appeal as do "cheap drinks" and "sports on TV."

Slow Bar

23 | 21 | 23 | M

Central Eastside | 533 SE Grand Ave. (Washington St.) | 503-230-7767 | www.slowbar.net

This "mellow" Central Eastside bar draws raves for its "fabulous" half-pound burger topped with onion rings, especially for a "late-night" nosh; its large red booths mean there's lots of room for groups, and its "moderately priced" drinks (cocktails, beer, wine) please, but it's the "big boy" patties that steal the show.

Someday Lounge

24 | 21 | 21 | I

Old Town-Chinatown | 125 NW Fifth Ave. (bet. Couch & Davis Sts.) | 503-248-1030 | www.somedaylounge.com

"Cool" and "laid-back", this Old Town venue plays host to an "eclectic" mix of entertainment, from jazz and hip-hop artists to DJs, "arty events" and more in rough-hewn environs with a "wooded look"; there's also a "comfortable" upstairs lounge, service is "friendly" and best of all, the drinks and veggie-focused eats "won't break the bank."

NEW Southeast Wine Collective

– | – | – | M

Division | 2425 SE 35th Pl. (Division St.) | 503-208-2061 | www.sewinecollective.com

Four local winemakers have set up shop in this Division winery and pour their wares until 10 PM (7 PM Sunday) at the tasting bar with house vintages on tap, beer and an extensive selection by the glass from producers that inspire the collective; it's creatively decked out in bottles and barrel staves, and there's cheese and charcuterie to cleanse the palate in between.

Spirit of 77
23 | 22 | 17 | M

Lloyd | 500 NE Martin Luther King Jr. Blvd. (bet. Hoyt St. & Lloyd Blvd.) | 503-232-9977 | www.spiritof77bar.com

"A Blazers bar through and through", this "industrial-sized" Lloyd district tavern is a tribute to the team's 1977 NBA championship, and with "loads of seating", "decent prices" and a "huge" projection screen it's "great for watching any major game"; when it's "packed wall to wall", "friendly" service can be "slow", but the "free arcade basketball" and pinball still mean "you'll stay much later than you initially planned."

Star Theater
23 | 22 | 20 | M

Old Town-Chinatown | 13 NW Sixth Ave. (bet. Burnside & Couch Sts.) | 503-248-4700 | www.startheaterportland.com

Once a "historic theater", this Old Town longtimer has been renovated into an "intimate" music and events venue with a "high-quality" sound system, "smallish stage" and "plush" surrounds complete with an "upstairs hidden balcony" and "huge" fire pit-enhanced patio; "fast" bartenders "know how to pour a drink", and prices are moderate.

Sweet Hereafter
24 | 24 | 18 | M

Belmont | 3326 SE Belmont St. (bet. 33rd & 34th Aves.) | no phone

"Delicious drinks" are complemented by "tasty" vegan bites at this midpriced Belmont hang; "servers who know what they're doing" contribute to a "pretty rad atmosphere" in the oft "busy" surrounds, and there's also a "spacious patio."

Swift Lounge
23 | 20 | 21 | M

Irvington | 1932 NE Broadway (bet. 19th & 21st Aves.) | 503-288-3333 | www.swift-lounge.com

"Hipsters" in the mood for some "awesome mason jar drinks" pile into this midpriced Irvington bar bolstered by a "cool" vibe; the space is "small", so it "can get pretty packed", and it might "take a while to get" your order, but the bartenders "work hard", and "you can taste the difference."

Teardrop Cocktail Lounge
24 | 24 | 22 | E

Pearl District | 1015 NW Everett St. (bet. 10th & 11th Aves.) | 503-445-8109 | www.teardroplounge.com

An "epicenter for classic cocktails", this "buzzing" Pearl District lounge is tended by "charming, knowledgeable" bartenders who "lovingly" craft "serious" drinks featuring an array of housemade ingredients, including an "impressive selection" of bitters, tinctures and its own tonic; the "small", "sleek" space features a curved bar, and though it's "kinda pricey", many find it "well worth" the cost, especially "if you're trying to impress someone."

Thirsty Lion Pub & Grill

22 | 21 | 20 | M

Downtown | 71 SW Second Ave. (Ash St.) | 503-222-2155
Tigard | 10205 SW Washington Square Rd. (Greenburg Rd.) |
503-352-4030
www.thirstylionpub.com

"British pub meets sports bar" at this "large" Downtown tavern (with sibs in Tigard and Arizona) that offers "good beer and cocktail selections" preferred by a "friendly" crew; there are "lots of TVs" for watching the game and prices are "reasonable", so even if a few sniff it's "nothing exceptional", it still works as a "place to hang out with friends" and can get "packed" on weekends.

Tony Starlight's Supperclub & Lounge

26 | 24 | 24 | M

Hollywood | 3728 NE Sandy Blvd. (37th Ave.) | 503-517-8584 |
www.tonystarlight.com

"Put on some red lipstick and take a trip back to the days of Sinatra" at this "nostalgic" Hollywood supper club where you can take in a "variety" of "entertaining" shows, including performances from the namesake owner that will help you "connect with your inner Rat Pack"; cover charges vary, but service is "attentive" and the drinks solid, so fans say it all adds up to a "one-of-a-kind experience."

Tugboat Brewing Company

24 | 21 | 22 | I

Downtown | 711 SW Ankeny St. (B'way) | 503-226-2508 |
www.d2m.com

One of the more "divey microbreweries" in Portland, this "tiny" Downtown pub brews its own beer and serves it up alongside other international selections in a "warm", "cozy" space with "walls of old books and board games" that help lend a "laid-back" "living room"–like vibe; "personable" bartenders and "reasonable prices" further explain why fans "will be back."

Upright Brewing ⌷

24 | 21 | 23 | I

Boise-Eliot | Leftbank | 240 N. Broadway (Weidler St.) | 503-735-5337 |
www.uprightbrewing.com

Those who find their way through the "downstairs labyrinth" of Boise-Eliot's Leftbank building to this microbrewery tasting room are rewarded with "interesting" "Belgian-inflected beers" at "cheap" prices; the servers are often the brewers, and the scant seating is located "in the midst of it all" with "brewing equipment and aging beer in barrels" acting as the decor; P.S. no cards and it's open Friday–Sunday only.

Uptown Billiards Club

25 | 23 | 22 | E

Northwest Portland | 120 NW 23rd Ave. (bet. Burnside & Everett Sts.) |
503-226-6909 | www.uptownbilliards.com

"A legitimate pool house", this "classy" NW Portland destination hidden behind an unmarked door appeals with "high-quality tables" and a "swanky" setting complete with a burnished antique bar; "accommodating" staffers pour cocktails and "expertly selected" wines, and while it's not cheap, fans say it makes for a "memorable evening."

Valentines

23 | 22 | 22 | M

Old Town-Chinatown | 232 SW Ankeny St. (bet. 2nd & 3rd Aves.) |
503-248-1600 | www.valentinespdx.com

"Cozy" and "intimate", this "lovely little hipster bar" is a bohemian
enclave in a touristy part of Old Town with regular art shows and
"quality live music"; prices are generally "reasonable", and though it
can get "noisy and crowded" during performances, a "romantic" atmosphere reigns weeknights, when couples can canoodle at the
outdoor tables or in the "secluded space upstairs."

Vault Martini

24 | 24 | 21 | M

Pearl District | 226 NW 12th Ave. (bet. Davis & Everett Sts.) |
503-224-4909 | www.vault-martini.com

A "charmingly large cocktail menu", including a "plethora of fancy
martinis" and some "daring" choices, stars at this "small", "swanky"
Pearl District lounge with a "lively" nighttime scene and "straightforward" staff; it's a little "expensive", but "happy-hour prices are
great" – just be prepared for "limited" seating, especially on weekends.

Vie de Boheme

26 | 25 | 26 | M

Central Eastside | 1530 SE Seventh Ave. (Clay St.) | 503-360-1233 |
www.viedebohemepdx.com

Fans say this "classy" Central Eastside vino bar and winery is "a must
if you love good wine" thanks to a "great selection" of labels and
"snacky foods" in a "sprawling" space with "mismatched wooden tables and chairs"; the staff is "friendly" and "knowledgeable", prices
are moderate and there's often "fantastic" live music.

Voicebox Karaoke Lounge

25 | 23 | 23 | M

Northwest Portland | 2112 NW Hoyt St. (21st Ave.) | 503-303-8220 |
www.voiceboxpdx.com

You can "get your karaoke on with a group of friends" at this NW
Portland lounge with six "stylish" and "spacious" private rooms that
"erase a lot of the anxiety" while also "reducing the heckler count"
significantly; the "upbeat" staff dispenses midpriced drinks (you'll
"sound better by the glass"), and if you go just plan to "book in ad-
vance because weekend nights fill up fast."

Whiskey Bar

25 | 22 | 24 | I

Old Town-Chinatown | 31 NW First Ave. (bet. Ankeny & Burnside Sts.) |
503-227-0405 | www.whiskeybarpdx.com

"If you are into electronic dance music", this brick-heavy Old Town
club fits the bill, hosting DJs who pump beats through an "awesome
sound system" complemented by a "good amount of lights and lasers"; the staff is "quick" with "strong" drinks, and the "outdoor smok-
ing area is a perfect setup for getting to know friends and fresh air."

🆕 The Whiskey Room

25 | 24 | 24 | M

Alberta | The Modern Man Barber Shop | 5018 NE 22nd Ave.
(Alberta St.) | 503-284-6008 | www.themodernmanpdx.com

It's all about "whiskey, whiskey, whiskey" at this Alberta bar on the
second floor of The Modern Man Barber Shop, where drinkers can

sample "top-shelf" brown booze in a small, cozy space decorated with pelts, six-shooters and deer heads; it's not cheap, but a projection screen for Timbers' games (and more) adds appeal, and customers from downstairs receive a complimentary drink.

Whiskey Soda Lounge

| 23 | 21 | 22 | M |

Division | 3131 SE Division St. (32nd Ave.) | 503-232-0102 | www.whiskeysodalounge.com

Most consider this lounge a "saner alternative" to the "nutty-long lines" at its famous Division neighbor and sib Pok Pok, as it allows customers to try menu "essentials" alongside "inventive cocktails" made by bartenders who take their work "seriously"; colorful vinyl tablecloths and "Thai pop music" create a "fun atmosphere" that's "crowded and happening on the weekends."

Widmer Brothers Gasthaus Pub

| 24 | 23 | 24 | M |

Boise-Eliot | 955 N. Russell St. (Interstate Ave.) | 503-281-3333 | www.widmerbrothers.com

A "Portland institution", this Boise-Eliot brewery attracts hopsheads who go to sample the "tasty" brews (the "Widmer seasonal list is a wonder to behold"), even if it's in an environment that feels a touch "corporate"; a "friendly, knowledgeable" staff also turns out pub fare that's "better than your average", which would explain why you see "lots of regulars at the bar every night with a beer and a burger."

Wonder Ballroom

| 25 | 21 | 21 | I |

Boise-Eliot | 128 NE Russell St. (Rodney Ave.) | 503-284-8686 | www.wonderballroom.com

Housed in a near century-old historic building, this Boise-Eliot venue is a "favorite for local concerts" say fans praising its "large" space with a "nice open layout" and "reasonable ticket prices"; there's also a balcony with "limited seating" and a "cool" downstairs lounge where patrons can choose from a small food menu that's available starting at 5 PM (open to day-of ticketed guests only).

SHOPPING

Portland Favorites

This list is plotted on the map at the back of this book.

1 Made In Oregon
2 Nike
3 Columbia Sportswear
4 Kitchen Kaboodle
5 A Children's Place
6 Backyard Bird Shop
7 Fabric Depot
8 Dennis' 7 Dees
9 Mac Store
10 Bike Gallery

TOP QUALITY

APPAREL

29 Langlitz Leathers
28 Louis Vuitton
　 Pendleton
27 Upper Playground
26 Mario's

BEAUTY & GROOMING

27 Kiehl's
　 Blush
26 L'Occitane
　 M.A.C.
25 Sephora

FURNITURE & HOME

29 Canoe
27 Hive
　 Joinery
　 Pendleton Home
25 Design Within Reach

GARDEN

28 Urban Farm
　 Portland Nursery

27 Dennis' 7 Dees
　 Garden Fever!
26 Backyard Bird Shop

GIFTS & NOVELTIES

27 Real Mother Goose
　 Sleighbells
26 Made In Oregon
24 Ink & Peat
　 OSU Beaver Store

SHOES

28 John Fluevog
27 Portland Running Co.
　 Nike
26 Keen Garage
25 Imelda's & Louie's

SPORTING GOODS

27 River City
　 Bikeworks
26 REI
　 Bike Gallery
　 Next Adventure

ONLY IN PORTLAND

Beam & Anchor
Canoe
Cargo
City Liquidators
Kitchen Kaboodle

Lizard Lounge
OMSI Science Store
Real Mother Goose
Rejuvenation
Schoolhouse Electric

GOOD VALUES

Artemisia Garden
Betsy & Iya
Bikeworks
Fabric Depot
Free Geek

Lippman Co.
Next Adventure
ReBuilding Center
Rerun
W.C. Winks Hardware

Excludes places with low votes

Shopping: Merchandise

Includes store names, locations and Quality ratings. These lists include low vote places that do not qualify for top lists.

ACCESSORIES

(See also Department Stores)

NEW TUMI	Downtown	28
Louis Vuitton	Downtown	28
Queen Bee	Boise-Eliot	28
EYES! On Broadway	Irvington	27
Sock Dreams	Sellwood	27
Ellington	NW Portland	26
Coach	multi.	26
Portland Luggage	multi.	25
Reynolds Optical	multi.	25
Lille	multi.	24
WatchWorks	Downtown	24

ANTIQUES/ FLEA MARKETS

Lounge Lizard	Hawthorne	24
I Heart Retro	Hollywood	23
Sellwood Antique	Sellwood	22
Really Good Stuff	Hawthorne	21

APPAREL

(See also Department Stores)

Langlitz Leathers	Division	29
Louis Vuitton	Downtown	28
John Helmer	Downtown	28
Hanna Andersson	multi.	28
Mercantile	Downtown	28
Pendleton	multi.	28
Columbia	Downtown	27
Upper Playground	Old Town-Chinatown	27
Nike	Downtown	27
Patagonia	Pearl Dist.	27
Lululemon	multi.	26
Mario's	multi.	26
Next Adventure	Central E	26
Brooks Brothers	Downtown	26
Rerun	King	26
North Face	Pearl Dist.	25
Duck Store	multi.	25
Eileen Fisher	Tigard	25
Moulé	Pearl Dist.	25
Blake	NW Portland	25
OSU	Downtown	24
Lizard Lounge	Pearl Dist.	24
Magpie	Downtown	24
Black Wagon	Mississippi	24
Blackbird	W End	24

Mabel & Zora	Pearl Dist.	23
Frances May	W End	23
Anthropologie	multi.	23
Animal Traffic	multi.	22
Hillary Day	NW Portland	22
Crossroads	multi.	22
Parallel	W End	21
Red Light Clothing	Hawthorne	21

APPLIANCES

Stark's Vacuums	multi.	26

ART SUPPLIES

Utrecht	Pearl Dist.	27
Dava Bead & Trade	Irvington	25
Dick Blick Art Materials	multi.	25
Frame Central	multi.	25
Beard's Framing	multi.	25
Hand Eye	Old Town-Chinatown	22

BEAUTY/GROOMING

(See also Department Stores)

Kiehl's	NW Portland	27
Blush	NW Portland	27
L'Occitane	multi.	26
M.A.C.	multi.	26
Sephora	multi.	25
Perfume Hse.	Hawthorne	25
Blackbird	W End	24

BED/BATH LINENS

(See also Department Stores)

French Quarter	Pearl Dist.	26

BICYCLES

River City	multi.	27
Bikeworks	Mississippi	27
REI	multi.	26
Bike Gallery	multi.	26
21st Ave.	NW Portland	24
Fat Tire Farm	NW Portland	24
A Better Cycle	Division	23
Dick's Sporting	multi.	21
Bike Commuter	Sellwood	21

BRIDAL

Lena Medoyeff	NW Portland	24
Anna's Bridal	multi.	24
English Dept.	W End	22

CAMERAS/VIDEO

Pro Photo	**NW Portland**	28
Blue Moon	**St. Johns**	25

CIGAR/SMOKE SHOPS

Rich's Cigar	**multi.**	27

COOKWARE

(See also Department Stores)

Williams-Sonoma	**multi.**	26
Kitchen Kaboodle	**multi.**	26
SweetWares	**Hillsdale**	26
Excalibur	**multi.**	25
Sur La Table	**multi.**	25
Crate & Barrel	**Tigard**	22

DEPARTMENT STORES

Nordstrom	**multi.**	26
Mario's	**multi.**	26
Macy's	**multi.**	22

ELECTRONICS

Apple Store	**multi.**	29
Pro Photo	**NW Portland**	28
Bang & Olufsen	**Pearl Dist.**	28
Bose	**Downtown**	27
Mac Store	**multi.**	26
Blue Moon	**St. Johns**	25
Free Geek	**Central E**	23

FABRICS

Button Emporium	**Downtown**	27
Josephine's	**W End**	27
Bolt	**Alberta**	26
Fabric Depot	**SE Portland**	26
Pendleton/Mill	**Milwaukie**	25
Mill End Store	**multi.**	24

FURNITURE/ HOME FURNISHINGS

(See also Antiques)

Canoe	**W End**	29
Hive	**Pearl Dist.**	27
Joinery	**Woodstock**	27
Pendleton Home	**Old Town-Chinatown**	27
Cielo Home	**Pearl Dist.**	25
Design Within	**Pearl Dist.**	25
Storables	**multi.**	24
Crate & Barrel	**Tigard**	22
Container	**Tigard**	22
Hip Furniture	**NW Portland**	22
Cargo	**Pearl Dist.**	21
City Liq.	**E Industrial**	17

GARDEN ACCESSORIES/ FURNITURE

Urban Farm	**Buckman**	28
Portland Nursery	**multi.**	28
Dennis' 7 Dees	**multi.**	27
Garden Fever!	**Alameda**	27
Backyard Bird Shop	**multi.**	26
Dig Garden Shop	**Pearl Dist.**	23
Artemisia Garden	**Kerns**	20

GIFTS/NOVELTIES

Canoe	**W End**	29
Noun	**Belmont**	27
Real Mother	**Downtown**	27
Sleighbells	**Sherwood**	27
Made/Oregon	**multi.**	26
Duck Store	**multi.**	25
Portland Luggage	**multi.**	25
Ink & Peat	**Boise-Eliot**	24
OSU	**Downtown**	24
Presents/Mind	**Hawthorne**	24
Betsy & Iya	**NW Portland**	23
Alder & Co.	**W End**	23
3 Monkeys	**NW Portland**	23
Cargo	**Pearl Dist.**	21
Tender Loving	**W End**	21
Lippman Co.	**E Industrial**	21
Aster & Bee	**Division**	21

HARDWARE

Chown	**Pearl Dist.**	28
W.C. Winks	**E Industrial**	27
Hippo	**Lower Burnside**	24
ReBuilding Ctr.	**Mississippi**	22

JEANS

Blake	**NW Portland**	25

JEWELRY

(*Antique/Vintage specialist)

Tiffany & Co.	**Downtown**	28
Kassab Jewelers	**multi.**	26
Twist	**NW Portland**	26
Gilt*	**NW Portland**	25
Maloy's Jewelers*	**Downtown**	25
Betsy & Iya	**NW Portland**	23

KNITTING/ NEEDLEPOINT

Knit Purl	**W End**	27
Twisted	**Irvington**	27
Naked Sheep	**Overlook**	27
Close Knit	**Alberta**	25

LIGHTING

Schoolhse. Electric | **NW Portland** 28
Rejuvenation | **Central E** 27

MUSEUM SHOPS

Mus. Cont. Craft | **Pearl Dist.** 27
Portland Art Mus. | **Downtown** 27
OMSI | **E Industrial** 26

MUSIC/MUSICAL INSTRUMENTS

Rhythm | **King** 27
Music Mil. | **Kerns** 27
Centaur | **Kerns** 26
Portland Music | **multi.** 26
Everyday Music | **multi.** 25
Apple Music | **Old Town-Chinatown** 25
2nd Ave. Records | **Downtown** 23
Tender Loving | **W End** 21

PETS/PET SUPPLIES

Salty's | **Mississippi** 25
LexiDog | **multi.** 24
Pet Loft | **Johns Landing** 24
Hip Hound | **NW Portland** 23
Furever Pets | **Irvington** 23

SEX TOYS

She Bop | **Mississippi** 29

SHOES

(See also Department Stores)
John Fluevog | **W End** 28
Haggis | **Westmoreland** 27
Keen Garage | **Pearl Dist.** 26
Imelda's/Louie's | **multi.** 25

Halo Shoes | **Pearl Dist.** 23
Ped-X Shoes | **Alberta** 23

SNEAKERS

Portland Running | **multi.** 27
Nike | **Downtown** 27

SPORTING GOODS

(See also Bicycles)
Portland Running | **multi.** 27
Nike | **Downtown** 27
Patagonia | **Pearl Dist.** 27
REI | **multi.** 26
Next Adventure | **Central E** 26
Andy & Bax | **Central E** 23
Dick's Sporting | **multi.** 21

STATIONERY

Oblation | **Pearl Dist.** 27
Presents/Mind | **Hawthorne** 24

SWIMWEAR

(See also Department Stores)
Popina | **multi.** 26

TOYS

Thinker Toys | **Multnomah** 27
Finnegan's Toys | **multi.** 27
OMSI | **E Industrial** 26
Hobby Smith | **Hollywood** 25
A Children's Place | **Beaumont** 25
Black Wagon | **Mississippi** 24
Aster & Bee | **Division** 21

WATCHES

Tiffany & Co. | **Downtown** 28
Coach | **Happy Valley** 26
WatchWorks | **Downtown** 24

SHOPPING

MERCHANDISE

Shopping: Locations

Includes store names, merchandise type (if necessary) and Quality ratings.
These lists include low vote places that do not qualify for tops lists.

Portland

ALAMEDA/SABIN

Garden Fever!	*Garden*	27
Backyard Bird Shop	*Garden*	26

ALBERTA

Bolt	*Fabrics*	26
Close Knit	*Knitting/Needlept.*	25
Ped-X Shoes	*Shoes*	23

BEAUMONT

A Children's Place	*Books*	25
Anna's Bridal	*Bridal*	24

BELMONT

Noun	*Gifts/Novelties*	27

BOISE-ELIOT

Queen Bee	*Accessories*	28
Ink & Peat	*Gifts/Novelties*	24
NEW Beam/Anchor	*Furniture/Home*	21

BROOKLYN

Portland Music	*Musical Instruments*	26

BUCKMAN/KERNS

Urban Farm	*Garden*	28
Music Mil.	*Music/DVDs*	27
Centaur	*Musical Instruments*	26
Everyday Music	*Music/DVDs*	25
Artemisia Garden	*Garden*	20

CENTRAL EASTSIDE/ EAST INDUSTRIAL

Rejuvenation	*Hardware*	27
Portland Running	*Sporting Gds.*	27
W.C. Winks	*Hardware*	27
River City	*Sporting Gds.*	27
Next Adventure	*Sporting Gds.*	26
Stark's Vacuums	*Appliances*	26
OMSI	*Mus. Shops*	26
Portland Music	*Musical Instruments*	26
Free Geek	*Electronics*	23
Andy & Bax	*Sporting Gds.*	23
Lippman Co.	*Gifts/Novelties*	21
City Liq.	*Furniture/Home*	17

DIVISION

Langlitz Leathers	*Apparel*	29
A Better Cycle	*Sporting Gds.*	23
Aster & Bee	*Gifts/Novelties*	21

DOWNTOWN

Apple Store	*Electronics*	29
Tiffany & Co.	*Jewelry*	28
NEW TUMI	*Luggage*	28
Louis Vuitton	*Apparel*	28
John Helmer	*Apparel*	28
Mercantile	*Apparel*	28
Pendleton	*Apparel*	28
Columbia	*Activewear*	27
Real Mother	*Gifts/Novelties*	27
Nike	*Sporting Gds.*	27
Button Emporium	*Fabrics*	27
Finnegan's Toys	*Toys*	27
Bose	*Electronics*	27
Portland Art Mus.	*Mus. Shops*	27
Rich's Cigar	*Cigar/Smoke*	27
Bike Gallery	*Sporting Gds.*	26
Nordstrom	*Dept Stores*	26
Mario's	*Apparel*	26
Coach	*Accessories*	26
Kassab Jewelers	*Jewelry*	26
L'Occitane	*Beauty/Groom.*	26
Brooks Brothers	*Apparel*	26
Made/Oregon	*Gifts/Novelties*	26
Duck Store	*Activewear*	25
Maloy's Jewelers	*Jewelry*	25
Portland Luggage	*Luggage*	25
Sephora	*Beauty/Groom.*	25
Reynolds Optical	*Eyewear*	25
Beard's Framing	*Art*	25
OSU	*Gifts/Novelties*	24
WatchWorks	*Watches*	24
Magpie	*Vintage*	24
2nd Ave. Records	*Music/DVDs*	23
Macy's	*Dept Stores*	22

FOSTER-POWELL

Dennis' 7 Dees	*Garden*	27

HAWTHORNE

Imelda's/Louie's	*Shoes*	25
Reynolds Optical	*Eyewear*	25
Perfume Hse.	*Beauty/Groom.*	25

SHOPPING

LOCATIONS

Lululemon | *Activewear* 26

REI | *Sporting Gds.* 26

Popina | *Swimwear* 26

French Quarter | *Bed/Bath* 26

Keen Garage | *Shoes* 26

North Face | *Activewear* 25

Dick Blick Art Materials | *Art* 25

Everyday Music | *Music/DVDs* 25

Sur La Table | *Cookware* 25

Cielo Home | *Furniture/Home* 25

Moulé | *Apparel* 25

Imelda's/Louie's | *Shoes* 25

Design Within | *Furniture/Home* 25

Frame Central | *Art* 25

LexiDog | *Pets/Supplies* 24

Lizard Lounge | *Apparel* 24

Storables | *Furniture/Home* 24

Halo Shoes | *Shoes* 23

Dig Garden Shop | *Garden* 23

Mabel & Zora | *Apparel* 23

Anthropologie | *Apparel* 23

Cargo | *Gifts/Novelties* 21

RALEIGH HILLS

Beard's Framing | *Art* 25

SELLWOOD/WESTMORELAND

Sock Dreams | *Legwear/Lingerie* 27

Haggis | *Shoes* 27

Sellwood Antique | *Antiques* 22

Bike Commuter | *Sporting Gds.* 21

SE PORTLAND

Portland Nursery | *Garden* 28

Bike Gallery | *Sporting Gds.* 26

Fabric Depot | *Fabrics* 26

Portland Music | 26
Musical Instruments

ST. JOHNS

Blue Moon | *Cameras/Video* 25

SYLVAN

Beard's Framing | *Art* 25

WEST END

Canoe | *Furniture/Home* 29

John Fluevog | *Shoes* 28

Knit Purl | *Knitting/Needlept.* 27

Josephine's | *Fabrics* 27

Lille | *Legwear/Lingerie* 24

Blackbird | *Apparel* 24

Alder & Co. | *Gifts/Novelties* 23

Frances May | *Apparel* 23

Animal Traffic | *Vintage* 22

English Dept. | *Bridal* 22

Tender Loving | *Gifts/Novelties* 21

Parallel | *Apparel* 21

WOODSTOCK

Joinery | *Furniture/Home* 27

Bike Gallery | *Sporting Gds.* 26

Portland Suburbs

BEAVERTON

Portland Running | *Sporting Gds.* 27

Dennis' 7 Dees | *Garden* 27

Kitchen Kaboodle | *Cookware* 26

Bike Gallery | *Sporting Gds.* 26

Mac Store | *Electronics* 26

Backyard Bird Shop | *Garden* 26

Stark's Vacuums | *Appliances* 26

Portland Music | 26
Musical Instruments

Dick Blick Art Materials | *Art* 25

Portland Luggage | *Luggage* 25

Everyday Music | *Music/DVDs* 25

Frame Central | *Art* 25

Beard's Framing | *Art* 25

Mill End Store | *Fabrics* 24

CLACKAMAS/HAPPY VALLEY

Kitchen Kaboodle | *Cookware* 26

REI | *Sporting Gds.* 26

Nordstrom | *Dept Stores* 26

Coach | *Accessories* 26

Mac Store | *Electronics* 26

Backyard Bird Shop | *Garden* 26

Stark's Vacuums | *Appliances* 26

Made/Oregon | *Gifts/Novelties* 26

Duck Store | *Activewear* 25

Excalibur | *Cookware* 25

Sephora | *Beauty/Groom.* 25

Macy's | *Dept Stores* 22

Dick's Sporting | *Sporting Gds.* 21

GRESHAM

Stark's Vacuums | *Appliances* 26

Beard's Framing | *Art* 25

Dick's Sporting | *Sporting Gds.* 21

HILLSBORO

Kitchen Kaboodle | *Cookware* 26

REI | *Sporting Gds.* 26

Stark's Vacuums | *Appliances* 26

Share your reviews on plus.google.com/local

Beard's Framing | *Art* 25
Macy's | *Dept Stores* 22
Dick's Sporting | *Sporting Gds.* 21

LAKE OSWEGO

Pendleton | *Apparel* 28
Dennis' 7 Dees | *Garden* 27
Bike Gallery | *Sporting Gds.* 26
Kassab Jewelers | *Jewelry* 26
Backyard Bird Shop | *Garden* 26
Sur La Table | *Cookware* 25
LexiDog | *Pets/Supplies* 24
Anna's Bridal | *Bridal* 24
Dick's Sporting | *Sporting Gds.* 21

MILWAUKIE

Pendleton/Mill | *Fabrics* 25
Mill End Store | *Fabrics* 24

SHERWOOD/ TUALATIN

Sleighbells | *Gifts/Novelties* 27
Stark's Vacuums | *Appliances* 26
Beard's Framing | *Art* 25

TIGARD

Apple Store | *Electronics* 29
Hanna Andersson | *Children's* 28

Finnegan's Toys | *Toys* 27
Williams-Sonoma | *Cookware* 26
Lululemon | *Activewear* 26
REI | *Sporting Gds.* 26
Nordstrom | *Dept Stores* 26
Mario's | *Apparel* 26
Coach | *Accessories* 26
Kassab Jewelers | *Jewelry* 26
L'Occitane | *Beauty/Groom.* 26
M.A.C. | *Beauty/Groom.* 26
Made/Oregon | *Gifts/Novelties* 26
Duck Store | *Activewear* 25
Eileen Fisher | *Apparel* 25
Excalibur | *Cookware* 25
Sur La Table | *Cookware* 25
Sephora | *Beauty/Groom.* 25
Frame Central | *Art* 25
Storables | *Furniture/Home* 24
Anthropologie | *Apparel* 23
Crate & Barrel | *Furniture/Home* 22
Container | *Furniture/Home* 22
Macy's | *Dept Stores* 22
Dick's Sporting | *Sporting Gds.* 21

SHOPPING

LOCATIONS

Shopping

Ratings & Symbols

Quality, Display & **Service** are rated on a 30-point scale.

Cost reflects our surveyors' estimate of the price range:

⌐I⌐ Inexpensive   ⌐E⌐ Expensive
⌐M⌐ Moderate   ⌐VE⌐ Very Expensive

● usually open after 7 PM   Ⓜ closed on Monday
Ⓢ closed on Sunday

A Better Cycle ●   23 | 22 | 23 | M

Division | 2324 SE Division St. (bet 23rd & 25th Aves.) | 503-265-8595 |
www.abettercycle.com
Worker-owned and collectively run, this "super-helpful", relatively
"inexpensive" Division bike shop comes "highly recommended" for
its willingness to "meet you at your cycling level"; it sells new stock
from Civia, KHS and Surly and "turns out awesome rides" of its own,
plus used and refurbished wheels, as well as a litany of accessories –
a mix that earns it a reputation of being a "delightful place to shop."

A Children's Place   25 | 23 | 24 | M

Beaumont | 4807 NE Fremont St. (bet. 47th & 49th Aves.) |
503-284-8294 | www.achildrensplacebookstore.com
"A child's dream", this vibrant Beaumont bookstore has an "amazing
variety" of titles and a "knowledgeable, helpful" staff that makes
"spot-on recommendations" and is "willing to spend some time with
you to find a perfect book", even "festively wrapping" gift items; it's
also a "great community-building place" with author readings, story
time and occasional fund-raisers, and "as an added bonus it has an
adult fiction section."

Alder & Co.   23 | 22 | 22 | E

West End | 537 SW 12th Ave. (bet. Alder & Washington Sts.) |
503-224-1647 | www.alderandcoshop.com
There's a "lovely collection of accessories and home goods" in a
range of prices that fills the shelves of this West End gift boutique –
think handmade Argentinean baskets, locally made wool bunny
slippers and wear-everywhere gems from Rebecca Overmann and
Kathleen Whitaker; it's a "welcoming and friendly place" staffed by
a "good crew" who is happy to help shoppers uncover its "unique
and unusual contemporary" gifts.

Andy & Bax Ⓢ   23 | 20 | 22 | M

Central Eastside | 324 SE Grand Ave. (bet. Oak & Pine Sts.) |
503-234-7538 | www.andyandbax.com
With its "tremendous selection of classic outdoor gear", including
survival equipment, plus a "fascinating collection of cast-off military
goods", this longtime Central Eastside shop is reminiscent of a "crazy

granddad's garage"; many prices are "below market", and the staff "knows it all", but its key charm is that "so many weird and awesome things" are "tucked away."

Animal Traffic
22 | 22 | 22 | M

Mississippi | 4000 N. Mississippi Ave. (bet. Mason & Shaver Sts.) | 503-249-4000
NEW West End | 429 SW 10th Ave. (bet. Stark & Washington Sts.) | 503-241-5427
www.animaltrafficpdx.com

This "quality vintage" clothing and Western-wear store on Mississippi and in the West End is a "good place for bandanas and cowboy boots", decades-old Pendleton button-ups or pre-loved denim jackets, and it also stocks new items like Minnetonka moccasins and locally made jewelry (most of the baubles are at the 10th Avenue stop); fans like it "because you don't have to sort through lots of junk" and say the moderate price tags are "comparable with less curated shops."

Anna's Bridal
24 | 23 | 22 | E

NEW Beaumont | 4819 NE Fremont St. (bet. 48th & 49th Aves.) | 503-481-2490
Lake Oswego | 17050 Pilkington Rd. (bet. Boones Ferry Rd. & Rosewood St.) | 503-636-1474 🖂
www.annasbridal.com

Brides flock to this "easy" "one-stop" bridal boutique in Lake Oswego (the Beaumont location is almost entirely sample stock) to find "beautiful" designer gowns à la Pronovias and Matthew Christopher as well as to accessorize, outfit their bridesmaids and attend to alterations; add in "patient" and "enthusiastic" service and many betrothed report landing their "dream dress" and say the "price fits the occasion."

Anthropologie ◑
23 | 26 | 20 | E

Pearl District | 1115 NW Couch St. (11th Ave.) | 503-274-0293
Tigard | Bridgeport Vill. | 7203 SW Bridgeport Rd. (Hazelfern Rd.) | 503-620-0682
www.anthropologie.com

For the "boho-chic aesthetic" (think *New Girl*'s Zooey Deschanel's "adorkable" wardrobe) look no further than this "whimsically" "quirky" chain; you'll find everything from "unique" "springtime frocks to fall layers to winter jackets", plus "killer accessories" and "eclectic" housewares "made for the rom-com heroine"; a visit "transports you" to a "lifestyle you aspire to live – isn't that what fashion is supposed to do?"

Apple Music
25 | 25 | 23 | M

Old Town-Chinatown | 225 SW First Ave. (bet. Oak & Pine Sts.) | 503-226-0036 | www.applemusicrow.com

Music mavens pluck "quality" gear from this "huge" independent Old Town store (circa 1975) with "rooms dedicated to guitars, drums, keyboards and more", including a 'museum' of "not-for-sale" rare and vintage instruments; prices are "on the mark or cheaper", staff is "helpful and kind" and gear rental, repairs and lessons are all available.

Apple Store ●

| 29 | 27 | 26 | E |

Downtown | Pioneer Pl. | 700 SW Fifth Ave. (Taylor St.) | 503-265-2010
Tigard | Bridgeport Vill. | 7293 SW Bridgeport Rd. (Upper Boones Ferry Rd.) | 503-670-8400
Tigard | Washington Sq. | 9530 SW Washington Square Rd. (Blum Rd.) | 503-495-2080
www.apple.com

You'll "wish you were a nerd all along" at these "jaw-dropping" showrooms for Apple's "tantalizing" devices, combining "flashy" "hands-on displays" with "one-stop shopping and support" from a staff of "egghead maestros" who are "unfailingly" helpful to "techies and nontechies alike"; the "cutting-edge" wares "command a hefty price", and the crowds of "e-nuts" "can be maddening", but "once bitten", it's "futile to resist."

Artemisia Garden Ⓜ

| 20 | 20 | 20 | M |

Kerns | 110 SE 28th Ave. (bet. Ankeny & Ash Sts.) | 503-232-8224 | www.collagewithnature.com

A "quaint shop" overrun with "bonsai, air plants, art items and more", this Kerns "diamond in the rough" attracts all types of plant lovers, with a special lure for those "into terrariums and everything related" (including kits and DIY workshops); prices are relatively "affordable" and the staff is "nice", but mostly shoppers are bowled over by a curated "beauty" that's like something "out of a children's book."

Aster & Bee Ⓩ

| 21 | 21 | 20 | M |

Division | 4819 SE Division St. (bet. 48th & 49th Aves.) | 503-236-8537 | www.asterandbee.com

"Whimsy and fun poke out of every corner" of this "cheerful, bright" Division gift shop "packed full of fantastic goodies, including "cool toys you won't likely find elsewhere" (some for "grown-up children"), "local jewelry", art and clothing; the "friendly" staff will help you sift through the "creative" wares, most of which are moderately priced.

Backyard Bird Shop

| 26 | 25 | 25 | E |

Sabin | 1419 NE Fremont St. (14th Ave.) | 503-445-2699
Beaverton | 11429 SW Beaverton-Hillsdale Hwy. (Oleson Rd.) | 503-626-0949
Clackamas | Clackamas Promenade | 8960 SE Sunnyside Rd. (bet. 84th & 93rd Aves.) | 503-496-0908
Lake Oswego | 16949 SW 65th Ave. (bet. Bradbury Ct. & Lower Boones Ferry Rd.) | 503-620-7454
www.backyardbirdshop.com

There's a "real menagerie of items to feed, entertain and attract your feathery backyard chirpers, squawkers and warblers" at this multibranched Portland shop that's "definitely for the birds"; the "wonderful" staff is "patient with incessant questions" even when it's "crowded", and most find prices "fair."

Bang & Olufsen

| 28 | 26 | 24 | VE |

Pearl District | 634 NW 12th Ave. (Hoyt St.) | 503-206-7438 |
www.bang-olufson.com

The "epitome of style" for the "hi-fi buff", this "audio-visual experience" is known for "sleek" Danish "designs matched with top-
quality" equipment, from "quintessential" sound systems to TVs;
the "classic showroom" is overseen by "personally invested" sales-
people, and while the merchandise is "ultraexpensive", if you seek
"the 'wow' factor" you "can't go wrong" here.

NEW Beam & Anchor M

∇ 21 | 19 | 22 | E |

Boise-Eliot | 2710 N. Interstate Ave. (bet. Graham & Knott Sts.) |
503-367-3230 | www.beamandanchor.com

Housed in a renovated 7,000-sq.-ft. industrial Boise-Eliot building, this shop/studio combo fits right in with the city's handmade
vibe, offering a careful selection of primarily local home goods, gifts
and accessories, including Wood&Faulk leather items, Robert Rahm
furniture (he owns the space with his wife, Jocelyn) and Lilith
Rockett ceramics; upstairs, there are open studios for several of the
city's most well-known artisans.

Beard's Framing

| 25 | 23 | 23 | E |

Sylvan | 7545 SW Barnes Rd. (bet. Leahy & Miller Rds.) | 503-203-2516
Downtown | 832 SW Fourth Ave. (Taylor St.) | 503-228-6250
Lloyd | Lloyd Ctr. | 1025 Lloyd Ctr. (bet. 9th & 15th Aves.) |
503-287-9126 ●
Raleigh Hills | 4715 SW 77th Ave. (Beaverton-Hillsdale Hwy.) |
503-297-2573
Beaverton | 11413 SW Beaverton-Hillsdale Hwy. (bet. Lombard &
110th Aves.) | 503-643-6664
Hillsboro | 2219 NW Allie Ave. (bet. Cornell Rd. & Stucki Ave.) |
503-690-7782 Ⓢ
Gresham | 1088 NW Civic Dr. (bet. Division & 13th Sts.) |
503-667-5700
Tualatin | 19200 SW Martinazzi Ave. (bet. Tualatin-Sherwood Rd. &
Warm Springs St.) | 503-692-0707
www.beards.com

The doors of this "excellent" string of frame shops first opened in
1974, and longtime customers say they're "always happy and impressed" with the "knowledgeable" staff's suggestions as well as the
"final products"; a few find it a "bit expensive", but most say the
price is "competitive" and the "work is wonderful."

Betsy & Iya

| 23 | 24 | 24 | M |

Northwest Portland | 2403 NW Thurman St. (24th Ave.) |
503-227-5482 | www.betsyandiya.com

This "wild and wonderful" NW Portland jewelry boutique stocks
plenty of its own "cool", "trendy" pieces ("from dog tags to definitely evening"), as well as an edited stock of clothing and accessory
lines such as Uzi and Make It Good; prices are relatively "affordable", and the "friendly" staff "will help you make the right decision"
on a bauble.

	QUALITY	DISPLAY	SERVICE	COST

Bike Commuter
`21` `21` `22` `M`

Sellwood | 8301 SE 13th Ave. (Umatilla St.) | 503-505-9200 |
www.pdxbikecommuter.com

Two-wheeled commuters head to this "local family-run" Sellwood
cycle shop for its "above-and-beyond" staff, "whether you're buying
or getting repairs" – even offering information on "how to fix it"
yourself; there are also new and used bikes and gear from the likes
of Fuji and Raleigh, and you can rent by the hour, day or week (hel-
met and lock included).

Bike Gallery
`26` `25` `25` `E`

Downtown | 1001 SW 10th Ave. (Salmon St.) | 503-222-3821
Woodstock | 4235 SE Woodstock Blvd. (43rd Ave.) | 503-774-3531
Hollywood | 5329 NE Sandy Blvd. (bet. 52nd & 54th Aves.) |
503-281-9800
Southeast Portland | 10950 SE Division St. (bet. 109th & 111th Aves.) |
503-254-2663
Beaverton | 12345 SW Canyon Rd. (Hall Blvd.) | 503-641-2580
Lake Oswego | 200 B Ave. (2nd St.) | 503-636-1600
www.bikegallery.com

At this "powerhouse" local chain of "community bike shops", riders find cycle "nerds" who offer "friendly help", "fast repair" and
"no-pressure sales" of mountain, city and road models that are
"perfectly fitted" to individual needs; while the "cost range is
wide", the products are "not cheap", but it's still a "favorite" for
rides and accessories.

Bikeworks
`27` `25` `26` `M`

Mississippi | 3978 N. Mississippi Ave. (Shaver St.) | 503-287-1098 |
www.northportlandbikeworks.org

This "cozy" nonprofit Mississippi bike shop is a "pleasure to stop by,
even if it's just to use their floor pump" say fans who herald the "low-
key", "awesome mechanics" "who enjoy working" on two-wheelers
(especially "old steel beauties"); particularly, it specializes in commuter bikes and parts from Jamis and Linus and offers repair workshops for the novice, all for a "really good" price.

Blackbird
`24` `22` `21` `E`

West End | 1306 W. Burnside St. (13th Ave.) | 503-227-1825 |
www.blackbirdballard.com

Perfect for "all you male fashionistas", this high-end men's shop in the
West End is a "great place" for designer wares from A.P.C., Comme
des Garçons and other top brands; fans love its "modern subculture"
feel, although they admit the price tags skew "expensive."

Black Wagon
∇ `24` `24` `21` `E`

Mississippi | 3964 N. Mississippi Ave. (bet. Failing & Shaver Sts.) |
866-916-0004 | www.blackwagon.com

Shop for your little ones at this "hip" Mississippi store, just be
warned: "your children will look better than you" thanks to "trendy"
infant and young kids' clothing (it also stocks a bevy of "creative
baby announcements", toys and just plain "good gifts"); "expect

to pay a lot", but take heart that the "customer service will beat your highest expectations."

Blake
25 | 21 | 23 | E

Northwest Portland | 26 NW 23rd Pl. (bet. Burnside St. & Westover Rd.) | 503-222-4848 | www.loveblake.com

"If you love denim" and want to buy it from "people who are passionate", "you won't go wrong" at this NW Portland shop, its walls stocked floor-to-ceiling with "high-quality" men's and women's jeans from J Brand, Raleigh Denim, Rogan and dozens more, plus an "expansive collection of other solid menswear options" – think Pendleton Portland Collection and RRL; "sure, the stuff is expensive", but if you desire what some say will be your "best-fitting pair", "it's worth it."

Blue Moon Camera & Machine ☒
25 | 21 | 24 | E

St. Johns | 8417 N. Lombard St. (bet. John & Leavitt Aves.) | 503-978-0333 | www.bluemooncamera.com

For those who "still enjoy shooting with film", this "museum"-like St. Johns camera shop and optical printing lab is the place as it deals exclusively in the retro format, stocking cameras of all shapes, sizes and prices, including pinhole kits, Holgas and Fuji Instax cameras – and the film to go with them; a "super-smart" staff that "cares about photography" can help with "hard-to-find" equipment, giving "dedicated photogeeks" a "reason to go" to this area of town.

Blush Beauty Bar
27 | 25 | 24 | E

Northwest Portland | 513 NW 23rd Ave. (bet. Glisan & Hoyt Sts.) | 503-227-3390 | www.blushbeautybar247.com

"So many kinds of cosmetics" swoon makeup connoisseurs over this NW Portland shop that keeps its stock of everything from "high-end" brands like Nars and Stila to "indie and hard-to-find" lines "very organized" in "cute displays"; the "incredibly helpful" staffers (aka "instant best friends") assist with product application, making "you look beautiful in a way you are comfortable with", and are known as "eyebrow specialists", as well as for their facials and hair-removal services.

Bolt Neighborhood Fabric Boutique
26 | 26 | 24 | M

Alberta | 2136 NE Alberta St. (22nd Ave.) | 503-287-2658 | www.boltfabricboutique.com

Though in a "teensy" space, this Alberta fabric shop packs in a lot of "fun, funky" prints and "all the newest bolts from every designer you crave" (Liberty of London, Kokka), including sustainable, organic and limited-edition runs, plus plenty of "spiffy notions"; prices are "fair", and most find the staff "helpful, especially to those new to sewing."

Bose ◗
27 | 24 | 23 | VE

Downtown | Pioneer Pl. | 340 SW Morrison St. (bet. 3rd & 4th Aves.) | 503-224-5772 | www.bose.com

Choosy audiophiles find "incredible" "aural experiences" at this "boutique" outlet for the "king of high fidelity", which offers "unsurpassed" speakers, Wave music systems and "noise-canceling headphones"; of course such "quality" commands a "premium price", but "they stand behind the product", and the "enthusiastic" salesfolk treat everyone as a "valued customer."

Brooks Brothers
26 | 24 | 24 | E

Downtown | 921 SW Morrison St. (9th Ave.) | 503-223-4039 | www.brooksbrothers.com

"A bastion of old-school style without living in the past", this "classic" chain hasn't lost its touch, with devotees calling it "the gold standard for all-American tailored clothing" thanks to "quality" suits, "wrinkle-free" dress button-downs and preppy rep ties; edgier sorts call the women's fashions "staid", but "excellent service" and "interesting bargains" come sale time keep customers loyal.

Button Emporium & Ribbonry
27 | 25 | 23 | M

Downtown | 1016 SW Taylor St. (bet. 10th & 11th Aves.) | 503-228-6372 | www.buttonemporium.com

It's "heaven for the crafty" at this "tiny" Downtown stockist "crammed full of, "you guessed it, buttons and ribbons", in addition to trim and other sewing embellishments; the "nice" displays are "grandma-y" in look, and an "intensely focused staff" is "willing to offer advice on projects."

Canoe Ⓜ
29 | 28 | 25 | E

West End | 1136 SW Alder St. (12th Ave.) | 503-889-8545 | www.canoeonline.net

Known as a "design geek's dream", this "cool, sophisticated" West End shop wows with its modern displays and "contemporary" selections of "trendy home goods" and the "most clever office accessories"; the staff shows "no pretense", and fans favor it for "impressive gifts", with some confessing a wish for "more money" in order to "burn a lot of it here."

Cargo
21 | 22 | 20 | M

Pearl District | 380 NW 13th Ave. (Flanders St.) | 503-209-8349 | www.cargoinc.com

This "eclectic", two-floor importer is a standout in the Pearl District for its eye-catching storefront, and it's "packed to the gills" with "treats from around the world" "in every price range", from furniture to home goods to jewelry and more (picture "unique" items like an "alabaster Buddha" next to "chairs made out of old tires"); just as it's easy to "get lost for an hour" among the "overwhelming" displays, it's also "[hard to] leave here cargo-less."

Centaur Guitar
26 | 23 | 25 | M

Kerns | 2833 NE Sandy Blvd. (bet. 28th & 29th Aves.) | 503-236-8711 | www.centaurguitar.com

"Look no further" if you're "obsessed with effects pedals, vintage gear and weird noise" say enthusiastic followers of this Kerns guitar shop that stocks used (and some new) instruments, amps and accessories; the "cool dudes" behind the counter are "knowledgeable, experienced musicians" who create a "low-pressure atmosphere" – and all at "punk prices."

QUALITY · DISPLAY · SERVICE · COST

Chown Hardware
28 | 25 | 25 | VE

Pearl District | 333 NW 16th Ave. (Flanders St.) | 503-243-6500 | www.chown.com

"When you can't find it [elsewhere] it's here", at this "quality" Pearl District hardware shop established in 1879, which stocks some of the "best plumbing and cabinetry hardware" in the area from "upper-end" lines such as Baldwin and Waterworks; the "extensive show-room" and "excellent displays" make it a "great place for decorating ideas", and the "customer-oriented" staff contributes to the "good old-fashioned" experience.

Cielo Home 🖲Ⓜ
▽ 25 | 24 | 22 | E

Pearl District | 528 NW 12th Ave. (bet. Glisan & Hoyt Sts.) | 503-445-0111 | www.shopcielo.com

Design buffs swoon for the European goodies at this Pearl District home boutique that showcases its owners' "fantastic taste" and "uncanny knack for scouring out unique items" – like John Derian decoupage, Juliska ceramic dishware, Diptyque candles and more; though somewhat "pricey" overall, there are many small items for sale, and folks are often willing to splurge for loved ones listed with the store's bridal/gift registry.

City Liquidators Furniture Warehouse
17 | 15 | 17 | M

Eastside Industrial | 823 SE Third Ave. (bet. 2nd & 3rd Aves.) | 503-238-4477 | www.cityliquidators.com

Resembling an "unplanned garage sale", this "huge" three-floor fur-niture showroom in Eastside Industrial has long been a "bargain-hunter's paradise" with its "endless" "hodgepodge" of furniture, yes, but also everything from kitchen utensils to pianos; you often "get what you pay for here" when it comes to quality, and service can be "hard to find", but it's a "total Portland experience" – and you just might unearth a "treasure."

Close Knit
25 | 25 | 24 | M

Alberta | 2140 NE Alberta St. (22nd Ave.) | 503-288-4568 | www.closeknitportland.com

This "jewel box" of a knitting shop on Alberta is filled with skeins of "gorgeous yarn", needles and pattern books displayed in a "warm", "inviting" setting decorated with "always-inspiring" sample projects; the "staff knows its stuff", and its stamp-card program "helps save" on the supplies; P.S. inquire about classes for beginners and beyond.

Coach ❶
26 | 25 | 24 | VE

Downtown | Pioneer Pl. | 700 SW Fifth Ave. (Taylor St.) | 503-294-0772
Happy Valley | Clackamas Town Ctr. | 12000 SE 82nd Ave. (Sunnyside Rd.) | 503-353-0088
Tigard | Washington Sq. | 9689 SW Washington Square Rd. (Blum Rd.) | 503-968-1772
www.coach.com

The "smell of sumptuous leather" wafts across the threshold of this "enduring standard-bearer" of "impeccably made" handbags, wallets, shoes and accessories, which always impresses with its "time-less" yet "creative designs" that "hold up through thick and thin"; factor in "elegant displays" and "old-school customer service", and it's no wonder that shopping here, though "expensive", is always a "positive experience."

Columbia Sportswear
27 | 25 | 24 | E

Downtown | 911 SW Broadway (Taylor St.) | 503-226-6800
www.columbia.com

A "Portland institution" since its beginnings as the Columbia Hat Company in 1938, this homegrown chain stocks "everything for the adventurous", including an "excellent selection of sportswear" and "good hiking and camping" accoutrements – all backed by a "knowledgeable" staff; the products might be "on the pricey side", but most feel it's "worth the money" as the "quality of clothing is impeccable and the gear lasts for a very long time."

Container Store ◑
22 | 22 | 20 | M

Tigard | Bridgeport Vill. | 7417 SW Bridgeport Rd. (Upper Boones Ferry Rd.) | 503-620-5700 | www.containerstore.com

It's hard to "contain yourself" at this "temple of organization", offering "stylish" "stuff for your stuff" from "floor to ceiling", including "under the bed" and "closets too"; with layouts "spacious enough so you don't feel overwhelmed" and staff to "help you find what you need", the only question is how much to "pay for empty boxes."

Crate & Barrel ◑
22 | 24 | 20 | M

Tigard | Bridgeport Vill. | 7267 SW Bridgeport Rd. (72nd Ave.) | 503-598-9005 | www.crateandbarrel.com

This national chain boasts "everything from furniture to dishes to home decor", all "dazzlingly displayed" in "color-coordinated and themed" sets that let shoppers have a whole new "made-up life in every corner of the store"; stocked with "tasteful designs", it's a wedding registry "stalwart" and also where many "set up house post-Ikea."

Crossroads Trading Co. ◑
22 | 19 | 18 | M

Hawthorne | 3736 SE Hawthorne Blvd. (bet. 37th & 38th Aves.) | 503-239-8099

NEW **Northwest Portland** | 128 NW 23rd Ave. (bet. Burnside & Everett Sts.) | 503-241-2545
www.crossroadstrading.com

For "secondhand" and "new resale" clothing that's relatively "mainstream" (think Diesel, Marc Jacobs, 7 For All Mankind) clothes hounds head to this Hawthorne–NW Portland duo that's part of a chain based in Berkeley, CA; there's a "lack" of decor and staff can be "a little scarce" at times, but the recycled pieces are "reasonably priced" and "sorted by color"; P.S. sell your own stuff for cash or trade.

Dava Bead & Trade
25 | 24 | 24 | E

Irvington | 2121 NE Broadway (bet. 17th St. & 19th Ave.) | 503-288-3991 | www.davabead.com

"Very cool" say crafty folks who appreciate this Irvington shop for its "huge selection" of "great" beads and related supplies; although it's "easy to spend a lot and leave with a very small bag" the staff is "always willing to help with a design", and workshops on all manner of jewelry-making are on offer.

Dennis' 7 Dees
27 | 26 | 25 | E

Foster-Powell | 6025 SE Powell Blvd. (bet. 59th & 62nd Aves.) | 503-777-1421
Beaverton | 10455 SW Butner Rd. (Park Way) | 503-297-1058
Lake Oswego | 1090 McVey Ave. (bet. Laurel & Oak Sts.) | 503-636-4660
www.dennis7dees.com

"Beautiful and healthy plants and everything you need to grow them" are available at this "wonderful" Portland-area nursery and landscape design mini-chain that first opened in 1956; with a "knowledgeable staff that makes shopping a genuine pleasure", "green thumbs" (and those who "wish they were") say it's "expensive but generally worth it."

Design Within Reach
25 | 23 | 20 | VE

Pearl District | 1200 NW Everett St. (12th Ave.) | 503-220-0200 | www.dwr.com

"Brilliant" home design spotlighting "iconic modern furniture" from the likes of Herman Miller and Isamu Noguchi is the forte of this high-end chain; while some pieces offer a retro spin "without buying vintage", others add a "creative new" edge to every room; either way it's worth "going into your reserve account or eating ramen noodles" because "you'll probably keep" these "real McCoys" forever.

Dick Blick Art Materials ◗
25 | 23 | 22 | M

NEW **Pearl District** | 1115 NW Glisan St. (bet. 11th & 12th Aves.) | 503-223-3724
Beaverton | Walker Ctr. | 2710 SW Cedar Hills Blvd. (Walker Rd.) | 503-646-9347
www.dickblick.com

Artists attest the Pearl District and Beaverton links of this national chain are "packed full" of "goodies", with an "array of supplies" in all mediums for creatives – "from beginner to professional"; surveyors report having "no problems finding" what they needed and say the prices are "fair", especially considering it stocks "all the ingredients to jump-start your imagination" in one place.

Dick's Sporting Goods ◗
21 | 19 | 15 | M

Kenton | Hayden Meadows Sq. | 1140 N. Hayden Meadows Dr. (bet. Kerby Ave. & Whitaker Rd.) | 503-285-5040
Hillsboro | Crossroads | 7280 NW Butler St. (Cornell Rd.) | 503-547-2904
Happy Valley | Johnson Creek Crossing | 9600 SE 82nd St. (Overland St.) | 503-788-7616
Gresham | Gresham Town Fair | 700 NW Eastman Pkwy. (Division St.) | 503-667-1950
Lake Oswego | Meridian Sq. | 17799 Lower Boones Ferry Rd. (65th Ave.) | 503-635-3800

(continued)

(continued)
Dick's Sporting Goods
Tigard | Washington Sq. | 9402 SW Washington Square Rd. (Blum Rd.) |
503-598-3081
www.dickssportinggoods.com
Dick Stack started his bait-and-tackle shop in 1948 in Binghamton,
New York, and today it's a national "big-box" chain catering to "all your
sporting goods needs" for fishing, golf, soccer and more; proponents
praise plentiful "bargains" on a "wide variety" of equipment and activewear, while caustic critics contend it's a bit "overpriced"; still,
most agree that staffers are "friendly", if you can find them.

Dig Garden Shop Ⓜ
23 | 23 | 21 | VE
Pearl District | 425 NW 11th Ave. (bet. Flanders & Glisan Sts.) |
503-223-4443 | www.diggardenshop.com
"Not your traditional garden shop", this "funky" Pearl District stop
stands out with its stock of "unusual" "city gardening" items such as
wheeled planters and outdoor furniture by Loll and Fermob; the
"charming" owner is "fun to chat with", and though they can be "expensive", the goods add "character" to small urban green spaces.

The Duck Store
25 | 25 | 23 | E
Downtown | White Stag Block Complex | 70 NW Couch St.
(bet. Naito Pkwy. & 2nd Ave.) | 503-412-3712
Happy Valley | Clackamas Town Ctr. | 12130 SE 82nd Ave.
(bet. Monterey Ave. & Sunnyside Rd.) | 503-908-0798 ◑
Tigard | Washington Sq. | 9378 SW Washington Square Rd. (Blum Rd.) |
503-431-6903 ◑
www.uoduckstore.com
Stocked with an "unrivaled" selection of team memorabilia ("from
knickknacks to awesome hoodies"), this "delightful" University of
Oregon trio will have you feeling as if you're "in the middle of
Duckville"; expect mostly "enthusiastic" service, and though items can
be "spendy", fans say it's "totally worth it" "for the Duck in all of us."

Eileen Fisher ◑
25 | 23 | 23 | E
Tigard | Bridgeport Vill. | 7353 SW Bridgeport Rd. (Upper Boones Ferry Rd.) |
503-620-9095 | www.eileenfisher.com
The quest for that perfect balance of "comfortable yet chic" ends at
this "favorite" chain for the "fashionable over-40" set, with "confident,
timeless" separates for "work and play" crafted from "excellent fabrics"; "helpful" staffers and "beautiful displays" enhance the experience, and, yes, it's "expensive", but the sales offer "real savings."

Ellington Handbags
26 | 24 | 25 | E
Northwest Portland | 1211 NW 23rd Ave. (bet. Northrup & Overton Sts.) |
503-542-3149 | www.ellingtonhandbags.com
This NW-area shop boasts "classic" "high-quality handbags" designed in-house using eco-friendly leathers and washed nylon twill,
plus there's an "impressive array" of wallets, small accessories and
"specialty bags"; despite high price tags, the items are "worth it",
especially considering they're styles "you'll want to take with you
everywhere for the rest of your life."

	QUALITY	DISPLAY	SERVICE	COST

The English Dept. 🖼 Ⓜ

22 | 22 | 23 | E

West End | 1128 SW Alder St. (bet. 11th & 12th Aves.) | 503-224-0724 | www.theenglishdept.com

"Tiny" but "fabulous", this West End bridal salon offers "beautiful" gowns from designer-owner Elizabeth Dye, plus a handful of mostly indie brands like Ivy & Aster and Love, Yu; blushing brides advise "make an appointment" with the "insightful" staff to secure a "dream dress."

Everyday Music ❶

25 | 23 | 22 | M

Kerns | 1931 NE Sandy Blvd. (19th St.) | 503-239-7610
Pearl District | 1313 W. Burnside St. (14th Ave.) | 503-274-0961
Beaverton | 3290 SW Cedar Hills Blvd. (bet. Fairfield St. & Hall Blvd.) | 503-350-0907
www.everydaymusic.com

This local chainlet, a "must-visit for music lovers", boasts a "huge, well-organized" selection of new and used CDs, DVDs and LPs with an emphasis on "older music" and "obscure" sounds; the generally "supportive" staff can usually "help you find what you need", and there are plenty of "bargains", especially in the scuff bins; P.S. there's a separate room for jazz and classical music in Kerns.

Excalibur Cutlery & Gifts ❶

25 | 25 | 22 | E

Lloyd | Lloyd Ctr. | 931 Lloyd Ctr. (bet. 9th & 15th Aves.) | 503-282-6575
Happy Valley | Clackamas Town Ctr. | 12000 SE 82nd Ave. (Sunnyside Rd.) | 503-786-6192
Tigard | Washington Sq. | 9759 SW Washington Square Rd. (Palmblad Rd.) | 503-639-2151
www.excaliburcutlery.com

"A cut above the rest", this blade shop fills its shelves with "beautiful, high-quality" kitchen cutlery (Forschner, Henckels, Wüsthof), pocket knives, razors, manicure sets and "unique" items like throwing knives and swords; even if some products are "spendy", most are "priced to beat" the competition, and "kind associates" who are "more than happy to help" give it an edge.

EYES! On Broadway 🖼

27 | 28 | 25 | E

Irvington | 2300 NE Broadway (bet. 22nd & 24th Aves.) | 503-284-2300 | www.eyesonbroadway.com

"Picking out glasses is actually fun" for the optically challenged customers who dig the "spectacular selection" of "hip" frames and "knowledgeable", "friendly" staffers who have a "great eye for what looks good" at this Irvington specs specialist; some say prices are "comparable" while others insist they're "costly", but it's one-stop shopping as eye exams, specialty lenses and contacts are all on offer.

Fabric Depot ❶

26 | 23 | 23 | M

Southeast Portland | 700 SE 122nd Ave. (Stark St.) | 503-252-9530 | www.fabricdepot.com

"Quilters" and other "crafty souls" are "overwhelmed" by the "feast of fabrics" at this "huge" "sewing nut's dream" of a shop in SE Portland with "everything for the seamstress", including an assortment of "unique buttons and different types of fringes"; prices are moderate and it also has "great sales", plus the "staff knows its stuff", so aficionados liken a trip here to a "pilgrimage."

Fat Tire Farm

| 24 | 21 | 23 | E |

Northwest Portland | 2714 NW Thurman St. (27th Ave.) | 503-222-3276 | www.fattirefarm.com

Bikers who put in "thousands of muddy, cruddy miles" "love going" to this NW Portland shop that "only deals with mountain bikes" and stocks an "amazing selection" of brands (Giant, Santa Cruz, Specialized) that covers models from entry level through professional, plus accessories and rentals; the staff is "passionate" and repairs are met with "expertise" and a "smile."

Finnegan's Toys ●

| 27 | 26 | 24 | M |

Downtown | 820 SW Washington St. (bet. 9th & Park Aves.) | 503-221-0306

Finnegan's Village Toys ●

Tigard | Bridgeport Vill. | 7439 SW Bridgeport Rd. (bet. Hazelfern & Upper Boones Ferry Rds.) | 503-747-4387
www.finnegansvillagetoys.com

"Chock-full" of amusements, this Downtown-Tigard toy shop is for "anyone who's a kid at heart", with an "eclectic variety" of playthings ("vintage-type", "modern" and "educational") that "you won't find at big-box stores"; it's independently owned and has a staff that will "help you pick out excellent gifts" at midrange prices "for all of the fun-freaks in your life."

Frame Central

| 25 | 22 | 22 | M |

Johns Landing | 6639 SW Macadam Ave. (bet. Idaho & Vermont Sts.) | 503-245-1000
Northwest Portland | 3265 NW Yeon Ave. (bet. Nicolai St. & 29th Ave.) | 503-219-9222
Pearl District | 1238 NW Davis St. (13th Ave.) | 503-546-9087 ●
Beaverton | 16157 NW Cornell Rd. (Bethany Blvd.) | 503-439-8961
Tigard | 12260 SW Main St. (Commercial St.) | 503-968-2668
www.framecentral.com

For a "huge selection" of "high-quality" picture frames (both premade and custom), aficionados recommend this local chainlet that gets the work "done fast" and has DIY options; it's "reasonably priced" considering the staff is "terrifically knowledgeable" and able to steer you "to just the right" solution for showcasing your artwork or memories.

Frances May Ⓜ

| ▽ 23 | 22 | 21 | E |

West End | 1013 SW Washington St. (bet. 10th & 11th Aves.) | 503-227-3402 | www.francesmay.com

Style hounds extol the "one-of-a-kind clothes for both men and women", shoes and accessories at this West End boutique, which values "quality fabric and craftsmanship" and carries "small-run, independent designers", plus well-known lines like Rachel Comey and Steven Alan; browsers praise the staff for "suggesting merchandise" "while not being overbearing", but you may need "tons of money" to get outfitted here regularly.

Free Geek �⌐ Ⓜ

23 | 19 | 25 | I

Central Eastside | 1731 SE 10th Ave. (bet. Market & Mill Sts.) | 503-232-9350 | www.freegeek.org

This "incredible" "community-friendly" Central Eastside nonprofit hosts a recycling program, education center and a bare-bones thrift store where those in need go to "buy used or refurbished computers and computer parts" at "incredibly low prices"; the staff and volunteers are "friendly and welcoming", and its "do-it-yourself" ethos is "so very Portland."

French Quarter Linens

26 | 26 | 23 | E

Pearl District | 530 NW 11th Ave. (bet. Glisan & Hoyt Sts.) | 503-282-8200 | www.frenchquarterlinens.com

For some of the "finest linens in all of Portland", this Pearl District boutique (relocated summer 2012, possibly outdating the Display rating) pleases with "classic", "luscious" bedding from the likes of Peacock Alley and Signoria Firenze, alongside bath towels, kitchen linens and related home goods; maybe prices are "not for the faint of heart", but thanks to a "friendly and helpful" staff, regulars "highly recommend it."

Furever Pets ◗

23 | 23 | 22 | E

Irvington | 1902 NE Broadway (19th Ave.) | 503-282-4225 | www.fureverpets.com

Crazy cat ladies and devoted dog dudes hit this "cute" animal-supply boutique in Irvington for everything "from poo bags to doggie backpacks", high-nutrition food brands like Nature's Variety and Vital Essentials plus the "latest in sportswear" for your furry friend; the staff appears to "love your pet as much or more than you do", and though it's a little pricey, it's all "excellent quality."

Garden Fever!

27 | 25 | 26 | E

Alameda | 3433 NE 24th Ave. (bet. Fremont & Klickitat Sts.) | 503-287-3200 | www.gardenfever.com

A "gardener's paradise" in Alameda, this small, "serene" nursery boasts "everything you need to have the perfect garden" with "healthy plants", flowers and vegetable starts plus plenty of tools and accessories in the "fun-to-wander-around" store and outdoor area; the staff provides "superb service", and there are regular classes and lectures for enrichment.

Gilt Ⓜ

25 | 23 | 21 | E

Northwest Portland | 720 NW 23rd Ave. (bet. Irving & Johnson Sts.) | 503-226-0629 | www.giltjewelry.com

"Magical" and "intimate", this NW Portland boutique draws gem aficionados with its "wide array of high-end jewelry" that ranges from antiques, including a "large selection of vintage diamond wedding and engagement rings", to new collections from local designers; the staff has plenty of "knowledge in all things gilded" and though items can be "pricey", the quality is "excellent."

	QUALITY	DISPLAY	SERVICE	COST

Haggis McBaggis

27 | 26 | 25 | E

Westmoreland | 6802 SE Milwaukie Ave. (bet. Bybee Blvd. & Claybourne St.) | 503-234-0849 | www.haggismcbaggis.com

The "high-quality" children's shoes at this Westmoreland retailer put a focus on "cute" and "comfortable" with names like EMU, Camper for Kids, pediped and Tsukihoshi lining the shelves; the kicks may be a "little pricey", but the staffers "know their stuff", and regulars advise to look out for "phenomenal sales."

Halo Shoes

23 | 22 | 21 | E

Pearl District | 938 NW Everett St. (bet. 9th & 10th Aves.) | 503-331-0366 | www.haloshoes.com

A "truly dangerous shoe store", this Pearl District spot stocks a "grand selection" of "top-quality" men's and women's footwear with lines including Costume National, Dries Van Noten and Timberland; devotees say the goods are "worth the expense" but wish there were a "few more pairs on the affordable end of the scale" in order to "indulge" "more often."

Hand Eye Supply

22 | 21 | 20 | M

Old Town-Chinatown | 23 NW Fourth Ave. (bet. Burnside & Couch Sts.) | 503-575-9769 | www.handeyesupply.com

This "quirky" Old Town supply shop for hipster artisans stocks workwear with an "impeccable" eye for "style" (e.g. "hard-to-find" tops and bottoms from U.S.-based Pointer Brand and shop coats from Denmark-based Mascot are in the mix) as well as design implements, books and other accessories, most at moderate prices; a "rad" staff helps make it "overall a fun place to visit" and "buy something random."

Hanna Andersson

28 | 26 | 25 | E

Pearl District | 327 NW 10th Ave. (Flanders St.) | 503-321-5275

Tigard | Washington Sq. | 9640 SW Washington Square Rd. (Blum Rd.) | 503-214-2332 ●

www.hannaandersson.com

Parents who want "adorable" yet "classic" kids' clothes able to "last through hand-me-downs" head to the understated Pearl District and Tigard outposts of the Portland-based chain where vibrant pops of color come from the merchandise; though the outfits are "pricey", note that "you get what you pay for."

Hillary Day ⊠Ⓜ

▽ 22 | 20 | 15 | E

Northwest Portland | 925 NW 19th Ave. (bet. Kearney & Lovejoy Sts.) | 503-913-0933 | www.hillaryday.com

Known for its line of feminine rainwear made from high-performance waterproof fabric, this NW Portland studio offers the eponymous designer's high-cost coat styles in a range of fabrics and colors; while its selection is small, the styles are meant to suit a range of figures and withstand any weather the city's notoriously wet winters can dish out; P.S. hours are limited but appointments can be scheduled.

Hip Furniture
22 | 22 | 20 | E

Northwest Portland | 1829 NW 25th Ave. (bet. Thurman & Upshur Sts.) | 503-225-5017 | www.ubhip.com

For home decorators seeking "fancy-pants furniture" that's "urban", "European" in style and definitely "modern", this NW Portland shop lives up to its name with its array of sleek sofas, storage units, beds, lighting and accessories; other bonuses: the pieces are "quality", and the staff doles out "lots of attention and help."

Hip Hound
23 | 22 | 20 | E

Northwest Portland | 610 NW 23rd Ave. (bet. Hoyt & Irving Sts.) | 503-841-5410 | www.hiphoundpdx.com

Pet lovers hit this spacious NW Portland paw shop for "high-end healthy natural foods for your dog" (including "grain-free and raw foods"), an "awesome" range of beds, coats, collars and toys plus, despite the name, a "good selection of cat stuff"; the owner is "knowledgeable" and welcomes furry friends, who like the "treats and lovin'."

Hippo Hardware
24 | 19 | 22 | E

Lower Burnside | 1040 E. Burnside St. (11th Ave.) | 503-231-1444 | www.hippohardware.com

"Indispensible for old-house" "renovators", this Lower Burnside salvage shop (since 1976) has an "incredible selection of vintage and vintagelike light fixtures", including "all the doorknobs you could want", in its 30,000-sq.-ft. space; you've got to be "in the mood for a scavenger hunt" among the "many rooms of strange, forgotten household items", but the staff is "sure to help" you "find that unfindable thing."

Hive
27 | 24 | 21 | VE

Pearl District | 820 NW Glisan St. (bet. 9th & Park Aves.) | 503-242-1967 | www.hivemodern.com

This "high-end" furniture and home accessories showroom in the Pearl District is a "great place to get design ideas", with "modern, fun" options from names like Eames, Corbusier and Alexander Girard; the staff's solid "customer service" is a plus too, making this a natural stop for contemporary-design devotees feathering their nest, er hive.

Hobby Smith Ⓜ
25 | 23 | 22 | E

Hollywood | 1809 NE Cesar E. Chavez Blvd. (bet. B'way & Hancock St.) | 503-284-1912 | www.hobbysmith.com

Ferroequinologists frequent this "old-time" Hollywood hobby shop that's many a fan's "first stop for model-railroading supplies", including N, HO, HOn3, Z and Lionel locomotives, plus topical magazines, books and DVDs; the staff's "not pushy", and there's an in-store operating layout and a friendly "community" of folks shopping that often chats about the "older-style hobbies" the store supplies.

I Heart Retro
23 | 23 | 19 | M

Hollywood | 1914 NE 42nd Ave. (Hancock St.) | 503-287-3764 | www.iheartretro.com

"My dream is for my living room to look like their display floor" says one surveyor smitten by this Hollywood vintage furniture and accessories shop featuring a "beautifully arranged" collection of mostly midcentury-modern and contemporary finds; other reasons to 'heart' it: the prices are "reasonable" and the staff is "willing to help when needed."

Imelda's & Louie's Shoes

25 | 24 | 22 | E

Hawthorne | 3426 SE Hawthorne Blvd. (bet. 34th & 35th Aves.) | 503-233-7476
Pearl District | 935 NW Everett St. (bet. 9th & 10th Aves.) | 503-595-4970
www.imeldasandlouies.com

The "stunning" selection of "beautiful, well-crafted shoes" (Børn, Clarks, Frye) impress at this "fab" pair in the Pearl District and Hawthorne that specializes in "comfy, quirky" footwear for women and men, and also stocks a selection of leather bags and accessories; other draws: the well-heeled say "you get what you pay for" and find the service "engaging."

Ink & Peat

24 | 24 | 23 | E

Boise-Eliot | 3808 N. Williams Ave. (bet. Beech & Failing Sts.) | 503-282-6688 | www.inkandpeat.com

Besides modern flower arrangements, this "exquisite" Boise-Eliot floral-design/gift shop carries an "excellent assortment" of "interesting" "pastoral-themed" items (many from local designers) including jewelry, fragrances and home decor; shoppers say they "love to browse here" and if prices are somewhat "elevated", at least it's for products that "grab your attention."

John Fluevog

28 | 28 | 25 | E

West End | 1224 SW Stark St. (bet. 12th & 13th Aves.) | 503-241-3338 | www.fluevog.com

For the namesake Canadian designer's "unusual shoes" with "lots of character", this West End footwear boutique is *the* place as it's the only Portland store to carry the distinctive brand; with an "amazing" interior designed by Fluevog that includes a reworked '64 Jaguar XKE, the environs match its attention-drawing wares, which may be "expensive", but are likely to get "compliments from strangers on the street."

John Helmer Haberdasher

28 | 26 | 26 | E

Downtown | 969 SW Broadway (Salmon St.) | 503-223-4976 | www.johnhelmer.com

It's "like stepping back in time" at this family-run Downtown haberdashery established in 1921, which still stocks a "natty" selection of "high-end" men's and women's toppers from fedoras to berets, alongside an "old-school collection of classic menswear"; the store itself is a "little confined", but service is "fabulous", leading devotees to declare "hats off."

The Joinery

27 | 25 | 22 | VE

Woodstock | 4804 SE Woodstock Blvd. (48th Ave.) | 503-788-8547 | www.thejoinery.com

"Everything is made so well" at this upscale Woodstock shop that you may think you're in an "art museum", though one spotlighting "gorgeous", "elegant" handcrafted furniture that's "timeless in design" (think Shaker, modern, Mission and Pacific styles); naturally, items are priced in accordance with their master craftsman origins, but no matter: admirers are in "love with the place."

Josephine's Dry Goods   27 | 24 | 24 | E

West End | 521 SW 11th Ave. (bet. Alder & Washington Sts.) | 503-224-4202 | www.josephinesdrygoods.com

"Designer fabrics of the best quality" swathe this spacious West End purveyor, a "longtime Portland favorite" with "fabulous silks", velvets, cashmere and more "beautiful" designs from big names like Calvin Klein, Dana Buchman and Donna Karan, plus notions and an impressive button collection; prices are high, but service is well regarded and there are numerous classes to improve one's skill.

Kassab Jewelers   26 | 24 | 24 | VE

Downtown | 529 SW Broadway (bet. Alder & Washington Sts.) | 503-295-0705 🖬

Lake Oswego | 310 N. State St. (bet. A Ave. & Northshore Rd.) | 503-635-8383 🖬

Tigard | Washington Sq. | 9306 SW Washington Square Rd. (bet. Blum & Greenburg Rds.) | 503-639-1177 ●
www.kassabjewelers.com

Gem-seekers – from first-timers "picking out 'the ring'" to those "looking for an upgrade" – recommend this family-owned jewelry chainlet for its "out-of-the-ordinary" pieces, which include custom designs and a "wonderful selection" of big names like Tacori and Verragio; the "helpful, professional" staff is "not pushy" and will help customers find the "right diamond" or other bauble "within a person's budget."

Keen Garage   26 | 26 | 25 | E

Pearl District | 926 NW 13th Ave. (Lovejoy St.) | 503-542-5560 | www.keenfootwear.com

The outdoor-shoe company's first retail store, this "small" Pearl District shop resembles a garage with concrete floors and "cool", space-maximizing rotating racks made from old bike chains that display "comfortable" footwear for men, women and children; an "eager-to-help" staff uses ladders to access hard-to-reach boxes, and fetishists say the "supreme" product is "worth the splurge."

Kiehl's   27 | 24 | 24 | E

Northwest Portland | 712 NW 23rd Ave. (Irving St.) | 503-223-7676 | www.kiehls.com

Bringing dull complexions "back to life" since 1851, this "time-warp chemist" peddles "hard-to-live-without" cosmetics, "natural" shampoos, "herbal" toners and body butter ("Crème de Corps: nothing moisturizes better") in an "old-school" setting; "as luxuries go, it's comparatively cheap", and the "ego-boosting" staff is "generous" with both kind words and free samples.

Kitchen Kaboodle   26 | 25 | 23 | E

Irvington | 1520 NE Broadway (16th Ave.) | 503-288-1500

(continued)

(continued)

Kitchen Kaboodle

Northwest Portland | 404 NW 23rd Ave. (Flanders St.) |
503-241-4040
Hillsboro | 1415 NE 61st Ave. (Cornell Rd.) | 503-846-1515
Beaverton | 8788 SW Hall Blvd. (bet. Fairview Pl. & Scholls Ferry Rd.) |
503-643-5491
Happy Valley | Clackamas Town Ctr. | 11860 SE 82nd Ave.
(Monterey Ave.) | 503-652-2567
www.kitchenkaboodle.com

"Foodies" love "puttering around" in this "cramped and cluttered"
locally owned chainlet stocked with "everything under the sun" including "obscure kitchen gadgets", table settings and "high-end
home wares" plus furniture; if it's "on the expensive side" all is forgiven for the "great" selection and "friendly" staff that "really listens
to your needs."

Knit Purl
27 | 26 | 24 | E

West End | 1101 SW Alder St. (11th Ave.) | 503-227-2999 |
www.knit-purl.com

"Creativity abounds" in this "beautiful" West End yarn shop, where
devoted knitters "go gaga" over the "amazing" "fairly pricey" selection of some of the "most luxurious and fashion-forward yarn in the
area", including silk, cashmere and alpaca; it also offers classes, and
a "welcoming" staff doles out "lots of helpful advice" for new and
experienced crafters alike.

Langlitz Leathers ⌧
29 | 23 | 28 | VE

Division | 2443 SE Division St. (bet. 24th & 26th Aves.) | 503-235-0959 |
www.langlitz.com

"Still the best" boast customers of this "PDX original", a family-owned
"famous maker of motorcycle leathers" on Division that got its start
in 1947 and has continuously put out "top-quality" protective gear,
namely jackets, vests and pants, plus other riding accessories;
though off-the-rack garments are available, "they prefer to make
each piece [custom]", which takes time and is "very expensive", but
fans say it's "worth" the wait for "American-made craftsmanship"
that "could save your hide"; P.S. Saturdays are by appointment only.

Lena Medoyeff Studio
24 | 23 | 22 | E

Northwest Portland | 710 NW 23rd Ave. (bet. Irving & Johnson Sts.) |
503-227-0011 | www.lenadress.com

"Exquisite", "one-of-a-kind" traditional and nontraditional bridal
and special-occasion gowns (with plenty of color and prints) are the
hallmark of this NW Portland boutique showcase for local designer
Lynn Medoff; though the "selection is small", the "sweet", "no-
pressure" staff "really listens" and creates a "special environment"
that makes customers "feel really good about buying."

LexiDog
24 | 23 | 23 | E

Johns Landing | 6100 SW Macadam Ave. (Iowa St.) | 503-245-4363
Pearl District | 416 NW 10th Ave. (bet. Flanders & Glisan Sts.) |
503-243-6200

(continued)

LexiDog

Lake Oswego | 366 Third St. (bet. A Ave. & Evergreen Rd.) | 503-635-3733 🗷
www.lexidog.com

A "must" if you treat pets "like children", this trio of "dog boutiques"/ daycares has plenty of "cute clothes and wonderful toys" and is run by a staff that "really loves you and your" furry ones; the Johns Landing shop has the largest retail selection plus a full-sized exercise pool and animals up for adoption from the Oregon Humane Society.

Lille Boutique

24 | 23 | 26 | E

Lower Burnside | 1007 E. Burnside St. (bet. 10th & 11th Aves.) | 503-232-0333

Lille Trousseau 🗷Ⓜ

West End | 1124 SW Alder St. (bet. 11th & 12th Aves.) | 503-222-2702
www.lilleboutique.com

If you "want to feel sexy", brassiere buffs recommend this "niche" Lower Burnside boutique (and its West End cousin, which focuses on bridal lingerie) for an "on-point" selection of "quality, some-times vintage-inspired" underpinnings that runs "naughty to nice"; if the "pretty things" have "hefty prices", the "helpful, sweet" staff lessens the sting.

Lippman Company 🗷

21 | 22 | 23 | M

Eastside Industrial | 50 SE Yamhill St. (bet. 2nd & Water Aves.) | 503-239-7007 | www.lippmancompany.com

"Everything you need for party planning" is packed into this 12,000-sq.-ft. Eastside Industrial powerhouse that's "unbelievably tacky and delightful" with wares running from simple "tchotchkes to whole thematic party setups"; a "helpful" staff and relatively "cheap" prices add to the festivities and a separate room for helium balloons also occasions a visit.

Lizard Lounge

24 | 24 | 22 | E

Pearl District | 1323 NW Irving St. (bet. 13th & 14th Aves.) | 503-416-7476 | www.lizardloungepdx.com

"On trend for the preppy hipster", this Pearl District boutique stocks "quality" men's and women's heritage brands (Filson, Pendleton, Woolrich) plus its house line, Horny Toad, along with footwear, bags and other accessories; items are "expensive", but the "nice" staff, free wireless and Stumptown coffee encourage an easygoing "hangout vibe."

L'Occitane ●

26 | 24 | 23 | E

Downtown | Pioneer Pl. | 340 SW Morrison Ave. (4th Ave.) | 503-295-9000
Tigard | Washington Sq. | 9520 SW Washington Square Rd. (Blum Rd.) | 503-443-4283
www.loccitane.com

This ubiquitous "aromatherapy haven" purveys some of the "best body-care potions" around, including "gorgeous shower gels" and "lovely, long-lasting" soaps and hand creams, which "smell like the South of France"; yes, the "balms" "come at a price", nevertheless they're an "affordable luxury" and also make for "welcome hostess gifts."

Louis Vuitton ⊠ Ⓜ

28 | 28 | 25 | VE

Downtown | Pioneer Pl. | 703 SW Fifth Ave. (Morrison St.) | 503-226-3280 | www.louisvuitton.com

"Exquisite, expensive and exclusive", this haute "high-end" French leather goods store "oozes luxury" with "timeless classics" in "traditional LV-logo" handbags and luggage "that get passed down the generations" and chic Marc Jacobs–designed apparel; service reviews range from "superb" to "snooty", though perhaps not surprisingly since the status covetables set "a standard by which others can be judged."

Lounge Lizard

24 | 24 | 23 | M

Hawthorne | 1310 SE Hawthorne Blvd. (bet. Ladd & Maple Aves.) | 503-232-7575

There's "lots and lots" of "hip vintage furniture" at this packed Hawthorne reseller with "amazing values" on furnishings and decor, much of it dating from the '50s through '70s; the staff is "helpful", but be warned that "it's like a whole new store every time you're in", so "if you like it, buy it"; P.S. delivery is available for a fee.

Lululemon Athletica

26 | 23 | 24 | E

Pearl District | 1231 NW Couch St. (12th Ave.) | 503-274-0007
Tigard | Bridgeport Vill. | 7381 SW Bridgeport Rd. (Upper Boones Ferry Rd.) | 503-620-7438 ✆
www.lululemon.com

"Get your sweat on in style" at this "yoga heaven", where the "amazing activewear makes you want to" bend and stretch, and the "high-end" prices are "worth it" thanks to "fabulous" quality and those "flattering" "pants that make every butt look great"; the "staff of perky yogis" is "skilled and sweet", and you might even find them downward dogging in "storefront windows."

Mabel & Zora

23 | 22 | 20 | E

Pearl District | 748 NW 11th Ave. (bet. Hoyt & Johnson Sts.) | 503-241-5696 | www.mabelandzora.com

"Darling dresses" and other "beautiful" women's apparel draw fashionistas to this elegant, retro-inspired haven near the Pearl's Jamison Square that also stocks gift items like Voluspa candles and jewelry by Portland-based Grayling; while not cheap, the fact that the "nice" staff is always on hand to offer "no-pressure" advice adds allure.

M.A.C. Cosmetics

26 | 24 | 22 | M

Northwest Portland | 615 NW 23rd Ave. (Hoyt St.) | 503-222-1943
Tigard | Bridgeport Vill. | 7239 SW Bridgeport Rd. (Hazelfern Rd.) | 503-639-6287 ✆
www.maccosmetics.com

Makeup junkies go wild at this cosmetics chain that's a "grown-up's playland" with its house brand of "all the new lipstick colors", "richly pigmented" blushes and "a rainbow assortment of look-at-me shadows and liners"; stylists "know their stuff" and stand ready "to give you a new look" – they'll even do makeovers on the spot.

The Mac Store   26 | 25 | 23 | E

Lloyd | 700 NE Multnomah St. (bet. 7th & 9th Aves.) | 800-689-8191
Beaverton | 3205 SW Cedar Hills Blvd. (bet. Hall Blvd. & Jenkins Rd.) | 800-689-8191 ◗
Happy Valley | Clackamas Town Ctr. | 12000 SE 82nd Ave. (bet. Flanders & Glisan Sts.) | 800-689-8191 ◗
www.themacstore.com

A "local independent Apple reseller" for decades, this Pacific NW chain with three Portland locations is "nice and bright", stocked with the latest new and used models and "lots of options for customizing gadgets"; it's "not crazy busy", making it an "alternative" to the official retailer, and surveyors appreciate its staff of "real Mac geeks" who provide "incredibly helpful" service.

Macy's ◗   22 | 20 | 17 | M

Downtown | 621 SW Fifth Ave. (Alder St.) | 503-223-0512
Lloyd | Lloyd Ctr. | 1100 Lloyd Ctr. (Halsey St.) | 503-281-4797
Hillsboro | The Streets | 2055 NW Allie Ave. (Cornell Rd.) | 503-617-6999
Happy Valley | Clackamas Town Ctr. | 12100 SE 82nd Ave. (Monterey Ave.) | 503-653-8811
Tigard | Washington Sq. | 9300 SW Washington Square Rd. (Blum Rd.) | 503-620-3311
www.macys.com

Established in 1858, this iconic brand sells "anything you could possibly want" at its "reliable" "mid-tier" department stores, where the "wide selection" is offered at prices "for every pocketbook"; staffers "could be more attentive" and some locations feel "cluttered" and "crowded", but no one complains about the "fantastic" sales.

Made In Oregon ◗   26 | 25 | 23 | M

Downtown | Pioneer Pl. | 340 SW Morrison St. (bet. 3rd & 4th Aves.) | 503-241-3630
Lloyd | Lloyd Ctr. | 1017 Lloyd Ctr. (11th Ave.) | 503-282-7636
Happy Valley | Clackamas Town Ctr. | 12000 SE 82nd Ave. (bet. Monterey Ave. & Sunnyside Rd.) | 503-659-3155
Tigard | Washington Sq. | 9589 SW Washington Square Rd. (Blum Rd.) | 503-620-4670
www.madeinoregon.com

It's "one-stop shopping" for "all things Oregon" at this well-known chainlet that's Portland's Most Popular retailer, vending a "delightful collection of locally made products", including arts and crafts, Pendleton designs, a "fairly large wine selection" and foodstuffs "from salmon to truffles"; sure, there's plenty of "kitsch", but items are available in a "variety of price points", and it's a "great choice for sending a bit of Oregon anywhere."

Magpie   24 | 23 | 22 | M

Downtown | 520 SW Ninth Ave. (bet. Alder & Washington Sts.) | 503-220-0920

For an "exciting wonderland" of "well-curated" vintage clothing, "especially for men", there's this Downtown fixture, which "holds amazing treasures", including "beautiful items from the turn of the century", "groovy threads from the '70s" and "lots of hats", shoes and jewelry; most of its items are a "great deal" and "if you hunt, you can find some interesting pieces."

Maloy's Jewelers ⊠

| 25 | 22 | 26 | E |

Downtown | 717 SW 10th Ave. (bet. Morrison & Yamhill Sts.) | 503-223-4720 | www.maloys.com

With its focus on fine vintage jewelry, custom designs and repairs, this "old-fashioned" Downtown jeweler displays a "discerning collection" of "beautiful, interesting" pieces with guidance from a "special staff that really knows jewelry"; the "expensive" price points are considered "reasonable" given the quality, resulting in "high recommendations" all around.

Mario's

| 26 | 25 | 24 | VE |

Downtown | 833 SW Broadway (bet. Taylor & Yamhill Sts.) | 503-227-3477

Mario's 3.10

Tigard | Bridgeport Vill. | 17031 SW 72nd Ave. (bet. Bridgeport & Durham Rds.) | 503-601-7310
www.marios.com

A serene ode to "upper-end" women's fashion (Alexander McQueen, Lanvin, Narciso Rodriguez) as well as "quality gentlemen's clothing", this "swanky" Downtown department store also impresses the local gentry with its "amazingly friendly" staff; at its Bridgeport Village offshoot, more contemporary brands fill the shelves (Clu, Rag & Bone, Theyskens' Theory) – but at either location, expect "steep" price tags.

Mercantile Portland

| 28 | 27 | 25 | VE |

Downtown | 729 SW Alder St. (bet. B'way & Park Ave.) | 503-223-6649 | www.mercantileportland.com

Specializing in contemporary and high-end women's fashion, this simple, spacious Downtown atelier gets props as one of the "best women's clothing stores in the area" and caters to youthful and mature audiences alike with a broad mix of labels (e.g. Diane von Furstenberg, J Brand, MaxMara); along with the "excellent quality" of its threads come "high" price tags, causing one cost-conscious browser to sigh "if only I could afford the clothes."

Mill End Store

| 24 | 20 | 21 | M |

Beaverton | 4955 SW Western Ave. (5th Ave.) | 503-646-3000
Milwaukie | 9701 SE McLoughlin Blvd. (Milport Rd.) | 503-786-1234
www.millendstore.com

This "venerable" Milwaukie textile emporium (there's also a smaller Beaverton outpost) is a "must-visit for those who sew, upholster or do anything with fabric" and has a huge "array of fine wools, linens, silks and dress goods" as well as yarn, notions and the like housed in a warehouselike space boasting an "astounding square footage"; the staff is "polite", and most find prices "affordable" and, of the "tremendous" selection, say "if they don't have it, no one does."

	QUALITY	DISPLAY	SERVICE	COST

Moulé
▽ 25 | 25 | 25 | E

Pearl District | 1225 NW Everett St. (bet. 12th & 13th Aves.) | 503-227-8530 | www.moulestores.com

The only U.S. outpost of the Canadian department store, this Pearl District rebel stocks "wonderful" contemporary clothing for women and men from hard-to-find designers like Rachel Mara, Scotch & Soda and Ulla Johnson; "trendy" gifts and home accessories are also on offer, and though prices can be "expensive", the occasional sales offer legendary bargains.

Museum of Contemporary Craft Gift Shop ⑤Ⓜ
27 | 27 | 23 | E

Pearl District | Museum of Contemporary Craft | 724 NW Davis St. (8th Ave.) | 503-223-2654 | www.museumofcontemporarycraft.org

A "wonderful" stock of wares from a range of local artisans is showcased at this Pearl District shop located in the lobby of the Museum of Contemporary Craft; even with the occasional "just weird" standouts, appreciators feel "lucky to have" the institution housing this store, which never fails to "highlight creativity"; P.S. it generally follows museum hours, but you can access without paying admission.

Music Millennium ⦿
27 | 25 | 25 | M

Kerns | 3158 E. Burnside St. (32nd Ave.) | 503-231-8926

Classical Millennium ⦿
Kerns | 3144 E. Burnside St. (32nd Ave.) | 503-231-8909 www.musicmillennium.com

"One of the last great music stores", this local Kerns "treasure" (since 1969) stocks a "fantastic", "fairly priced" mix of new and used CDs and LPs "from all genres", including a deep classical catalog, plus DVDs; and "in an era when music is all going online" it offers brick-and-mortar niceties like free in-store concerts from "local and nationally touring artists" and a staff that's a "wealth of information."

Naked Sheep Knit Shop Ⓜ
27 | 28 | 26 | M

Overlook | 2142 N. Killingsworth St. (bet. Denver & Gay Aves.) | 503-283-2004 | www.thenakedsheepknitshop.com

"Cute, bright" and "organized", this Overlook knitting nexus appeals with its "inspiring" yarn, lots of patterns, "ideas for gifts" and "great classes", with offerings for crocheters too; smitten stitchers praise the "welcoming" staff and insist the "best way to spend an afternoon is knitting on the big blue couch" here.

Next Adventure
26 | 22 | 25 | M

Central Eastside | 426 SE Grand Ave. (Stark St.) | 503-233-0706

Next Adventure Paddle Sports Center
Central Eastside | 704 SE Washington St. (7th Ave.) | 503-233-0706 www.nextadventure.net

Outdoor gear is "bursting at the seams" of this Central Eastside sporting goods mecca, which has a "massive selection" of equipment for year-round activities from camping and hiking to skiing and snowboarding; though the layout can seem "chaotic", most herald the "incredible prices" of the used stuff on the lower level and praise

the "knowledgeable" staff, "avid outdoor enthusiasts" themselves;
P.S. the Washington Street location carries gear for water sports.

Nike Portland ❷   27 | 27 | 24 | E

Downtown | 638 SW Fifth Ave. (Morrison St.) | 503-221-6453 |
www.nike.com

This "beautiful", "modern" Downtown flagship location of what's
perhaps "Portland's most beloved company" is a sure bet with its
signature "baller kicks" and the "latest" clothing and gear filling its
26,000-sq.-ft. space; service shows "attention to detail", and if it's
"slightly pricey", most insist the goods are "worth it" – so "just do it."

Nordstrom ❷   26 | 24 | 26 | E

Downtown | 701 SW Broadway (Morrison St.) | 503-224-6666
Lloyd | Lloyd Ctr. | 1001 Lloyd Ctr. (Halsey St.) | 503-287-2444
Happy Valley | Clackamas Town Ctr. | 11900 SE 82nd Ave.
(Monterey Ave.) | 503-652-1810
Tigard | Washington Sq. | 9700 SW Washington Square Rd. (Blum Rd.) |
503-620-0555
www.nordstrom.com

Starting off as a Seattle shoe store back in 1901, this "lovely", "civilized" national department store chain now offers "tasteful" fashions for the whole family, a "fabulous" footwear department and
service that is "second to none" – it's no wonder fans call it "god's
gift to retail"; still, the wares can be "pricey", which is why many
"live for their sales."

The North Face ❷   25 | 21 | 20 | E

Pearl District | 1202 NW Davis St. (12th Ave.) | 503-727-0200 |
www.thenorthface.com

Famous for its "quality outdoor gear", this Portland branch of the na-
tionwide chain stocks an "extensive line" of sports clothes and out-
erwear along with "excellent" technical equipment and footwear;
though the merchandise may be "costly", for most it's "worth the
price in warmth" whether they're facing "sub-zero temperatures" or
merely a "cold day."

Noun: A Person's Place For Things Ⓜ   ▽ 27 | 27 | 25 | E

Belmont | 3300 SE Belmont St. (33rd Ave.) | 503-235-0078 |
www.shopnoun.com

"Cute and quirky", this SE Belmont gift shop stocks "local goods,
unique vintage items" and a "fun selection of decor and jewelry"; the
owner's care shows in the "cute descriptions" that accompany the
pieces, and the overall effect makes fans "feel good every time" they
visit; P.S. there's an outpost of bakery Saint Cupcake located inside.

Oblation Papers & Press   27 | 25 | 23 | E

Pearl District | 516 NW 12th Ave. (bet. Glisan & Hoyt Sts.) |
503-223-1093 | www.oblationpapers.com

It's the "artisanal feel" of the "gorgeous" letterpress cards and handmade papers at this Pearl District stationer that sends folks flocking
for "classy" correspondence, invites and announcements plus writing
implements and gifts; the tabs are "high-end", but the staffers

	QUALITY	DISPLAY	SERVICE	COST

show "pride in their product" so it's the place to go if you want your recipient "to be impressed."

OMSI Science Store ◐
26 | 25 | 23 | E

Eastside Industrial | Oregon Museum of Science & Industry (OMSI) | 1945 SE Water Ave. (Hawthorne Blvd.) | 503-797-4626 | www.omsi.edu

"Mom, can I have that?" is a familiar refrain at this "quality" companion store to the Oregon Museum of Science and Industry that offers up the "world of science for you to take home", including "gadgets, experiments and trinkets that cannot be found just anywhere"; fans advise braving the "pricey" tabs to be rewarded with "cool toys."

OSU Beaver Store
24 | 24 | 23 | E

Downtown | 538 SW Sixth Ave. (Alder St.) | 503-525-2678 | www.osubeaverstore.com

"From mugs to sweatshirts to knickknacks", it's "everything Beaver" at this Oregon State University gear shop Downtown loaded with "tons" of officially licensed merch; the staff is "friendly", and fanatics say it's a "fun place to get your inner cheerleader or team geek on."

Parallel
▽ 21 | 22 | 22 | E

West End | 1016 SW Washington St. (bet. 10th & 11th Aves.) | 503-274-8882 | www.parallelportland.com

A "well-edited selection" of wardrobe basics, fashion-forward picks (e.g. Clu, Hansel from Basel, Rag & Bone) and accessories fill this trendy women's boutique that recently relocated to the West End; the staff is "friendly" and "helpful", leading style-conscious shoppers to declare it a "must-stop."

Patagonia
27 | 22 | 23 | E

Pearl District | 907 NW Irving St. (10th Ave.) | 503-525-2552 | www.patagonia.com

"Outdoorsy" sorts call this "superior" international chain a "top choice" for "practical" activewear that's "stylish" yet "rugged" and manufactured with the "environment" in mind; it'll cost some "green", but the "crunchy-granola staff" provides plenty of assistance, and "these clothes perform" rain, snow or shine.

Ped-X Shoes
23 | 24 | 23 | E

Alberta | 2230 NE Alberta St. (bet. 22nd & 23rd Aves.) | 503-460-0760 | www.pedxshoes.com

Fans of comfortable yet stylish women's shoes laud this cheery Alberta emporium for its "spot-on" selection of "middle- and high-end" footwear (think Campers, Frye, Tsubo) plus bags and accessories; the sale balcony is the place to head for "best buys", and most find the staff "helpful, even when it gets busy."

Pendleton
28 | 26 | 25 | E

Downtown | 900 SW Fifth Ave. (Taylor St.) | 503-242-0037
Lake Oswego | 385 First St. (A Ave.) | 503-675-7626
www.pendleton-usa.com

"Quality" is the hallmark of the clothing and signature blankets on offer at these "bright" Downtown and Lake Oswego retail outlets of the well-known Oregon woolen mill; sure, it's a "little pricey", but a staff that "goes above and beyond to help" plus the brand's caché ("it's Pendleton . . . enough said") make it a "lovely place to browse" if not always to buy.

Pendleton Home Store ⊠

| 27 | 25 | 24 | E |

Old Town-Chinatown | 220 NW Broadway (Davis St.) | 503-535-5444 | www.pendleton-usa.com

This Old Town home furnishings shop stocks "lots" of its famous parent's "beautiful" signature "Western-themed" fabrics on blankets, throws, pillows and the like, as well as furniture and larger home goods; though woolen-gatherers admit that "shopping here all the time" could "break the bank", the "incredible quality" is "hard to beat."

Pendleton Woolen Mill Store

| 25 | 22 | 23 | E |

Milwaukie | 8500 SE McLoughlin Blvd. (Springwater Corridor Trail) | 503-535-5786 | www.pendleton-usa.com

"If you need it they have it" among the "huge selection of yarns, fabrics and notions" at this Milwaukie textile outlet from the renowned woolen mill that also showcases the signature Native American-themed patterns in blankets, decor and tabletop items from its namesake Home collection; the warehouse space is nothing fancy, but on-site quilting, crocheting and rug-making classes where you can "build a keepsake" are a plus.

The Perfume House ⊠

| 25 | 24 | 23 | E |

Hawthorne | 3328 SE Hawthorne Blvd. (33rd Ave.) | 503-234-5375 | www.theperfumehouse.com

"Scentsational" say fragrance-philes of this "exquisite" Hawthorne shop with "high-quality" scents that will "blow your mind", including "hard-to-find, out-of-production and rare" perfumes and colognes; it's staffed by expert "noses" that "know the product" and will help you "find what you love" in an environment that "feels like you're in Paris."

Pet Loft

| 24 | 26 | 26 | M |

Johns Landing | 6333 SW Macadam Ave. (bet. Carolina & Dakota Sts.) | 503-244-9538 | www.petloft.net

"Two thumbs and four paws up" for the "personal service" at this Johns Landing pet shop say devoted customers who also appreciate the "fantastic selection" of dog and cat food, including raw options, plus an "amazing" roundup of pet essentials including gear for tropical fish; prices are commensurate with the brands, and surveyors say "you get what you pay for" and are happy to keep "making the trip back."

Popina Swimwear Boutique

| 26 | 21 | 23 | E |

Northeast Portland | 4831 NE 42nd Ave. (Alberta Ct.) | 503-282-5159
Pearl District | 318 NW 11th Ave. (bet. Everett & Flanders Sts.) | 503-243-7946
www.popinaswimwear.com

"Many choices" "for real women's bodies" abound at this Pearl District and NE Portland swimwear specialist owned by a local designer, which highlights its own "functional and fun" retro-inspired

designs alongside other brands; the "wonderful" staff can custom-
ize suits too, so while prices are "on the expensive side" you can "go
to the beach feeling awesome."

Portland Art Museum Shop

27 | 26 | 23 | E

Downtown | Portland Art Museum | 1219 SW Park Ave. (Jefferson St.) |
503-226-2811 | www.portlandartmuseum.org

A "beautiful" shop that's an "exhibit in itself", this annex to the
Portland Art Museum is "packed to the gills" with "interesting design
objects", including "cool toys, beautiful fabrics, stunning jewelry" and
"wonderful books"; whether for a "special memento" after a museum
visit or a "unique" gift for someone else, prices are "reasonable" for
the wares – especially for those with a membership discount.

Portland Luggage Company

25 | 22 | 22 | E

Downtown | 440 SW Fourth Ave. (Washington St.) | 888-695-8180
Beaverton | 11645 SW Beaverton-Hillsdale Hwy. (bet. Grift Dr. &
Lombard Ave.) | 503-641-3456
www.portlandluggage.com

Packing "high-quality luggage" (e.g. Ghurka, Tumi, Victorinox),
briefcases, messenger and laptop bags and "tough-to-find" travel
accessories, this venerable Downtown-Beaverton emporium is a
destination for sojurners – though even fans say "there's nothing
cheap here"; opinions on service are mixed, but many nod to "excellent repair work", and frequent fliers say they'll be "making
another trip soon."

Portland Music Company

26 | 23 | 24 | E

Brooklyn | 1010 SE Powell Blvd. (bet. 10th & 11th Aves.) |
503-775-0800 Ⓢ
Central Eastside | 531 SE Martin Luther King Jr. Blvd. (Washington St.) |
503-226-3719
Irvington | 2502 NE Broadway (25th Ave.) | 503-228-8437
Southeast Portland | 12334 SE Division St. (bet. 10th & 11th Aves.) |
503-760-6881
Beaverton | 10075 SW Beaverton-Hillsdale Hwy. (bet. 99th Ave. &
101st Ct.) | 503-641-5505
www.portlandmusiccompany.com

There's a "ton of instruments" (for purchase or rental) including
plenty of "cool stuff on consignment" and an "unbeatable array of
sheet music" at these locally owned Portland-area music centers,
which are an "excellent resource for teachers, aspiring learners and
gigging practitioners"; the "knowledgeable" staff is ready to help
you "trade in your old Bronco and get a Stratocaster", with an overall
effect that's "music to the ears."

Portland Nursery

28 | 27 | 27 | E

Mt. Tabor | 5050 SE Stark St. (bet. 49th & 52nd Aves.) | 503-231-5050
Southeast Portland | 9000 SE Division St. (bet. 89th & 92nd Aves.) |
503-788-9000
www.portlandnursery.com

A "well-known staple for all your garden needs", this "awesome" SE
Portland and Mt. Tabor duo impresses with a "massive, sprawling

complex of indoor/outdoor plants" helpfully laid out "with similar species and microclimate conditions together" plus a "wonderful native plants section"; it's a "little expensive but the customer service makes up for the price", and fans confess becoming greenery "addicts."

Portland Running Company ⦿ | 27 | 25 | 27 | E |

Central Eastside | 800 SE Grand Ave. (Morrison St.) | 503-232-8077
Beaverton | 10029 SW Nimbus Ave. (Scholls Ferry Rd.) | 503-524-7570
www.portlandrunningcompany.com
A "go-to for all your running needs", this Central Eastside–Beaverton purveyor is marked by its "patient", "knowledgeable" staff that will "take its time" and "watch you run" to ensure a "good-fitting pair" of shoes that's "appropriate for the activity" and "your form"; besides the "broad product selection", there are group runs and events to "bring people in the community together."

Presents of Mind | 24 | 24 | 23 | M |

Hawthorne | 3633 SE Hawthorne Blvd. (bet. 36th & 37th Aves.) | 503-230-7740 | www.presentsofmind.tv
This "playful" gift emporium in the heart of Hawthorne offers a "selection of oddities", including "clever presents for the jokester", "snarky" greeting cards, "toys and tchotchkes" plus some "tony jewelry" that's locally made; it's a "favorite place to browse", but the "reasonable" prices and "down-to-earth" staff also make it a lock "when you get the urge to buy."

Pro Photo Supply ⌁ | 28 | 24 | 25 | VE |

Northwest Portland | 1112 NW 19th Ave. (bet. Marshall & Northrup Sts.) | 503-241-1112 | www.prophotosupply.com
"Photo geeks" swear this NW Portland supplier is one of the "best camera shops in town", with its "awesome" gear, "fantastic film selection" and plenty of used and rental equipment at a "reasonable cost" for the high quality; otherwise, the focus is on its "top-notch" staff who really "knows the industry", offers "excellent product support" and is able, for instance, to dive into "obscure technical details on old digital cameras."

Queen Bee Creations | 28 | 26 | 25 | E |

Boise-Eliot | 3961 N. Williams Ave. (bet. Failing & Shaver Sts.) | 503-232-1755 | www.queenbee-creations.com
"They 'put a bird on it' long before *Portlandia*" say fans of this Boise-Eliot accessories shop known for its line of "distinctive" leather goods – bike panniers, wallets, bags, purses and the like – adorned with an array of feathered friends and other "beautiful designs"; it's "expensive", but "like fine shoes" the "high-quality" products "will wear well for years."

Really Good Stuff | 21 | 19 | 21 | I |

Hawthorne | 1322 SE Hawthorne Blvd. (bet. Ladd & Maple Aves.) | 503-238-1838
While it "doesn't look like much", this Hawthorne thrift store is piled to the rafters with a "great selection of old stuff" – everything from musical instruments and vintage electronics to bins of old photos

and random housewares, much of it cheap; while it can feel "dusty", it's got a staff that's "super-passionate about its junk" and oversees some real "finds", even if "it can take a few trips to find what you want."

The Real Mother Goose ⊠

27 | 26 | 24 | E

Downtown | 901 SW Yamhill St. (9th Ave.) | 503-223-9510 | www.therealmothergoose.com

"Unique items made by Pacific NW artists" are on display at this "inspiring" Downtown shop showcasing a collection of "stunning jewelry", pottery, woodworking, "superb furniture" and other "artsy goodies", much of it "expensive"; shopping here can feel "like finding treasure", and even if you're just browsing, there's always something "to drool over."

ReBuilding Center

22 | 18 | 24 | M

Mississippi | 3625 N. Mississippi Ave. (bet. Beech & Fremont Sts.) | 503-331-1877 | www.rebuildingcenter.org

"What could possibly be more Portland?" than this nonprofit "reuse, recycle and repurpose" construction-supply center in Mississippi with an "expansive" selection of "inexpensive", "random" materials ranging from old light fixtures to cabinets and lumber; some of the "amazing" staff are volunteers, and even if finding what you need can be like looking for "a needle in a haystack, it's a really great haystack."

Red Light Clothing Exchange ◗

21 | 20 | 17 | M

Hawthorne | 3590 SE Hawthorne Blvd. (36th Ave.) | 503-963-8888 | www.redlightclothingexchange.com

For "unique", "quirky" clothing ranging from the "'50s era to now", this Hawthorne vintage shop and "Portland institution" has "bargains galore" among the crowded racks; it can be "a lot to wade through", and some shoppers give the service low marks, but for "good-quality and perhaps unorthodox" wardrobe pieces it's "worth visiting"; P.S. bring your old clothes to sell or trade.

REI ◗

26 | 23 | 24 | M

Pearl District | 1405 NW Johnson St. (14th Ave.) | 503-221-1938
Hillsboro | 2235 NW Allie Ave. (Stucki Ave.) | 503-617-6072
Happy Valley | Clackamas Town Ctr. | 12160 SE 82nd Ave. (Sunnyside Rd.) | 503-659-1156
Tigard | Bridgeport Vill. | 7410 SW Bridgeport Rd. (Upper Boones Ferry Rd.) | 503-624-8600
www.rei.com

"Activities" addicts turn to the branches of Seattle's reigning sporting goods champ for "excellent" outdoor clothes and gear "galore" that provide "inspiration for doing exercise" and propel you "into the wild"; add "top-notch service" and "fair" pricing (with "a healthy rebate" for members), and the "adventure" "fix" "is complete."

Rejuvenation

27 | 26 | 24 | VE

Central Eastside | 1100 SE Grand Ave. (Taylor St.) | 503-238-1900 | www.rejuvenation.com

A "destination" for "fancy" period lighting and interior fixtures, this "high-priced" Central Eastside specialist has "all the good old stuff you need for a restoration project" or just to add a retro touch; it's a "place of inspiration", and the "knowledgeable" staff will "make you feel right at home."

Rerun

26 | 24 | 22 | I

King | 707 NE Fremont St. (7th Ave.) | 503-517-3786 | www.portlandrerun.com

There are "some great treasures" hiding in this "small" King consignment store stocked with a "well-curated" assortment of "eclectic merchandise" from "funky clothes" to "nice furniture" at "reasonable prices"; the owners are "nice" too, and even if "you can't always find the item you went in looking for", you often leave with "something fabulous" anyway; P.S. closed Tuesdays.

Reynolds Optical

25 | 23 | 23 | E

Downtown | 800 SW Alder St. (Park Ave.) | 503-223-8813 ⑤
Hawthorne | 3535 SE Hawthorne Blvd. (bet. 35th & 36th Aves.) | 503-232-3222
Hollywood | 4344 NE Sandy Blvd. (bet. 43rd & 44th Aves.) | 503-546-4193 ⑤

Reynolds Specialty Store

Northwest Portland | 524 NW 23rd Ave. (bet. Glisan & Hoyt Sts.) | 503-221-6539
www.reynoldsopticalco.com

This long-lived local optics chainlet (circa 1910) garners praise for a "fantastic selection" of "cool, quirky" and "stylish eyewear", including frames that are designed in Portland, displayed in an "organized and accessible" layout; the staff is "kind" and "quite helpful", and eye exams are available at the Hawthorne and Downtown locales.

Rhythm Traders

27 | 24 | 26 | E

King | 3904 NE Martin Luther King Jr. Blvd. (Failing St.) | 503-288-6950 | www.rhythmtraders.com

Sure, this "moderately expensive" "percussionist's heaven" in King stocks the "normal drum-set fare", with plenty of "high-quality new and used equipment", but "stringing and tuning djembes by hand" clues shoppers in to the depth and breadth of its expertise; indeed, the staffers are "some of the most enthusiastic professionals you could hope for", making it the "best friend of any drummer in the city."

Rich's Cigar Store

27 | 25 | 24 | M

Downtown | 820 SW Alder St. (9th Ave.) | 503-228-1700
Northwest Portland | 706 NW 23rd Ave. (bet. Irving & Johnson Sts.) | 503-227-6907
Pearl District | 922 NW Flanders St. (bet. 9th & 10th Aves.) | 503-595-5556 ⑤
www.richscigarstore.com

"If you smoke you know" that this trio of "truly dedicated tobacconists" is the "place for cigar connoisseurs" and those with an affinity for "exotic pipes and tobaccos" – especially the Downtown stop where you can light up inside; it's also "magazine heaven", with everything from "mainstream to obscure international titles", but regardless of your interest the "knowledgeable" staff provides "great service" and prices are "on par" with similar shops.

River City Bicycles ❷

27 | 25 | 25 | E

Central Eastside | 706 SE Martin Luther King Jr. Blvd. (bet. Alder & Morrison Sts.) | 503-233-5973 | www.rivercitybicycles.com

River City Bicycles Outlet

Eastside Industrial | 534 SE Belmont St. (6th Ave.) | 503-446-2205 | www.rivercitybicyclesoutlet.com

With a "staggering" inventory of "high-end bikes and accessories", this "busy" Central Eastside peddler has something for everyone, including "casual riders", "commuters" and "professional racers"; its "very knowledgeable" crew presides over repairs, an indoor test track upstairs and free espresso on the weekends, and most feel it really "captures the spirit and energy of cycling"; P.S. for deals, try the outlet on Belmont.

Salty's Dog & Cat Shop

25 | 24 | 25 | M

Mississippi | 4039 N. Mississippi Ave. (bet. Mason & Shaver Sts.) | 503-249-1432 | www.saltysdogshop.com

"Thank you for being awesome" purr fans of this Mississippi pet shop offering chow with no fillers or preservatives, plus treats and "eco-conscious" toys – and with "excellent pricing" and "loyalty perks" for regular customers to boot; it's all overseen by "helpful" folks who are always "knowledgeable, congenial" and ready to "give your dogs lots of lovin'."

Schoolhouse Electric

28 | 27 | 25 | VE

Northwest Portland | 2181 NW Nicolai St. (bet. Sherlock & Yeon Aves.) | 503-230-7113 | www.schoolhouseelectric.com

Best known for its "authentic" reproduction light fixtures with shades "formed in original period molds", this "intimidatingly cool" (and pricey) NW Portland shop also carries "superb" pieces for the home, including furniture, hardware and textiles; with "informative", "professional" staffers and "drool"-worthy displays, it's easy to see why fans are "sold on the store."

2nd Avenue Records ❷

23 | 21 | 22 | M

Downtown | 400 SW Second Ave. (Stark St.) | 503-222-3783 | www.2ndavenuerecords.com

A "realm for music junkies", this packed Downtown record shop has been a "Portland staple" since 1982 and "keeps the die-hard collectors from going the way of the buffalo" with its stock of "vintage" LPs, 45s and 78s plus new and used CDs; some "bargains can be found" amid the many bins, and the staff "will help you hunt down" "rare or hard-to-find releases."

Sellwood Antique Mall ⊠Ⓜ

22 | 20 | 20 | M

Sellwood | 7875 SE 13th Ave. (bet. Bidwell & Lexington Sts.) | 503-389-7670 | www.sellwoodantiquemall.com

In an area known for antiques, this Sellwood collective stocks a "little bit of everything from past to present" with plenty of "unique conversation starters" in the mix; the "close quarters" can feel "disheveled", but it's a "fun place to look around" – and if you're willing to "dig for the treasures", you may discover "something you've never seen before"; P.S. there's a food-cart pod next door.

Sephora
25 | 24 | 22 | M

Downtown | 413 SW Morrison St. (4th Ave.) | 503-224-1742 Ⓢ Ⓜ
Happy Valley | Clackamas Town Ctr. | 12300 SE 82nd Ave. (Sunnyside Rd.) | 503-653-8830 ◗
Tigard | Washington Sq. | 9329 SW Washington Square Rd. (Blum Rd.) | 503-684-9693 ◗
www.sephora.com

All hail the "candy store of cosmetics" carrying "your favorite brands" in makeup, skin treatments, haircare, fragrance and beauty tools for every age and ethnicity; reviewers adore the "well-trained" staff, loyalty card "perks" and return policy, not to mention the on-site makeup artists – just "be careful, it's seductive" and the "impulse to buy" reigns supreme.

She Bop
29 | 28 | 29 | E

Mississippi | 909 N. Beech St. (bet. Michigan & Mississippi Aves.) | 503-473-8018 | www.sheboptheshop.com

The "tearoom of exotic boutiques", this "comfortable" Mississippi sex shop offers "every kind of toy, lotion and potion, all in exquisite good taste" and in a "woman-friendly" environment (read: no "creepo vibe"); "disarming" staffers who provide "giggle-free attention" to both neophytes and those "more well versed" ensure that "you've never felt better and healthier" about erotic products.

Sleighbells
27 | 26 | 24 | E

Sherwood | 23855 SW 195th Pl. (Chapman Rd.) | 503-625-6052 | www.sleighbells.biz

It's like the "perfect Santa's workshop" at this Sherwood Christmas shop that will get you into the "spirit" with "decorations for various holidays", though the yuletide is the focus with "every decoration and ornament" imaginable (e.g. Christopher Radko collectibles) and a Christmas tree farm on-site; it's open year-round with many "different rooms and halls" to wander, and though it can get "crowded" in December, it's "well worth a visit."

Sock Dreams
27 | 25 | 25 | M

Sellwood | 8005 SE 13th Ave. (Nehalem St.) | 503-232-3330 | www.sockdreams.com

"Who can say no to a store devoted to awesome socks?" muse rabid fans of this "friendly" Sellwood emporium for "funky and functional" "footsie fun" that comes "in all colors of the rainbow" (with lots of knee- and thigh-highs), plus a smattering of gloves, hats and scarves; the exhaustive stock means that "if you can't find your favorite here", you likely "won't find it anywhere."

Stark's Vacuums
26 | 22 | 24 | M

Central Eastside | 107 NE Grand Ave. (Davis St.) | 503-232-4101

(continued)

Stark's Vacuums

Montavilla | 8326 SE Stark St. (84th Ave.) | 503-251-6912 ◗
Beaverton | 12920 SW Canyon Rd. (B'way) | 503-626-3699
Hillsboro | 2139 NE Cornell Rd. (21st Ave.) | 503-648-5493
Happy Valley | 9640 SE 82nd Ave. (bet. Jackson Creek Blvd. & Otty Rd.) | 503-654-1517
Gresham | 240 NW Division St. (Victoria Ave.) | 503-661-0128
Sherwood | 16074 SW Tualatin-Sherwood Rd. (bet. Olds Pl. & Pacific Hwy.) | 503-625-2958
www.starks.com

Ok, it's "not romantic", but this "longtime local business" with hubs across town is the "place to go when you need a vacuum or repair", with an "amazing selection" of "high-end suckers", plus bags and filters for "new and vintage models"; the "old-fashioned customer service" means they assist and do "quick fixes" "without trying to up-sell you"; P.S. Central Eastside includes a Vacuum Museum ("how cool is that?").

Storables

24 | 24 | 21 | E

Pearl District | 105 NW 13th Ave. (Couch St.) | 503-221-4500 🗷
Tigard | 9140 SW Hall Blvd. (bet. Greenburg & Palmblad Rds.) | 503-624-9500 ◗
www.storables.com

These "organization paradises" in the Pearl District and Tigard provide "clever solutions" for storage problems with a "great selection of quality merchandise" that helps put home and office in order; if some gripe about "high prices", the "easy-to-navigate" spaces and "knowledgeable" staffers are pluses at stores that "have what you are looking for" when the bug hits.

Sur La Table

25 | 22 | 21 | E

Pearl District | 1102 NW Couch St. (11th Ave.) | 503-295-9679 ◗
Lake Oswego | 390 N. State St. (A Ave.) | 503-636-2181
Tigard | Bridgeport Vill. | 7479 SW Bridgeport Rd. (Upper Boones Ferry Rd.) | 503-968-8015 ◗
www.surlatable.com

You'll "feel like a kid in a candy store" at these "foodie" specialists offering "first-rate" (read: pricey) "kitchen paraphernalia", from "pretty-colored spatulas" and small appliances to "gadgets and gorgeous linens", plus a "gracious staff"; besides the cookware, most locations feature cooking classes, which will "inspire" you to whip up a meal "when you leave."

SweetWares Ⓜ

∇ 26 | 27 | 19 | E

Hillsdale | 6306 SW Capitol Hwy. (bet. 18th Dr. & Sunset Blvd.) | 503-546-3737 | www.sweetwares.com

Located near its sister bread and pastry shop (Baker & Spice), this "cute" Hillsdale culinary boutique is where dough punchers find "just the right rolling pin or mixing bowl", alongside hard-to-find tools for serious bakers and decorative items like "vintage"-inspired cake plates; if it's a bit "expensive", it's also "fun for looking."

Tender Loving Empire

21 | 24 | 23 | M

West End | 412 SW 10th Ave. (bet. Stark & Washington Sts.) |
503-243-5859 | www.tenderlovingempire.com

What started as a local recording label has grown into a small, "chillin'" shop in the West End stocking a "uniquely Portland showcase of crafts, music and art", most of which is locally produced and often "hand-made" from "reclaimed materials"; service rates favorably, and it's recommended even if you're "just stopping in for the eye candy."

Thinker Toys

27 | 26 | 26 | E

Multnomah Village | 7784 SW Capitol Hwy. (35th Ave.) |
503-245-3936 | www.thinkertoysoregon.com

In the "heart of Multnomah Village", this "go-to" toy shop eschews "plastic crap" for "high-quality", "unusual" diversions "for all ages", with lots of "hands-on" areas for in-store play; sure, prices are "commensurate" with the high-end brands, but staffers will "gor-geously wrap" items if requested, all of which leads the child-free to venture it "makes you wish you had kids."

3 Monkeys

23 | 23 | 21 | M

Northwest Portland | 811 NW 23rd Ave. (bet. Johnson & Kearney Sts.) |
503-222-5160

Fans say that this "fascinating" NW Portland boutique is "packed to the gills" with an "eclectic mix" of "collectables and gifts" (including imports and antiques) plus clothing, jewelry and accessories, which range from "cutesy" to "quirky" at "fair" prices; the staff is "polite", and fans say "if you have the time" it's a "true treasure hunt."

Tiffany & Co.

28 | 28 | 26 | VE

Downtown | 330 SW Yamhill St. (4th Ave.) | 503-221-5565 |
www.tiffany.com

Founded in NYC in 1837, this "iconic" jeweler with outposts around the world continues to set the "gold standard" for "classic" jewelry in-cluding "sparkling" engagement rings, as well as silver and crystal "gifts to impress"; while there's "a markup for the name", most say the happy reaction to that "distinctive blue box" makes it "well worth it."

NEW TUMI ⊘

28 | 24 | 24 | VE

Downtown | Pioneer Pl. | 702 SW Fifth Ave. (bet. Morrison & Yamhill Sts.) |
503-241-5614 | www.tumi.com

"You just feel cool" toting the "fab" bags from this global standout known for furnishing "the hard-core road warrior" with "sturdy and fashionable" luggage in "stylish" designs, plus "beautiful" leather goods and accessories; service is "attentive", and while it may be "over-the-top pricewise", given "impeccable" quality that "truly lasts", "you won't regret" the "investment."

21st Avenue Bicycles

24 | 22 | 24 | E

Northwest Portland | 916 NW 21st Ave. (bet. Kearney & Lovejoy Sts.) |
503-222-2851 | www.21stbikes.com

This "rad" NW Portland shop gets props for its "experienced", "sharp" staff of mechanics who can get a "bike back up and running" and will "take time to walk through options" on its new commuter cycles, including "pricey but good" names like Specialized and Surly; free pinball and the sense that "they care about building a better cycling community" makes it a "favorite"; P.S. sibling Fat Tire Farm specializes in mountain bikes.

Twist

26 | 26 | 21 | E

Northwest Portland | 30 NW 23rd Pl. (Westover Rd.) | 503-224-0334 | www.twistonline.com

The "out-of-the-ordinary" jewelry and "extraordinary gifts" (ceramics, scarves, table accessories) at this NW Portland shop come courtesy of a "fantastic array of designers", including Cathy Waterman, Pippa Small and Melissa Joy Manning; it's "expensive" and the "gallery"-like setting is conducive for a "wander", but it's also a recommended "go-to" for "special-occasion" presents.

Twisted ●

27 | 26 | 26 | M

Irvington | 2310 NE Broadway (23rd Ave.) | 503-922-1150 | www.twistedpdx.com

"Knitaholics" are in "heaven" at this "inviting" Irvington shop offering a "wide variety" of "beautiful" fibers (including piles of sock yarns), "tons of patterns" and "lots of tools and accessories"; everything is "well displayed", the "kindly staff" is quick with "advice" and regular classes and knitting nights come with "yummy tea."

Upper Playground ●

27 | 27 | 23 | M

Old Town-Chinatown | 23 NW Fifth Ave. (bet. Burnside & Couch Sts.) | 503-548-4835 | www.upperplayground.com

At this "little gem hiding in Chinatown" (the Portland branch of the international chainlet), "overall hipsterness" rules the day, what with its collection of "whimsical" – and "one-of-a-kind" – "urban and sk8" gear, including "cool" T-shirts, hoodies, namesake hats and even tops for babies emblazoned with its signature walrus; "affordable" prices sweeten the deal, while a "sweet" art gallery showcasing West Coast artists cements its rep as one "sick store."

Urban Farm Store

28 | 24 | 28 | M

Buckman | 2100 SE Belmont St. (bet. 20th & 23rd Aves.) | 503-234-7733 | www.urbanfarmstore.com

"Your urban chicken brood" rules the roost at this "charming" citified farming "gem" in Buckman, which stocks "gorgeous" live birds, organic feed and "plenty" of garden accessories, including heirloom seeds – all at reasonable prices; a "friendly, helpful staff" overseen by a husband-and-wife team and "cats lounging about" offer further enticement, "making a trip here more of a treat than a chore."

Utrecht Art Supplies

27 | 24 | 24 | M

Pearl District | 1122 NW Everett St. (bet. 11th & 12th Sts.) | 503-417-8024 | www.utrechtart.com

"Crafty" types paint a rosy picture of this well-"organized" Pearl District chain link, which serves a cadre of students and teachers who appreciate its "wide" selection of "everything you need" for an art project – including a "great selection" of paints, canvases and the like; a generally "helpful" staff assists budding Rembrandts, but it's the "reasonable" prices and "good sales" that keep them coming back.

WatchWorks ☒ | 24 | 23 | 21 | VE |

Downtown | 711 SW 10th Ave. (bet. Morrison & Yamhill Sts.) | 503-223-1368 | www.watchworkspdx.com

"Watch geeks" tick off the reasons they "love" this Downtown family-run jeweler, starting with its "fabulous" selection of "amazing time-pieces" (including Bell & Ross and numerous "vintage" options) and a "helpful, not pushy" team that executes "flawless" repair work; while prices may be "fair" for the "high-quality" goods, it helps to shop here after a "lottery win."

W.C. Winks Hardware ☒ | 27 | 23 | 26 | M |

Eastside Industrial | 200 SE Stark St. (2nd Ave.) | 503-227-5536 | www.winkshardware.com

The "hardware store of your dreams", this Eastside Industrial "institution" has been around since 1909 (after originating on the Westside) and boasts one of the "most detailed and meticulous selections" in town; it's overseen by an "experienced staff" that's happy to act as a "tour guide" to anyone browsing the shop's "rows and rows of shelves", but "beware of the hours of operation" – it's closed weekends and shuts early on weeknights.

Williams-Sonoma ◗ | 26 | 25 | 23 | E |

Northwest Portland | 38 NW 23rd Ave. (Flanders St.) | 503-946-2300
Tigard | Washington Sq. | 9367 SW Washington Square Rd. (Blum Rd.) | 503-684-2784
www.williams-sonoma.com

An "indispensable" source of "kitchen fantasy fulfillment", this popular chain is guaranteed to "lend culinary cachet" with a "comprehensive selection" of "first-rate" cookware "classics" and "obscure" gadgets; between the "customer service" and "enticing displays", "discerning" home chefs "don't mind paying top dollar" – "case closed."

SHOPPING: FOOD & WINE

Portland Favorites

This list is plotted on the map at the back of this book.

1 New Seasons Market | *Major Market*

2 Dave's Killer Bread | *Baked Goods*

3 Elephants Delicatessen | *Specialty Shops*

4 Uwajimaya | *Specialty Shops*

5 Bob's Red Mill | *Specialty Shops*

6 Moonstruck Chocolate* | *Candy & Nuts*

Top Quality

29 Dave's Killer Bread
Bob's Red Mill

28 Phil's Uptown Meat
Moonstruck Chocolate
New Seasons Market

Gartner's Country Meat
Foster & Dobbs
Clear Creek Distillery
Main Street Homebrew
Original Bavarian Sausage

Top Display

27 Meadow
Moonstruck Chocolate
Original Bavarian Sausage
Benessere Olive Oils
Penzeys Spices

New Seasons Market

26 Foster & Dobbs
Pearl Specialty Market*
City Market
Phil's Uptown Meat

Top Service

28 Phil's Uptown Meat

27 Newman's Fish Company

26 Helen Bernhard Bakery
Gartner's Country Meat
New Seasons Market

Piece of Cake Bakery
Bob's Red Mill
Spicer Brothers Produce
Main Street Homebrew
JaCiva's Bakery

GOOD VALUES

ABC Seafood Market
Cash & Carry
Cherry Sprout Produce
Cork
Edelweiss Sausage

Gartner's Country Meat
Kruger's Farm Market
La Espiga Dorada
Uwajimaya
Vino

Excludes places with low votes; * indicates a tie with property above

Shopping: Food & Wine – Types

Listings cover the best in each category and include names, locations and Quality ratings. These lists include low vote places that do not qualify for top lists.

BAKED GOODS

Dave's Killer Bread	**Milwaukie**	29
Piece of Cake	**Sellwood**	27
JaCiva's Bakery	**Hawthorne**	27
La Espiga Dorada	**Beaverton**	27
Saint Cupcake	**multi.**	27
Two Tarts Bakery	**NW Portland**	27
German Bakery	**NE Portland**	27
NEW Spielman	**Division**	27
Dovetail Bakery	**Alberta**	26
Delphina's Bakery	**Beaumont**	26
Cupcake Jones	**Pearl Dist.**	26
Helen Bernhard	**Irvington**	26
Bliss Cupcake	**Bethany**	26
NEW Bakeshop	**Hollywood**	25
NEW Blue Collar	**Downtown**	24
NEW Fressen	**Kerns**	-

CANDY & NUTS

Moonstruck	**multi.**	28
Cacao	**multi.**	28
Van Duyn	**NW Portland**	27
Alma Chocolate	**Kerns**	26
NEW Candy Babel	**Alberta**	26
Candy Basket	**Gresham**	26
NEW Cosmic	**Belmont**	25

CHEESE & DAIRY

Blackbird	**Beaumont**	26
Cheese Bar	**Mt. Tabor**	26

COFFEE & TEA

Portland Roasting	**multi.**	27
Steven Smith Tea	**NW Portland**	27
Mr. Green Beans	**Mississippi**	27
NEW Spielman	**Division**	27
Townshend's	**multi.**	26
Spice & Tea	**Downtown**	26
World Cup Coffee	**multi.**	26
Cellar Door	**Central E**	25
Tea Chai Te	**NW Portland**	25

HERBS & SPICES

Penzeys Spices	**multi.**	28
Meadow	**Mississippi**	27
Spice & Tea	**Downtown**	26
Stone Cottage	**SE Portland**	24

MAJOR MARKETS

New Seasons Mkt.	**multi.**	28
City Mkt.	**NW Portland**	27
People's Co-op	**Clinton**	27
Zupan's	**multi.**	27
Market of Choice	**SW Portland**	26
Sheridan	**E Industrial**	26
Barbur	**SW Portland**	26
Food Front Co-op	**multi.**	26
Alberta Co-op	**Alberta**	25
Food Fight!	**Buckman**	25
Cash & Carry	**multi.**	24

MEAT, POULTRY & GAME

Phil's Uptown	**NW Portland**	28
Gartner's	**NE Portland**	28
Original Bav.	**Tigard**	28
Edelweiss	**Brooklyn**	27
Nicky USA	**E Industrial**	27
Zenner's	**NW Portland**	26
Chop	**multi.**	-

PRODUCE

Spicer Bros.	**Oregon City**	27
Sheridan	**E Industrial**	26
Kruger's Farm Mkt.	**multi.**	26
Cherry Sprout	**Humboldt**	23

SEAFOOD

Newman's	**NW Portland**	27
Pacific Seafood	**Foster-Powell**	26
Flying Fish Co.	**multi.**	24
ABC Seafood	**Foster-Powell**	23

SPECIALTY SHOPS

Bob's Red Mill	**Milwaukie**	29
Foster & Dobbs	**Irvington**	28
Woodstock	**Woodstock**	26
Pastaworks	**multi.**	27
Benessere	**multi.**	27
Elephants Deli	**multi.**	27

Uwajimaya | **Beaverton**	27
Martinotti's | **W End**	25
Food Fight! | **Buckman**	25
Decorette Shop | **Foster-Powell**	24
Anzen Hiroshi's | **Lloyd**	24
NEW Woodsman | **Division**	24
Fubonn | **82nd Ave**	22
G Mart | **Beaverton**	22
H Mart | **Tigard**	21

WINES, BEER & LIQUOR

Clear Creek | **NW Portland**	28
Main St. | **Hillsboro**	28
New Deal | **Central E**	28
Vino | **Kerns**	27

Pearl Specialty | **Pearl Dist.**	27
Vinopolis | **W End**	27
Woodstock | **Woodstock**	26
Liner & Elsen | **NW Portland**	26
Blackbird | **Beaumont**	26
House Spirits | **Central E**	26
Cork | **Alberta**	26
Let's Brew | **Montavilla**	25
Oregon Wines | **Downtown**	25
E&R Wine | **Johns Landing**	25
John's Mkt. | **Multnomah**	25
Uptown Liquor | **NW Portland**	25
Homebrew | **Kenton**	24
F.H. Steinbart | **Buckman**	24
10th Ave. | **Downtown**	23
11th Ave. | **Hawthorne**	22

Shopping: Food & Wine – Locations

Includes names, categories and Quality ratings. These lists include low vote places that do not qualify for top lists.

Portland

ALBERTA

Townshend's | *Coffee/Tea*	26
Dovetail Bakery | *Baked Gds.*	26
NEW Candy Babel | *Candy/Nuts*	26
Cork | *Wine/Beer/Liq.*	26
Alberta Co-op | *Maj. Mkt.*	25

BEAUMONT

Blackbird | *Wine/Beer/Liq.*	26
Delphina's Bakery | *Baked Gds.*	26

BELMONT

Zupan's | *Maj. Mkt.*	27
Saint Cupcake | *Baked Gds.*	27
NEW Cosmic | *Candy/Nuts*	25

BETHANY

Bliss Cupcake | *Baked Gds.*	26

BOISE-ELIOT

Chop | *Meat/Poultry*	-

BROOKLYN

Edelweiss | *Meat/Poultry*	27

BUCKMAN/KERNS

Vino | *Wine/Beer/Liq.*	27
Alma Chocolate | *Candy/Nuts*	26
Food Fight! | *Spec. Shops*	25
F.H. Steinbart | *Wine/Beer/Liq.*	24
NEW Fressen | *Baked Gds.*	-

CENTRAL EASTSIDE/ EAST INDUSTRIAL

New Deal | *Wine/Beer/Liq.*	28
Portland Roasting | *Coffee/Tea*	27
Nicky USA | *Meat/Poultry*	27
Sheridan | *Maj. Mkt.*	26
House Spirits | *Wine/Beer/Liq.*	26
Cellar Door | *Coffee/Tea*	25
Cash & Carry | *Maj. Mkt.*	24

CLINTON/DIVISION

New Seasons Mkt. | *Maj. Mkt.*	28
People's Co-op | *Maj. Mkt.*	27

NEW Spielman | *Coffee/Tea*	27
Townshend's | *Coffee/Tea*	26
NEW Woodsman | *Spec. Shops*	24

CONCORDIA

New Seasons Mkt. | *Maj. Mkt.*	28

DOWNTOWN

Moonstruck | *Candy/Nuts*	28
Cacao | *Candy/Nuts*	28
Benessere | *Spec. Shops*	27
Elephants Deli | *Spec. Shops*	27
Spice & Tea | *Herbs/Spices*	26
Oregon Wines | *Wine/Beer/Liq.*	25
NEW Blue Collar | *Baked Gds.*	24
10th Ave. | *Wine/Beer/Liq.*	23

82ND AVENUE

Fubonn | *Spec. Shops*	22

FOSTER-POWELL/ MT. SCOTT

Pacific Seafood | *Seafood*	26
Decorette Shop | *Spec. Shops*	24
ABC Seafood | *Seafood*	23

HAWTHORNE

New Seasons Mkt. | *Maj. Mkt.*	28
Pastaworks | *Spec. Shops*	27
JaCiva's Bakery | *Baked Gds.*	27
Kruger's Farm Mkt. | *Produce*	26
Flying Fish Co. | *Seafood*	24
11th Ave. | *Wine/Beer/Liq.*	22

HILLSDALE/ MULTNOMAH VILL.

Food Front Co-op | *Maj. Mkt.*	26
John's Mkt. | *Wine/Beer/Liq.*	25

HOLLYWOOD

NEW Bakeshop | *Baked Gds.*	25

HUMBOLDT

Cherry Sprout | *Produce*	23

IRVINGTON/LLOYD

Foster & Dobbs | *Spec. Shops*	28
Benessere | *Spec. Shops*	27

Portland Roasting | *Coffee/Tea* 27
Helen Bernhard | *Baked Gds.* 26
Anzen Hiroshi's | *Spec. Shops* 24

JOHNS LANDING

Zupan's | *Maj. Mkt.* 27
E&R Wine | *Wine/Beer/Liq.* 25

KENTON

Homebrew | *Wine/Beer/Liq.* 24

MISSISSIPPI

Pastaworks | *Spec. Shops* 27
Meadow | *Herbs/Spices* 27
Mr. Green Beans | *Coffee/Tea* 27

MONTAVILLA/
MT. TABOR

Cheese Bar | *Cheese/Dairy* 26
Let's Brew | *Wine/Beer/Liq.* 25

NE PORTLAND

Gartner's | *Meat/Poultry* 28
German Bakery | *Baked Gds.* 27

NORTH PORTLAND

New Seasons Mkt. | *Maj. Mkt.* 28
Cash & Carry | *Maj. Mkt.* 24

NW PORTLAND

Phil's Uptown | *Meat/Poultry* 28
Moonstruck | *Candy/Nuts* 28
Clear Creek | *Wine/Beer/Liq.* 28
Pastaworks | *Spec. Shops* 27
City Mkt. | *Maj. Mkt.* 27
Zupan's | *Maj. Mkt.* 27
Newman's | *Seafood* 27
Elephants Deli | *Spec. Shops* 27
Two Tarts Bakery | *Baked Gds.* 27
Van Duyn | *Candy/Nuts* 27
Steven Smith Tea | *Coffee/Tea* 27
Liner & Elsen | *Wine/Beer/Liq.* 26
Zenner's | *Meat/Poultry* 26
World Cup Coffee | *Coffee/Tea* 26
Food Front Co-op | *Maj. Mkt.* 26
Uptown Liquor | *Wine/Beer/Liq.* 25
Tea Chai Te | *Coffee/Tea* 25
Chop | *Meat/Poultry* -

PEARL DISTRICT

Penzeys Spices | *Herbs/Spices* 28
Pearl Specialty | *Wine/Beer/Liq.* 27

World Cup Coffee | *Coffee/Tea* 26
Cupcake Jones | *Baked Gds.* 26
Cash & Carry | *Maj. Mkt.* 24

RALEIGH HILLS

New Seasons Mkt. | *Maj. Mkt.* 28

SAUVIE ISLAND

Kruger's Farm Mkt. | *Produce* 26

SELLWOOD

New Seasons Mkt. | *Maj. Mkt.* 28
Piece of Cake | *Baked Gds.* 27
Tea Chai Te | *Coffee/Tea* 25

SE PORTLAND

Stone Cottage | *Herbs/Spices* 24

ST. JOHNS

Moonstruck | *Candy/Nuts* 28
Kruger's Farm Mkt. | *Produce* 26
Flying Fish Co. | *Seafood* 24

SW PORTLAND

Market of Choice | *Maj. Mkt.* 26
Barbur | *Maj. Mkt.* 26

WEST END

Cacao | *Candy/Nuts* 28
Saint Cupcake | *Baked Gds.* 27
Vinopolis | *Wine/Beer/Liq.* 27
Martinotti's | *Spec. Shops* 25

WOODSTOCK

Woodstock | *Wine/Beer/Liq.* 26

Portland Suburbs

BEAVERTON

Moonstruck | *Candy/Nuts* 28
New Seasons Mkt. | *Maj. Mkt.* 28
Penzeys Spices | *Herbs/Spices* 28
La Espiga Dorada | *Baked Gds.* 27
Uwajimaya | *Spec. Shops* 27
G Mart | *Spec. Shops* 22

CLACKAMAS/
HAPPY VALLEY

New Seasons Mkt. | *Maj. Mkt.* 28
Penzeys Spices | *Herbs/Spices* 28
Cash & Carry | *Maj. Mkt.* 24

GRESHAM

Candy Basket | *Candy/Nuts* 26
Cash & Carry | *Maj. Mkt.* 24

HILLSBORO

New Seasons Mkt. | *Maj. Mkt.* 28
Main St. | *Wine/Beer/Liq.* 28

LAKE OSWEGO

Moonstruck | *Candy/Nuts* 28
New Seasons Mkt. | *Maj. Mkt.* 28
Zupan's | *Maj. Mkt.* 27
Elephants Deli | *Spec. Shops* 27

MILWAUKIE

Dave's Killer Bread | *Baked Gds.* 29
Bob's Red Mill | *Spec. Shops* 29

OREGON CITY

Spicer Bros. | *Produce* 27

TIGARD

Original Bav. | *Meat/Poultry* 28
Cash & Carry | *Maj. Mkt.* 24
H Mart | *Spec. Shops* 21

LOCATIONS

Shopping: Food & Wine

Ratings & Symbols

Quality, Display & **Service** are rated on a 30-point scale.

Cost reflects our surveyors' estimate of the price range:

| I | Inexpensive | E | Expensive |
| M | Moderate | VE | Very Expensive |

● open until 8:30 PM or later

ABC Seafood Market ● *Seafood*　　　23 | 20 | 21 | M
Foster-Powell | 6509 SE Powell Blvd. (bet. 65th & 66th Aves.) | 503-771-5802

"Selection" is the thing at this utilitarian Foster-Powell seafood market, offering an "out-of-this-world" variety of "fresh-as-it-gets" fish, along with a limited supply of fruits, veggies and herbs; "decent" pricing helps keep it "busy on the weekends", but at least the service is "fast."

Alberta Cooperative Grocery *Major Market*　25 | 22 | 23 | M
Alberta | 1500 NE Alberta St. (15th Ave.) | 503-287-4333 | www.albertagrocery.coop

"Local organic produce" and other "eclectic" items turn up at this "hip" Alberta grocery cooperative with a "farmer's market feel" and a "focused" section of goods; "well run", it stocks items "at a reasonable price", and fans say it's worth it for the "interesting bulk items" alone.

Alma Chocolate *Candy & Nuts*　　　26 | 24 | 23 | E
Kerns | 140 NE 28th Ave. (bet. Couch & Davis Sts.) | 503-517-0262 | www.almachocolate.com

Sarah Hart's "adorable" Kerns sweets shop turns out "remarkable" chocolates and truffles that are "almost too beautiful to eat" and come in "unique" flavors; sure, they're "pricey", but devotees say they're "worth every penny"; P.S. an expansion is in the works.

Anzen Hiroshi's *Specialty Shops*　　　24 | 19 | 23 | M
Lloyd | 736 NE Martin Luther King Jr. Blvd. (bet. Irving & Oregon Sts.) | 503-233-5111

This "old-fashioned" Japanese grocery store has been in Portland since 1905 and enjoys a "loyal following" at its current Lloyd location by stocking supplies for all the "basics of Asian cooking" along with "authentic" cookware; the store is "not large", but the goods are "well chosen" and there are always "new tastes to investigate."

NEW Bakeshop *Baked Goods*　　　25 | 22 | 23 | E
Hollywood | 5351 NE Sandy Blvd. (54th Ave.) | 503-946-8884 | www.bakeshoppdx.com

"Gourmet baker" Kim Boyce showcases "simply luscious pastries" and an "ever-changing" array of "whole-grain goodies" at her light-filled Hollywood shop; everything's as "delish" as it smells, so even though the pricing skews "expensive", fans feel it's "truly a find."

Barbur World Foods *Major Market*

26 | 22 | 24 | M

Southwest Portland | 9845 SW Barbur Blvd. (Taylors Ferry Rd.) | 503-244-0670 | www.barburworldfoods.com

Offering a "phenomenal" variety of goods that "spans the globe", this specialty market in SW Portland is especially touted for its "fantastic" deli with "homestyle Mediterranean treats" including fresh-baked pita bread; the setting is "unassuming", the owners "personable" and the overall experience like going to the "Middle East without traveling."

Benessere Olive Oils & Vinegars *Specialty Shops*

27 | 27 | 26 | E

Downtown | 907 SW Ninth Ave. (Taylor St.) | 503-206-5317
Irvington | 1428 NE Broadway (bet. 14th & 15th Aves.) | 503-281-6389
www.benessereoil.com

A "mecca for olive oils", this "quality" Downtown-Irvington duo showcases varieties "you've never heard of", along with an "impressive array" of artisanal vinegars; while it's "fairly expensive", most agree it's "worth the extra cost", especially given that the "helpful" staff doles out "free samples" and answers questions in a "down-to-earth" way.

Blackbird Wineshop & Atomic Cheese *Wines, Beer & Liquor*

26 | 23 | 23 | E

Beaumont | 4323 NE Fremont St. (bet. 43rd & 44th Aves.) | 503-282-1887 | www.blackbirdwine.com

There's a "diverse" roster of wines along with "nice" cheese selections at this Beaumont shop that's one of the "best in town"; the "open atmosphere", "knowledgeable" staffers and overall "quality" mean the "expensive" tabs are easier to swallow, while "weekly tastings" keep oenophiles "coming back."

Bliss Cupcake Shop *Baked Goods*

26 | 25 | 25 | E

Bethany | 4708 NW Bethany Blvd. (Central Dr.) | 503-645-6000 | www.blisscupcakeshop.com

"Delicious" treats fill the display cases at this "cute" Bethany bakery that lives up to its name with "yummy" cupcakes ("get there early if you want red velvet") and custom wedding cakes, as well as vegan and gluten-free items; though the goods "aren't cheap", fans feel it's "worth the splurge."

NEW Blue Collar Baking Company *Baked Goods*

24 | 24 | 26 | M

Downtown | 319 SW Pine St. (bet. 3rd & 4th Aves.) | 503-227-3249 | www.bluecollarbaking.com

Hewing close to its slogan 'we're not afraid of butter', this Downtown bakery dishes up "excellent" goodies (cookies, scones and "tasty Bundt cakes") to a receptive crowd; "attentive" service, a "mellow" setting, free WiFi and plenty of seating make it "perfect for doing work on your laptop or sitting with friends."

QUALITY | DISPLAY | SERVICE | COST

Bob's Red Mill Whole Grain Store *Specialty Shops*

29 | 25 | 26 | M

Milwaukie | 5000 SE International Way (bet. Freeman Way & Lake Rd.) | 503-607-6455 | www.bobsredmill.com

"All-natural grains" are the specialty of this longtime Milwaukie mill offering everything from "superior baking products" to "hard-to-find" flours and gluten-free items; the "happy-to-be-there" staff and "not unreasonable" prices please locals, though its massive, barn-like building is also a "lively tourist destination."

Cacao *Candy & Nuts*

28 | 26 | 25 | E

Downtown | Heathman Hotel | 712 SW Salmon St. (bet. B'way & Park Ave.) | 503-274-9510

West End | 414 SW 13th Ave. (bet. Stark & Washington Sts.) | 503-241-0656

www.cacaodrinkchocolate.com

For "chocolate that would make the Mayan gods and goddesses blush", surveyors recommend this West End retailer (and its "jewel box" Heathman Hotel offshoot) for its "exotic" imports from around the world that fans sample as "you would wines" along with a "sinful" housemade drinking chocolate; the "passionate" staff really "knows its stuff", making "spending some extra money on quality" totally "worth it."

NEW Candy Babel *Candy & Nuts*

26 | 25 | 26 | M

Alberta | 1237 NE Alberta St. (bet. 12th & 13th Aves.) | 503-867-0591 | www.candybabel.com

Old-fashioned "candies from everywhere" are the specialty of this Alberta sweets shop where the "delicious" product, much of it Scandinavian, has no genetically modified ingredients or trans fats; freshly spun cotton candy in a variety of flavors ices the cake.

Candy Basket Chocolates *Candy & Nuts*

26 | 23 | 24 | E

Gresham | 1924 NE 181st Ave. (San Rafael St.) | 503-666-2000

This longtime old-fashioned Gresham sweet shop is renowned for the "cool chocolate fountain" near the entrance and its extensive array of "handmade" chocolates and taffies; although the pricing is "a bit high end", the goods are "quality" and the staffers all "nice people."

Cash & Carry *Major Market*

24 | 20 | 22 | I

Central Eastside | 731 SE Stephens St. (bet. 7th & 8th Aves.) | 503-232-7157

North Portland | 910 N. Hayden Meadows Dr. (bet. Kerby Ave. & Whitaker Rd.) | 503-528-1022

Pearl District | 1420 NW 14th Ave. (bet. Pettygrove & Quimby Sts.) | 503-221-1049

Clackamas | 15700 SE 82nd Dr. (Bonaventure Ln.) | 503-655-6045

Gresham | 2521 NW Division St. (Birdsdale Ave.) | 503-666-6868

Tigard | 11745 SW Pacific Hwy. (Dartmouth St.) | 503-639-3226

www.smartfoodservice.com

One of the "best places to get a gallon of nacho cheese sauce", this grocery-supply chain is geared toward food-service folks but open to anyone looking for "cheap, bulk" products, everything from "cookware to food"; it's "exactly what you'd expect" down to the "giant rolling carts", but "contrary to the name, they take credit cards."

Cellar Door Coffee Roasters *Coffee & Tea* | 25 | 20 | 24 | M |

Central Eastside | 2001 SE 11th Ave. (Harrison St.) | 503-234-7155 |
www.cellardoorcoffee.com

It's all about the "good stuff to wake up to" at this Central Eastside coffee vendor set in a Victorian house where "fabulous" house-roasted java is "served with love" by "master baristas"; food items like pastries and quiche mean you'll have more excuses to settle in and enjoy the "great atmosphere."

Cheese Bar ⬤ *Cheese & Dairy* | 26 | 25 | 25 | E |

Mt. Tabor | 6031 SE Belmont St. (61st Ave.) | 503-222-6014 |
www.cheese-bar.com

The "opportunity to try dozens of cheeses" draws fromage fans to this "attractive" Mt. Tabor shop with a bar dispensing a selection of "finely chosen beer and wine" plus a "tasty light menu"; the "high quality" is reflected in the high prices, but at least the "patient" staffers "let you sample their wares liberally."

Cherry Sprout Produce Market *Produce* | 23 | 22 | 23 | I |

Humboldt | 722 N. Sumner St. (bet. Albina & Kerby Aves.) |
503-445-4959 | www.cherrysprout.com

A "fantastic selection" of "local, organic" produce is yours at this Humboldt grocer that seals the deal with "great quality" and "unbeatable prices"; granted, it's somewhat small and the offerings rather "limited", but the "basics are covered" and the staff is "gracious."

Chop Butchery & Charcuterie *Meat & Poultry* | - | - | - | E |

Boise-Eliot | 3808 N. Williams Ave. (bet. Beech & Failing Sts.) |
503-288-1901
Northwest Portland | City Mkt. | 735 NW 21st Ave. (Johnson St.) |
503-221-3012
www.chopbutchery.com

"Have an actual conversation with the butcher" at these City Market and Boise-Eliot shops where a knowledgeable staff will walk you through a selection of "incredible" locally sourced meats and house-made sausages, pâtés and salami, plus "some of the best sandwiches in town", like the Friday-only porchetta (Saturdays too, if there's any left); both outposts have an old-fashioned feel and somewhat "pricey" bills, but the NW Portland locale boasts a larger selection.

City Market *Major Market* | 27 | 26 | 25 | E |

Northwest Portland | 735 NW 21st Ave. (bet. Irving & Johnson Sts.) |
503-221-3007

NW Portland's "boutique-style" collection of specialty grocers groups a handful of retailers together "under one roof", including Chop Butchery & Charcuterie, Newman's Fish Company, Pasta-works and Raw Raw Raw Produce; granted, the "jaw-droppingly gorgeous" products come at "jaw-breaking prices", but at least the staffers are "knowledgeable" and its "one-stop shopping" aspect is convenient.

QUALITY | DISPLAY | SERVICE | COST

Clear Creek Distillery *Wines, Beer & Liquor*   28 | 23 | 24 | E

Northwest Portland | 2389 NW Wilson St. (bet. 23rd & 24th Aves.) |
503-248-9470 | www.clearcreekdistillery.com

Owner Steve McCarthy is "passionate" about the "exquisitely created"
small batch spirits available to buy and taste at this "fabulous" NW
Portland distillery, a "true Oregon treasure"; made primarily from local
fruits in European pot stills, all of the offerings are "delish", but insiders
say the pear-in-a-bottle brandy is the "real conversation piece."

Cork *Wines, Beer & Liquor*   26 | 24 | 22 | M

Alberta | 2901 NE Alberta St. (bet. 29th & 30th Aves.) | 503-281-2675 |
www.corkwineshop.com

For "wines from all over the world" – and a "nice selection under
$20" – Alberta oenophiles head to this "beautiful" bottle shop that
also offers a variety of beers, chocolates, vinegars and olive oils, all
dispatched by a "friendly, hands-on" crew; regulars recommend
"joining the Cork club" for "special offers" and discounts.

NEW Cosmic Soda Pop &   25 | 24 | 25 | M
Candy Shop *Candy & Nuts*

Belmont | 817 SE 34th Ave. (bet. Belmont & Morrison Sts.) |
503-894-8980 | www.cosmicsodacandy.com

"Relive your childhood" at this "cute little soda shop" in Belmont
with a "whimsical" candy selection and lots of "hard-to-find sodas";
the owners are "sweet", and there's plenty of space to relax on counter stools and leather couches.

Cupcake Jones *Baked Goods*   26 | 25 | 25 | E

Pearl District | 307 NW 10th Ave. (bet. Everett & Flanders Sts.) |
503-222-4404 | www.cupcakejones.net

The "just plain delicious" cupcakes that go "beyond the usual
chocolate and vanilla" draw fans to this Pearl District bakery offering a product so "amazing" that "you forget about the calories"; alright, the tabs are a bit "pricey", but at least the "upbeat"
owners are "sweet."

Dave's Killer Bread *Baked Goods*   29 | 24 | 26 | M

Milwaukie | 5209 SE International Way (Mallard Way) | 503-335-8077 |
www.daveskillerbread.com

"Phenomenal" organic breads (including high-fiber, high-protein
and gluten-free options) that are both "tasty" and "healthy" earn this
"bare minimum" Milwaukie bakery outlet the top rating for Quality
among Portland food shops; though the tabs are a little "spendy",
bargain-hunters show up for "discounted prices" on day-olds, im-
perfects and store returns, many with the company's signature "seeds
and other goodies sprinkled on top."

Decorette Shop *Specialty Shops*   24 | 20 | 24 | E

Foster-Powell | 5338 SE Foster Rd. (54th Ave.) | 503-774-3760 |
www.thedecoretteshop.com

All your "cake decorating needs" – not to mention "unusual party
supplies" and "hard-to-find" candy-making products – are on of-

fer at this "classic" 40-year-old shop in Foster-Powell; "helpful" staffers give patrons "lots of new ideas" and compensate for the somewhat "expensive" tabs.

Delphina's Bakery *Baked Goods*

26 | 24 | 25 | M

Beaumont | 4636 NE 42nd Ave. (Wygant St.) | 503-281-1373 | www.delphinasbakerycafe.com

"Go for the marble rye" but "stay for the breakfast sandwiches" say aficionados of this family-run Beaumont bakery that's been serving up "fresh-baked breads and pastries" since 1983; a bonus counter-service cafe supplies "mellow" vibrations and plenty of "natural light."

Dovetail Bakery *Baked Goods*

26 | 22 | 23 | E

Alberta | 3039 NE Alberta St. (31st Ave.) | 503-288-8839

Regulars swear "you won't be able to tell" that this "higher-end" Alberta bakery is "all vegan" given the "over-the-top deliciousness" of its pies, cookies, cinnamon rolls and "amazing" sticky buns; though sweets are the focus here, some say it also offers some of the "best biscuits and gravy in town."

E&R Wine Shop *Wines, Beer & Liquor*

25 | 22 | 23 | E

Johns Landing | 6141 SW Macadam Ave. (bet. Carolina & Iowa Sts.) | 503-246-6101

Filling the shelves at this Johns Landing venue is a "fabulous selection" of wines from around the world at "all price levels"; there's "no snobbery" here – the "expert" staff welcomes everyone from "novices" to "oenophiles" – while the vinos are organized by region for an "easy" shopping experience.

Edelweiss Sausage & Delicatessen *Meat & Poultry*

27 | 23 | 23 | M

Brooklyn | 3119 SE 12th Ave. (bet. Kelly St. & Powell Blvd.) | 503-238-4411 | www.edelweissdeli.com

A "genuine slice of Germany" in Brooklyn, this "family-owned" butcher/delicatessen offers "seductive" European-style cured meats and sausages along with "imported cheeses" and "beer from the oldest breweries in Bavaria"; the "little lunch counter" in back is so "popular" that "long lines" at prime times are the norm.

Elephants Delicatessen *Specialty Shops*

27 | 25 | 25 | E

Downtown | 812 SW Park Ave. (bet. Taylor & Yamhill Sts.) | 503-546-3166

Northwest Portland | 115 NW 22nd Ave. (bet. Burnside & Everett Sts.) | 503-299-6304 ◗

Lake Oswego | 5885 SW Meadows Rd. (bet. Kruse Oaks Blvd. & Kruse Woods Dr.) | 503-620-2444

www.elephantsdeli.com

Portland's version of "Dean & DeLuca", these "destination" delis (the NW flagship is largest) offer a "dizzying variety of food" for eat-in or takeout, and are famed for "ridiculously good" sandwiches and "must-try" orange-tomato soup; sure, it's "expensive" and "bustlingly busy at lunch", but ultimately "worth it for the quality."

11th Avenue Liquor *Wines, Beer & Liquor*   22 | 21 | 22 | M

Hawthorne | 1040 SE Hawthorne Blvd. (11th Ave.) | 503-236-2076
"Everyone always seems to be in good spirits" at this "typical"
Hawthorne liquor store that's stocked with a "well-chosen selection" of booze (particularly bourbons and vodkas), abetted by an
"awesome collection of cigars"; a few note it looks "kind of dumpy"
on the outside, but inside the service is "fast and friendly."

F.H. Steinbart *Wines, Beer & Liquor*   24 | 20 | 22 | M

Buckman | 234 SE 12th Ave. (Pine St.) | 503-232-8793 |
www.fhsteinbart.com
In business since 1918, this Buckman homebrew supply shop boasts
an "expansive" selection of beer- and wine-making equipment; the
"knowledgeable" staff is "happy to nerd out about hops", and diehards
say there's "no other place for brewing supplies that comes close."

Flying Fish Company *Seafood*   24 | 21 | 22 | E

Hawthorne | Kruger's Farm Mkt. | 2310 SE Hawthorne Blvd. (bet. 23rd &
24th Aves.) | 503-260-6552
St. Johns | 7316 N. Lombard St. (Burr Ave.) | 503-260-4872
www.flyingfishcompany.com
"Amazingly fresh", "sushi-grade" seafood is yours at this tiny
Hawthorne store next to Kruger's Farm Market (there's also a St.
Johns truck); as well, its "friendly" owners stock grass-fed and other
humanely raised meats, along with eggs, cheese and condiments.

Food Fight! Vegan Grocery *Major Market*   25 | 24 | 22 | M

Buckman | 1217 SE Stark St. (bet. 12th & 13th Aves.) | 503-233-3910 |
www.foodfightgrocery.com
"You never have to wonder if it's truly vegan" at this "animal product"–
free Buckman grocer that stocks everything from the "essentials" to
"junk food"; the "down-to-earth" staff is "cool enough", and if "some
things are a little pricey", that just "comes with the territory."

Food Front Cooperative   26 | 22 | 23 | M
Grocery ◑ *Major Market*

Hillsdale | 6344 SW Capitol Hwy. (bet. Bertha Ct. & Sunset Blvd.) |
503-546-6559
Northwest Portland | 2375 NW Thurman St. (bet. 23rd Pl. & 24th Ave.) |
503-222-5658
www.foodfront.coop
Shoppers "trust the staff to stock quality items from ethical sources"
at these cooperative groceries vending "beautiful produce", "fabulous" meats, an "amazing" bulk section and a "fantastic" deli; the
mood is "welcoming", the merchandise "a bit spendy" and it's open
to all, though members enjoy "extra discounts."

Foster & Dobbs Authentic   28 | 26 | 25 | E
Foods *Specialty Shops*

Irvington | 2518 NE 15th Ave. (Brazee St.) | 503-284-1157 |
www.fosteranddobbs.com
A "good place to put together a fancy picnic", this Irvington shop
specializes in "high-end" cheeses, wines and "gourmet food items",

plus "super-tasty sandwiches" and "hard-to-find" oils and vinegars; true, it's "very expensive", but the staff is "helpful" and many of the goods can "not be found elsewhere in Portland."

NEW Fressen Artisan Bakery *Baked Goods* | _-_ | _-_ | _-_ | M |

Kerns | 523 NE 19th Ave. (Glisan St.) | 503-953-3222 | www.fressenartisanbakery.com

German treats are the star at this small, spare Kerns bakery and cafe whose goods are already standards at area farmer's markets; there's usually several rustic traditional breads on offer (the soft pretzels are popular), along with house pastries, soups, sandwiches, Ristretto Roasters coffee and deli items like potato salad and spaetzle.

Fubonn Supermarket *Specialty Shops* | 22 | 20 | 17 | M |

82nd Avenue | 2850 SE 82nd Ave. (bet. Brooklyn & Woodward Sts.) | 503-517-8877 | www.fubonn.com

"Disneyland" for Asian food fans, this "huge" 82nd Avenue supermarket is known for its "exotic vegetables" and "rare imported candy", not to mention "cuts of meat that some don't want to hear about"; its "sheer size" can be overwhelming and there's not much service, but at least the "prices are great."

Gartner's Country Meat Market *Meat & Poultry* | 28 | 26 | 26 | M |

Northeast Portland | 7450 NE Killingsworth St. (75th Ave.) | 503-252-7801 | www.gartnersmeats.com

"It's worth taking a number and waiting in line" at this NE Portland butcher shop that's been slicing an "outstanding" selection of "high-quality" meats since 1959; even though items cost "a bit more than the supermarket", the "efficient" staff and "pristine cases" compensate.

German Bakery *Baked Goods* | 27 | 24 | 25 | M |

Northeast Portland | 10528 NE Sandy Blvd. (106th Ave.) | 503-252-1881 | www.the-german-bakery.com

"*Das ist gut*" proclaim fans of the "wonderful" breads and "authentic" pastries, cookies and cakes sold at this "old-world" German bakery in NE Portland; dry goods line the shelves, while the deli area offers Bavarian meats and cheeses; P.S. it shares an owner with Original Bavarian Sausage.

G Mart ◑ *Specialty Shops* | 22 | 20 | 20 | M |

Beaverton | 3975 SW 114th Ave. (bet. Canyon Rd. & Center St.) | 503-641-3313

This "small" Beaverton market offers a "good selection" of Korean and Asian produce, meat and other "basics" (there's an entire aisle of dried seaweed); surveyors cite the mezzanine level's casual Spring Restaurant as a good choice for a "quick bite."

Helen Bernhard Bakery *Baked Goods* | 26 | 25 | 26 | M |

Irvington | 1717 Broadway St. (17th St.) | 503-287-1251 | www.helenbernhardbakery.com

Since 1924, this "old-school" Irvington bakery has been turning out "all the traditional treats", ranging from pastries, breads, pies and cookies to "outstanding" custom cakes; although a "deserved Portland institution", it's not fancy, but prices are "reasonable" and the staffers "friendly."

H Mart ● *Specialty Shops* `21` `20` `19` `M`

Tigard | 13600 SW Pacific Hwy. (Park St.) | 503-620-6120 | www.hmart.com

This "well-appointed" "hypermart", a Tigard link of the national chain, gets kudos for its "amazing" selection of Korean and Asian groceries in departments devoted to meats, seafood, produce and housewares; given the relatively "inexpensive" price tags, the experience reminds some of "being back in Seoul."

Homebrew Exchange *Wines, Beer & Liquor* `24` `22` `23` `M`

Kenton | 1907 N. Kilpatrick St. (bet. Denver & Fenwick Aves.) | 503-286-0343 | www.homebrewexchange.net

Specializing in supplies for home brewing beer, wine, soda and cheese, this Kenton shop also offers classes for "learning how to brew your own"; "sweet", "patient" service and "affordable" prices seal the deal.

House Spirits *Wines, Beer & Liquor* `26` `26` `25` `E`

Central Eastside | 2025 SE Seventh Ave. (bet. Harrison & Lincoln Sts.) | 503-235-3174 | www.housespirits.com

Known as the "home of Aviation gin", this "master" Central Eastside distillery also soars with its "amazing" aquavit and "one-of-a-kind" whiskey; the elegant tasting room is staffed by "helpful" employees who make you want to snap up their booze as a "classy gift for the sophisticated drunk in your life"; P.S. tours are offered on Saturdays at 1 and 3 PM.

JaCiva's Bakery & Chocolatier *Baked Goods* `27` `25` `26` `E`

Hawthorne | 4733 SE Hawthorne Blvd. (48th Ave.) | 503-234-8115 | www.jacivas.com

An "old-fashioned bakery" with "incredible cakes" and "to-die-for" chocolates, this Hawthorne "institution" is "as good as the newer bakeries" and renowned for its custom creations for "special occasions"; the staff is "sweet" and most items are "reasonably priced", plus it's open late Friday–Saturday for hot drinks and "exquisite desserts."

John's Market ● *Wines, Beer & Liquor* `25` `21` `22` `E`

Multnomah Village | 3535 SW Multnomah Blvd. (35th Ave.) | 503-244-2617 | www.johnsmarketplace.com

"If you love beer, worship" at this bottle shop "temple" that's been open in Multnomah Village since 1923 and stocks an "astounding" selection of "brews and microbrews from all over the globe", as well as kegs, wine and a few basic grocery items; even if the decor is "nothing to write home about", shoppers appreciate the "knowledgeable" service with "helpful" recommendations.

Kruger's Farm Market *Produce* `26` `24` `24` `M`

Sauvie Island | 17100 NW Sauvie Island Rd. (bet. Howell Park & Reeder Rds.) | 503-621-3489

(continued)

Kruger's Farm Stand *Produce*

Hawthorne | 2310 SE Hawthorne Blvd. (bet. 23rd & 24th Aves.) |
503-235-0314
St. Johns | 7316 N. Lombard St. (bet. Buchanan & Burr Aves.) |
503-289-2535
www.krugersfarmmarket.com

"A trip to Sauvie Island would not be complete without a stop at
Kruger's" say fans of the "family-friendly" farm and its stand (the
Hawthorne and St. Johns outposts also sell its produce), where you
can "pick your own berries" in season, wander a "well-thought-out"
corn maze and take in "magical" summer concerts; the staff is "enthusiastic", prices are "way below your average farmer's market"
and the baskets are filled with "warts 'n' all fresh veggies and fruit."

La Espiga Dorada ● *Baked Goods*   ▽ 27 | 24 | 24 | I

Beaverton | 18350 SW Tualatin Valley Hwy. (185th Ave.) |
503-591-9859

"Eat like a king" for cheap at this "amazing" Mexican bread and
pastry shop turning out "wonderful treats" in Beaverton; it can be
"busy" and it's self-serve (grab a tray and tongs), but fans love
the "freshly baked" goods, including *conchas* (sweet rolls) "hot out
of the oven."

Let's Brew *Wines, Beer & Liquor*   25 | 20 | 23 | M

Montavilla | 8235 SE Stark St. (bet. 82nd & 83rd Aves.) | 503-256-0205 |
www.letsbrew.net

There's "all kinds of useful equipment and a huge selection of brewing supplies" at this Montavilla shop, where you can "cut your teeth"
on beer-making in its kitchen; though a few find the staffers "off-
putting", others say they "know what they're talking about" and
you're "likely to learn something new."

Liner & Elsen *Wines, Beer & Liquor*   26 | 23 | 23 | E

Northwest Portland | 2222 NW Quimby St. (bet. 22nd & 23rd Aves.) |
503-241-9463 | www.linerandelsen.com

This NW Portland wine shop, a "vinified find", has a reputation as
one of the city's "best" for its "grand array of wines" from "around
the world" and "interesting tastings"; some commend the "helpful"
service and "varied price range", though a few find it "cliquish" and
warn not to expect a "basement bargain."

Main Street Homebrew   28 | 26 | 26 | M
Supply Co. *Wines, Beer & Liquor*

Hillsboro | 23596 NW Clara Ln. (Jacobsen Rd.) | 503-648-4254 |
www.mainbrew.com

Offering a "large selection" of supplies, this "outstanding homebrew
store" in Hillsboro is sweetened by a "patient crew" that's "always
willing to go the extra mile" and answer "all kinds of novice questions" pertaining to making beer, wine and cider (not to mention
mead and cheese), even when "super busy"; "decent prices" and a
"huge" cooler of suds are the malt in the brew.

Market of Choice ● *Major Market* | 26 | 24 | 24 | E |
Southwest Portland | 8502 SW Terwilliger Blvd. (Taylors Ferry Rd.) |
503-892-7331 | www.marketofchoice.com

"Small" but mighty with a "top selection", this "handy" SW Portland
link in the Oregon chain has "everything you need", including "quality
meat and seafood", "organic produce" (check out the "wild mushrooms") and "outstanding beer, wine and deli choices"; it's "not
cheap but it's also high-end eatin'", with a "professional" touch and
"lots of items not found elsewhere."

Martinotti's Cafe & Deli *Specialty Shops* | ▽ 25 | 21 | 23 | M |
West End | 404 SW 10th Ave. (bet. Stark & Washington Sts.) |
503-224-9028

"It's like walking into an old deli in Italy" at this family-owned West
End shop and cafe, offering "imported meats and cheeses", top-
notch sandwiches and "anything traditional" from The Boot (including wine); staffers who "remember you" make it extra "pleasant", so
fans who "supect not enough people know about the place" say it's
"worth a visit."

The Meadow *Herbs & Spices* | 27 | 27 | 23 | E |
Mississippi | 3731 N. Mississippi Ave. (bet. Beech & Failing Sts.) |
503-288-4633 | www.atthemeadow.com

An "extraordinary variety" of "gourmet finishing salts" in "every color"
from all over the globe is the draw at this "beautiful little boutique"
on Mississippi, which gets top marks for Display among Portland
food shops; overseen by a staff that's "passionate about educating"
(one of the owners literally wrote the book on salt), it's "expensive
but worth it" considering the "unique" treasures, which also include
an "awe"-inspiring chocolate trove as well as wine and flowers, making it a go-to for "wonderful gifts."

Moonstruck Chocolate Cafe *Candy & Nuts* | 28 | 27 | 26 | E |
Downtown | 608 SW Alder St. (bet. B'way & 6th Ave.) |
503-241-0955
Downtown | 700 SW Fifth Ave. (bet. Taylor & Yamhill Sts) |
503-219-9118
Northwest Portland | 526 NW 23rd Ave. (bet. Glisan & Hoyt Sts.) |
503-542-3400 ●
St. Johns | 6600 N. Baltimore Ave. (Crawford St.) | 503-247-3448 |
800-557-6666
Beaverton | 11705 SW Beaverton-Hillsdale Hwy. (Lombard Ave.) |
503-352-0835 ●
Lake Oswego | 45 S. State St. (Leonard St.) | 503-697-7097
www.moonstruckchocolate.com

"Adorable" handmade truffles in the "best flavor combinations"
plus "amazing drinking chocolate" at this "pricey" sweets mini-
chain are "just the right thing for a dreary, cloudy day"; the crew
is "up to date on their chocolate-mongering" and "makes you
feel welcome" with samples – just be aware that one bite may
"ruin your taste buds" so you'll "never again appreciate the average
store-bought bar."

QUALITY DISPLAY SERVICE COST

Mr. Green Beans *Coffee & Tea*   `27` `24` `26` `M`

Mississippi | 3932 N. Mississippi Ave. (bet. Failing & Shaver Sts.) | 503-288-8698 | www.mrgreenbeanspdx.com

It's a "domestic arts extravaganza" at this "pleasant" Mississippi coffee-supply hub catering to "all levels of home roasters", as well as customers making soap, cheese, candy and more; the "encouraging" staff "will stop at nothing to show you how easy and inexpensive" DIY can be – so "eat your heart out", java chains.

New Deal Distillery *Wines, Beer & Liquor*   `28` `23` `25` `M`

Central Eastside | 1311 SE Ninth Ave. (bet. Madison & Main Sts.) | 503-234-2513 | www.newdealdistillery.com

"One of the big names in Portland's microdistillery scene", this Central Eastside small-batch producer creates "excellent, unusual" vodkas and gins that are "handmade with care" with a focus on local (the coffee liqueur "smells and tastes just like NW" premium) at a "fair" price; a "knowledgeable" staff runs the "small" but "nice" tasting room and gives "excellent tours and demonstrations" on a limited schedule.

Newman's Fish Company *Seafood*   `27` `24` `27` `E`

Northwest Portland | City Market | 735 NW 21st Ave. (bet. Irving & Johnson Sts.) | 503-227-2700 | www.newmansfish.com

Considered by many to be "the place to acquire the freshest catch" in town, this NW Portland seafood retailer in City Market boasts an "impressive offering of fresh and smoked fish" from nearby and far-flung waters, including live lobster, crab and plenty of oysters; prices are appropriate, and the staff will "happily take the time" to share "wonderful recipes."

New Seasons Market ◗ *Major Market*   `28` `27` `26` `E`

Division | 1954 SE Division St. (bet. 18th & 20th Aves.) | 503-445-2888
Concordia | 5320 NE 33rd Ave. (Emerson St.) | 503-288-3838
Hawthorne | 4034 SE Hawthorne Blvd. (bet. 40th & 41st Aves.) | 503-236-4800
North Portland | 6400 N. Interstate Ave. (bet. Holman St. & Rosa Parks Way) | 503-467-4777
Raleigh Hills | Raleigh Hills Plaza | 7300 SW Beaverton-Hillsdale Hwy. (Scholls Ferry Rd.) | 503-292-6838
Sellwood | 1214 SE Tacoma St. (bet. 11th & 13th Aves.) | 503-230-4949
Beaverton | 14805 SW Barrows Rd. (Horizon Blvd.) | 503-597-6777
Hillsboro | 1453 NE 61st Ave. (Cornell Rd.) | 503-648-6968
Happy Valley | 15861 SE Happy Valley Town Center Dr. (bet. Misty Dr. & Sunnyside Rd.) | 503-558-9214
Lake Oswego | 3 SW Monroe Pkwy. (Boones Ferry Rd.) | 503-496-1155
www.newseasonsmarket.com
Additional locations throughout the Portland area

This "superior" chain of grocery stores – voted Most Popular among Portland food shops – pleases those on an "organic, local and sustainable food kick" with its "fantastically fresh", "freakishly delicious" fare and "great selection of specialty items", including a "lovely array of wines and cheese"; sure, parking can be a "pain" and it's a "bit pricey", but "you get what you pay for", and a "super-friendly staff" will help you find "every ingredient" to make your "most esoteric recipe ever."

Nicky USA *Meat & Poultry*   ▽ 27 | 19 | 23 | E

Eastside Industrial | 223 SE Third Ave. (Pine St.) | 503-234-4263 | www.nickyusa.com

This primarily wholesale company in Eastside Industrial carries "some of the best quality game, beef and butchered products that you can get", with a specialization in "local and exotic", "hard-to-find" meats (think wild boar, elk, rattlesnake, kangaroo and then some); call ahead for appointment-only, individual dock sales.

Oregon Wines   25 | 24 | 22 | E
on Broadway *Wines, Beer & Liquor*

Downtown | 515 SW Broadway (bet. Alder & Washington Sts.) | 503-228-4655 | www.oregonwinesonbroadway.com

An "amazing selection of Oregon Pinots" are available at this Downtowner focusing on in-state and Washington wines for take-out, as well as offering tastes, glasses and bottles at its bar (for no corkage); "prices vary", but the "quality is golden" and the "good-natured yet sassy" staff is there to "help you through your day or celebrate its finish", especially in the case of Friday champagne flights.

Original Bavarian Sausage *Meat & Poultry*   28 | 27 | 25 | M

Tigard | 8705 SW Locust St. (bet. Hall Blvd. & Jefferson Ave.) | 503-892-5152 | www.originalbavariansausage.com

When in "need of some German soul food", this Tigard deli and grocery fits the bill with a meaty array of sausages, salamis, wursts and a "good choice of German products" including canned and dry goods, chocolates and beer; a "patient" staff accommodates take-out and dine-in orders for sandwiches that "sing with TLC"; P.S. it shares an owner with German Bakery.

Pacific Seafood *Seafood*   26 | 22 | 24 | M

Foster-Powell | 3380 SE Powell Blvd. (34th Ave.) | 503-233-4891 | www.pacseafood.com

The genesis of what is now a large wholesale fish supplier, this Foster-Powell seafooder has been around since 1941, and though minuscule, it delivers an "exceptional selection" of "fresh" sea-faring fare ("they will probably have it in the back" if you need "something specific"); the service makes you "feel important" and it's "affordable" to boot, so overall surveyors "definitely recommend."

Pastaworks *Specialty Shops*   27 | 25 | 24 | E

Hawthorne | 3735 SE Hawthorne Blvd. (bet. 37th & 38th Aves.) | 503-232-1010

Mississippi | 4212 N. Mississippi Ave. (bet. Mason & Skidmore Sts.) | 503-445-1303

Northwest Portland | City Market | 735 NW 21st Ave. (bet. Irving & Johnson Sts.) | 503-221-3002

www.pastaworks.com

For "fresh pasta that can't be beat unless you make it yourself", noodle lovers recommend this "expensive-but-worth-it" mini-chain devoted to "those Italian specialties you've been craving", including "fantastic charcuterie", "cheeses from absolutely everywhere" and "top-notch produce"; some "wish it had pull-out couches for overnight guests", but "otherwise it's wonderful" down to the "great folks behind the counter"; P.S. the Hawthorne branch houses Kevin Gibson's well-regarded eatery, Evoe.

Pearl Specialty Market & Spirits ● *Wines, Beer & Liquor*

27 | 26 | 21 | M

Pearl District | 900 NW Lovejoy St. (bet. 9th & 10th Aves.) | 503-477-8604 | www.pearlspecialty.com

"From bitters to hard alcohol" and "champagne to cigars", the "offerings are immense" at this "pleasant" Pearl District liquor store boasting "better brands" and a "sleek design"; the staff can always "lend a hand if you have a question", and the late hours (open till 10 PM every day but Sunday) bring an "aww yeah" from last-minute shoppers.

Penzeys Spices *Herbs & Spices*

28 | 27 | 26 | M

Pearl District | 120 NW 10th Ave. (bet. Couch & Davis Sts.) | 503-227-6777
Beaverton | 11787 SW Beaverton-Hillsdale Hwy. (bet. Griffith Dr. & Lombard Ave.) | 503-643-7430
Happy Valley | 11322 SE 82nd Ave. (bet. Boyer Dr. & Causey Ave.) | 503-653-7779
www.penzeys.com

"Who knew there were five types of cinnamon" say fans who "delight" in "every single spice you can think of and more" at this "destination" trio, where you can "smell samples" and purchase "smaller portions" to assure your dried herbs, rubs and salts are "always fresh"; giving a nod to "helpful" service, "reasonable" prices and "easy-to-navigate" racks, not to mention some "pretty darn amazing" house blends, many agree "you'll never buy spices at the grocery store again."

People's Co-op ● *Major Market*

27 | 24 | 25 | M

Clinton | 3029 SE 21st Ave. (bet. Brooklyn & Tibbetts Sts.) | 503-674-2642 | www.peoples.coop

This Clinton food cooperative is where "grassroots ideals" of "organic, fair trade and fair wage" meet a "commitment to bulk items and local produce" – "bulk tofu for the win" cheer vegetarians and vegans who don't mind the lack of meat; it's "full of positive energy" with "excellent prices on staples", plus the Wednesday farmer's market (from 2 to 7 PM) "brings the life of Portland into the neighborhood."

Phil's Uptown Meat Market *Meat & Poultry*

28 | 26 | 28 | M

Northwest Portland | 17 NW 23rd Pl. (bet. Burnside St. & Westover Rd.) | 503-224-9541

"Instant, delicious gratification" courtesy of the "popular bento cart" out front is a solid hook, but it's the "high-quality", "well-cut" meat and fish and tasty medley of prepared foods served up by a "super-friendly" team that defines this NW Portland butcher shop and earns it the No. 1 Service rating among the city's food shops; though the street level market is petite, there's a "high-quality" "wine cellar downstairs" with a "vast and excellent" selection.

QUALITY DISPLAY SERVICE COST

Piece of Cake Bakery *Baked Goods*   27 | 25 | 26 | E

Sellwood | 8306 SE 17th Ave. (Umatilla St.) | 503-234-9445 |
www.pieceofcakebakery.net

Those with special sweet needs – vegan, gluten-free – "recommend" this "funky, old" Sellwood bakery that's also known for its
Fantasy Cake (part chocolate, part cheesecake), "unique" wedding
cakes and cupcakes; some mention "quirky" service and note "if
you're not familiar with the Portland vibe, you probably won't get
the eclectic decor."

Portland Roasting Coffee *Coffee & Tea*   27 | 24 | 25 | M

Central Eastside | 340 SE Seventh Ave. (Oak St.) |
800-949-3898
NEW Lloyd | Oregon Convention Ctr. | 777 NE Martin Luther King Jr. Blvd.
(Holladay St.) | no phone
www.portlandroasting.com

"A damned good cup of joe" awaits at this Central Eastside roaster
whose "excellent" coffees (including organic and single-origin
choices) can be sampled and purchased both whole-bean and
ground at the small retail shop; customers also "like that it's a carbon-
neutral company" and delivers "great customer service"; P.S. the
Convention Center cafes are only open when the center is.

Saint Cupcake Deluxe *Baked Goods*   27 | 26 | 24 | E

Belmont | Noun: A Person's Place for Things | 3300 SE Belmont St.
(33rd Ave.) | 503-235-0078
Saint Cupcake Galore *Baked Goods*
West End | 1138 SW Morrison St. (12th Ave.) | 503-473-8760
www.saintcupcake.com

"Amazing", "adorable" cupcakes are on constant rotation at these
bright, "stinking cute" shops in West End and Belmont, where regulars also go "dotty" for the minis – "it's really hard not to eat more
than one"; the Galore branch serves the sweets alongside tarts,
sandwiches and salads, while Deluxe keeps to cupcakes, cookies
and party supplies, and though either one could "eat a hole in your
pocket", "if you're going to indulge, do it right."

Sheridan Fruit Company *Major Market*   26 | 23 | 24 | M

Eastside Industrial | 409 SE Martin Luther King Jr. Blvd. (Oak St.) |
503-236-2114 | www.sheridanfruit.com

"Long one of Portland's favorite produce stores", this "affordable",
"old-fashioned grocery" in Eastside Industrial offers a "feel-good
retro-shopping experience" with "always-fresh" veggies", "first-
class" wine and cheese and a "tremendous selection of sausages",
as well as "hard-to-find bulk items"; staffers lend it an "inviting"
vibe, and despite the "limited space", it's "packed full of surprises."

Spice & Tea Exchange *Herbs & Spices*   26 | 26 | 25 | E

Downtown | 536 SW Broadway (bet. Alder & Washington Sts.) |
503-208-2886 | www.spiceandtea.com
Suggested for tea drinkers "interested in expanding their repertoire",
this Downtown chain link stocks "all kinds of teas" and accessories,

plus spices from around the world; it's small and well-manicured, and though some find the selection "limited", the "knowledgeable" staff ensures "quality" purchases.

Spicer Brothers Produce *Produce*　　27 | 25 | 26 | M

Oregon City | 508 14th St. (bet. Center & Washington Sts.) | 503-656-7061 | www.spicerbrothersproduce.com

For "fresh, local produce", supplemented by a small selection of dairy, bread and other staples from area purveyors, Oregon City folks turn to this locally owned, longtime indoor/outdoor market that's "cheaper" than comparable shops; "welcoming" and "community"-conscious, it has a "close-knit feel" that's hard to find elsewhere.

NEW Spielman Coffee　　　　　　　27 | 24 | 24 | M
Roasters *Coffee & Tea*

Division | 2128 SE Division St. (22nd Ave.) | 503-467-0600

"Heck yes" say customers to the combo of "fresh-every-day" sour-dough bagels and "excellent" house-roasted coffee at this "ultra-casual" Division shop that "brings them together"; with a pleasant "neighborhood" vibe rounding it out, it's the "perfect pick-me-up to start the day."

Steven Smith Teamaker *Coffee & Tea*　▽ 27 | 23 | 23 | E

Northwest Portland | 1626 NW Thurman St. (bet. 16th & 17th Aves.) | 503-719-8752 | www.smithtea.com

"Handcrafted teas from the man who started the whole upscale" boom draw fans to this "quiet", "fairly priced" NW Portland shop by Steven Smith (a founder of both Tazo and Stash Tea) with a focus on premium full leaf and varietals; there's a lot to choose from, so to "get ideas of what you really like", steeped regulars suggest to "do a tasting."

Stone Cottage Spices *Herbs & Spices*　▽ 24 | 23 | 23 | M

Southeast Portland | 3844 SE Gladstone St. (39th Ave.) | 503-719-6658 | www.herbsspicesteas.com

SE Portlanders are "happy to have this gem", providing "one-stop shopping" on an "amazing" array of spices and teas as well as items like produce, coffee, handmade pasta, soaps and "beautiful tea sets"; a "dedicated" team provides "personal" service in the "Zen-like" space, and the "reasonable to super-cheap" prices don't hurt either.

Tea Chai Te *Coffee & Tea*　　　　　25 | 24 | 24 | M

Northwest Portland | 734 NW 23rd Ave. (bet. Irving & Johnson Sts.) | 503-228-0900 ◗

NEW Sellwood | 7983 SE 13th Ave. (Nehalem St.) | 503-432-8747 www.teachaite.com

Perched on the second floor of an old Victorian, this NW Portland "bastion of relaxation" is "one of the best tea shops" in the city, with a "fantastic" selection of 100-plus, largely organic choices, plus there's kombucha on tap; sippers "love the staff" and say "prices aren't that bad" for specialty items; P.S. the newer Sellwood stop in an old caboose has the same baked goods, light fare and free WiFi.

10th Avenue Liquor Store *Wines, Beer & Liquor*   23 | 21 | 22 | M
Downtown | 925 SW 10th Ave. (bet. Salmon & Taylor Sts.) | 503-227-3391
In business since the '60s, this "convenient" Downtown liquor store vends a "solid selection" with an especially "wide-ranging" array of single-malt scotches, dispatched by a "helpful" staff in "roomy" digs; ok, it's "not very fancy", but if you're looking for an "oddball" brand, chances are "they've got it."

Townshend's Teahouse ❶ *Coffee & Tea*   26 | 23 | 22 | M
Alberta | 2223 NE Alberta St. (bet. 22nd & 23rd Aves.) | 503-445-6699
NEW **Division** | 3531 SE Division St. (35th Pl.) | no phone
www.townshendstea.com
"Craft teas from around the world" impress at this warm, cozy Portland duo with "a lot of different fusions and flavors", "excellent tea lattes", bubble tea and "incredible" Brew Dr. Kombucha on tap; with everything "made to order", no wonder it's a "favorite hangout"; P.S. they've got a tea bar inside the Hollywood Whole Foods Market.

Two Tarts Bakery *Baked Goods*   27 | 24 | 26 | M
Northwest Portland | 2309 NW Kearney St. (23rd Ave.) | 503-312-9522 | www.twotartsbakery.com
"Made throughout the day", the "adorably tiny" treats "packing so much flavor" are the "perfect size, taste and price" at this NW Portland bakery; though its petite tarts, brownies and bars are available "all over town", the "relaxing" shop is staffed by "good people" and it's a "fun trip."

Uptown Liquor *Wines, Beer & Liquor*   25 | 22 | 22 | M
Northwest Portland | 1 NW 23rd Pl. (Burnside St.) | 503-227-0338
"Keyed to the neighborhood", this "reliable" NW Portland liquor store has top-shelf items out on display for browsing, including rums, grappas, bitters and local microdistillery spirits, along with "bargain vodka"; it's helmed by a "motley crew of friendly folks", and diehards note that samples and demos are sometimes available on Friday and Saturday nights.

Uwajimaya ❶ *Specialty Shops*   27 | 24 | 22 | M
Beaverton | 10500 SW Beaverton-Hillsdale Hwy. (Western Ave.) | 503-643-4512 | www.uwajimaya.com
"A must for esoteric Asian ingredients", this "spectacular" "superstore" in Beaverton (part of the Seattle-based chainlet) specializing in Japanese foods offers an almost "overwhelming" variety, including "fresh, even live, fish", meats, produce, household goods and "yummy readymade" items; while it "can get expensive", most find it "reasonable", and the "staff is always willing to help" those unfamiliar with the fare.

Van Duyn Chocolates *Candy & Nuts*   27 | 26 | 25 | E
Northwest Portland | 2360 NW Quimby St. (bet. Pettygrove & Quimby Sts.) | 503-227-1927 | www.vanduyns.com
This old-school NW Portland chocolatier (with a production facility behind the tiny storefront) has been a "chocolate lover's

paradise" since 1927 and turns out plentiful, "traditional" boxed varieties, including some of the "best dark-chocolate truffles" and even sugar-free options; it's "mildly expensive but delicious", so just try going in "without buying at least half a pound."

Vino *Wines, Beer & Liquor*

| 27 | 24 | 24 | M |

Kerns | 137 SE 28th Ave. (Ash St.) | 503-235-8545 | www.vinobuys.com

"You'll learn a story to share with your friends about what you're drinking" at this "relaxing" Buckman wine shop where the well-versed staff can guide you through vino "from all major regions"; on Fridays, locals "make an event" of the "fun" $10 tasting flights (five wines per session).

Vinopolis Wine Shop *Wines, Beer & Liquor*

| 27 | 24 | 23 | E |

West End | 1025 SW Washington St. (bet. 10th & 11th Aves.) | 503-223-6002 | www.vinopoliswineshop.com

A staff that "knows and loves its wine" and is "happy to offer advice" is a boon at this sizable, well-stocked West End shop with everything from midpriced to "very, very high-end" vino; surveyors don't seem to mind that bottles are showcased in crates and boxes, and simply wish to "become independently wealthy" so they can "go and buy one of everything."

NEW Woodsman Market *Specialty Shops*

| ∇ 24 | 24 | 24 | E |

Division | 4529 SE Division St. (bet. 45th & 46th Aves.) | 971-373-8267 | www.woodsmantavern.com

"Insanely good deli meats and cheeses" and special-occasion "treats from around the world" (including beer and wine) fill this small, Euro-hip but hospitable Division specialty market next to its cousin, the much buzzed about Woodsman Tavern; you won't one-stop shop here and it seems "expensive" to some, but there are soups and sandwiches for takeout until 3:30 PM daily.

Woodstock Wine & Deli Co. *Wines, Beer & Liquor*

| 26 | 24 | 23 | M |

Woodstock | 4030 SE Woodstock Blvd. (41st Ave.) | 503-777-2208

Locals love the "excellent" array of wine and beer, enjoyable tastings and "nice" "neighborhood" feel at this well-stocked Woodstock shop; in addition to its alcohol, fans "love the food" – sandwiches, soups, cheeses and the like – for dining in and "visiting with friends" or taking out for a "light dinner."

World Cup Coffee & Tea *Coffee & Tea*

| 26 | 23 | 25 | M |

Northwest Portland | 1740 NW Glisan St. (18th Ave.) | 503-228-4152

Pearl District | Powell's City of Books | 1005 W. Burnside St. (10th Ave.) | 503-228-4651 ●

www.worldcupcoffee.com

Devotees say their "day cannot begin without a cuppa" (both espresso drinks and drip) at this "comfortable" "go-to" duo where the crew's "friendly" and the "prices are all right"; roasting of the mostly organic, often shade-grown beans happens at the NW Portland stop, while the second branch inside Powell's City of Books includes tea, coffee and nibbles.

Zenner's Quality Sausage & Smoked Meats *Meat & Poultry*

26 | 22 | 26 | M

Northwest Portland | 2131 NW Kearney St. (Lovejoy St.) | 503-241-4113 | www.zenners.com

Though not technically a retail location, shoppers can still stop by this "old-school" NW Portland meatery, which has been crafting small-batch "delicious sausages" (some claim the "best in the NW") in natural casings since 1927; it primarily serves restaurants and markets, but individuals are welcome as long as they're willing to abide by limited hours, order ahead and purchase a case or more.

Zupan's ◗ *Major Market*

27 | 26 | 25 | E

Belmont | 3301 SE Belmont St. (33rd Ave.) | 503-239-3720
Johns Landing | 7221 SW Macadam Ave. (bet. Nevada St. & Taylors Ferry Rd.) | 503-244-5666
Northwest Portland | 2340 W. Burnside St. (Vista Ave.) | 503-497-1088
NEW **Lake Oswego** | 16380 Boones Ferry Rd. (bet. Bryant & Upper Drs.) | 503-210-4190
www.zupans.com

This family-owned "boutique market" chainlet (since 1975) wows with its "vast" selection of "marvelous" produce, "real fish and meat department" and "splendid take-home dishes", as well as "fantastic flowers" and a "superior" wine selection; though "you pay for" the "quality", it's a "pleasure to shop" in the "elegant", "tidy" surrounds and the staff is the "happiest."

SITES & ATTRACTIONS

Most Popular

The top five on this list are plotted on the map at the back of this book.

1 Multnomah Falls
2 Powell's City of Books
3 OMSI
4 Oregon Zoo
5 International Rose
    Test Garden

6 Portland Japanese Garden
7 Lan Su Chinese Garden
8 Forest Park
9 Portland Saturday Market
10 Oaks Amusement Park
11 Portland Farmers Market*

TOP APPEAL

29] Multnomah Falls
Powell's City of Books

28] OMSI
Portland Japanese Garden
Oregon Garden

Forest Park
International Rose Test Gdn.
Mt. Tabor
Lan Su Chinese Garden
Portland Farmers Market

TOP FACILITIES

27] OMSI
Evergreen Aviation Museum
Rose Quarter
Lan Su Chinese Garden

26] World Forestry Center

Oregon Garden
Portland Japanese Garden
Central Library
Washington Park
Powell's City of Books

TOP SERVICE

26] OMSI
World Forestry Center
Powell's City of Books

25] Portland Farmers Market
Rose Quarter

Oregon Zoo
Portland Children's Museum
Portland Japanese Garden
Lan Su Chinese Garden
Tryon Creek State Park

Excludes places with low votes; * indicates a tie with place above

Share your reviews on plus.google.com/local

Sites & Attractions Types

Includes names, locations and Appeal ratings. These lists include low vote places that do not qualify for tops lists.

GARDENS

Elk Rock Gdn. | **SW Portland**   28

Portland Japanese Gdn. | **SW Portland**   28

Oregon Gdn. | **Silverton**   28

Int'l Rose Test Gdn. | **SW Portland**   28

Lan Su Chinese Gdn. | **Old Town-Chinatown**   28

Crystal Springs Gdn. | **Eastmoreland**   27

HISTORICAL HOUSES

Pittock Mansion | **NW Portland**   25

HISTORIC LANDMARKS

Old Church | **Downtown**   28

Pioneer Courthse. Sq. | **Downtown**   23

LIBRARIES

Central Library | **Downtown**   25

MUSEUMS

OMSI | **E Industrial**   28

Evergreen Aviation Mus. | **McMinnville**   27

World Forestry Ctr. | **SW Portland**   26

Portland Art Mus. | **Downtown**   26

Portland Children's Mus. | **SW Portland**   26

Oregon History Mus. | **Downtown**   25

24-Hr. Church/Elvis | **Old Town-Chinatown**   24

OTHER

Powell's City/Books | **Pearl Dist.**   29

Burnside Skate Park | **E Industrial**   25

Oaks Amusement Park | **Sellwood**   25

OUTDOOR MARKETS

Portland Farmers Mkt. | **PSU**   28

Portland Saturday Mkt. | **Old Town-Chinatown**   26

PARKS

Multnomah Falls | **Corbett**   29

Forest Park | **NW Portland**   28

Mt. Tabor | **SE Portland**   28

Tryon Creek | **SW Portland**   28

Washington Park | **SW Portland**   27

Gov. Tom McCall Park | **Downtown**   27

Hoyt Arboretum | **SW Portland**   26

Vera Katz/Esplanade | **E Industrial**   25

PLANETARIUMS

OMSI | **E Industrial**   28

RELIGIOUS SITES

Grotto | **NE Portland**   26

SPORTS: SPECTATOR VENUES

Rose Quarter | **Lloyd**   27

Jeld-Wen Field | **Goose Hollow**   26

TRANSPORT

Portland Aerial Tram | **SW Portland**   25

ZOOS/ ANIMAL PARKS

Oregon Zoo | **SW Portland**   27

Sites & Attractions Locations

Includes names and Appeal ratings. These lists include low vote places that do not qualify for tops lists.

Portland

DOWNTOWN

Old Church	28
Gov. Tom McCall Park	27
Portland Art Mus.	26
Oregon History Mus.	25
Central Library	25
Pioneer Courthse. Sq.	23

EAST INDUSTRIAL

OMSI	28
Burnside Skate Park	25
Vera Katz/Esplanade	25

EASTMORELAND

Crystal Springs Gdn.	27

GOOSE HOLLOW

Jeld-Wen Field	26

LLOYD

Rose Quarter	27

NE PORTLAND

Grotto	26

NW PORTLAND

Forest Park	28
Pittock Mansion	25

OLD TOWN-CHINATOWN

Lan Su Chinese Gdn.	28
Portland Saturday Mkt.	26
24-Hr. Church/Elvis	24

PEARL DISTRICT

Powell's City/Books	29

PSU

Portland Farmers Mkt.	28

SELLWOOD

Oaks Amusement Park	25

SE PORTLAND

Mt. Tabor	28

SW PORTLAND

Elk Rock Gdn.	28
Portland Japanese Gdn.	28
Int'l Rose Test Gdn.	28
Tryon Creek	28
Washington Park	27
Oregon Zoo	27
World Forestry Ctr.	26
Hoyt Arboretum	26
Portland Children's Mus.	26
Portland Aerial Tram	25

Outlying Areas

CORBETT

Multnomah Falls	29

MCMINNVILLE

Evergreen Aviation Mus.	27

SILVERTON

Oregon Gdn.	28

Sites & Attractions

Ratings & Symbols

Appeal, Facilities & **Service** are rated on a 30-point scale.

Cost reflects the attraction's high-season price range for one adult admission, indicated as follows:

$0	Free	E	$26 to $40
I	$10 and below	VE	$41 or above
M	$11 to $25		

Burnside Skate Park
`25 | 21 | 18 | $0`

Eastside Industrial | SE Ankeny St. & Second Ave., under Burnside Bridge | no phone | www.skateoregon.com

"Where skating all began" in Portland, this massive concrete public park under the Burnside Bridge in the gritty Eastside Industrial district is a "rad place to shred"; built without permission by skateboarders and later sanctioned by the city, it draws an "impressive" array of talent, but "don't expect to feel overly welcomed" if you just hang around to "people-watch."

Central Library
`25 | 26 | 24 | $0`

Downtown | 801 SW 10th Ave. (bet. Taylor & Yamhill Sts.) | 503-988-5123 | www.multcolib.org

A "tribute to Portland's book scene", the Central Library's "magnificent" circa-1913 Downtown home impresses with "artistic adornments" and "minute details that make it special", including a "grand marble staircase etched with quotes" and a bronze tree in the "remarkable children's section"; its 17 miles of shelves delight bookworms, as do the "pleasant" staff, "plenty of seating" and "open stacks that beckon one to linger", especially on "rainy days."

Crystal Springs Rhododendron Garden
`27 | 23 | 22 | I`

Eastmoreland | SE 28th Ave. & Woodstock Blvd. | 503-771-8386 | www.portlandonline.com

"Clouds of flowers seemingly float in space" during blooming season (early spring through summer) at this "beautiful" Eastmoreland garden showcasing a "riot of color" from more than 2,500 rhododendrons, azaleas and companion plants; if it's "not as striking" during the remainder of the year, the trails, bridges and water features still "delight"; P.S. adult admission is free Tuesdays and Wednesdays and the day after Labor Day through February, while those under 12 never pay.

Elk Rock Garden of the Bishop's Close
`▽ 28 | 24 | 18 | $0`

Southwest Portland | 11800 SW Military Ln. (Riverside Dr.) | 503-636-5613 | www.elkrockgarden.com

For "peace, quiet and beauty", head to this "stroll"-worthy English-style garden set on a high bluff in SW Portland; originally part of a private estate and now owned by the city's Episcopal Diocese, it's hailed by admirers as one of the area's "best-kept secrets", offering some six acres filled with a "diverse selection of plants" of "year-round interest", plus "breathtaking views of the Willamette River" as a "bonus"; P.S. no public restrooms or picnicking.

Evergreen Aviation & Space Museum   27 | 27 | 24 | M

McMinnville | 460 NE Capt. Michael King Smith Way (Salmon River Hwy.) | 503-434-4006 | www.evergreenmuseum.org

There's a "wonderful display of science and history" that awaits at this "top-notch" aviation museum in McMinnville (some 40 miles southwest of Portland) featuring an "extensive collection" of "unique aircraft", including Howard Hughes' "impressive" Spruce Goose, a wooden prototype flying boat with a 320-ft. wingspan; if it's a bit "spendy", fans deem it "totally worth" it since there's plenty to keep both kids and adults "interested and engaged", including a 3-D theater and the "amazing" attached indoor Wings & Waves Waterpark for those looking to "leave soaking wet."

Forest Park   28 | 23 | 21 | $0

Northwest Portland | 4099 NW Thurman St. (St. Helens Rd.) | 503-223-5449 | www.forestparkconservancy.org

An urban "treasure", this "vast" 5,100-acre park in NW Portland is just minutes from Downtown but "feels like a trip to the mountains" with its extensive tree canopy, "pretty waterfalls", 70 miles of "excellent trails" for hiking, biking and horseback riding and more than 100 bird species among other flora and fauna; it's a "perfect place to shake off the city" and the "scenic" grounds are "well mapped" – just "be warned, some of the wildlife is human."

Governor Tom McCall Waterfront Park   27 | 22 | 21 | $0

Downtown | SW Naito Pkwy. (bet. NW Glisan & SW Harrison Sts.) | 503-823-7529 | www.portlandonline.com

Enjoy "beautiful views of the riverfront", bridges and Mt. Hood at this Downtown public park occupying some 30 acres along the west bank of the Willamette and offering a paved waterside walkway, "kid-friendly" fountains and green space plus an opportunity to observe the "interesting characters" who are "part of the show"; it also hosts some "wonderful festivals", including ones focused on blues, beer and food.

The Grotto   26 | 23 | 22 | $0

(aka The National Sanctuary of Our Sorrowful Mother)

Northeast Portland | 8840 NE Skidmore St. (Sandy Blvd.) | 503-254-7371 | www.thegrotto.org

This "lush" NE Portland shrine and 62-acre green space is "Catholic in foundation" but "appreciated by anyone" seeking a "tranquil retreat from the city"; the free lower plaza area features Our Lady's Grotto (a rock cave with a replica of the Pietà at its center) and visitor facilities, but devotees recommend taking the inexpensive elevator ride up 110 feet to the top level, where the "manicured" grounds include a chapel "hanging off the side of a cliff"; P.S. it's particularly "incredible at Christmastime" during the Festival of Lights.

APPEAL | FACIL. | SERVICE | COST

Hoyt Arboretum

| 26 | 24 | 24 | $0 |

Southwest Portland | 4000 SW Fairview Blvd. (Knights Blvd.) | 503-865-8733 | www.hoytarboretum.org

A "meticulously planned" arboretum that "seems utterly natural", this "educational" SW Portland forested park within Washington Park was founded in 1928 to conserve trees and plant species from around the world; enthusiasts say its 187 acres and 12 miles of trails are ideal for "running, walking, picnics and playing", and the "lovely" ridgetop setting is equally "beautiful" during blooming season and after the "leaves have fallen", when the grounds are "carpeted with vivid berries"; P.S. it also offers children's programs and "worth-it" workshops.

International Rose Test Garden

| 28 | 24 | 20 | $0 |

Southwest Portland | 400 SW Kingston Ave. (Burnside St.) | 503-823-3636 | www.rosegardenstore.org

"Luscious" scents waft through the air during blooming season at this "gorgeous" SW Portland hilltop haven, the oldest continuously operated public rose test garden in the U.S., founded in 1917 and today home to more than 10,000 plantings of 500-plus varieties of "every color, size and shape"; though the display is most "spectacular" in June, the "lovely, relaxing" 4.5-acre setting within Washington Park offers "incredible" city and mountain views year-round.

Jeld-Wen Field

| 26 | 25 | 22 | M |

Goose Hollow | 1844 SW Morrison St. (bet. 18th & 20th Aves.) | 503-553-5400 | www.jeld-wenfield.com

"Go Timbers!" shout "devoted fans" who cheer on the city's Major League Soccer team at this "wild" and "wonderful" Goose Hollow stadium that also hosts the Portland State University Vikings during football season; with a long history and multiple remodels under its belt (most recently in 2010–11), it pleases devotees who deem it "big enough to get that energetic atmosphere, but small enough to feel unintimidating and cozy", lending it "one of the greatest sports vibes in North America"; P.S. ticket prices vary by event.

Lan Su Chinese Garden

| 28 | 27 | 25 | I |

Old Town-Chinatown | 239 NW Everett St. (3rd Ave.) | 503-228-8131 | www.lansugarden.org

A "stunning" "sanctuary within the city", this inexpensive "authentic Suzhou-style" garden occupying an Old Town city block is so "serene and beautiful", it's like entering "another world"; it boasts a host of "exquisite touches" such as hundreds of plants native to China, "mesmerizing" stonework "hauled over" from the motherland and a "wonderful" tearoom, Tao of Tea, all of which make learning about Chinese culture an "inspiring" "treat."

Mt. Tabor

| 28 | 24 | 21 | $0 |

Southeast Portland | SE Salmon St. & 60th Ave. | 503-823-7529 | www.portlandonline.com

"Panoramic views" of Portland and beyond await those who are willing to "work up a little sweat" by hiking, cycling or simply driving to the summit of SE Portland's "gorgeous", "well-forested" Mt. Tabor, a 636-ft. dormant volcano within city limits; the "quiet" park topping the cinder cone is ideal for picnicking, enjoying the kids' playground or just "erupting with awe" while taking in a summer concert or watching the "overwhelmingly beautiful" sunsets from its peak.

Multnomah Falls

29 | 24 | 23 | $0

Corbett | 5000 Historic Columbia River Hwy. (Crown Point Hwy.) | 503-695-2376 | www.oregon.com

"Hydrophiles" are "hypnotized" by this "breathtaking" 620-ft., two-tiered cascading waterfall near Corbett (an "easy" 30-mile drive east of Portland), voted the area's Most Popular attraction and tops for Appeal; it "can be viewed with or without a hike" and on "paved paths for the mobility challenged", and if you have to "wade through crowds" at peak times, fans say it's "worth" it, especially since it's part of the "spectacular" Columbia River Gorge National Scenic Area, with other "lovely" trails nearby.

Oaks Amusement Park

25 | 23 | 23 | $0

Sellwood | 7805 SE Oaks Park Way (Spokane St.) | 503-233-5777 | www.oakspark.com

This circa-1905 amusement park "throwback" on the banks of the Willamette River in Sellwood proves the "appeal of the carnival never wanes", with modestly priced rides "for the whole family", a "fun" miniature golf course and a "fantastic" old-fashioned wooden skating rink with music from a "live pipe organ" to complete the "nostalgia"; though some say it "shows its age", most affirm that it's still "great to watch little kids' eyes light up" here.

Old Church

∇ 28 | 28 | 23 | $0

Downtown | 1422 SW 11th Ave. (Clay St.) | 503-222-2031 | www.oldchurch.org

Completed in 1883 and listed on the National Register of Historic Places, this "beautiful, small" Carpenter Gothic–style church-turned-performance and events space Downtown is kitted out with a Victorian parlor, intricate stained-glass windows and curved wooden pews, but the highlight is the massive Hook & Hastings pipe organ; locals appreciate it for the free recitals at noon on Wednesdays in its 300-seat auditorium as well as special ticketed shows (and weddings, of course) throughout the year.

The Oregon Garden

28 | 26 | 24 | M

Silverton | 879 W. Main St. (Rte. 213) | 503-874-8100 | www.oregongarden.org

"If you love gardens, you have to go" to this "beautiful" 80-acre Silverton destination (about a 40-minute drive south from Portland) featuring more than 20 specialty gardens dedicated to everything from roses to conifers, with highlights including a giant 400-year-old oak tree and a children's section with an in-ground Hobbit House, plus the only Frank Lloyd Wright–designed home in Oregon; moderate admission fees add to its appeal.

	APPEAL	FACIL.	SERVICE	COST

Oregon History Museum

| 25 | 25 | 23 | M |

Downtown | 1200 SW Park Ave. (Madison St.) | 503-222-1741 | www.ohs.org

"History buffs love" this modestly priced Downtown museum (part of the Oregon Historical Society) that offers "good insight" into the state's past with a "variety of changing exhibits" covering art, culture, geology, politics and more; two eight-story-tall Richard Haas murals near the entrance depict area history and make the center easy to find; P.S. admission is free for Multnomah County residents and OHS members.

Oregon Museum of Science & Industry (OMSI)

| 28 | 27 | 26 | M |

Eastside Industrial | 1945 SE Water Ave. (Caruthers St.) | 503-797-4000 | 800-955-6674 | www.omsi.edu

"Kids love it, and parents learn things as well" while exploring the "huge world of science" and technology at this "educational" Eastside Industrial museum, rated tops for Facilities and Service among Portland Attractions; besides "engaging", "hands-on" exhibits and a "friendly" staff, it boasts a planetarium, IMAX Dome theater and "terrific" traveling shows, and while over 21ers tout the monthly 'After Dark' events (complete with wine, beer and "nerds"), fans say everyone will find "something new to challenge and amaze" at every visit.

Oregon Zoo

| 27 | 25 | 25 | M |

Southwest Portland | 4001 SW Canyon Rd. (Sunset Hwy.) | 503-226-1561 | www.oregonzoo.org

"Amazing" elephants ("Packy just turned 50!") are among the highlights at this affordable zoo set on 64 "beautiful" acres with "windy trails through lots of greenery" in SW Portland's Washington Park; it showcases a "variety" of exhibits that emphasize "conservation and habitat preservation", and though it draws "crowds" and "lots of kids" on "sunny days", some contend it's "best on a cool day" because "more animals are out and about."

Pioneer Courthouse Square

| 23 | 20 | 20 | $0 |

Downtown | 701 SW Sixth Ave. (Yamhill St.) | 503-223-1613 | www.pioneercourthousesquare.org

It's known as "Portland's living room", and with more than 300 events per year (beer fests, outdoor movies, farmer's markets) there's "always something interesting happening" at this brick-paved "open square" occupying a Downtown city block opposite the historic Pioneer Courthouse; even fans admit that "sometimes it smells and you'll run into a sidewalk preacher", but it's a "true melting pot" and a fine place to "watch the world go by"; P.S. "don't miss the weather machine, the mile post sign, the echo chamber or the keystone lectern."

Pittock Mansion

| 25 | 24 | 23 | I |

Northwest Portland | 3229 NW Pittock Dr. (Burnside Rd.) | 503-823-3623 | www.pittockmansion.com

Perched on a bluff overlooking the city, this "graceful" NW Portland manor was completed in 1914 as a residence for Henry Pittock, former publisher of *The Oregonian* newspaper, and his wife, Georgiana, and opened to the public in 1965 after a "magnificent" restoration; with 23 period-decorated rooms, it offers a "historical snapshot" of the era and visitors who want an in-depth look can spring for the occasional "behind-the-scenes" tours (not recommended for children under 10), but some just "go for the views" from the "well-tended", 46-acre picnic-friendly grounds.

Portland Aerial Tram
25 | 23 | 20 | I

Southwest Portland | 3303 SW Bond Ave. (Whitaker St.) | 503-494-8283 | www.portlandtram.org

For an "amazing view" of the Willamette River, the city's bridges and distant mountain peaks, take a "quick", inexpensive ride aboard this aerial tram that rises 500 feet as it travels up Marquam Hill from SW Portland's South Waterfront docking station (adjacent to a Streetcar line and with bike parking); the experience in the sleek, Swiss-designed cabins is "fun for kids and grown-ups alike", although many passengers are simply headed to and from Oregon Health & Science University facilities.

Portland Art Museum
26 | 25 | 24 | M

Downtown | 1219 SW Park Ave. (bet. Jefferson & Main Sts.) | 503-226-2811 | www.portlandartmuseum.org

"Remarkable" collections of Asian, American and Native American art and "impressive" touring shows are highlights at this Downtown institution, founded in 1892 and known as the "starting place" for abstract painter Mark Rothko, who held his first museum exhibit here in 1933; it boasts a collection of more than 42,000 objects displayed in 112,000 sq. ft. of galleries, and the building's "crazy mix of levels" includes the Northwest Film Center theater in the basement, whose "large" screen and "comfy" seats make for a "wonderful movie-going experience."

Portland Children's Museum
26 | 25 | 25 | I

Southwest Portland | 4015 SW Canyon Rd. (Knights Blvd.) | 503-223-6500 | www.portlandcm.org

This children's museum in SW Portland's Washington Park is "full of creative and educational activities" for "younger kids", including a pet hospital, clay studio and outdoor maze that keep little ones "busy and happy"; sure, "hordes of children" await, so some advise "prepare for this place like you would for battle", while others appreciate that you can just "let 'em loose" here.

Portland Farmers Market
28 | 23 | 25 | $0

PSU | Park Ave. & SW Montgomery St. | 503-241-0032 | www.portlandfarmersmarket.org

"Rain or shine", visiting this outdoor market in the Park Blocks at Portland State University is a "Saturday morning ritual" for loyalists who browse an "outstanding variety" of vendors proffering "marvelous local foods" (fruits, vegetables, meats, seafood, baked goods, cheese, flowers) from mid-March through mid-December; admirers call it a "best of Portland" experience and "arguably the best in the country", adding it's "hard to know what to love most": the things you'll buy or the "characters" you'll see.

Portland Japanese Garden

28 | 26 | 25 | I

Southwest Portland | 611 SW Kingston Ave. (Burnside Rd.) | 503-223-1321 | www.japanesegarden.com

There's a "masterful celebration of Japanese culture and gardening" at this "exquisite", inexpensive 5.5-acre retreat set in SW Portland's Washington Park that features five "peaceful, meditative" Japanese gardens – "each is unique but flows well into the next" – with "views that are part and parcel" of its "beauty"; it's "not to be missed" when the cherry trees blossom in spring, but it's "outstanding at any time of year" and you'll leave with an appreciation for the "enormous effort and skill" that goes into its upkeep.

Portland Saturday Market

26 | 21 | 22 | $0

Old Town-Chinatown | 108 W. Burnside St. (Naito Pkwy.) | 503-222-6072 | www.portlandsaturdaymarket.com

"It's like Etsy in real life" at this open-air arts and crafts market, a "Portland tradition" near the waterfront in Old Town where local artisans proffer "varied, fantastic and weird" wares Saturday–Sunday from March through late December; it gets "crowded" and some cite a lot of "schlock", but most agree that "character and liveliness" abound, making it "one of the best people-watching places in the city."

Powell's City of Books

29 | 26 | 26 | $0

Pearl District | 1005 W. Burnside St. (10th Ave.) | 503-228-4651 | www.powells.com

Occupying a full city block in the Pearl District, this "Portland institution" is a "mecca" for bibliophiles thanks to its "amazing selection" of more than one million new, used and rare books all "under one roof", plus "plenty of unique gifts"; even with "wide" aisles, "color-coded" signs and an "über-knowledgeable" staff, it's still easy to "get lost" and "lose track of time" exploring its "incredible maze"; P.S. "bring your credit card" because "you will not leave empty-handed."

Rose Quarter

27 | 27 | 25 | E

Lloyd | 1 N Center Ct. (Interstate Ave.) | 503-797-9619 | www.rosequarter.com

From sporting events to concerts, there's "always something fun going on" at this huge Lloyd-area entertainment complex that boasts two arenas (the Rose Garden and Memorial Coliseum) and serves as a home to Portland's Trail Blazers basketball and Winterhawks hockey teams; while tickets and concessions are "spendy", fanatics appreciate that "views are unobstructed from just about any seat", so you can "follow the arc of the ball" even if you're seated "all the way up in the rafters."

Tryon Creek State Park

28 | 25 | 25 | $0

Southwest Portland | 11321 SW Terwilliger Blvd. (Rte. 43) | 503-636-4398 | 800-551-6949 | www.tryonfriends.org

A "beautiful" piece of "wilderness" in SW Portland, this forested 670-acre state park "welcomes all – runners, horse riders, walkers" – to explore its "well-kept" trails and partake in family programs and guided hikes, which "teach and reach" both "young and old"; the popular annual spring Trillium Festival is "not the only reason to visit" say devotees who extol its simple "naturalness" as a "relief" from the urban grind.

24-Hour Church of Elvis

| 24 | 16 | 17 | $0 |

Old Town-Chinatown | 408 NW Couch St. (bet. 4th & 5th Aves.) | 503-226-3671 | www.24hourchurchofelvis.com

Experience "Portland's weirdness" at this "quirky" '24-hour coin-operated art gallery' set on the exterior of an Old Town storefront ("don't expect an announcement that you've left the building" since "you can't get in"); whether you drop in a quarter and have your fortune told, opt for a "quickie" faux marriage or just admire the displays of "kitsch" (not much of it Elvis themed), it's a "cool" stop, especially for "post-barhopping meditation."

Vera Katz Eastbank Esplanade

| 25 | 20 | 17 | $0 |

Eastside Industrial | East bank of Willamette River (bet. Hawthorne & Steel Bridges) | 503-823-7529 | www.portlandonline.com

This 1.5-mile-long esplanade with its 1,200-ft.-long "partially floating" public promenade on the banks of the Willamette River in the Eastside Industrial area is a "great place to bike or stroll" while taking in "lovely" views of the water and Downtown; it's also "worth walking" an extra mile or so to do the loop that connects to Governor Tom McCall Waterfront Park on the west side via the Steel and Hawthorne bridges, while people-watching all the way.

Washington Park

| 27 | 26 | 23 | $0 |

Southwest Portland | SW Douglas & Park Pls. | 503-823-7529 | www.washingtonparkpdx.org

There's "beauty around every turn" at this 400-acre SW Portland public park "just minutes from Downtown" that's home to key attractions (including the International Rose Test Garden, Oregon Zoo and Portland Japanese Garden) and offers playgrounds, 15 miles of nature trails "to wander" and much more; though "on a sunny day it seems the whole of Portland" comes here to "catch some rays", it's still "big enough to find a private spot."

World Forestry Center Discovery Museum

| 26 | 26 | 26 | I |

Southwest Portland | 4033 SW Canyon Rd. (Sunset Hwy.) | 503-228-1367 | www.worldforestry.org

Gain a "new appreciation for and understanding of the forests" at this museum in SW Portland's Washington Park; focusing on forests in the Pacific NW as well as worldwide, it features "amazing" "interactive exhibits" (including a canopy lift ride and river raft adventure simulator) plus "educational components" that make it "super fun for big'uns and littl'uns alike."

ZAGAT
2013

Portland Map

Portland Most Popular

Listed in order of popularity within each category; map coordinates follow names. For multi-location places, only central locations are plotted. Sections A-K show places in Downtown Portland (see adjacent map). Sections L-S show places in the greater Portland area (see reverse side of map).

Dining

1. Gustav's† (P-3)
2. Andina (G-2)
3. Flying Pie† (Q-4)
4. Higgins (G-5)
5. Jake's Famous Crawfish (G-3)
6. RingSide Steak (E-3, S-4)
7. Portland City Grill (H-3)
8. 3 Doors Down Café (P-4)
9. Apizza Scholls (Q-4)
10. Toro Bravo (O-3)
11. Heathman (G-5)
12. Jake's Grill* (G-4)
13. Paley's Place (E-1)
14. Salty's (P-1)
15. Screen Door (P-4)
16. Pok Pok (P-3, P-4)
17. Painted Lady (M-7)
18. Nostrana (P-4)
19. Rheinlander (Q-3)
20. Fire on the Mountain† (Q-3)

Dining Chains

21. McMenamins† (P-2)
22. Old Spaghetti Factory† (O-5)
23. Pizzicato† (D-2)
24. Mio Sushi† (G-2)
25. Original Pancake House (N-6)

Nightlife

26. Crystal Ballroom (G-3)
27. Deschutes Brewery (G-3)
28. Aladdin Theater (O-5)
29. Doug Fir (O-4)
30. Acropolis Steak/Strip (P-6)
31. C.C. Slaughters (H-3)
32. Darcelle XV Showplace (I-3)
33. Horse Brass Pub* (P-4)
34. Widmer Brothers (O-3)
35. Jimmy Mak's (G-3)

Shopping

36. Made In Oregon† (H-5)
37. Nike (H-4)
38. Columbia Sportswear (G-5)
39. Kitchen Kaboodle† (D-2)
40. A Children's Place (Q-3)
41. Backyard Bird Shop† (P-3)
42. Fabric Depot (S-4)
43. Dennis' 7 Dees† (Q-5)
44. Mac Store† (O-3)
45. Bike Gallery† (G-5)

Shopping: Food & Wine

46. New Seasons Market† (P-4)
47. Dave's Killer Bread (Q-7)
48. Elephants Delicatessen† (E-3)
49. Uwajimaya (L-5)
50. Bob's Red Mill (Q-7)
51. Moonstruck Chocolate†* (D-2)

Sites & Attractions

52. Multnomah Falls (S-3)
53. Powell's City of Books (G-3)
54. OMSI (J-7)
55. Oregon Zoo (B-7)
56. Int. Rose Test Garden (C-4)
57. Portland Japanese Garden (C-4)
58. Lan Su Chinese Garden (I-2)
59. Forest Park (A-1)
60. Portland Saturday Market (I-3)
61. Oaks Amusement Park (O-6)
62. Portland Farmers Market* (G-6)

---

*Indicates tie with above   † Indicates multiple branches